INTRODUCTION TO LOGIC CIRCUITS & LOGIC DESIGN

WITH VHDL

PRELIMINARY EDITION

Brock J. LaMeres, Ph.D.

For JoAnn, Alexis, and Kylie

Founded in 1807, John Wiley & Sons, Inc. has been a valued source of knowledge and understanding for more than 200 years, helping people around the world meet their needs and fulfill their aspirations. Our company is built on a foundation of principles that include responsibility to the communities we serve and where we live and work. In 2008, we launched a Corporate Citizenship Initiative, a global effort to address the environmental, social, economic, and ethical challenges we face in our business. Among the issues we are addressing are carbon impact, paper specifications and procurement, ethical conduct within our business and among our vendors, and community and charitable support. For more information, please visit our website: www.wiley.com/go/citizenship.

Printing identification and country of origin will either be included on this page and/or the end of the book. In addition, if the ISBN on this page and the back cover do not match, the ISBN on the back cover should be considered the correct ISBN.

ISBN 978-1-119-17118-8

Printed in the United States of America

Table of Contents

Preface

The purpose of this new book is to fill a void that has appeared in the instruction of digital circuits over the past decade due to the rapid abstraction of system design. Up until the mid 1980's, digital circuits were designed using *classical* techniques. Classical techniques relied heavily on manual design practices for the synthesis, minimization and interfacing of digital systems. Corresponding to this design style, academic textbooks were developed that taught classical digital design techniques. Around 1990, large scale digital systems began being designed using hardware description languages (HDL) and automated synthesis tools. Broad scale adoption of this *modern design* approach spread through the industry during this decade. Around 2000, hardware description languages and the modern digital design approach began to be taught in universities, mainly at the senior and graduate level. There were a variety of reasons that the modern digital design approach did not penetrate the lower levels of academia. First, the design and simulation tools were difficult to use and overwhelmed freshman and sophomore students. Second, the ability to implement the designs in a laboratory setting was infeasible. The modern design tools at the time were targeted at custom integrated circuits, which are cost and time prohibitive to implement in a university setting. Between 2000 and 2005, rapid advances in programmable logic and design tools allowed the modern digital design approach to be implemented in a university setting, even in lower level courses. This allowed students to learn the modern design approach based on HDLs and prototype their designs in real hardware, mainly Field Programmable Gate Arrays (FPGAs). This spurred an abundance of textbooks to be authored teaching hardware description languages and higher levels of design abstraction. This trend has continued until today. While abstraction is a critical tool for engineering design, the rapid movement toward teaching only the modern digital design techniques has left a void for freshman and sophomore level courses in digital circuitry. Legacy textbooks that teach the classical design approach are outdated and do not contain sufficient coverage of HDLs to prepare the students for follow-on classes. Newer textbooks that teach the modern digital design approach move immediately into high-level behavioral modeling with minimal or no coverage of the underlying hardware used to implement the systems. As a result, students are not being provided the resources to understand the fundamental hardware theory that lies beneath the modern abstraction such as interfacing, gate level implementation, and technology optimization. Students moving too rapidly into high levels of abstraction have little understanding of what is going on when they click the "compile & synthesize" button of their design tool. This leads to graduates who can model a breadth of different systems in an HDL, but have no depth into how the system is implemented in hardware. This becomes problematic when an issue arises in a real design and there is no foundational knowledge for the students to fall back on in order to debug the problem.

This new book addresses the lower level foundational void by providing a comprehensive, bottoms-up, coverage of digital systems. The book begins with a description of lower level hardware including binary representations, gate-level implementation, interfacing and simple combinational logic design. Only after a foundation has been laid in the underlying hardware theory is the VHDL language introduced. The VHDL introduction gives only the basic concepts of the language in order to model, simulate and synthesize combinational logic. This allows the students to gain familiarity with the language and the modern design approach without getting overwhelmed by the full capability of the language. The book then covers sequential logic and finite state machines at the component level. Once this secondary foundation has been laid, the remaining capabilities of VHDL are presented that allow sophisticated, synchronous systems to be modeled. An entire chapter is then dedicated to examples of sequential system modeling, which allows the students to learn by example. The second part of the textbook introduces the details of programmable logic, semiconductor memory and arithmetic circuits. The book culminates with a discussion of computer system design, which incorporates all of the knowledge gained in the previous chapters. Each component of a computer system is described with an accompanying VHDL implementation, all while continually reinforcing the underlying hardware beneath the HDL abstraction.

Written the Way it is Taught

The organization of this book is designed to follow the way in which the material is actually learned. Topics are presented only once sufficient background has been provided by earlier chapters to fully understand the material. An example of this *learning-oriented* organization is how the VHDL language is broken into two chapters. Chapter 5 presents an introduction to VHDL and the basic constructs to model combinational logic. This is an ideal location to introduce the language because the reader has just learned about combinational logic theory in Chapter 4. This allows the student to begin gaining experience using the VHDL simulation tools on basic combinational logic circuits. The more advanced constructs of VHDL such as sequential modeling and test benches are presented in Chapter 8 only after a thorough background in sequential logic is presented in Chapter 7. Another example of this learning-oriented approach is how arithmetic circuits are not introduced until Chapter 12. While technically the arithmetic circuits in Chapter 12 are combinational logic circuits and could be presented in Chapter 4, the student does not have the necessary background in Chapter 4 to fully understand the operation of the arithmetic circuitry so its introduction is postponed.

This incremental, *just-in-time* presentation of material allows the book to follow the way the material is actually taught in the classroom and/or learned when reading the material by itself. This design also avoids the need for the instructor to assign sections that move back-and-forth through the text. This not only reduces course design effort for the instructor but allows the student to know where they are in the sequence of learning. At any point, the student should know the material in prior chapters and be moving toward understanding the material in subsequent ones.

An additional advantage of this book's organization is that it supports giving the student hands-on experience with digital circuitry for courses with an accompanying laboratory component. The flow is designed to support lab exercises that begin using discrete logic gates on a breadboard and then move into HDL-based designs implemented on off-the-shelf FPGA boards. Using this approach to a laboratory experience gives the student experience with the basic electrical operation of digital circuits, interfacing, and HDL-based designs.

Learning Outcomes

Each chapter begins with an explanation of the learning goals and objectives followed by a brief preview of the chapter topics. The specific learning outcomes are then presented for the chapter in the form of concise statements about the measurable knowledge and/or skills the student will possess by the end of the chapter. There are 600+ exercise problems and concept check questions for each section tied directly to specific learning outcomes for both formative and summative assessment.

Teaching by Example

With over 200 worked examples, concept checks for each section, 200+ supporting figures, and 600+ exercise problems, students are provided with multiple ways to learn. Each topic is described in a clear, concise written form with accompanying figures as necessary. This is then followed by annotated worked examples that match the form of the exercise problems at the end of each chapter. Additionally, concept check questions are placed at the end of each section in the book to measure the student's general understanding of the material using a concept inventory assessment style. These features provide the student multiple ways to learn the material and build an understanding of digital circuitry.

Course Design

The book can be used in multiple ways. The first is to use the book to cover two, semester-based college courses in digital logic. The first course in this sequence is an *introduction to logic circuits* and covers chapters 1-7. This introductory course, which is found in nearly all accredited electrical and computer engineering programs, gives students a basic foundation in digital hardware and interfacing. Chapters 1-7 only cover relevant topics in digital circuits to make room for a thorough introduction to VHDL. At the end of this course students have a solid foundation in digital circuits and are able to design and simulate VHDL models of concurrent and hierarchical systems. The second course in this sequence covers *logic design* using chapters 8-13. In this second course, students learn the advanced features of VHDL such as packages, sequential behavioral modeling, and test benches. This provides the basis for building larger digital systems such as registers, finite state machines, and arithmetic circuits. Chapter 13 brings all of the concepts together through the design of a simple 8-bit computer system that can be simulated and implemented using many off-the-shelf FPGA boards.

This book can also be used in a more accelerated digital logic course that reaches a higher level of abstraction in a single semester. This is accomplished by skipping some chapters and moving quickly through others. In this use model, it is likely that Chapter 2 on numbers systems and Chapter 3 on digital circuits would be quickly referenced but not covered in detail. Chapter 4 and 7 could also be covered quickly in order to move rapidly into VHDL modeling without spending significant time looking at the underlying hardware implementation. This approach allows a higher level of abstraction to be taught but provides the student with the reference material so that they can delve in the details of the hardware implementation if interested.

All exercise and concept problems that do not involve a VHDL model are designed so that they can be implemented as a multiple choice or numeric entry question in a standard course management system. This allows the questions to be automatically graded. For the VHDL design questions, it is expected that the students will upload their VHDL source files and screenshots of their simulation waveforms to the course management system for manual grading by the instructor or teaching assistant.

Instructor Resources

Instructors can download a solution manual that contains a graphic-rich description of the solutions for each of the 600+ exercise problems. Instructors are also provided with the VHDL solutions and test benches for each VHDL design exercise. A lab manual is also provided that gives potential lab exercises based on the 74HC discrete logic family and an off-the-shelf FPGA board based. This manual is provided separately from the book in order to support the ever changing technology options available for laboratory exercises.

Chapter 1: Introduction – Analog vs. Digital

We often hear that we live in a digital age. This refers to the massive adoption of computer systems within every aspect of our lives from smart phones to automobiles to household appliances. This statement also refers to the transformation that has occurred to our telecommunications infrastructure that now transmits voice, video and data using 1's and 0's. There are a variety of reasons that digital systems have become so prevalent in our lives. In order to understand these reasons, it is good to start with an understanding of what a digital system is and how it compares to its counterpart, the analog system.

Learning Outcomes – After completing this chapter, you will be able to:

1.1   Describe the fundamental differences between analog and digital systems.
1.2   Describe advantages of digital systems compared to analog systems.
1.3   Identify digital systems in use today.
1.4   Identify analog systems in use today.

1.1 Differences between Analog and Digital Systems

Let's begin by looking at signaling. In electrical systems, signals represent information that is transmitted between devices using an electrical quantity (voltage or current). An analog signal is defined as a continuous, time-varying quantity that corresponds directly to the information it represents. An example of this would be a barometric pressure sensor that outputs an electrical voltage corresponding to the pressure being measured. As the pressure goes up, so does the voltage. While the range of the input (pressure) and output (voltage) will have different spans, there is a direct mapping between the pressure and voltage. Another example would be sound striking a traditional analog microphone. Sound is a pressure wave that travels through a medium such as air. As the pressure wave strikes the diaphragm in the microphone, the diaphragm moves back and forth. Through the process of inductive coupling, this movement is converted to an electric current. The characteristics of the current signal produced (e.g., frequency and magnitude) correspond directly to the characteristics of the incoming sound wave. The current can travel down a wire and go through another system that works in the opposite manner by inductively coupling the current onto another diaphragm, which in turn moves back and forth forming a pressure wave and thus sound (i.e., a speaker). In both of these examples, the electrical signal represents the *actual* information that is being transmitted and is considered *analog*. Analog signals can be represented mathematically as a function with respect to time.

In digital signaling the electrical signal itself is not directly the information it represents, instead, the information is encoded. The most common type of encoding is binary (1's and 0's). The 1's and 0's are represented by the electrical signal. The simplest form of digital signaling is to define a threshold voltage directly in the middle of the range of the electrical signal. If the signal is above this threshold, the signal is representing a 1. If the signal is below this threshold, the signal is representing a 0. This type of signaling is not considered continuous as in analog signaling, instead, it is considered to be *discrete* because the information is transmitted as a series of distinct values. The signal transitions between a 1 to 0 or 0 to 1 are assumed to occur instantaneously. While this is obviously impossible, for the purposes of information transmission, the values can be interpreted as a series of discrete values. This is a *digital* signal and is not the actual information, but rather the binary encoded representation of the original information. Digital signals are not represented using traditional mathematical functions, instead, the digital values are typically held in tables of 1's and 0's.

Figure 1.1 shows an example analog signal (left) and an example digital signal (right). While the digital signal is in reality continuous, it represents a series of discrete 1 and 0 values.

Figure 1.1
Analog (left) vs. Digital (right) Signals

CONCEPT CHECK

CC1.1   If a digital signal is only a discrete representation of real information, how is it possible to produce high quality music without hearing "gaps" in the output due to the digitization process?

A)   The gaps are present but they occur so quickly that the human ear can't detect them.

B)   When the digital music is converted back to analog sound the gaps are smoothed out since an analog signal is by definition *continuous*.

C)   Digital information is a continuous, time-varying signal so there aren't gaps.

D)   The gaps can be heard if the music is played slowly, but at normal speed, they can't be.

1.2 Advantages of Digital Systems over Analog Systems

There are a variety of reasons that digital systems are preferred over analog systems. First is their ability to operate within the presence of noise. Since an analog signal is a direct representation of the physical quantity it is transmitting, any noise that is coupled onto the electrical signal is interpreted as noise on the original physical quantity. An example of this is when you are listening to an AM/FM radio and you hear distortion of the sound coming out of the speaker. The distortion you hear is not due to actual distortion of the music as it was played at the radio station, but rather electrical noise that was coupled onto the analog signal transmitted to your radio prior to being converted back into sound by the speakers. Since the signal in this case is analog, the speaker simply converts it in its entirety (noise + music) into sound. In the case of digital signaling, a significant amount of noise can be added to the signal while still preserving the original 1's and 0's that are being transmitted. For example, if the signal is representing a 0, the receiver will still interpret the signal as a 0 as long as the noise doesn't cause the level to exceed the threshold. Once the receiver interprets the signal as a 0, it stores the encoded value as a 0 thus ignoring any noise present during the original transmission. Figure 1.2 shows the exact same noise added to the analog and digital signals from Figure 1.1. The analog signal is distorted; however, the digital signal is still able to transmit the 0's and 1's that represent the information.

Figure 1.2
Noise on Analog (left) and Digital (right) Signals

Another reason that digital systems are preferred over analog ones is the simplicity of the circuitry. In order to produce a 1 and 0, you simply need an electrical switch. If the switch connects the output to a voltage below the threshold, then it produces a 0. If the switch connects the output to a voltage above the threshold, then it produces a 1. It is relatively simple to create such a switching circuit using modern transistors. Analog circuitry, however, needs to perform the conversion of the physical quantity it is representing (e.g., pressure, sound) into an electrical signal all the while maintaining a direct correspondence between the input and output. Since analog circuits produce a direct, continuous representation of information, they require more complicated designs to achieve linearity in the presence of environmental variations (e.g., power supply, temperature, fabrication differences). Since digital circuits only produce a discrete representation of the information, they can be implemented with simple switches that are only altered when information is produced or retrieved. Figure 1.3 shows an example comparison between an analog inverting amplifier and a digital inverter. The analog amplifier uses dozens of transistors (inside the triangle) and two resistors to perform the inversion of the input. The digital inverter uses two transistors that act as switches to perform the inversion.

Figure 1.3
Analog (left) vs. Digital (right) Circuits

A final reason that digital systems are being widely adopted is their reduced power consumption. With the advent of Complementary Metal Oxide Transistors (CMOS), electrical switches can be created that consume very little power to *turn* on or off and consume relatively negligible amounts of power to *keep* on or off. This has allowed large scale digital systems to be fabricated without excessive levels of power consumption. For stationary digital systems such as servers and workstations, extremely large and complicated systems can be constructed that consume reasonable amounts of power. For portable digital systems such as smart phones and tablets, this means useful tools can be designed that are able to run on portable power sources. Analog circuits, on the other hand, require continuous power to accurately convert and transmit the electrical signal representing the physical quantity. Also, the circuit techniques that are required to compensate for variances in power supply and fabrication processes in analog systems require additional power consumption. For these reasons, analog systems are being replaced with digital systems wherever possible to exploit their noise immunity, simplicity and low power consumption. While analog systems will always be needed at the transition between the physical (e.g., microphones, camera lenses, sensors, video displays) and the electrical world, it is anticipated that the push toward digitization of everything in between (e.g., processing, transmission, storage) will continue.

CONCEPT CHECK

CC1.2   When does the magnitude of electrical noise on a digital signal prevent the original information from being determined?

A)   When it causes the system to draw too much power.

B)   When the shape of the noise makes the digital signal look smooth and continuous like a sine wave.

C)   When the magnitude of the noise is large enough that it causes the signal to inadvertently cross the threshold voltage.

D)   It doesn't. A digital signal can withstand any magnitude of noise.

Summary

❖   An analog system uses a direct mapping between an electrical quantity and the information being processed. A digital system, on the other hand, uses a discrete representation of the information.

❖   Using a discrete representation allows the digital signals to be more immune to noise in addition to requiring simple circuits that require less power to perform the computations.

Exercise Problems

Section 1.1 – Differences between Analog and Digital Systems

1.1.1   If an electrical signal is a direct function of a physical quantity, is it considered analog or digital?

1.1.2   If an electrical signal is a discrete representation of information, is it considered analog or digital?

1.1.3   What part of any system will always require an analog component?

1.1.4   Is the sound coming out of earbuds analog or digital?

1.1.5   Is the MP3 file stored on an iPod analog or digital?

1.1.6   Is the circuitry that reads the MP3 file from memory in an iPod analog or digital?

1.1.7   Is the electrical signal that travels down earphone wires analog or digital?

1.1.8   Is the voltage coming out of the battery in an iPod analog or digital?

1.1.9   Is the physical interface on the touch display of an iPod analog or digital?

1.1.10   Take a look around right now and identify two digital technologies in use.

1.1.11   Take a look around right now and identify two analog technologies in use.

Section 1.2 – Advantages of Digital Systems over Analog Systems

1.2.1   Give three advantages of using digital systems over analog.

1.2.2   Name a technology or device that has evolved from analog to digital in your lifetime.

1.2.3   Name an analog technology or device that has become obsolete in your lifetime.

1.2.4   Name an analog technology or device that has been replaced by digital technology but is still in use due to nostalgia.

1.2.5   Name a technology or device *invented* in your lifetime that could not have been possible without digital technology.

Chapter 2: Number Systems

Logic circuits are used to generate and transmit 1's and 0's to compute and convey information. This two-valued number system is called *binary*. As presented earlier, there are many advantages of using a binary system; however, the human brain has been taught to count, label and measure using the *decimal* number system. The decimal number system contains 10 unique symbols $(0 \rightarrow 9)$ commonly referred to as the *Arabic numerals*. Each of these symbols is assigned a relative magnitude to the other symbols. For example, 0 is less than 1, 1 is less than 2, etc. It is often conjectured that the 10 symbol number system that we humans use is due to the availability of our 10 fingers (or *digits*) to visualize counting up to 10. Regardless, our brains are trained to think of the real world in terms of a decimal system. In order to bridge the gap between the way our brains think (decimal) and how we build our computers (binary), we need to understand the basics of number systems. This includes the formal definition of a positional number system and how it can be extended to accommodate any arbitrarily large (or small) value. This also includes how to convert between different number systems that contain different numbers of symbols. In this chapter, we cover 4 different number systems: decimal (10 symbols), binary (2 symbols), octal (8 symbols), and hexadecimal (16 symbols). The study of decimal and binary is obvious as they represent how our brains interpret the physical world (decimal) and how our computers work (binary). Hexadecimal is studied because it is a useful means to represent large sets of binary values using a manageable number of symbols. Octal is rarely used but is studied as an example of how the formalization of the number systems can be applied to all systems regardless of the number of symbols they contain. This chapter will also discuss how to perform basic arithmetic in the binary number system and represent negative numbers.

Learning Outcomes – After completing this chapter, you will be able to:

2.1   Convert unsigned binary numbers to decimal.
2.2   Convert unsigned hexadecimal numbers to decimal.
2.3   Convert unsigned decimal numbers to binary.
2.4   Convert unsigned decimal numbers to hexadecimal.
2.5   Convert unsigned binary numbers to hexadecimal.
2.6   Convert unsigned hexadecimal numbers to binary.
2.7   Perform unsigned binary addition by hand.
2.8   Perform unsigned binary subtraction by hand.
2.9   Determine the range of an n-bit two's complement number.
2.10   Convert a signed decimal number to binary using two's complement representation.
2.11   Convert a signed two's complement binary number into decimal.
2.12   Perform signed binary addition by hand using two's complement representation.

2.1 Positional Number Systems

A positional number system allows the expansion of the original set of symbols so that they can be used to represent any arbitrarily large (or small) value. For example, if we use the 10 symbols in our decimal system, we can count from 0 to 9. Using just the individual symbols we do not have enough symbols to count beyond 9. To overcome this, we use the same set of symbols but assign a different value to the symbol based on its position within the number. The *position* of the symbol with respect to other symbols in the number allows an individual symbol to represent greater (or lesser) values. We can use this approach to represent numbers larger than the original set of symbols. For example, let's say we want to count from 0 upward by 1. We begin counting 0, 1, 2, 3, 4, 5, 6, 7, 8 to 9. When we are out of symbols and wish to go higher, we bring on a symbol in a different position with that position being valued higher and then start counting over with our original symbols (e.g., ..., 9, 10, 11,... 19, 20, 21,...). This is repeated each time a position runs out of symbols (e.g., ..., 99, 100, 101... 999, 1000, 1001,...).

First, let's look at the formation of a number system. The first thing that is needed is a set of symbols. The formal term for one of the symbols in a number system is a *numeral*. One or more numerals are used to form a *number*. We define the number of numerals in the system using the terms *radix* or *base*. For example, our decimal number system is said to be *base 10*, or have a *radix of 10* because it consists of 10 unique numerals or symbols.

Radix = Base ≡ the number of numerals in the number system

The next thing that is needed is the relative value of each numeral with respect to the other numerals in the set. We can say 0 < 1 < 2 < 3 etc. to define the relative magnitudes of the numerals in this set. The numerals are defined to be greater or less than their neighbors by a magnitude of 1. For example, in the decimal number system each of the subsequent numerals is greater than its predecessor by exactly 1. When we define this relative magnitude we are defining that the numeral 1 is greater than the numeral 0 by a magnitude of 1; the numeral 2 is greater than the numeral 1 by a magnitude of 1, etc. At this point we have the ability to count from 0 to 9 by 1's. We also have the basic structure for mathematical operations that have results that fall within the numeral set from 0 to 9 (e.g., 1+2=3). In order to expand the values that these numerals can represent, we need define the rules of a positional number system.

2.1.1 Generic Structure

In order to represent larger or smaller numbers than the lone numerals in a number system can represent, we adopt a positional system. In a positional number system, the relative position of the numeral within the overall number dictates its value. When we begin talking about the position of a numeral, we need to define a location to which all of the numerals are positioned with respect to. We define the *radix point* as the point within a number to which numerals to the left represent whole numbers and numerals to the right represent fractional numbers. The radix point is denoted with a period (i.e., "."). A particular number system often renames this radix point to reflect its base. For example, in the base 10 number system (i.e., decimal), the radix point is commonly called the *decimal point*; however, the term *radix point* can be used across all number systems as a generic term. If the radix point is not present in a number, it is assumed to be to the right of number. Figure 2.1 shows an example number highlighting the radix point and the relative positions of the whole and fractional numerals.

Figure 2.1
Definition of Radix Point

Next, we need to define the position of each numeral with respect to the radix point. The position of the numeral is assigned a whole number with the number to the left of the radix point having a position value of 0. The position number increases by 1 as numerals are added to the left (2, 3, 4…) and decreased by 1 as numerals are added to the right (-1, -2, -3). We will use the variable p to represent position. The position number will be used to calculate the value of each numeral in the number based on its relative position to the radix point. Figure 2.2 shows the example number with the position value of each numeral highlighted.

```
Definition of Position        1   3   2 . 6   5   4
                              ↑   ↑   ↑   ↑   ↑   ↑
                  Position (p) 2   1   0  -1  -2  -3
```

Figure 2.2
Definition of Position Number (p) within the Number

In order to create a generalized format of a number, we assign the term *digit* (d) to each of the numerals in the number. The term digit signifies that the numeral has a position. The position of the digit within the number is denoted as a subscript. The term *digit* can be used as a generic term to describe a numeral across all systems, although some number systems will use a unique term instead of digit which indicates its base. For example, the binary system uses the term *bit* instead of digit; however, using the term digit to describe a generic numeral in any system is still acceptable. Figure 2.3 shows the generic subscript notation used to describe the position of each digit in the number.

Figure 2.3
Digit Notation

We write a number from left to right starting with the highest position digit that is greater than 0 and end with the lowest position digit that is greater than 0. This reduces the amount of numerals that are written; however, a number can be represented with an arbitrary number of 0's to the left of the highest position digit greater than 0 and an arbitrary number of 0's to the right of the lowest position digit greater than 0 without affecting the value of the number. For example, the number 132.654 could be written as 0132.6540 without affecting the value of the number. The 0's to the left of the number are called *leading 0's* and the 0's to the right of the number are called *trailing 0's*. The reason this is being stated is because when a number is implemented in circuitry, the number of numerals is fixed and each numeral must have a value. The variable n is used to represent the number of numerals in a number. If a number is defined with $n=4$, that means 4 numerals are always used. The number 0 would be represented as 0000 with both representations having an equal value.

2.1.2 Decimal Number System (Base 10)

As mentioned earlier, the decimal number system contains 10 unique numerals (0, 1, 2, 3, 4, 5, 6, 7, 8 and 9). This system is thus a base 10 or a radix 10 system. The relative magnitudes of the symbols are $0 < 1 < 2 < 3 < 4 < 5 < 6 < 7 < 8 < 9$.

2.1.3 Binary Number System (Base 2)

The binary number system contains 2 unique numerals (0 and 1). This system is thus a base 2 or a radix 2 system. The relative magnitudes of the symbols are $0 < 1$. At first glance, this system looks very limited in its ability to represent large numbers due to the small number of numerals. When counting up, as soon as you count from 0 to 1, you are out of symbols and must increment the p+1 position in order to represent the next number (e.g., 0, 1, 10, 11, 100, 101, …); however, magnitudes of each position scale quickly so that circuits with a reasonable amount of digits can represent very large numbers. The term *bit* is used instead of *digit* in this system to describe the individual numerals and at the same time indicate the base of the number.

Due to the need for multiple bits to represent meaningful information, there are terms dedicated to describe the number of bits in a group. When 4 bits are grouped together, they are called a **nibble**. When 8 bits are grouped together, they are called a **byte**. Larger groupings of bits are called **words.** The size of the word can be stated as either an *n-bit word* or omitted if the size of the word is inherently implied. For example, if you were using a 32-bit microprocessor, using the term *word* would be interpreted as a *32-bit word.* For example, if there was a 32-bit grouping, it would be referred to as a 32-bit word. The leftmost bit in a binary number is called the ***Most Significant Bit*** **(MSB)**. The rightmost bit in a binary number is called the **Least Significant Bit (LSB)**.

2.1.4 Octal Number System (Base 8)

The octal number system contains 8 unique numerals (0, 1, 2, 3, 4, 5, 6, 7). This system is thus a base 8 or a radix 8 system. The relative magnitudes of the symbols are $0 < 1 < 2 < 3 < 4 < 5 < 6 < 7$. We use the generic term *digit* to describe the numerals within an octal number.

2.1.5 Hexadecimal Number System (Base 16)

The hexadecimal number system contains 16 unique numerals. This system is most often referred to in spoken word as "hex" for short. Since we only have 10 Arabic numerals in our familiar decimal system, we need to use other symbols to represent the remaining 6 numerals. We use the alphabetic characters A-F in order to expand the system to 16 numerals. The 16 numerals in the hexadecimal system are 0, 1, 2, 3, 4, 5, 6, 7, 8, 9, A, B, C, D, E and F. The relative magnitudes of the symbols are 0 < 1 < 2 < 3 < 4 < 5 < 6 < 7 < 8 < 9 < A < B < C < D < E < F. We use the generic term digit to describe the numerals within a hexadecimal number.

At this point, it becomes necessary to indicate the base of a written number. The number 10 has an entirely different value if it is a decimal number or binary number. In order to handle this, a subscript is typically included at the end of the number to denote its base. For example, 10_{10} indicates that this number is decimal "ten". If the number was written as 10_2, this number would represent binary "one zero". Table 2.1 lists the equivalent values in each of the 4 number systems just described for counts from 0_{10} to 15_{10}. The left side of the table does not include leading 0's. The right side of the table contains the same information but includes the leading zero's. The equivalencies of decimal, binary and hexadecimal in this table are typically committed to memory.

Equivalency Between Different Number Systems

Decimal	Binary	Octal	Hex	Decimal	Binary	Octal	Hex
0	0	0	0	00	0000	00	0
1	1	1	1	01	0001	01	1
2	10	2	2	02	0010	02	2
3	11	3	3	03	0011	03	3
4	100	4	4	04	0100	04	4
5	101	5	5	05	0101	05	5
6	110	6	6	06	0110	06	6
7	111	7	7	07	0111	07	7
8	1000	10	8	08	1000	10	8
9	1001	11	9	09	1001	11	9
10	1010	12	A	10	1010	12	A
11	1011	13	B	11	1011	13	B
12	1100	14	C	12	1100	14	C
13	1101	15	D	13	1101	15	D
14	1110	16	E	14	1110	16	E
15	1111	17	F	15	1111	17	F
(Without Leading 0's)				(With Leading 0's)			

Table 2.1
Number System Equivalency

CONCEPT CHECK

CC2.1 The base of a number system is arbitrary and is commonly selected to match a particular aspect of the physical system in which it is used (e.g., base 10 corresponds to our 10 fingers, base 2 corresponds to the 2 states of a switch). If a physical system contained 3 unique modes and a base of 3 was chosen for the number system, what is the base 3 equivalent of the decimal number 3?

A) $3_{10} = 11_3$ B) $3_{10} = 3_3$ C) $3_{10} = 10_3$ D) $3_{10} = 21_3$

2.2 Base Conversion

Now we look at converting between bases. There are distinct techniques for converting to and from decimal. There are also techniques for converting between bases that are powers of 2 (e.g., base 2, 4, 8, 16, etc.).

2.2.1 Converting to Decimal

The value of each digit within a number is based on the individual digit value and the digit's position. Each position in the number contains a different *weight* based on its relative location to the radix point. The weight of each position is based on the radix of the number system that is being used. The weight of each position in decimal is defined as:

Weight = (Radix)^p

This expression gives the number system the ability to represent fractional numbers since an expression with a negative exponent (e.g., x^{-y}) is evaluated as one over the expression with the exponent change to positive (e.g., $1/x^y$). Figure 2.4 shows the generic structure of a number with its positional weight highlighted.

Definition of Positional Weight

$$d_2 \; d_1 \; d_0 \; . \; d_{-1} \; d_{-2} \; d_{-3}$$

Weight = (radix)^p

$(radix)^2 \quad (radix)^0 \quad (radix)^{-2}$
$(radix)^1 \quad (radix)^{-1} \quad (radix)^{-3}$

Figure 2.4
Weight Definition

In order to find the decimal value of each of the numerals in the number, its individual numeral value is multiplied by its positional weight. In order to find the value of the entire number, each value of the individual numeral-weight products is summed. The generalized format of this conversion is written as:

$$Total\ Decimal\ Value = \sum_{i=p_{min}}^{p_{max}} d_i \cdot (radix)^i$$

In this expression, p_{max} represents the highest position number that contains a numeral greater than 0. The variable p_{min} represents the lowest position number that contains a numeral greater than 0. These limits are used to simplify the hand calculations; however, these terms theoretically could be $+\infty$ to $-\infty$ with no effect on the result since the summation of every leading 0 and every trailing 0 contributes nothing to the result.

As an example, let's evaluate this expression for a decimal number. The result will yield the original number but will illustrate how positional weight is used. Let's take the number 132.654_{10}. To find the decimal value of this number, each numeral is multiplied by its positional weight and then all of the products are summed. The positional weight for the digit 1 is (radix)^p or $(10)^2$. In decimal this is called the hundred's position. The positional weight for the digit 3 is $(10)^1$, referred to as the ten's position. The positional weight for digit 2 is $(10)^0$, referred to as the one's position. The positional weight for digit 6 is $(10)^{-1}$, referred to as the tenth's position. The positional weight for digit 5 is $(10)^{-2}$, referred to as the hundredth's position. The positional weight for digit 4 is $(10)^{-3}$, referred to as the thousandth's position.

When these weights are multiplied by their respective digits and summed, the result is the original decimal number 132.654_{10}. Example 2.1 shows this process step-by-step.

Example: Convert 132.654_{10} to Decimal:

$$1 \quad 3 \quad 2 \;.\; 6 \quad 5 \quad 4_{10}$$

Position (p) → $2 \quad 1 \quad 0 \quad \text{-}1 \quad \text{-}2 \quad \text{-}3$

Weight → $(10)^2 \; (10)^1 \; (10)^0 \; (10)^{-1} (10)^{-2} (10)^{-3}$

$$\text{Value} = \sum_{i=-3}^{2} d_i \cdot 10^{\,i}$$

$$\text{Value} = 1 \cdot 10^2 + 3 \cdot 10^1 + 2 \cdot 10^0 + 6 \cdot 10^{-1} + 5 \cdot 10^{-2} + 4 \cdot 10^{-3}$$

$$\text{Value} = 1 \cdot (100) + 3 \cdot (10) + 2 \cdot (1) + 6 \cdot (^1/_{10}) + 5 \cdot (^1/_{100}) + 4 \cdot (^1/_{1000})$$

$$\text{Value} = 100 + 30 + 2 + 0.6 + 0.05 + 0.004$$

$$\text{Value} = 132.654_{10}$$

Example 2.1
Converting Decimal to Decimal

This process is used to convert between any other base to decimal.

2.2.1.1 Binary to Decimal

Let's convert 101.11_2 to decimal. The same process is followed with the exception that the base in the summation is changed to 2. Converting from binary to decimal can be accomplished quickly in your head due to the fact that the bit values in the products are either 1 or 0. That means any bit that is a 0 has no impact on the outcome and any bit that is a 1 simply yields the weight of its position. Example 2.2 shows the step-by-step process converting a binary number to decimal.

Example 2.2
Converting Binary to Decimal

2.2.1.2 Octal to Decimal

When converting from octal to decimal, the same process is followed with the exception that the base in the weight is changed to 8. Example 2.3 shows an example of converting an octal number to decimal.

Example: Convert 17.17_8 to Decimal:

$$1 \quad 7 \quad . \quad 1 \quad 7_8$$

Position (p) ⟶ 1 0 -1 -2

Weight ⟶ $(8)^1$ $(8)^0$ $(8)^{-1}$ $(8)^{-2}$

$$\text{Value} = \sum_{i=-2}^{1} d_i \cdot 8^i$$

$$\text{Value} = 1 \cdot 8^1 + 7 \cdot 8^0 + 1 \cdot 8^{-1} + 7 \cdot 8^{-2}$$

$$\text{Value} = 1 \cdot (8) + 7 \cdot (1) + 1 \cdot (1/8) + 7 \cdot (1/64)$$

$$\text{Value} = 8 + 7 + 0.125 + 0.109375$$

$$\text{Value} = 15.234375_{10}$$

Example 2.3
Converting Octal to Decimal

2.2.1.3 Hexadecimal to Decimal

Let's convert $1AB.EF_{16}$ to decimal. The same process is followed with the exception that the base is changed to 16. When performing the conversion, the decimal equivalent of the numerals A-F need to be used. Example 2.4 shows the step-by-step process converting a hexadecimal number to decimal.

Example 2.4
Converting Hexadecimal to Decimal

2.2.2 Converting from Decimal

The process of converting from decimal to another base consists of two separate algorithms. There is one algorithm for converting the whole number portion of the number and another algorithm for converting the fractional portion of the number. The process for converting the whole number portion is to divide the decimal number by the base of the system you wish to convert to. The division will result in a quotient and a whole number remainder. The remainder is recorded as the *least significant numeral* in the converted number. The resulting quotient is then divided again by the base, which results in a new quotient and new remainder. The remainder is recorded as the next higher order numeral in the new number. This process is repeated until a quotient of 0 is achieved. At that point the conversion is complete. The remainders will always be within the numeral set of the base being converted to.

The process for converting the fractional portion is to multiply just the fractional component of the number by the base. This will result in a product that contains a whole number and a fraction. The whole number is recorded as the *most significant digit* of the new converted number. The new fractional portion is then multiplied again by the base with the whole number portion being recorded as the next lower order numeral. This process is repeated until the product yields a fractional component equal to zero or the desired level of accuracy has been achieved. The level of accuracy is specified by the number of numerals in the new converted number. For example, the conversion would be stated as "convert this decimal number to binary with a fractional accuracy of 4 bits". This means the algorithm would stop once 4-bits of fraction had been achieved in the conversion.

2.2.2.1 Decimal to Binary

Let's convert 11.375_{10} to binary. Example 2.5 shows the step-by-step process converting a decimal number to binary.

Example: Convert 11.375_{10} to Binary:

$$1\,1\,.\,3\,7\,5_{10}$$

Part 1: Converting the whole number portion:

	Quotient	Remainder	
Step 1: $2\,\overline{\smash{)}\,11}$	5	1	LSB
Step 2: $2\,\overline{\smash{)}\,5}$	2	1	Next highest order bit
Step 3: $2\,\overline{\smash{)}\,2}$	1	0	Next highest order bit
Step 4: $2\,\overline{\smash{)}\,1}$	0	1	MSB
	Done		Converted Whole Number = 1011_2

Part 2: Converting the fractional number portion:

	Product	Whole Number	
Step 1: $2 \cdot (0.375)$	0.75	0	MSB
Step 2: $2 \cdot (0.75)$	1.50	1	Next lower order bit
Step 3: $2 \cdot (0.5)$	1.00	1	LSB
	Done		Converted Fractional Number = $.011_2$

Part 3: Combine the two components to form the new number:

$$1\,0\,1\,1\,.\,0\,1\,1_2$$

Example 2.5
Converting Decimal to Binary

2.2.2.2 Decimal to Octal

Let's convert 10.4_{10} to octal with an accuracy of 4 fractional digits. When converting the fractional component of the number, the algorithm is continued until 4 digits worth of fractional numerals has been achieved. Once the accuracy has been achieved, the conversion is finished even though a product with a zero fractional value has not been obtained. Example 2.6 shows the step-by-step process converting a decimal number to octal with a fractional accuracy of 4 digits.

Example: Convert 10.4_{10} to Octal with an Accuracy of 4 fractional digits:

$$10 \cdot 4_{10}$$

Part 1: Converting the whole number portion:

	Quotient	Remainder	
Step 1: 8 ⟌ 10	1	2	Least significant digit
Step 2: 8 ⟌ 1	0	1	Most significant digit
	Done	Converted Whole Number = 12_8	

Part 2: Converting the fractional number portion:

	Product	Whole Number	
Step 1: 8 · (0.4)	3.2	3	Most significant digit
Step 2: 8 · (0.2)	1.6	1	Next lower order digit
Step 3: 8 · (0.6)	4.8	4	Next lower order digit
Step 4: 8 · (0.8)	6.4	6	Least significant digit

Converted Fractional Number = $.3146_8$

Done because we have achieved the desired accuracy

Part 3: Combine the two components to form the new number:

$$1\,2 \cdot 3\,1\,4\,6_8$$

Example 2.6
Converting Decimal to Octal

2.2.2.3 Decimal to Hexadecimal

Let's convert 254.655_{10} to hexadecimal with an accuracy of 3 fractional digits. When doing this conversion, all of the divisions and multiplications are done using decimal. If the results end up between 10_{10} and 15_{10}, then the decimal numbers are substituted with their hex symbol equivalent (i.e., A to F). Example 2.7 shows the step-by-step process of converting a decimal number to hex with a fractional accuracy of 3 digits.

Example: Convert 254.655_{10} to Hexadecimal with an Accuracy of 3 fractional digits:

$$254 . 655_{10}$$

Part 1: Converting the whole number portion:

		Quotient	Remainder	
Step 1:	16 $\overline{)254}$	15 (F_{16})	14 (E_{16})	Least significant digit
Step 2:	16 $\overline{)15}$	0	15 (F_{16})	Most significant digit
		Done	Converted Whole Number = FE_{16}	

Part 2: Converting the fractional number portion:

		Product	Whole Number	
Step 1:	16 · (0.655)	10.48	10 (A_{16})	Most significant digit
Step 2:	16 · (0.48)	7.68	7	Next lower order digit
Step 3:	16 · (0.68)	10.88	10 (A_{16})	Least significant digit
			Converted Fractional Number = $.A7A_{16}$	

Done because we have achieved the desired accuracy

Part 3: Combine the two components to form the new number:

$$F E . A 7 A_{16}$$

Example 2.7
Converting Decimal to Hexadecimal

2.2.3 Converting Between 2^n Bases

Converting between 2^n bases (e.g., 2, 4, 8, 16, etc.) takes advantage of the direct mapping that each of these bases has back to binary. Base 8 numbers take exactly 3 binary bits to represent all 8 symbols (i.e., $0_8 = 000_2$, $7_8 = 111_2$). Base 16 numbers take exactly 4 binary bits to represent all 16 symbols (i.e., $0_{16} = 0000_2$, $F_{16} = 1111_2$).

When converting *from* binary to any other 2^n base, the whole number bits are grouped into the appropriate-sized sets starting from the radix point and working left. If the final leftmost grouping does not have enough symbols, it is simply padded on left with leading 0's. Each of these groups is then directly substituted with their 2^n base symbol. The fractional number bits are also grouped into the appropriate-sized sets starting from the radix point, but this time working right. Again, if the final rightmost grouping does not have enough symbols, it is simply padded on the right with trailing 0's. Each of these groups is then directly substituted with their 2^n base symbol.

2.2.3.1 Binary to Octal

Example 2.8 shows the step-by-step process of converting a binary number to octal.

Example: Convert 10111.01_2 to Octal:

$$10111.01_2$$

Part 1: Form groups of 3 bits representing octal symbols.

$$(0\ 1\ 0)\ (1\ 1\ 1)\ .\ (0\ 1\ 0)_2$$

Whole number groupings start at the radix point and work left. Leading 0's are added as necessary.

Fractional number groupings start at the radix point and work right. Trailing 0's are added as necessary.

Part 2: Perform a direct substitution of the bit groupings with the equivalent octal symbol.

$$(0\ 1\ 0)\ (1\ 1\ 1)\ .\ (0\ 1\ 0)_2$$

$$2\ 7\ .\ 2_8$$

Example 2.8
Converting Binary to Octal

2.2.3.2 Binary to Hexadecimal

Example 2.9 shows the step-by-step process of converting a binary number to hexadecimal.

Example: Convert 111011.11111_2 to Hexadecimal:

$$111011.11111_2$$

Part 1: Form groups of 4 bits representing hex symbols.

$$(0\ 0\ 1\ 1)\ (1\ 0\ 1\ 1)\ .\ (1\ 1\ 1\ 1)\ (1\ 0\ 0\ 0)_2$$

Whole number groupings start at the radix point and work left. Leading 0's are added as necessary.

Fractional number groupings start at the radix point and work right. Trailing 0's are added as necessary.

Part 2: Perform a direct substitution of the bit groupings with the equivalent hex symbol.

$$(0\ 0\ 1\ 1)\ (1\ 0\ 1\ 1)\ .\ (1\ 1\ 1\ 1)\ (1\ 0\ 0\ 0)_2$$

$$3\ B\ .\ F\ 8_{16}$$

Example 2.9
Converting Binary to Hexadecimal

2.2.3.3 Octal to Binary

When converting *to* binary from any 2^n base, each of the symbols in the originating number are replaced with the appropriate-sized number of bits. An octal symbol will be replaced with 3 binary bits while a hexadecimal symbol will be replaced with 4 binary bits. Any leading or trailing 0's can be removed from the converted number once complete. Example 2.10 shows the step-by-step process of converting an octal number to binary.

Example: Convert 347.12_8 to Binary:

$$347 . 12_8$$

Part 1: Each of the octal symbols is replaced with its 3 bit binary equivalent.

$$347 . 12_8$$

$$(0\ 1\ 1)\ (1\ 0\ 0)\ (1\ 1\ 1)\ .\ (0\ 0\ 1)\ (0\ 1\ 0)_2$$

Leading and Trailing 0's can be removed

$$11100111 . 00101_2$$

Example 2.10
Converting Octal to Binary

2.2.3.4 Hexadecimal to Binary

Example 2.11 shows the step-by-step process of converting a hexadecimal number to binary.

Example: Convert $1B.A_{16}$ to Binary:

Part 1: Each of the hex symbols is replaced with its 4 bit binary equivalent.

$$1\ B . A_{16}$$

$$(0\ 0\ 0\ 1)\ (1\ 0\ 1\ 1)\ .\ (1\ 0\ 1\ 0)_2$$

Part 2: Leading and trailing zeros can be removed.

$$11011 . 101_2$$

Example 2.11
Converting Hexadecimal to Binary

2.2.3.5 Octal to Hexadecimal

When converting between 2^n bases (excluding binary) the number is first converted into binary and then converted from binary into the final 2^n base using the algorithms described before. Example 2.12 shows the step-by-step process of converting an octal number to hexadecimal.

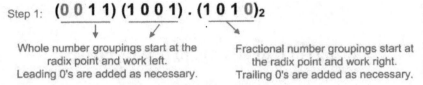

Example: Convert 71.5_8 to Hexadecimal:

Part 1: Convert the octal number into binary. Each octal symbol is represented with 3 bits.

$$7\ 1\ .\ 5_8$$

$$(1\ 1\ 1)\ (0\ 0\ 1)\ .\ (1\ 0\ 1)_2$$

$$111001\ .\ 101_2$$

Part 2: Convert the binary number into hexadecimal. Form groups of 4 bits representing hex symbols.

Step 1: $(0\ 0\ 1\ 1)\ (1\ 0\ 0\ 1)\ .\ (1\ 0\ 1\ 0)_2$

Whole number groupings start at the radix point and work left.
Leading 0's are added as necessary.

Fractional number groupings start at the radix point and work right.
Trailing 0's are added as necessary.

Step 2: $(0\ 0\ 1\ 1)\ (1\ 0\ 0\ 1)\ .\ (1\ 0\ 1\ 0)_2$

$$3\ 9\ .\ A_{16}$$

Example 2.12
Converting Octal to Hexadecimal

2.2.3.6 Hexadecimal to Octal

Example 2.13 shows the step-by-step process of converting a hexadecimal number to octal.

Example: Convert $AB.C_{16}$ to Octal:

$$AB\ .\ C_{16}$$

Part 1: Convert the hex number into binary. Each hex symbol is represented with 4 bits.

$$AB\ .\ C_{16}$$

$$(1\ 0\ 1\ 0)\ (1\ 0\ 1\ 1)\ .\ (1\ 1\ 0\ 0)_2$$

$$10101011\ .\ 11_2$$

Part 2: Convert the binary number into octal. Form groups of 3 bits representing octal symbols.

Step 1: $(0\ 1\ 0)\ (1\ 0\ 1)\ (0\ 1\ 1)\ .\ (1\ 1\ 0)_2$

Step 2: $2\ 5\ 3\ .\ 6_8$

Example 2.13
Converting Hexadecimal to Octal

CONCEPT CHECK

CC2.2 A "googol" is the term for the decimal number 1e100. When written out manually this number is a 1 with 100 zero's after it (e.g., 10,000,000,000,000,000,000,000, 000,000,000,000,000,000,000,000,000,000,000,000,000,000,000,000,000,00 0,000,000,000,000,000). This term is more commonly associated with the search engine company Google, which uses a different spelling but is pronounced the same. How many bits does it take to represent a googol in binary?

A) 100 bits   B) 256 bits   C) 332 bits   D) 333 bits

2.3 Binary Arithmetic

2.3.1 Addition (Carries)

Binary addition is a straightforward process that mirrors the approach we have learned for longhand decimal addition. The two numbers (or terms) to be added are aligned at the radix point and addition begins at the least significant bit. If the sum of the least significant position yields a value with two bits (e.g., 10_2), then the least significant bit is recorded and the most significant bit is *carried* to the next higher position. The sum of the next higher position is then performed including the potential *carry bit* from the prior addition. This process continues from the least significant position to the most significant position. Example 2.14 shows how addition is performed on two individual bits.

Example: Single Bit Binary Addition

There are four possible results when adding two bits.

0	0	1	1
+ 0	+ 1	+ 0	+ 1
0	1	1	Carry → 1 0

Example 2.14
Single Bit Binary Addition

When performing binary addition, the width of the inputs and output is fixed (i.e., n-bits). Carries that exist within the n-bits are treated in the normal fashion of including them in the next higher position sum; however, if the highest position summation produces a carry, this is a uniquely named event. This event is called a *carry out* or the sum is said to *generate a carry*. The reason this type of event is given special terminology is because in real circuitry, the number of bits of the inputs and output is fixed in hardware and the carry out is typically handled by a separate circuit. Example 2.15 shows this process when adding two 4-bit numbers.

Example: What is the sum of 1010.1_2 and 1110.1_2? Did this addition generate a carry?

The two numbers are aligned at the radix point and addition begins at the least significant position. Carries are recorded at each position and used in the addition of the next higher position.

The addition starts in the least significant position

The bitwise summation continues to the most significant position.

If a carry results, it is used in the next higher order position summation.

The sum of these two numbers is 11001.0_2. Since the inputs each had n=5 but the sum required n=6, we say that this addition "generated a carry". Another way of stating the result is "1001_2 with a carry".

Example 2.15
Multiple Bit Binary Addition

The largest decimal sum that can result from the addition of two binary numbers is given by $2 \cdot (2^n-1)$. For example, two 8-bit numbers to be added could both represent their highest decimal value of (2^n-1) or 255_{10} (i.e., $1111\ 1111_2$). The sum of this number would result in 510_{10} or ($1\ 1111\ 1110_2$). Notice that the largest sum achievable would only require one additional bit. This means that a single carry bit is sufficient to handle all possible magnitudes for binary addition.

2.3.2 Subtraction (Borrows)

Binary subtraction also mirrors longhand decimal subtraction. In subtraction, the formal terms for the two numbers being operated on are *minuend* and *subtrahend*. The subtrahend is subtracted from the minuend to find the *difference*. In longhand subtraction, the minuend is the top number and the subtrahend is the bottom number. For a given position if the minuend is less than the subtrahend, it needs to *borrow* from the next higher order position to produce a difference that is positive. If the next higher position does not have a value that can be borrowed from (i.e., 0), then it in turn needs to borrow from the next higher position, and so forth. Example 2.16 shows how subtraction is performed on two individual bits.

Example: Single Bit Binary Subtraction

There are four possible results when subtracting two bits.

Example 2.16
Single Bit Binary Subtraction

As with binary addition, binary subtraction is accomplished on fixed widths of inputs and output (i.e., n-bits). The minuend and subtrahend are aligned at the radix point and subtraction begins at the least significant bit position. Borrows are used as necessary as the subtractions move from the least significant position to the most significant position. If the most significant position requires a borrow, this is a uniquely named event. This event is called a *borrow in* or the subtraction is said to *require a borrow*. Again, the reason this event is uniquely named is because in real circuitry, the number of bits of the input and output is fixed in hardware and the borrow in is typically handled by a separate circuit. Example 2.17 shows this process when subtracting two 4-bit numbers.

Example: What is the difference between 1011.0_2 and 0100.1_2? Did this subtraction require a borrow in?

The way this question is phrased indicates that 1011.0_2 is the minuend and 0100.1_2 is the subtrahend. The two numbers are aligned at the radix point and subtraction begins at the least significant position. Borrows are taken as needed from the next higher order position.

The subtraction starts in the least significant position

The difference of these two numbers is 0110.1_2 and it did not require a borrow in. To double-check if this subtraction worked, we can look at the decimal equivalents of the numbers: 1011.0_2 (11_{10}) - 0100.1_2 (4.5_{10}) = 0110.1_2 (6.5_{10}), which verifies the subtraction was correct.

Example 2.17
Multiple Bit Binary Subtraction

Notice that if the minuend is less than the subtrahend, then the difference will be negative. At this point, we need a way to handle negative numbers.

CONCEPT CHECK

CC2.3 If an 8-bit computer system can only perform unsigned addition on 8-bit inputs and produce an 8-bit sum, how is it possible for this computer to perform addition on numbers that are larger than what can be represented with 8-bits (e.g., $1{,}000_{10} + 1{,}000_{10} = 2{,}000_{10}$)?

A) There are multiple 8-bit adders in a computer to handle large numbers.

B) The result is simply rounded to the nearest 8-bit number.

C) The computer returns an error and requires smaller numbers to be entered.

D) The computer keeps track of the carry out and uses it in a subsequent 8-bit addition, which enables larger numbers to be handled.

2.4 Unsigned and Signed Numbers

All of the number systems presented in the prior sections were positive. We need to also have a mechanism to indicate negative numbers. When looking at negative numbers, we only focus on the mapping between decimal and binary since octal and hexadecimal are used as just another representation of a binary number. In decimal, we are able to use the negative *sign* in front of a number to indicate it is negative (e.g., -34_{10}). In binary, this notation works fine for writing numbers on paper (e.g., -1010_2), but we need a mechanism that can be implemented using real circuitry. In a real digital circuit, the circuits can only deal with 0's and 1's. There is no "-" in a digital circuit. Since we only have 0's and 1's in the hardware, we use a bit to represent whether a number is positive or negative. This is referred to as the *sign bit*. If a binary number is not going to have any negative values, then it is called an **unsigned** number and it can only represent positive numbers. If a binary number is going to allow negative numbers, it is called a **signed** number. It is important to always keep track of the type of number we are using as the same bit values can represent very different numbers depending on the coding mechanism that is being used.

2.4.1 Unsigned Numbers

An unsigned number is one that does not allow negative numbers. When talking about this type of code, the number of bits is fixed and stated up front. We use the variable n to represent the number of bits in the number. For example, if we had an 8-bit number, we would say, "This is an 8-bit, unsigned number".

The number of unique codes in an unsigned number is given by 2^n. For example, if we had an 8-bit number, we would have 2^8 or 256 unique codes (e.g., $0000\ 0000_2$ to $1111\ 1111_2$).

The *range* of an unsigned number refers to the decimal values that the binary code can represent. If we use the notation $N_{unsigned}$ to represent any possible value that an n-bit, unsigned number can take on, the range would be defined as: $0 < N_{unsigned} < (2^n - 1)$

$$\textbf{Range of an UNSIGNED number} \quad \Rightarrow \quad 0 \leq N_{unsigned} \leq (2^n - 1)$$

For example, if we had an unsigned number with n=4, it could take on a range of values from $+0_{10}$ (0000_2) to $+15_{10}$ (1111_2). Notice that while this number has 16 unique possible codes, the highest decimal value it can represent is 15_{10}. This is because one of the unique codes represents 0_{10}. This is the reason that the highest decimal value that can be represented is given by (2^n-1). Example 2.18 shows this process for a 16-bit number.

Example: What is the range of decimal numbers that an 16-bit, unsigned word can represent?

The term "16-bit word" means that the binary number has n=16. We can plug this into the equation for the range of an unsigned numbers directly.

$$0 \leq N_{unsigned} \leq (2^n - 1)$$
$$\downarrow$$
$$0 \leq N_{unsigned} \leq (2^{16} - 1)$$
$$\downarrow$$
$$0 \leq N_{unsigned} \leq (65{,}536 - 1)$$
$$\downarrow$$
$$0 \leq N_{unsigned} \leq 65{,}535$$

An unsigned 16-bit word can represent decimal numbers from 0 to 65,535.

Example 2.18
Finding the Range of an Unsigned Number

2.4.2 Signed Numbers

Signed numbers are able to represent both positive and negative numbers. The most significant bit of these numbers is always the *sign bit*, which represents whether the number is positive or negative. The sign bit is defined to be a **0 if the number is positive** and **1 if the number is negative**. When using signed numbers, the number of bits is fixed so that the sign bit is always in the same position. There are a variety of ways to encode negative numbers using a sign bit. The encoding method used exclusively in modern computers is called *two's complement*. There are two other encoding techniques called *signed magnitude* and *one's complement* that are rarely used but are studied to motivate the power of two's complement. When talking about a signed number, the number of bits and the type of encoding is always stated. For example, we would say, "This is an 8-bit, two's complement number".

2.4.2.1 Signed Magnitude

Signed Magnitude is the simplest way to encode a negative number. In this approach, the most significant bit (i.e., leftmost bit) of the binary number is considered the sign bit (0=positive, 1=negative). The rest of the bits to the right of the sign bit represent the magnitude or absolute value of the number. As an example of this approach, let's look at the decimal values that a 4-bit, signed magnitude number can take on. These are shown in Example 2.19.

Example: What decimal values can a 4-bit "Signed Magnitude" code represent?

Decimal	4-bit Signed Magnitude
-7	1111
-6	1110
-5	1101
-4	1100
-3	1011
-2	1010
-1	1001
-0	1000
0	0000
1	0001
2	0010
3	0011
4	0100
5	0101
6	0110
7	0111

└─Sign bit

Example 2.19
Decimal Values that a 4-bit, Signed Magnitude Code Can Represent

There are drawbacks of signed magnitude encoding that are apparent from this example. First, the value of 0_{10} has two signed magnitude codes (0000_2 and 1000_2). This is an inefficient use of the available codes and leads to complexity when building arithmetic circuitry since it must account for two codes representing the same number.

The second drawback is that addition using the negative numbers does not directly map to how decimal addition works. For example, in decimal if we added (-5) + (1), the result would be -4. In signed magnitude, adding these numbers using a traditional adder would produce (-5) + (1) = (-6). This is because the traditional addition would take place on the magnitude portion of the number. A 5_{10} is represented with 101_2. Adding 1 to this number would result in the next higher binary code 110_2 or 6_{10}. Since the sign portion is separate, the addition is performed on |5|, thus yielding 6. Once the sign bit is included, the resulting number is -6. It is certainly possible to build an addition circuit that works on signed magnitude numbers, but it is more complex than a traditional adder because it must perform a different addition operation for the negative numbers versus the positive numbers. It is advantageous to have a single adder that works across the entire set of numbers.

Due to the duplicate codes for 0, the range of decimal numbers that signed magnitude can represent is reduced by 1 compared to unsigned encoding. For an n-bit number, there are 2^n unique binary codes available but only $2^n - 1$ can be used to represent unique decimal numbers. If we use the notation N_{SM} to represent any possible value that an n-bit, signed magnitude number can take on, the range would be defined as:

Range of a SIGNED MAGNITUDE number $\Rightarrow$ $-(2^{n-1} - 1) \leq N_{SM} \leq +(2^{n-1} - 1)$

Example 2.20 shows how to use this expression to find the range of decimal values that an 8-bit, signed magnitude code can represent.

> Example: What is the range of decimal numbers that an 8-bit, signed magnitude number can represent?
>
> The term "8-bit" means that n=8. We can plug this into the equation for the range of a signed magnitude number directly.
>
> $$-(2^{n-1}-1) \leq N_{SM} \leq +(2^{n-1}-1)$$
>
> $$\downarrow$$
>
> $$-(2^{8-1}-1) \leq N_{SM} \leq +(2^{8-1}-1)$$
>
> $$\downarrow$$
>
> $$-127 \leq N_{SM} \leq +127$$
>
> An 8-bit, signed magnitude number can represent decimal numbers from -127 to +127.

Example 2.20
Finding the Range of a Signed Magnitude Number

The process to determine the decimal value from a signed magnitude binary code involves treating the sign bit separately from the rest of the code. The sign bit provides the polarity of the decimal number (0=Positive, 1=Negative). The remaining bits in the code are treated as unsigned numbers and converted to decimal using the standard conversion procedure described in the prior sections. This conversion yields the magnitude of the decimal number. The final decimal value is found by applying the sign. Example 2.21 shows an example of this process.

> Example: What is the decimal value of the 5-bit, signed magnitude code 11010_2?
>
> The most significant bit of this 5-bit number is a 1, which indicates that the number is negative.
>
> Sign Bit ⟶ **1**1010 ⟵ Magnitude
>
> The remaining 4-bits are the magnitude of the decimal number and are converted directly to decimal.
>
> $$1\ 0\ 1\ 0_2$$
>
> $$\downarrow$$
>
> $$|\text{Value}| = \sum_{i=0}^{3} d_i \cdot 2^i$$
>
> $$\downarrow$$
>
> $$|\text{Value}| = 1 \cdot 2^3 + 0 \cdot 2^2 + 1 \cdot 2^1 + 0 \cdot 2^0$$
>
> $$\downarrow$$
>
> $$|\text{Value}| = 1 \cdot (8) + 0 \cdot (4) + 1 \cdot (2) + 0 \cdot (1)$$
>
> $$\downarrow$$
>
> $$|\text{Value}| = 8 + 0 + 2 + 0$$
>
> $$\downarrow$$
>
> $$|\text{Value}| = 10_{10}$$
>
> The negative sign is then added back to the converted number giving a decimal value of -10_{10}

Example 2.21
Finding the Decimal Value of a Signed Magnitude Number

2.4.2.2 One's Complement

One's complement is another simple way to encode negative numbers. In this approach, the negative number is obtained by taking its positive equivalent and flipping all of the 1's to 0's and 0's to 1's. This procedure of *flipping the bits* is called a **complement** (notice the two *e*'s). In this way, the most significant bit of the number is still the sign bit (0=positive, 1=negative). The rest of the bits represent the value of the number, but in this encoding scheme the negative number values are less intuitive. As an example of this approach, let's look at the decimal values that a 4-bit, one's complement number can take on. These are shown in Example 2.22.

Example: What decimal values can a 4-bit "One's Complement" code represent?

Decimal	4-bit One's Complement
-7	1000
-6	1001
-5	1010
-4	1011
-3	1100
-2	1101
-1	1110
-0	1111
0	0000
1	0001
2	0010
3	0011
4	0100
5	0101
6	0110
7	0111

$\llcorner$ Sign bit

Example 2.22
Decimal Values that a 4-bit, One's Complement Code Can Represent

Again, we notice that there are two different codes for 0_{10} (0000_2 and 1111_2). This is a drawback of one's complement because it reduces the possible range of numbers that can be represented from 2^n to (2^n-1) and requires arithmetic operations that take into account the gap in the number system. There are advantages of one's complement, however. First, the numbers are ordered such that traditional addition works on both positive and negative numbers (excluding the double 0 gap). Taking the example of (-5) + (1) again, in one's complement the result yields -4, just as in a traditional decimal system. Notice in one's complement, -5_{10} is represented with 1010_2. Adding 1 to this entire binary code would result in the next higher binary code 1011_2 or -4_{10} from the above table. This makes addition circuitry less complicated, but still not as simple as if the double 0 gap was eliminated. Another advantage of one's complement is that as the numbers are incremented beyond the largest value in the set, they *roll over* and start counting at the lowest number. For example, if you increment the number 0111_2 (7_{10}), it goes to the next higher binary code 1000_2, which is -7_{10}. The ability to have the numbers roll over is a useful feature for computer systems.

If we use the notation N_{1comp} to represent any possible value that an n-bit, one's complement number can take on, the range is defined as:

Range of a ONE'S COMPLEMENT number $\Rightarrow$ $-(2^{n-1} - 1) \leq N_{1's\ comp} \leq +(2^{n-1} - 1)$

Example 2.23 shows how to use this expression to find the range of decimal values that a 24-bit, one's complement code can represent.

Example: What is the range of decimal numbers that a 24-bit, one's complement number can represent?

The term "24-bit" means that n=24. We can plug this into the equation for the range of a one's complement number directly.

$$-(2^{n-1}-1) \leq N_{1comp} \leq +(2^{n-1} - 1)$$

$$\downarrow$$

$$-(2^{24-1}-1) \leq N_{1comp} \leq +(2^{24-1} - 1)$$

$$\downarrow$$

$$-8{,}388{,}607 \leq N_{1comp} \leq +8{,}388{,}607$$

A 24-bit, one's complement number can represent decimal numbers from -8,388,607 to +8,388,607.

Example 2.23
Finding the Range of a 1's Complement Number

The process of finding the decimal value of a one's complement number involves first identifying whether the number is positive or negative by looking at the sign bit. If the number is positive (i.e., the sign bit is 0), then the number is treated as an unsigned code and is converted to decimal using the standard conversion procedure described in prior sections. If the number is negative (i.e., the sign bit is 1), then the number sign is recorded separately and the code is complemented in order to convert it to its positive magnitude equivalent. This new positive number is then converted to decimal using the standard conversion procedure. As the final step, the sign is applied. Example 2.24 shows an example of this process.

Example: What is the decimal value of the 5-bit, one's complement code 11010_2?

The most significant bit of this 5-bit number is a 1, which indicates that the number is negative.

Sign Bit → **1**1010

To find the magnitude of the number, we first perform a complement on the entire number to find its positive equivalent.

$$1\ 1\ 0\ 1\ 0_2$$
$$\downarrow$$
$$0\ 0\ 1\ 0\ 1_2$$

A complement operation turns all 1's to 0's and all 0's to 1's

The number can now be converted into decimal to find its magnitude.

$$|Value| = \sum_{i=0}^{4} d_i \cdot 2^i$$

$$\downarrow$$

$$|Value| = 0 \cdot 2^4 + 0 \cdot 2^3 + 1 \cdot 2^2 + 0 \cdot 2^1 + 1 \cdot 2^0$$

$$\downarrow$$

$$|Value| = 0 \cdot (16) + 0 \cdot (8) + 1 \cdot (4) + 0 \cdot (2) + 1 \cdot (1)$$

$$\downarrow$$

$$|Value| = 0 + 0 + 4 + 0 + 1 = 5_{10}$$

The negative sign is then added back to the converted number giving a decimal value of -5_{10}

Example 2.24
Finding the Decimal Value of a 1's Complement Number

2.4.2.3 Two's Complement

Two's complement is an encoding scheme that addresses the double 0 issue in signed magnitude and 1's complement representations. In this approach, the negative number is obtained by subtracting its positive equivalent from 2^n. This is identical to performing a complement on the positive equivalent and then adding one. If a carry is generated, it is discarded. This procedure is called "*taking the two's complement of a number*". The procedure of complementing each bit and adding one is the most common technique to perform a two's complement. In this way, the most significant bit of the number is still the sign bit (0=positive, 1=negative) but all of the negative numbers are in essence *shifted up* so that the double 0 gap is eliminated. Taking the two's complement of a positive number will give its negative counterpart and vice versa. Let's look at the decimal values that a 4-bit, two's complement number can take on. These are shown in Example 2.25.

Example: What decimal values can a 4-bit "Two's Complement" code represent?

Decimal	4-bit Two's Complement
-8	1000
-7	1001
-6	1010
-5	1011
-4	1100
-3	1101
-2	1110
-1	1111
0	0000
1	0001
2	0010
3	0011
4	0100
5	0101
6	0110
7	0111

└─Sign bit

Example 2.25
Decimal Values that a 4-bit, Two's Complement Code Can Represent

There are many advantages of two's complement encoding. First, there is no double 0 gap, which means that all possible 2^n unique codes that can exist in an n-bit number are used. This gives the largest possible range of numbers that can be represented. Another advantage of two's complement is that addition with negative numbers works exactly the same as decimal. In our example of (-5) + (1), the result (-4). Arithmetic circuitry can be built to mimic the way our decimal arithmetic works without the need to consider the double 0 gap. Finally, the rollover characteristic is preserved from one's complement. Incrementing +7 by +1 will result in -8.

If we use the notation N_{2comp} to represent any possible value that an n-bit, two's complement number can take on, the range is defined as:

$$\text{Range of a TWO'S COMPLEMENT number} \Rightarrow -(2^{n-1}) \leq N_{2's\,comp} \leq +(2^{n-1} - 1)$$

Example 2.26 shows how to use this expression to find the range of decimal values that a 32-bit, two's complement code can represent.

Example: What is the range of decimal numbers that a 32-bit, two's complement number can represent?

The term "32-bit" means that n=32. We can plug this into the equation for the range of a two's complement number directly.

$$-(2^{n-1}) \leq N_{2comp} \leq +(2^{n-1} - 1)$$

$$\downarrow$$

$$-(2^{32-1}) \leq N_{2comp} \leq +(2^{32-1} - 1)$$

$$\downarrow$$

$$-2{,}147{,}483{,}648 \leq N_{2comp} \leq +2{,}147{,}483{,}647$$

$$\downarrow$$

A 32-bit, two's complement number can represent decimal numbers from -2,147,483,648 to +2,147,483,647.

Example 2.26
Finding the Range of a Two's Complement Number

The process of finding the decimal value of a two's complement number involves first identifying whether the number is positive or negative by looking at the sign bit. If the number is positive (i.e., the sign bit is 0), then the number is treated as an unsigned code and is converted to decimal using the standard conversion procedure described in prior sections. If the number is negative (i.e., the sign bit is 1), then the number sign is recorded separately and a two's complement is performed on the code in order to convert it to its positive magnitude equivalent. This new positive number is then converted to decimal using the standard conversion procedure. The final step is to apply the sign. Example 2.27 shows an example of this process.

Example: What is the decimal value of the 5-bit, 2's complement code 11010_2?

The most significant bit of this 5-bit number is a 1, which indicates that the number is negative.

Sign Bit $\longrightarrow$ $\underline{1}1010$

To find the magnitude of the number, we take the 2's complement of the entire number to find its positive equivalent.

Step 1 – Complement the number $1\ 1\ 0\ 1\ 0_2$

$$\downarrow$$

$$0\ 0\ 1\ 0\ 1_2$$

Step 2 – Add 1, ignore carry out if any

$$0\ 0\ 1\ 0\ 1$$
$$+\qquad\qquad 1$$
$$\overline{0\ 0\ 1\ 1\ 0_2}$$

The number can now be converted into decimal to find its magnitude (i.e., $00110_2 = 6_{10}$). The negative sign is then added giving a final decimal value of -6_{10}.

Example 2.27
Finding the Decimal Value of a Two's Complement Number

To convert a decimal number into its two's complement code, the range is first checked to determine whether the number can be represented with the allocated number of bits. The next step is to convert the decimal number into unsigned binary. The final step is to apply the sign bit. If the original decimal number was positive, then the conversion is complete. If the original decimal number was negative, then the two's complement is taken on the unsigned binary code to find its negative equivalent. Example 2.28 shows this procedure when converting -99_{10} to its 8-bit, two's complement code.

Example: What is the 8-bit, 2's complement code for -99_{10}?

Step 1 – Determine if -99_{10} can be represented within the 2's complement number range

An 8-bit, 2's complement number has a range of:

$$-(2^{n-1}) \leq N_{2comp} \leq +(2^{n-1} - 1)$$

$$\downarrow$$

$$-(2^{8-1}) \leq N_{2comp} \leq +(2^{8-1} - 1)$$

$$\downarrow$$

$$-128 \leq N_{2comp} \leq +127$$

Yes, the number -99_{10} falls within the range that an 8-bit, 2's complement number.

Step 2 – Find the positive binary code for -99_{10}

		Quotient	Remainder	
2	99	49	1	LSB
2	49	24	1	
2	24	12	0	
2	12	6	0	
2	6	3	0	
2	3	1	1	
2	1	0	1	MSB

Done   The converted 8-bit number is $0110\ 0011_2$.

Step 3 – Perform 2's Complement on the positive equivalent of 99_{10}

First, complement the number $0\ 1\ 1\ 0\ \ 0\ 0\ 1\ 1_2$

$$\downarrow$$

$1\ 0\ 0\ 1\ \ 1\ 1\ 0\ 0_2$

Second, add 1, ignore carry out if any

$$
\begin{array}{r}
1\ 0\ 0\ 1\ \ 1\ 1\ 0\ 0 \\
+\ \ \ \ \ \ \ \ \ \ \ \ \ \ \ \ \ 1 \\
\hline
1\ 0\ 0\ 1\ \ 1\ 1\ 0\ 1_2
\end{array}
$$

The 8-bit, 2's complement code for -99_{10} is $1001\ 1101_2$

Example 2.28
Finding the Two's Complement Code of a Decimal Number

2.4.2.4 Arithmetic with Two's Complement

Two's complement has a variety of arithmetic advantages. First, the operations of addition, subtraction and multiplication are handled exactly the same as when using unsigned numbers. This means that duplicate circuitry is not needed in a system that uses both number types. Second, the ability to convert a number from positive to its negative representation by performing a *two's complement* means that an adder circuit can be used for subtraction. For example, if we wanted to perform the subtraction $13_{10} - 4_{10} = 9_{10}$, this is the same as performing $13_{10} + (-4_{10}) = 9_{10}$. This allows us to use a single adder circuit to perform both addition and subtraction as long as we have the ability to take the two's complement of a number. Creating a circuit to perform two's complement can be simpler and faster than building a separate subtraction circuit, so this approach can sometimes be advantageous.

There are specific rules for performing two's complement arithmetic that must be followed to ensure proper results. First, any carry or borrow that is generated is **ignored**. The second rule that must be followed is to always check if **two's complement overflow** occurred. Two's complement overflow refers to when the result of the operation falls outside of the range of values that can be represented by the number of bits being used. For example, if you are performing 8-bit, two's complement addition, the range of decimal values that can be represented is -128_{10} to $+127_{10}$. Having two input terms of 127_{10} ($0111\ 1111_2$) is perfectly legal because they can be represented by the 8-bits of the two's complement number; however, the summation of $127_{10} + 127_{10} = 254_{10}$ ($1111\ 1110_2$). This number does *not* fit within the range of values that can be represented and is actually the two's complement code for -2_{10}, which is obviously incorrect. Two's complement overflow occurs if any of the following occurs:

- The sum of like signs results in an answer with opposite sign
  (i.e., Positive + Positive = Negative or Negative + Negative = Positive)
- The subtraction of a positive number from a negative number results in a positive number
  (i.e., Negative – Positive = Positive)
- The subtraction of a negative number from a positive number results in a negative number
  (i.e., Positive – Negative = Negative)

Computer systems that use two's complement have a dedicated logic circuit that monitors for any of these situations and lets the operator know that overflow has occurred. These circuits are straightforward since they simply monitor the sign bits of the input and output codes. Example 2.29 shows how to use two's complement in order to perform subtraction using an addition operation.

Example: Use 4-bit, two's complement addition to find the differences between 6_{10} and 3_{10}.

The answer in decimal to this problem is $6_{10} - 3_{10} = 3_{10}$. Instead of using subtraction, we will use the two's complement representation of -3_{10} and add the two numbers.

$$\begin{array}{cc} 6_{10} & 6_{10} \\ -\ 3_{10} & =\quad +\ (-3_{10}) \\ \hline 3_{10} & 3_{10} \end{array}$$

Step 1 – Find the 4-bit, two's complement codes for $+6_{10}$ and -3_{10}.

Since 6 is positive, its code is simply its 4-bit binary equivalent ($+6_{10} = 0110_2$)

Since 3 is negative, we'll need to take the two's complement of its 4-bit positive binary equivalent ($+3_{10} = 0011_2$)

1) Complement the number

$$0011_2$$
$$\downarrow$$
$$1100_2$$

2) Add 1, ignore carry out if any

$$\begin{array}{r} 1100 \\ +\quad\quad 1 \\ \hline 1101_2 \end{array}$$

Step 2 – Add the two codes, ignore carry out if any

$$\begin{array}{cc} 6_{10} & 0110_2 \\ +\ (-3_{10}) & =\quad +\ 1101_2 \\ \hline 3_{10} & 10011_2 \end{array}$$

The sum resulted in a carry out, but in two's complement addition, this bit is ignored.

The result of the addition was 0011_2 or $+3_{10}$, verifying that this approach was correct. Also, two's complement overflow did not occur because the result of this operation was within the range of possible values that a 4-bit, two's complement number can represent (e.g., -8_{10} to $+7_{10}$).

Example 2.29
Two's Complement Addition

CONCEPT CHECK

CC2.4   A 4-bit, two's complement number has 16 unique codes and can represent decimal numbers between -8_{10} to $+7_{10}$. If the number of unique codes is even, why is it that the range of integers it can represent is not symmetrical about zero?

A)   One of the positive codes is used to represent zero. This prevents the highest positive number from reaching $+8_{10}$ and being symmetrical.

B)   It is asymmetrical because the system allows the numbers to roll over.

C)   It isn't asymmetrical if zero is considered a positive integer. That way there are eight positive numbers and eight negatives numbers.

D)   It is asymmetrical because there are duplicate codes for 0.

Summary

❖   The base, or radix, of a number system refers to the number of unique symbols within its set. The definition of a number system includes both the symbols used and the relative values of each symbol within the set.

❖   The most common number systems are base 10 (decimal), base 2 (binary), and base 16 (hexadecimal). Base 10 is used because it is how the human brain has been trained to treat numbers. Base 2 is used because the two values are easily represented using electrical switches. Base 16 is a convenient way to describe large groups of bits.

❖   A positional number system allows larger (or smaller) numbers to be represented beyond the values within the original symbol set. This is accomplished by having each position within a number have a different *weight*.

❖   There are specific algorithms that are used to convert any base to or from decimal. There are also algorithms to convert between number systems that contain a power-of-two symbols (e.g., binary to hexadecimal and hexadecimal to binary).

❖   Binary arithmetic is performed on a fixed width of bits (n). When an n-bit addition results in a sum that cannot fit within n-bits, it generates a *carry out* bit. In an n-bit subtraction, if the minuend is smaller than the subtrahend, a *borrow in* can be used to complete the operation.

❖   Binary codes can represent both unsigned and signed numbers. For an arbitrary n-bit binary code, it is important to know the encoding technique and the range of values that can be represented.

❖   Signed numbers use the most significant position to represent whether the number is negative (0=positive, 1=negative). The width of a signed number is always fixed.

❖   Two's complement is the most common encoding technique for signed numbers. It has an advantage that there are no duplicate codes for zero and that the encoding approach provides a monotonic progression of codes from the most negative number that can be represented to the most positive. This allows addition and subtraction to work the same on two's complement numbers as it does on unsigned numbers.

❖   When performing arithmetic using two's complement codes, the carry bit is ignored.

❖   When performing arithmetic using two's complement codes, if the result lies outside of the range that can be represented it is called *two's complement overflow*. Two's complement overflow can be determined by looking at the sign bits of the input arguments and the sign bit of the result.

Exercise Problems

Section 2.1 – Positional Number Systems

2.1.1   What is the radix of the binary number system?

2.1.2   What is the radix of the decimal number system?

2.1.3   What is the radix of the hexadecimal number system?

2.1.4   What is the radix of the octal number system?

2.1.5   For the number 261.367, what position (p) is the number 2 in?

2.1.6   For the number 261.367, what position (p) is the number 1 in?

2.1.7   For the number 261.367, what position (p) is the number 3 in?

2.1.8   For the number 261.367, what position (p) is the number 7 in?

2.1.9   What is the name of the number system containing 10_2?

2.1.10   What is the name of the number system containing 10_{10}?

2.1.11 What is the name of the number system containing 10_{16}?

2.1.12 What is the name of the number system containing 10_8?

2.1.13 Which of the four number systems covered in this chapter (i.e., binary, decimal, hexadecimal, and octal) could the number 22 be part of? Give all that are possible.

2.1.14 Which of the four number systems covered in this chapter (i.e., binary, decimal, hexadecimal, and octal) could the number 99 be part of? Give all that are possible.

2.1.15 Which of the four number systems covered in this chapter (i.e., binary, decimal, hexadecimal, and octal) could the number 1F be part of? Give all that are possible.

2.1.16 Which of the four number systems covered in this chapter (i.e., binary, decimal, hexadecimal, and octal) could the number 88 be part of? Give all that are possible.

Section 2.2 – Base Conversions

2.2.1 If the number 101.111 has a radix of 2, what is the weight of the position containing the bit 0?

2.2.2 If the number 261.367 has a radix of 10, what is the weight of the position containing the numeral 2?

2.2.3 If the number 261.367 has a radix of 16, what is the weight of the position containing the numeral 1?

2.2.4 If the number 261.367 has a radix of 8, what is the weight of the position containing the numeral 3?

2.2.5 Convert $1100\ 1100_2$ to decimal. Treat all numbers as <u>unsigned</u>.

2.2.6 Convert 1001.1001_2 to decimal. Treat all numbers as <u>unsigned</u>.

2.2.7 Convert 72_8 to decimal. Treat all numbers as <u>unsigned</u>.

2.2.8 Convert 12.57_8 to decimal. Treat all numbers as <u>unsigned</u>.

2.2.9 Convert $F3_{16}$ to decimal. Treat all numbers as <u>unsigned</u>.

2.2.10 Convert $15B.CEF_{16}$ to decimal. Treat all numbers as <u>unsigned</u>. Use an accuracy of 7 fractional digits.

2.2.11 Convert 67_{10} to binary. Treat all numbers as <u>unsigned</u>.

2.2.12 Convert 252.987_{10} to binary. Treat all numbers as <u>unsigned</u>. Use an accuracy of 4 fractional bits and don't round up.

2.2.13 Convert 67_{10} to octal. Treat all numbers as <u>unsigned</u>.

2.2.14 Convert 252.987_{10} to octal. Treat all numbers as <u>unsigned</u>. Use an accuracy of 4 fractional digits and don't round up.

2.2.15 Convert 67_{10} to hexadecimal. Treat all numbers as <u>unsigned</u>.

2.2.16 Convert 252.987_{10} to hexadecimal. Treat all numbers as <u>unsigned</u>. Use an accuracy of 4 fractional digits and don't round up.

2.2.17 Convert $1\ 0000\ 1111_2$ to octal. Treat all numbers as <u>unsigned</u>.

2.2.18 Convert $1\ 0000\ 1111.011_2$ to hexadecimal. Treat all numbers as <u>unsigned</u>.

2.2.19 Convert 77_8 to binary. Treat all numbers as <u>unsigned</u>.

2.2.20 Convert $F.A_{16}$ to binary. Treat all numbers as <u>unsigned</u>.

2.2.21 Convert 66_8 to hexadecimal. Treat all numbers as <u>unsigned</u>.

2.2.22 Convert $AB.D_{16}$ to octal. Treat all numbers as <u>unsigned</u>.

Section 2.3 – Binary Arithmetic

2.3.1 Compute $1010_2 + 1011_2$ by hand. Treat all numbers as <u>unsigned</u>. Provide the 4-bit sum and indicate whether a *carry out* occurred.

2.3.2 Compute $1111\ 1111_2 + 0000\ 0001_2$ by hand. Treat all numbers as <u>unsigned</u>. Provide the 8-bit sum and indicate whether a *carry out* occurred.

2.3.3 Compute $1010.1010_2 + 1011.1011_2$ by hand. Treat all numbers as <u>unsigned</u>. Provide the 8-bit sum and indicate whether a *carry out* occurred.

2.3.4 Compute $1111\ 1111.1011_2 + 0000\ 0001.1100_2$ by hand. Treat all numbers as <u>unsigned</u>. Provide the 12-bit sum and indicate whether a *carry out* occurred.

2.3.5 Compute $1010_2 - 1011_2$ by hand. Treat all numbers as <u>unsigned</u>. Provide the 4-bit difference and indicate whether a *borrow in* occurred.

2.3.6 Compute $1111\ 1111_2 - 0000\ 0001_2$ by hand. Treat all numbers as <u>unsigned</u>. Provide the 8-bit difference and indicate whether a *borrow in* occurred.

2.3.7 Compute $1010.1010_2 - 1011.1011_2$ by hand. Treat all numbers as <u>unsigned</u>. Provide the 8-bit difference and indicate whether a *borrow in* occurred.

2.3.8 Compute $1111\ 1111.1011_2 - 0000\ 0001.1100_2$ by hand. Treat all numbers as <u>unsigned</u>. Provide the 12-bit difference and indicate whether a *borrow in* occurred.

Section 2.4 – Unsigned and Signed Numbers

2.4.1 What range of decimal numbers can be represented by <u>8-bit, two's complement</u> numbers?

2.4.2 What range of decimal numbers can be represented by <u>16-bit, two's complement</u> numbers?

2.4.3 What range of decimal numbers can be represented by <u>32-bit, two's complement</u> numbers?

2.4.4 What range of decimal numbers can be represented by <u>64-bit, two's complement</u> numbers?

2.4.5 What is the 8-bit, two's complement code for $+88_{10}$?

2.4.6 What is the 8-bit, two's complement code for -88_{10}?

2.4.7 What is the 8-bit, two's complement code for -128_{10}?

2.4.8 What is the 8-bit, two's complement code for -1_{10}?

2.4.9 What is the decimal value of the 4-bit, two's complement code 0010_2?

2.4.10 What is the decimal value of the 4-bit, two's complement code 1010_2?

2.4.11 What is the decimal value of the 8-bit, two's complement code $0111\ 1110_2$?

2.4.12 What is the decimal value of the 8-bit, two's complement code $1111\ 1110_2$?

2.4.13 Compute $1110_2 + 1011_2$ by hand. Treat all numbers as <u>4-bit, two's complement codes</u>. Provide the 4-bit sum and indicate whether *two's complement overflow* occurred.

2.4.14 Compute $1101\ 1111_2 + 0000\ 0001_2$ by hand. Treat all numbers as <u>8-bit, two's complement codes</u>. Provide the 8-bit sum and indicate whether *two's complement overflow* occurred.

2.4.15 Compute $1010.1010_2 + 1000.1011_2$ by hand. Treat all numbers as <u>8-bit, two's complement codes</u>. Provide the 8-bit sum and indicate whether *two's complement overflow* occurred.

2.4.16 Compute $1110\ 1011.1001_2 + 0010\ 0001.1101_2$ by hand. Treat all numbers as <u>12-bit, two's complement codes</u>. Provide the 12-bit sum and indicate whether *two's complement overflow* occurred.

2.4.17 Compute $4_{10} - 5_{10}$ using <u>4-bit two's complement</u> addition. You will need to first convert each number into its 4-bit two's complement code and then perform binary addition (i.e, $4_{10} + (-5_{10})$). Provide the 4-bit result and indicate whether two's complement overflow occurred. Check your work by converting the 4-bit result back to decimal.

2.4.18 Compute $7_{10} - 7_{10}$ using <u>4-bit two's complement</u> addition. You will need to first convert each decimal number into its 4-bit two's complement code and then perform binary addition (i.e, $7_{10} + (-7_{10})$). Provide the 4-bit result and indicate whether two's complement overflow occurred. Check your work by converting the 4-bit result back to decimal.

2.4.19 Compute $7_{10} + 1_{10}$ using <u>4-bit two's complement</u> addition. You will need to first convert each decimal number into its 4-bit two's complement code and then perform binary addition. Provide the 4-bit result and indicate whether two's complement overflow occurred. Check your work by converting the 4-bit result back to decimal.

2.4.20 Compute $64_{10} - 100_{10}$ using <u>8-bit two's complement</u> addition. You will need to first convert each number into its 8-bit two's complement code and then perform binary addition (i.e, $64_{10} + (-100_{10})$). Provide the 8-bit result and indicate whether two's complement overflow occurred. Check your work by converting the 8-bit result back to decimal.

2.4.21 Compute $(-99)_{10} - 11_{10}$ using <u>8-bit two's complement</u> addition. You will need to first convert each decimal number into its 8-bit two's complement code and then perform binary addition (i.e, $(-99_{10}) + (-11_{10})$). Provide the 8-bit result and indicate whether two's complement overflow occurred. Check your work by converting the 8-bit result back to decimal.

2.4.22 Compute $50_{10} + 100_{10}$ using <u>8-bit two's complement</u> addition. You will need to first convert each decimal number into its 8-bit two's complement code and then perform binary addition. Provide the 8-bit result and indicate whether two's complement overflow occurred. Check your work by converting the 8-bit result back to decimal.

Chapter 3: Digital Circuitry & Interfacing

Now we turn our attention to the physical circuitry and electrical quantities that are used to represent and operate on the binary codes 1 and 0. In this chapter we begin by looking at how logic circuits are described and introduce the basic set of gates used for all digital logic operations. We then look at the underlying circuitry that implements the basic gates including digital signaling and how voltages are used to represent 1's and 0's. We then look at interfacing between two digital circuits and how to ensure that when one circuit sends a binary code, the receiving circuit is able to determine which code was sent. Logic families are then introduced and the details of how basic gates are implemented at the switch level are presented. Finally, interfacing considerations are covered for the most common types of digital loads (i.e., other gates, resistors, and LEDs).

Learning Outcomes – After completing this chapter, you will be able to:

3.1	Describe the functional operation of a basic logic gate using truth tables, logic expressions, and logic waveforms.
3.2	Determine the noise margins for a logic family based on the DC operating conditions provided by a data sheet.
3.3	Determine the power supply currents of a driver when sourcing and/or sinking multiple loads.
3.4	Extract key switching characteristics from a logic gate's data sheet.
3.5	Draw the transistor-level schematic for basic CMOS gates.
3.6	Determine the output current of a driver when driving multiple gates from the same logic family.
3.7	Determine the output current of a driver when driving resistive loads.
3.8	Determine the output current of a driver when driving LED loads.

3.1 Basic Gates

The term *gate* is used to describe a digital circuit that implements the most basic functions possible within the binary system. When discussing the operation of a logic gate, we ignore the details of how the 1's and 0's are represented with voltages and manipulated using transistors. We instead treat the inputs and output as simply ideal 1's and 0's. This allows us to design more complex logic circuits without going into the details of the underlying physical hardware.

3.1.1 Describing the Operation of a Logic Circuit

3.1.1.1 The Logic Symbol

A logic symbol is a graphical representation of the circuit that can be used in a schematic to show how circuits in a system interface to one another. For the set of basic logic gates, there are uniquely shaped symbols that graphically indicate their functionality. For more complex logic circuits that are implemented with multiple basic gates, a simple rectangular symbol is used. Inputs of the logic circuit are typically shown on the left of the symbol and outputs are on the right. Figure 3.1 shows two example logic symbols.

Figure 3.1
Example Logic Symbols

3.1.1.2 The Truth Table

We formally define the functionality of a logic circuit using a *truth table.* In a truth table, each and every possible input combination is listed and the corresponding output of the logic circuit is given. If a logic circuit has n inputs, then it will have 2^n possible input codes. The binary codes are listed in ascending order within the truth table mimicking a binary count starting at 0. By always listing the input codes in this way, we can assign a *row number* to each input that is the decimal equivalent of the binary input code. Row numbers can be used to simplify the notation for describing the functionality of larger circuits. Figure 3.2 shows the formation of an example 3-input truth table.

Truth Table Formation

Input codes are always listed in ascending order.

Listing the input codes as a binary count allow each input's decimal equivalent to be used as the "row number"

row	A	B	C	F
0	0	0	0	0
1	0	0	1	1
2	0	1	0	1
3	0	1	1	0
4	1	0	0	1
5	1	0	1	0
6	1	1	0	0
7	1	1	1	1

The corresponding output of the circuit is listed for each possible input code

Figure 3.2
Truth Table Formation

3.1.1.3 The Logic Function

A logic *expression*, (also called a *logic function),* is an equation that provides the functionality of each output in the circuit as a function of the inputs. The logic operations for the basic gates are given a symbolic set of operators (e.g., $+$, $\cdot$, $\oplus$), the details of which will be given in the next sections. The logic function describes the operations that are necessary to produce the outputs listed in the truth table. A logic function is used to describe a single output that can take on only the values 1 and 0. If a circuit contains multiple outputs, then a logic function is needed for each output. The input variables can be included in the expression description just as in an analog function. For example, "F(A,B,C)=..." would state that "F is a function of the inputs A, B and C". This can also be written as "$F_{A,B,C}=...$". The input variables can also be excluded for brevity as in "F=...". Figure 3.3 shows the formation of an example 3-input logic expression.

Logic Expression Formation

A	B	C	F
0	0	0	0
0	0	1	1
0	1	0	1
0	1	1	0
1	0	0	1
1	0	1	0
1	1	0	0
1	1	1	1

$$F(A,B,C) = A \oplus B \oplus C$$

or

$$F_{A,B,C} = A \oplus B \oplus C$$

or

$$F = A \oplus B \oplus C$$

Figure 3.3
Logic Function Formation

3.1.1.4 The Logic Waveform

A logic *waveform* is a graphical depiction of the relationship of the output to the inputs with respect to time. This is often a useful description of behavior since it mimics the format that is typically observed when measuring a real digital circuit using test equipment such as an oscilloscope. In the waveform, each signal can only take on a value of 1 or 0. It is useful to write the logic values of the signal at each transition in the waveform for readability. Figure 3.4 shows an example logic waveform.

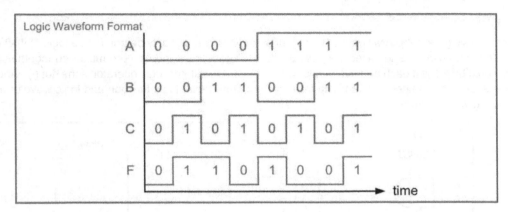

Figure 3.4
Example Logic Waveform

3.1.2 The Buffer

The first basic gate is the *buffer*. The output of a buffer is simply the input. The logic symbol, truth table, logic function and logic waveform for the buffer are given in Figure 3.5.

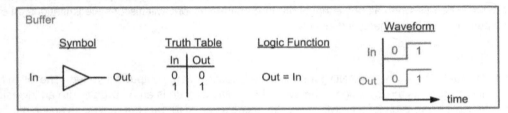

Figure 3.5
Buffer Symbol, Truth Table, Logic Function and Logic Waveform

3.1.3 The Inverter

The next basic gate is the *inverter*. The output of an inverter is the complement of the input. Inversion is also often called the *not* operation. In spoken word, we might say "A is equal to *not* B". thus this gate is also often called a *not* gate. The symbol for the inverter is the same as the buffer with the exception that an *inversion bubble* (i.e., a circle) is placed on the output. The inversion bubble is a common way to show inversions in schematics and will be used by many of the basic gates. In the logic function, there are two common ways to show this operation. The first way is by placing a prime (') after the input variable (e.g., Out = In'). This notation has the advantage that it is supported in all text editors but has the drawback that it can sometimes be difficult to see. The second way to indicate inversion in a logic function is by placing an *inversion bar* over the input variable (e.g., Out = $\overline{\text{In}}$). The advantage of this notation is that it is easy to see but has the drawback that it is not supported by many text editors. In this text, both conventions will be used to provide exposure to each. The logic symbol, truth table, logic function and logic waveform for the inverter are given in Figure 3.6.

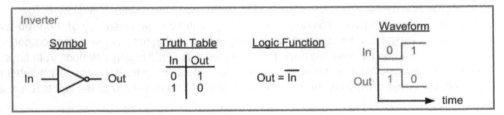

Figure 3.6
Inverter Symbol, Truth Table, Logic Function and Logic Waveform

3.1.4 The AND Gate

The next basic gate is the *AND gate*. The output of an AND gate will only be true (i.e., a logic 1) if **all of the inputs are true**. This operation is also called a *logical product* because if the inputs were multiplied together, the only time the output would be a 1 is if each and every input was a 1. As a result, the logic operator is the dot (·). Another notation that is often seen is the ampersand (&). The logic symbol, truth table, logic function and logic waveform for a 2-input AND gate are given in Figure 3.7.

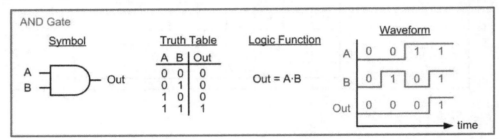

Figure 3.7
2-Input AND Gate Symbol, Truth Table, Logic Function and Logic Waveform

Ideal AND gates can have any number of inputs. The operation of an n-bit, AND gates still follows the rule that the output will only be true when all of the inputs are true. Later sections will discuss the limitations on expanding the number of inputs of these basic gates indefinitely.

3.1.5 The NAND Gate

The NAND gate is identical to the AND gate with the exception that the output is inverted. The "N" in NAND stands for "NOT", which represents the inversion. The symbol for a NAND gate is an AND gate with an inversion bubble on the output. The logic expression for a NAND gate is the same as an AND gate but with an inversion bar over the entire operation. The logic symbol, truth table, logic function and logic waveform for a 2-input NAND gate are given in Figure 3.8. Ideal NAND gates can have any number of inputs with the operation of an n-bit, NAND gate following the rule that the output is always the inversion of an n-bit, AND operation.

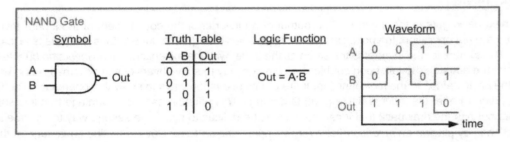

Figure 3.8
2-Input NAND Gate Symbol, Truth Table, Logic Function and Logic Waveform

3.1.6 The OR Gate

The next basic gate is the *OR gate*. The output of an OR gate will be true when **any of the inputs are true**. This operation is also called a *logical sum* because of its similarity to logical disjunction in which the output is true if *at least one* of the inputs is true. As a result, the logic operator is the plus sign (+). The logic symbol, truth table, logic function and logic waveform for a 2-input OR gate are given in Figure 3.9. Ideal OR gates can have any number of inputs. The operation of an n-bit, OR gates still follows the rule that the output will be true if any of the inputs are true.

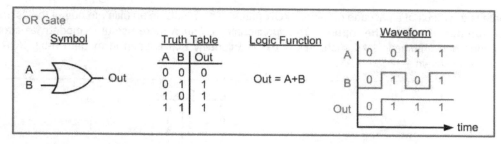

Figure 3.9
2-Input OR Gate Symbol, Truth Table, Logic Function and Logic Waveform

3.1.7 The NOR Gate

The NOR gate is identical to the OR gate with the exception that the output is inverted. The symbol for a NOR gate is an OR gate with an inversion bubble on the output. The logic expression for a NOR gate is the same as an OR gate but with an inversion bar over the entire operation. The logic symbol, truth table, logic function and logic waveform for a 2-input NOR gate are given in Figure 3.10. Ideal NOR gates can have any number of inputs with the operation of an n-bit, NOR gate following the rule that the output is always the inversion of an n-bit, OR operation.

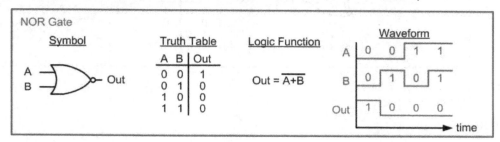

Figure 3.10
2-Input NOR Gate Symbol, Truth Table, Logic Function and Logic Waveform

3.1.8 The XOR Gate

The next basic gate is the *exclusive-OR gate*, or XOR gate for short. This gate is also called a *difference* gate because for the 2-input configuration, its output will be true when the **input codes are different from one another**. The logic operator is a circle around a plus sign ($\oplus$). The logic symbol, truth table, logic function and logic waveform for a 2-input XOR gate are given in Figure 3.11.

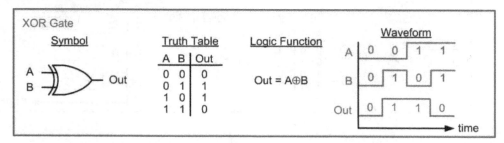

Figure 3.11
2-Input XOR Gate Symbol, Truth Table, Logic Function and Logic Waveform

Using the formal definition of an XOR gate (i.e., the output is true if any of the input codes are different from one another), an XOR gate with more than two inputs can be built. The truth table for a 3-bit, XOR gate using this definition is shown in Figure 3.12. In modern electronics, this type of gate has found little use since it is much simpler to build this functionality using a combination of AND and OR gates. As such, XOR gates with greater than two inputs do not implement the *difference* function. Instead, a more useful functionality has been adopted in which the output of the n-bit, XOR gate is the result of a cascade of 2-input XOR gates. This results in an ultimate output that is true when there is **an ODD number of 1's on the inputs**. This functionality is much more useful in modern electronics for error correction codes and arithmetic. As such, this is the functionality that is seen in modern n-bit, XOR gates. This functionality is also shown in Figure 3.12.

Figure 3.12
3-Input XOR Gate Implementation

3.1.9 The XNOR Gate

The exclusive-NOR gate is identical to the XOR gate with the exception that the output is inverted. This gate is also called an *equivalence* gate because for the 2-input configuration, its output will be true when the **input codes are equivalent to one another**. The symbol for an XNOR gate is an XOR gate with an inversion bubble on the output. The logic expression for an XNOR gate is the same as an XOR gate but with an inversion bar over the entire operation. The logic symbol, truth table, logic function and logic waveform for a 2-input XNOR gate are given in Figure 3.13. XNOR gates can have any number of inputs with the operation of an n-bit, XNOR gate following the rule that the output is always the inversion of an n-bit, XOR operation (i.e., the output is true if there is an ODD number of 1's on the inputs).

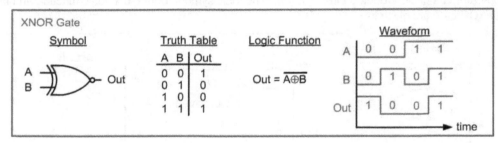

Figure 3.13
2-Input XNOR Gate Symbol, Truth Table, Logic Function and Logic Waveform

CONCEPT CHECK

CC3.1   Given the following logic diagram, which is the correct logic expression for F?

A) $F = (A \cdot B)' \oplus C$

B) $F = (A' \cdot B') \oplus C$

C) $F = (A' \cdot B' \oplus C)$

D) $F = A \cdot B' \oplus C$

3.2 Digital Circuit Operation

Now we turn our attention to the physical hardware that is used to build the basic gates just described and how electrical quantities are used to represent and communicate the binary values 1 and 0. We begin by looking at digital signaling. Digital signaling refers to how binary codes are generated and transmitted successfully between two digital circuits using electrical quantities (e.g., voltage and current). Consider the digital system shown in Figure 3.14. In this system, the sending circuit generates a binary code. The sending circuit is called either the *transmitter* (Tx) or *driver*. The transmitter represents the binary code using an electrical quantity such as voltage. The receiving circuit (Rx) observes this voltage and is able to determine the value of the binary code. In this way, 1's and 0's can be communicated between the two digital circuits. The transmitter and receiver are both designed to use the same digital signaling scheme so that they are able to communicate with each other. It should be noted that all digital circuits contain both inputs (Rx) and outputs (Tx) but are not shown in this figure for simplicity.

Figure 3.14
Generic Digital Transmitter / Receiver Circuit

3.2.1 Logic Levels

A *logic level* is the term to describe all possible states that a signal can have. We will focus explicitly on circuits that represent binary values so these will only have two finite states (1 and 0). To begin, we define a simplistic model of how to represent the binary codes using an electrical quantity. This model uses a voltage threshold (V_{th}) to represent the switching point between the binary codes. If the voltage of the signal (V_{sig}) is above this threshold, it is considered a *logic HIGH*. If the voltage is below this threshold, it is considered a *logic LOW*. A graphical depiction of this is shown in Figure 3.15. The terms HIGH and LOW are used to describe which logic level corresponds to the *higher* or *lower* voltage.

Figure 3.15
Definition of Logic HIGH and LOW

It is straightforward to have the HIGH level correspond to the binary code 1 and the LOW level correspond to the binary code 0; however, it is equally valid to have the HIGH level correspond to the binary code 0 and the LOW level correspond to the binary code 1. As such, we need to define how the logic levels HIGH and LOW map to the binary codes 1 and 0. We define two types of digital assignments: Positive Logic and Negative Logic. In **Positive Logic**, the logic HIGH level represents a binary 1 and the logic LOW level represents a binary 0. In **Negative Logic**, the logic HIGH level represents a binary 0 and the logic LOW level represents a binary 1. Table 3.1 shows the definition of positive and negative logic. There are certain types of digital circuits that benefit from using negative logic; however, we will focus specifically on systems that use positive logic since it is more intuitive when learning digital design for the first time. The transformation between positive and negative logic is straightforward and will be covered in Chapter 4.

Definition of Positive and Negative Logic

Logic Level	Logic Value	
	Positive Logic	Negative Logic
LOW	0	1
HIGH	1	0

Table 3.1
Definition of Positive and Negative Logic

3.2.2 Output DC Specifications

Transmitting circuits provide specifications on the range of output voltages (V_O) that they are guaranteed to provide when outputting a logic 1 or 0. These are called the DC output specifications. There are four DC voltage specifications that specify this range: $V_{OH\text{-}max}$, $V_{OH\text{-}min}$, $V_{OL\text{-}max}$, and $V_{OL\text{-}min}$. The $V_{OH\text{-}max}$ and $V_{OH\text{-}min}$ specifications provide the range of voltages the transmitter is guaranteed to provide when outputting a logic HIGH (or logic 1 when using positive logic). The $V_{OL\text{-}max}$ and $V_{OL\text{-}min}$ specifications provide the range of voltages the transmitter is guaranteed to provide when outputting a logic LOW (or logic 0 when using positive logic). In the subscripts for these specifications, the "O" signifies "output" and the "L" or "H" signifies "LOW" or "HIGH" respectively.

The maximum amount of current that can flow through the transmitter's output (I_O) is also specified. The specification $I_{OH\text{-}max}$ is the maximum amount of current that can flow through the transmitter's output when sending a logic HIGH. The specification $I_{OL\text{-}max}$ is the maximum amount of current that can flow through the transmitter's output when sending a logic LOW. When the maximum output currents are violated, it usually damages the part. Manufacturers will also provide a *recommended* amount of current for I_O that will guarantee the specified operating parameters throughout the life of the part. Figure 3.16 shows a graphical depiction of these DC specifications. When the transmitter output is providing current to the receiving circuit (a.k.a., the *load*), it is said to be ***sourcing*** current. When the transmitter output is drawing current from the receiving circuit, it is said to be ***sinking*** current. In most cases, the transmitter sources current when driving a logic HIGH and sinks current when driving a logic LOW. Figure 3.16 shows a graphical depiction of these specifications.

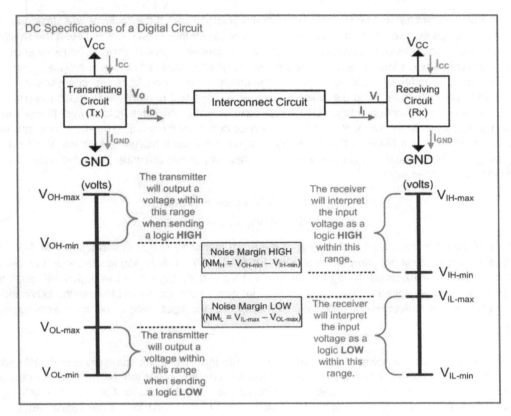

Figure 3.16
DC Specifications of a Digital Circuit

3.2.3 Input DC Specifications

Receiving circuits provide specifications on the range of input voltages (V_I) that they will interpret as either a logic HIGH or LOW. These are called the DC input specifications. There are four DC voltage specifications that specify this range: $V_{IH\text{-}max}$, $V_{IH\text{-}min}$, $V_{IL\text{-}max}$, and $V_{IL\text{-}min}$. The $V_{IH\text{-}max}$ and $V_{IH\text{-}min}$ specifications provide the range of voltages that the receiver will interpret as a logic HIGH (or logic 1 when using positive logic). The $V_{IL\text{-}max}$ and $V_{IL\text{-}min}$ specifications provide the range of voltages that the receiver will interpret as a logic LOW (or logic 0 when using positive logic). In the subscripts for these specifications, the "I" signifies "input".

The maximum amount of current that the receiver will draw, or take in, when connected is also specified I_I). The specification $I_{IH\text{-}max}$ is the maximum amount of current that the receiver will draw when it is being driven with a logic HIGH. The specification $I_{IL\text{-}max}$ is the maximum amount of current that the receiver will draw when it is being driven with a logic LOW. Again, Figure 3.16 shows a graphical depiction of these DC specifications.

3.2.4 Noise Margins

For digital circuits that are designed to operate with each other, the $V_{OH\text{-}max}$ and $V_{IH\text{-}max}$ specifications have equal voltages. Similarly, the $V_{OL\text{-}min}$ and $V_{IL\text{-}min}$ specifications have equal voltages. The $V_{OH\text{-}max}$ and $V_{OL\text{-}min}$ output specifications represent the *best case* scenario for digital signaling as the transmitter is sending the largest (or smallest) signal possible. If there is no loss in the interconnect between the transmitter and receiver, the full voltage levels will arrive at the receiver and be interpreted as the correct logic states (HIGH or LOW).

The *worst-case* scenario for digital signaling is when the transmitter outputs its levels at $V_{OH\text{-}min}$ and $V_{OL\text{-}max}$. These levels represent the furthest away from an *ideal* voltage level that the transmitter can send to the receiver and are susceptible to loss and noise that may occur in the interconnect system. In order to compensate for potential loss or noise, digital circuits have a predefined amount of margin built into their worst-case specifications. Let's take the worst-case example of a transmitter sending a logic HIGH at the level $V_{OH\text{-}min}$. If the receiver was designed to have $V_{IH\text{-}min}$ (i.e., the lowest voltage that would still be interpreted as a logic 1) equal to $V_{OH\text{-}min}$, then if even the smallest amount of the output signal was attenuated as it traveled through the interconnect, it would arrive at the receiver below $V_{IH\text{-}min}$ and would not be interpreted as a logic 1. Since there will always be some amount of loss in any interconnect system, the specifications for $V_{IH\text{-}min}$ is always less than $V_{OH\text{-}min}$. The difference between these two quantities is called the **Noise Margin**. More specifically, it is called the Noise Margin HIGH (or NM_H) to signify how much margin is built into the Tx/Rx circuit when communicating a logic 1. Similarly, the $V_{IL\text{-}max}$ specification is always higher than the $V_{OL\text{-}max}$ specification to account for any voltage added to the signal in the interconnect. The difference between these two quantities is called the Noise Margin LOW (or NM_L) to signify how much margin is built into the Tx/Rx circuit when communicating a logic 0. Noise margins are always specified as positive quantities, thus the order of the subtrahend and minuend in these differences.

$$NM_H = V_{OH\text{-}min} - V_{IH\text{-}min}$$
$$NM_L = V_{IL\text{-}max} - V_{OL\text{-}max}$$

Figure 3.16 includes the graphical depiction of the noise margins. Notice in this figure that there is a region of voltages that the receiver will not interpret as either a HIGH or LOW. This region lies between the $V_{IH\text{-}min}$ and $V_{IL\text{-}max}$ specifications. This is the **uncertainty region** and should be avoided. Signals in this region will cause the receiver's output to go to an unknown voltage. Digital transmitters are designed to transition between the LOW and HIGH states quickly enough so that the receiver does not have time to react to the input being in the uncertainty region.

3.2.5 Power Supplies

All digital circuits require a power supply voltage and a ground. There are some types of digital circuits that may require multiple power supplies. For simplicity, we will focus on digital circuits that only require a single power supply voltage and ground. The power supply voltage is commonly given the abbreviations of either V_{CC} or V_{DD}. The "CC" or "DD" have to do with how the terminals of the transistors inside of the digital circuit are connected (i.e., "collector to collector" or "drain to drain"). Digital circuits will specify the required power supply voltage. Ground is considered an ideal 0v. Digital circuits will also specify the maximum amount of DC current that can flow through the V_{CC} (I_{CC}) and GND (I_{GND}) pins before damaging the part.

There are two components of power supply current. The first is the current that is required for the functional operation of the device. This is called the *quiescent current* (I_q). The second component of the power supply current is the output currents (I_o). Any current that flows out of a digital circuit must also flow into it. When a transmitting circuit sources current to a load on its output pin, it must bring in that same amount of current on another pin. This is accomplished using the power supply pin (V_{CC}). Conversely, when a transmitting circuit sinks current from a load on its output pin, an equal amount of current must exit the circuit on a different pin. This is accomplished using the GND pin. This means that the amount of current flowing through the V_{CC} and GND pins will vary depending on the logic states that are being driven on the outputs. Since a digital circuit may contain numerous output pins, the maximum amount of current flowing through the V_{CC} and GND pins can scale quickly and care must be taken not to damage the device.

The quiescent current is often specified using the term I_{CC}. This should not be confused with the specification for the maximum amount of current that can flow through the V_{CC} pin, which is often called $I_{CC\text{-}max}$. It is easy to tell the difference because I_{CC} (or I_q) is much smaller than $I_{CC\text{-}max}$ for CMOS parts. I_{CC} (or I_q) is specified in the uA to nA range while the maximum current that can flow through the V_{CC} pin is specified in the mA range. Example 3.1 shows the process of calculating the I_{CC} and I_{GND} currents when sourcing multiple loads.

Example: Calculating I_{CC} and I_{GND} when Sourcing Multiple Loads

Given: The driver is specified to have a quiescent current of 1mA and is driving a logic HIGH on two of its output pins. Each of the two loads on the output pins is being sourced with 4mA of current from the driver.

Find: I_{CC} and I_{GND}

Solution: The current into the device must equal the current out of the device. The quiescent current of 1mA is used for the functional operation of the transistors within the transmitter and will flow into the device through the V_{CC} pin and out of the device on the GND pin. The output currents that are being sourced by the driver exit the circuit on the two output pins $V_{O(1)}$ and $V_{O(2)}$. An equal amount of current must also flow into the device ($I_{O(1)} + I_{O(2)} = 8mA$), which enters the device on the V_{CC} pin. This means the total amount of current flowing into the circuit on the V_{CC} pin is:

$$I_{CC} = I_q + I_{O(1)} + I_{O(2)} = 1mA + 4mA + 4mA = 9mA$$

The total amount of current flowing out of the circuit on the GND pin is simply the quiescent current I_q.

$$I_{GND} = I_q = 1mA$$

Check: Does the total amount of current entering the circuit equal the total amount of current exiting the circuit?

Yes, there is 9mA entering the circuit through the V_{CC} pin. There is also 9mA exiting the circuit using the $V_{O(1)}$, $V_{O(2)}$ and GND pins.

Example 3.1
Calculating I_{CC} and I_{GND} when Sourcing Multiple Loads

Example 3.2 shows the process of calculating the I_{CC} and I_{GND} currents when both sourcing and sinking loads.

Example: Calculating I_{CC} and I_{GND} When Both Sourcing and Sinking Loads

Given: The driver is specified to have a quiescent current of 0.5mA and is driving a logic HIGH on one of its output pins and a logic LOW on two of its output pins. The driver is sourcing 1mA when driving a HIGH and sinking 2mA when driving a LOW.

Find: I_{CC} and I_{GND}

Solution: The current into the device must equal the current out of the device. The quiescent current of 0.5mA enters the circuit on the V_{CC} pin and exits on the GND pin. The output current for $V_{O(1)}$ enters the circuit on the V_{CC} pin and exits the circuit on the $V_{O(1)}$ pin. The output current for $V_{O(2)}$ and $V_{O(3)}$ enters the circuit on the $V_{O(2)}$ and $V_{O(3)}$ pins and exits the circuit on the GND pin. This means the total amount of current flowing into the circuit on the V_{CC} pin is:

$$I_{CC} = I_q + I_{O(1)} = 0.5mA + 1mA = 1.5mA$$

The total amount of current flowing out of the circuit on the GND pin is the quiescent current I_q plus the current being sunk from the pins $V_{O(2)}$ and $V_{O(3)}$:

$$I_{GND} = I_q + I_{O(2)} + I_{O(3)} = 0.5mA + 2mA + 2mA = 4.5mA$$

Example 3.2
Calculating I_{CC} and I_{GND} When Both Sourcing and Sinking Loads

3.2.6 Switching Characteristics

Switching characteristics refer to the transient behavior of the logic circuits. The first group of switching specifications characterize the *propagation delay* of the gate. The propagation delay is the time it takes for the output to respond to a change on the input. The propagation delay is formally defined as the time it takes from the point at which the input has transitioned to 50% of its final value to the point at which the output has transitioned to 50% of its final value. The initial and final voltages for the input are defined to be GND and V_{CC}, while the output initial and final voltages are defined to be V_{OL} and V_{OH}. Specifications are given for the propagation delay when transitioning from a

LOW to HIGH (t_{PLH}) and from a HIGH to LOW (t_{PHL}). When these specifications are equal, the values are often given as a single specification of t_{pd}. These specifications are shown graphically in Figure 3.17.

The second group of switching specifications characterize how quickly the output switches between states. The *transition time* is defined as the time it takes for the output to transition from 10% to 90% of the output voltage range. The *rise time* (t_r) is the time it takes for this transition when going from a LOW to HIGH, and the *fall time* (t_f) is the time it takes for this transition when going from a HIGH to LOW. When these specifications are equal, the values are often given as a single specification of t_t. These specifications are shown graphically in Figure 3.17.

Figure 3.17
Switching Characteristics of a Digital Circuit

3.2.7 Data Sheets

The specifications for a particular part are given in its **data sheet**. The data sheet contains all of the operating characteristics for a part, in addition to functional information such as package geometries and pin assignments. The data sheet is usually the first place a designer will look when selecting a part. Figure 3.18, Figure 3.19 and Figure 3.20 show excerpts from an example data sheet highlighting some of the specifications just covered.

Data Sheet Excerpt (1)

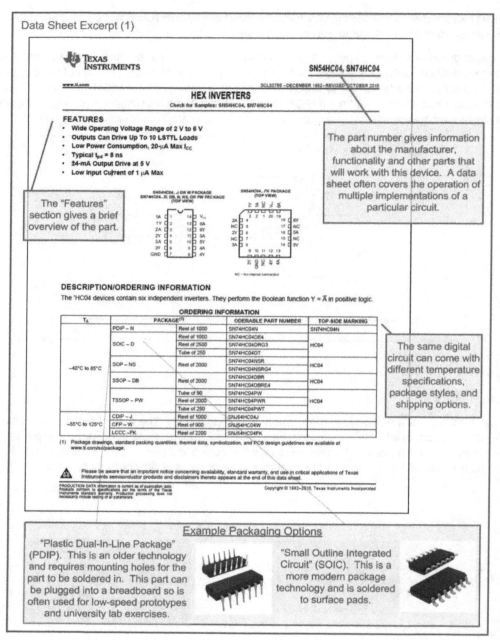

Figure 3.18
Example Data Sheet Excerpt (1)

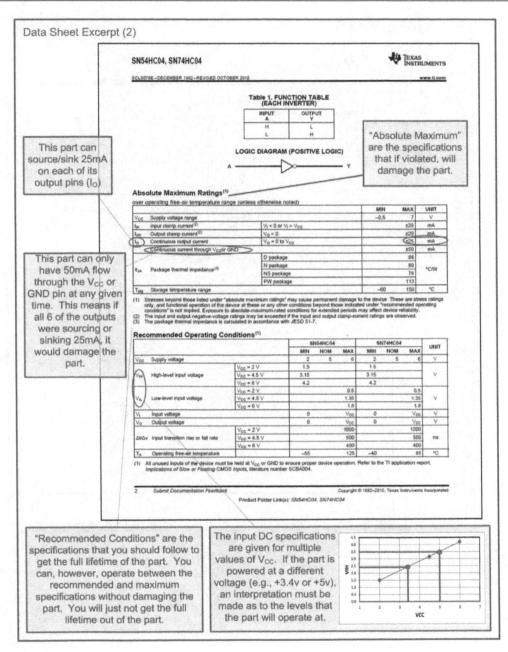

Figure 3.19
Example Data Sheet Excerpt (2)

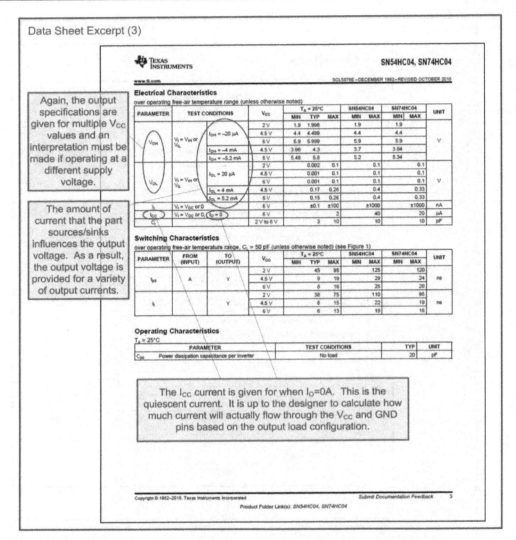

Figure 3.20
Example Data Sheet Excerpt (3)

CONCEPT CHECK

CC3.2(a) Given the following DC specifications for a driver/receiver pair, in what situation *may* a logic signal transmitted not be successfully received?

$V_{OH-max} = +3.4v$ $V_{IH-max} = +3.4v$

$V_{OH-min} = +2.5v$ $V_{IH-min} = +2.5v$

$V_{OL-max} = +1.5v$ $V_{IL-max} = +2.0v$

$V_{OL-min} = 0v$ $V_{IL-min} = 0v$

  A) Driving a HIGH with $V_o=+3.4v$

  B) Driving a HIGH with $V_o=+2.5v$

  C) Driving a LOW with $V_o=+1.5v$

  D) Driving a LOW with $V_o=0v$

CC3.2(b) For the following driver configuration, which of the following is a valid constraint that could be put in place to prevent a violation of the maximum power supply currents (I_{CC-max} and $I_{GND-max}$)?

  A) Modify the driver transistors so that they can't provide more than 5mA on any output.

  B) Apply a cooling system (e.g., a heat sink or fan) to the driver chip.

  C) Design the logic so that no more than half of the outputs are HIGH at any given time.

  D) Drive multiple receivers with the same output pin.

CC3.2(c) Why is it desirable to have the output of a digital circuit transition quickly between the logic LOW and logic HIGH levels?

  A) So that the outputs are not able to respond as the input transitions through the uncertainty region. This avoids unwanted transitions.

  B) So that all signals look like square waves.

  C) To reduce power by minimizing the time spent switching.

  D) Because the system can only have two states, a LOW and a HIGH.

3.3 Logic Families

It is apparent from the prior discussion of operating conditions that digital circuits need to have comparable input and output specifications in order to successfully communicate with each other. If a transmitter outputs a logic HIGH as +3.4v and the receiver needs a logic HIGH to be above +4v to be successfully interpreted as a logic HIGH, then these two circuits will not be able to communicate. In order to address this interoperability issue, digital circuits are grouped into *Logic Families*. A logic family is a group of parts that all adhere to a common set of specifications so that they work together. The logic family is given a specific name and once the specifications are agreed upon, different manufacturers produce parts that work within the particular family. Within a logic family, parts will all have the same power supply requirements and DC input/output specifications such that if connected *directly*, they will be able to successfully communicate with each other. The phrase "connected directly" is emphasized because it is very possible to insert an interconnect circuit between two circuits within the same logic family and alter the output voltage enough so that the receiver will not be able to interpret the correct logic level. Analyzing the effect of the interconnect circuit is part of the digital design process. There are many logic families that exist (up to 100 different types!) and more emerge each year as improvements are made to circuit fabrication processes that create smaller, faster and lower power circuits.

3.3.1 Complementary Metal Oxide Semiconductors (CMOS)

The first group of logic families we will discuss is called Complementary Metal Oxide Semiconductors, or CMOS. This is currently the most popular group of logic families for digital circuits implemented on the same integrated circuit (IC). An **integrated circuit** is where the entire circuit is implemented on a single piece of semiconductor material (or chip). The IC can contain transistors, resistors, capacitors, inductors, wires and insulators. Modern integrated circuits can contain billions of devices and meters of interconnect. The opposite of implementing the circuit on an integrated circuit is to use **discrete components**. Using discrete components refers to where every device (transistor, resistor, etc.) is its own part and is wired together externally using either a printed circuit board (PCB) or jumper wires as on a breadboard. The line between ICs and discrete parts has blurred in the past decades because modern discrete parts are actually fabricated as an IC and regularly contain multiple devices (e.g., 4 logic gates per chip). Regardless, the term *discrete* is still used to describe components that only contain a *few* components where the term IC typically refers to a much larger system that is custom designed.

The term CMOS comes from the use of particular types of transistors to implement the digital circuits. The transistors are created using a Metal Oxide Semiconductor (MOS) structure. These transistors are turned on or off based on an electric field, so they are given the name Metal Oxide Semiconductor *Field Effect* Transistors, or MOSFETs. There are two transistors that can be built using this approach that operate *complementary* to each other, thus the term *Complementary Metal Oxide Semiconductors*. To understand the basic operation of CMOS logic, we begin by treating the MOSFETs as ideal switches. This allows us to understand the basic functionality without diving into the detailed electronic analysis of the transistors.

3.3.1.1 CMOS Operation

In CMOS, there is a single power supply (V_{CC} or V_{DD}) and a single ground (GND). The ground signal is sometimes called V_{SS}. The maximum input and output DC specifications are equal to the power supply ($V_{CC} = V_{OH-max} = V_{IH-max}$). The minimum input and output DC specification are equal to ground (GND = 0v = V_{OL-min} = V_{IL-min}). In this way, using CMOS simplifies many of the specifications. If you state that you are using "CMOS with a +3.4v power supply", you are inherently stating that $V_{CC} = V_{OH-max} = V_{IH-max} = +3.4v$ and that $V_{OL-min} = V_{IL-min} = 0v$. Many times the name of the logic family will be associated with the power supply voltage. For example, a logic family may go by the name "+3.3v CMOS" or "+2.5v CMOS". These names give a first level description of the logic family operation, but more details about the operation must be looked up in the data sheet.

There are two types of transistors used in CMOS. The transistors will be closed or open based on an input logic level. The first transistor is called an N-type MOSFET, or **NMOS**. This transistor will turn on, or close, when the voltage between the gate and source (V_{GS}) is greater than its *threshold voltage*. The threshold voltage (V_T) is the amount of voltage needed to create a conduction path between the drain and the source terminals. The threshold voltage of an NMOS transistor is typically between 0.2v to 1v and much less than the V_{CC} voltage in the system. The second transistor is called a P-type MOSFET, or **PMOS**. This transistor turns on, or closes, when the voltage between the gate and the source (V_{GS}) is less than V_T, where the V_T for a PMOS is a negative value. This means that to turn on a PMOS transistor, the gate terminal needs to be at a lower voltage than the source. The type of transistor (i.e., P-type or N-type) has to do with the type of semiconductor material used to conduct current through the transistor. An NMOS transistor uses negative charge to conduct current (i.e., Negative-Type) while a PMOS uses positive charge (i.e., Positive-Type). Figure 3.21 shows the symbols for the PMOS and NMOS, the fabrication cross-sections, and their switch level equivalents.

Figure 3.21
CMOS Transistors

The basic operation of CMOS is that when driving a logic HIGH the switches are used to connect the output to the power supply (V_{CC}), and when driving a logic LOW the switches are used to connect the output to GND. In CMOS, V_{CC} is considered an ideal logic HIGH and GND is considered an ideal logic LOW. V_{CC} is typically much larger than V_T so using these levels can easily turn on and off the transistors. The design of the circuit must never connect the output to V_{CC} and GND at the same time or else the device itself will be damaged due to the current flowing directly from V_{CC} to GND through the transistors. Due to the device physics of the MOSFETS, PMOS transistors are used to form the network that will connect the output to V_{CC} (a.k.a., the pull-up network), and NMOS transistors are used to form the network that will connect the output to GND (a.k.a., the pull-down network). Since PMOS transistors are closed when the input is a 0 (thus providing a logic HIGH on the output) and NMOS transistors are closed when the input is a 1 (thus providing a logic LOW on the output), CMOS implements negative logic gates. This means CMOS can implement inverters, NAND and NOR gates but not buffers, AND and OR gates directly. In order to create a CMOS AND gate, the circuit would implement a NAND gate followed by an inverter and similarly for an OR gate and buffer.

3.3.1.2 CMOS Inverter

Let's now look at how we can use these transistors to create a CMOS inverter. Consider the transistor arrangement shown in Figure 3.22.

Figure 3.22
CMOS Inverter Schematic

The inputs of both the PMOS and NMOS are connected together. The PMOS is used to connect the output to V_{CC} and the NMOS is used to connect the output to GND. Since the inputs are connected together and the switches operate in a complementary manner, this circuit ensures that both transistors will never be on at the same time. When In=0, the PMOS switch is closed and the NMOS switch is open. This connects the output directly to V_{CC}, thus providing a logic HIGH on the output. When In=1, the PMOS switch is open and the NMOS switch is closed. This connects the output directly to GND, thus providing a logic LOW. This configuration yields an inverter. This operation is shown graphically in Figure 3.23.

Figure 3.23
CMOS Inverter Operation

3.3.1.3 CMOS NAND Gate

Let's now look at how we use a similar arrangement of transistors to implement a 2-input NAND gate. Consider the transistor configuration shown in Figure 3.24.

Figure 3.24
CMOS 2-Input NAND Gate Schematic

The pull-down network consists of two NMOS transistors in series (M1 and M2) and the pull-up network consists of two PMOS transistors in parallel (M3 and M4). Let's go through each of the input conditions and examine which transistors are on and which are off and how they impact the output. The first input condition is when A=0 and B=0. This condition turns *on* both M3 and M4 creating two parallel paths between the output and V_cc. At the same time, it turns *off* both M1 and M2 preventing a path between the output and GND. This input condition results in an output that is connected to V_cc resulting in a logic HIGH. The second input condition is when A=0 and B=1. This condition turns *on* M3 in the pull-up network and M2 in the pull-down network. This condition also turns *off* M4 in the pull-up network and M1 in the pull-down network. Since the pull-up network is a parallel combination of PMOS transistors, there is still a path between the output and V_cc through M3. Since the pull-down network is a series combination of NMOS transistors, both M1 and M2 must be on in order to connect the output to GND. This input condition results in an output that is connected to V_cc resulting in a logic HIGH. The third input condition is when A=1 and B=0. This condition again provides a path between the output and V_cc through M4 and prevents a path between the output and ground by having M2 open. This input condition results in an output that is connected to V_cc resulting in a logic HIGH. The final input condition is when A=1 and B=1. In this input condition, both of the PMOS transistors in the pull-up network (M3 and M4) are off preventing the output from being connected to V_cc. At the same time, this input turns on both M1 and M2 in the pull-down network connecting the output to GND. This input condition results in an output that is connected to GND resulting in a logic LOW. Based on the resulting output values corresponding to the four input codes, this circuit yields the logic operation of a 2-Input NAND gate. This operation is shown graphically in Figure 3.25.

Figure 3.25
CMOS 2-Input NAND Gate Operation

Creating a CMOS NAND gate with more than 2 inputs is accomplished by adding additional PMOS transistors to the pull-up network in parallel and additional NMOS transistors to the pull-down network in series. Figure 3.26 shows the schematic for a 3-Input NAND gate. This procedure is followed for creating NAND gates with larger numbers of inputs.

CMOS 3-Input NAND Gate Schematic

A	B	C	Out
0	0	0	1
0	0	1	1
0	1	0	1
0	1	1	1
1	0	0	1
1	0	1	1
1	1	0	1
1	1	1	0

Figure 3.26
CMOS 3-Input NAND Gate Schematic

If the CMOS transistors were ideal switches, the approach of increasing the number of inputs could be continued indefinitely. In reality, the transistors are not ideal switches and there is a limit on how many transistors can be added in series and continue to operate. The limitation has to do with ensuring that each transistor has enough voltage to properly turn on or off. This is a factor in the series network because the drain terminals of the NMOS transistors are not all connected to GND. If a voltage develops across one of the lower transistors (e.g., M3), then it takes more voltage on the input to turn on the next transistor up (e.g., M2). If too many transistors are added in series, then the uppermost transistor in the series may not be able to be turned on or off by the input signals. The number of inputs that a logic gate can have within a particular logic family is called its **fan-in** specification. When a logic circuit requires a number of inputs that exceeds the fan-in specification for a particular logic family, then additional logic gates must be used. For example, if a circuit requires a 5-input NAND gate but the logic family has a fan-in specification of 4, this means that the largest NAND gate available only has 4-inputs. The 5-input NAND operation must be accomplished using additional circuit design techniques that use gates with 4 or less inputs. These design techniques will be covered in Chapter 4.

3.3.1.4 CMOS NOR Gate

A CMOS NOR gate is created using a similar topology as a NAND gate with the exception that the pull-up network consists of PMOS transistors in series and the pull-down network that consists of NMOS transistors in parallel. Consider the transistor configuration shown in Figure 3.27.

Figure 3.27
CMOS 2-Input NOR Gate Schematic

The series configuration of the pull-up network will only connect the output to V$_{CC}$ when both inputs are 0. Conversely, the pull-down network prevents connecting the output to GND when both inputs are 0. When either or both of the inputs are true, the pull-up network is off and the pull-down network is on. This yields the logic function for a NOR gate. This operation is shown graphically in Figure 3.28. As with the NAND gate, the number of inputs can be increased by adding more PMOS transistors in series in the pull-up network and more NMOS transistors in parallel in the pull-down network.

Figure 3.28
CMOS 2-Input NOR Gate Operation

The schematic for a 3-input NOR gate is given in Figure 3.29. This approach can be used to increase the number of inputs up until the fan-in specification of the logic family is reached.

Figure 3.29
CMOS 3-Input NOR Gate Schematic

3.3.2 Transistor-Transistor Logic (TTL)

One of the first logic families that emerged after the invention of the integrated circuit was Transistor-Transistor Logic (TTL). This logic family uses bipolar junction transistor (BJT) as its fundamental switching item. This logic family defined a set of discrete parts that contained all of the basic gates in addition to more complex building blocks. TTL was used to build the first computer systems in the 1960's. TTL is not widely used today other than for specific applications because it consumes more power than CMOS and cannot achieve the density required for today's computer systems. TTL is discussed because it was the original logic family based on integrated circuits so it provides a historical perspective of digital logic. Furthermore, the discrete logic pin-outs and part-numbering schemes are still used today for discrete CMOS parts.

3.3.2.1 TTL Operation

TTL logic uses BJT transistors and resistors to accomplish the logic operations. The operation of a BJT transistor is more complicated than a MOSFET; however, it performs essentially the same switch operation when used in a digital logic circuit. An input is used to turn the transistor on, which in turn allows current to flow between two other terminals. Figure 3.30 shows the symbol for the two types of BJT transistors. The PNP transistor is analogous to a PMOS and the NPN is analogous to an NMOS. Current will flow between the Emitter and Collector terminals when there is a sufficient voltage on the Base terminal. The amount of current that flows between the Emitter and Collector is related to the current flowing into the Base. The primary difference in operation between BJTs and MOSFETs is that BJTs require proper voltage biasing in order to turn on and also draws current through the BASE in order to stay on. The detailed operation of BJTs is beyond the scope of this text, so an overly simplified model of TTL logic gates is given.

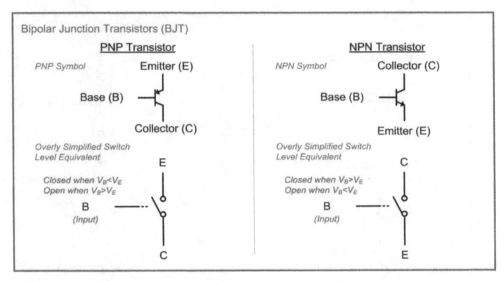

Figure 3.30
PNP and NPN Transistors

Figure 3.31 shows a simplified model of how TTL logic operates using BJTs and resistors. This simplified model does not show all of the transistors that are used in modern TTL circuits but instead is intended to provide a high level overview of the operation. This gate is an inverter that is created with an NPN transistor and a resistor. When the input is a logic HIGH, the NPN transistor turns on and conducts current between its collector and emitter terminals. This in effect closes the switch and connects the output to GND providing a logic LOW. During this state, current will also flow through the resistor to GND through Q1 thus consuming more power than the equivalent gate in CMOS. When the input is a logic LOW, the NPN transistor turns off and no current flows between its collector and emitter. This, in effect, is an open circuit leaving only the resistor connected to the output. The resistor pulls the output up to V_{CC} providing a logic HIGH on the output. One drawback of this state is that there will be a voltage drop across the resistor so the output is not pulled fully to V_{CC}.

Figure 3.31
TTL Inverter

3.3.3 The 7400 Series Logic Families

The 7400 series of TTL circuits became popular in the 1960's and 1970's. This family was based on TTL and contained hundreds of different digital circuits. The original circuits came in either plastic or ceramic Dual-In-Line packages (DIP). The 7400 TTL logic family was powered off of a +5v supply. As mentioned before, this logic family set the pin-outs and part-numbering schemes for modern logic families. There were many derivatives of the original TTL logic family that made modifications to improve speed, reliability, decrease power and reduce power supplies. Today's CMOS logic families within the 7400 series still use the same pin-outs and numbering schemes as the original TTL family. It is useful to understand the history of this series because these parts are often used in introductory laboratory exercises to learn how to interface digital logic circuits.

3.3.3.1 Part Numbering Scheme

The part numbering scheme for the 7400 series and its derivatives contains 5 different fields: 1) manufacturer, 2) temperature range, 3) logic family, 4) logic function and 5) package type. The breakdown of these fields is shown in Figure 3.32.

Figure 3.32
7400 Series Part Numbering Scheme

3.3.3.2 DC Operating Conditions

Table 3.2 gives the DC operating conditions for a few of the logic families within the 7400 series. Notice that the CMOS families consume much less power than the TTL families. Also notice that the TTL output currents are asymmetrical. The differences between the I_{OH} and I_{OL} within the TTL families has to do with the nature of the bipolar transistors and the resistors used to create the pull-up networks within the devices. CMOS has symmetrical drive currents due to using complementary transistors for the pull-up (PMOS) and pull-down networks (NMOS).

Logic Family	Year	DC Operating Condition											Speed (MHz)
		V_{CC}	V_{OHmax}	V_{OHmin}	V_{OLmax}	V_{OLmin}	V_{IHmax}	V_{IHmin}	V_{ILmax}	V_{ILmin}	I_{CC}	$I_{Omax\ (H/L)}$	
Orig. (TTL)	1964	+5	+5	+2.4	+0.4	GND	+5	+2	+0.8	GND	40m	-4/+16m	25
LS (TTL)	1976	+5	+5	+2.4	+0.4	GND	+5	+2	+0.8	GND	8.8m	-4/+8m	40
HC (CMOS)	1982	+2-6	V_{CC}	$0.8 \cdot V_{CC}$	0.33	GND	V_{CC}	$0.7 \cdot V_{CC}$	$0.3 \cdot V_{CC}$	GND	40u	+/-25m	50
AC (CMOS)	1985	+2-6	V_{CC}	$0.8 \cdot V_{CC}$	0.33	GND	V_{CC}	$0.7 \cdot V_{CC}$	$0.3 \cdot V_{CC}$	GND	80u	+/-50m	125

DC Operating Conditions for a Sample of 7400 Series Logic Families

Note 1: All voltage specifications have units of volts. All current specifications have units of amps.

Note 2: The V_O and V_I specifications for the AC and HC logic families are worst case and vary depending on the V_{CC} selection and the output current.

Note 3: All specifications are given for the commercial temperature range (74 series).

Table 3.2
DC Operating Conditions for a Sample of 7400 Series Logic Families

3.3.3.3 Pin-out Information for the DIP Packages

Figure 3.33 shows the pin-out assignments for a subset of the basic gates from the 74HC logic family in the Dual-In-Line package form factor. Most of the basic gates within the 7400 series follow these assignments. Notice that each of these basic gates comes in a 14-pin DIP package, each with a single V_{CC} and single GND pin. It is up to the designer to ensure that the maximum current flowing through the V_{CC} and GND pins does not exceed the maximum specification. This is particularly important for parts that contain numerous gates. For example, the 74HC00 part contains four, 2-Input NAND gates. If each of the NAND gates was driving a logic HIGH at its maximum allowable output current (i.e., 25mA from Figure 3.19), then a total of 4·25mA + I_q = ~100mA would be flowing through its V_{CC} pin. Since the V_{CC} pin can only tolerate a maximum of 50mA of current (from Figure 3.19), the part would be damaged since the output current of ~100mA would also flow through the V_{CC} pin. The pin-outs in Figure 3.33 are useful when first learning to design logic circuits because the DIP packages plug directly into a standard breadboard.

Figure 3.33
Pin-outs for a subset of Basic Gates from the 74HC Logic Family in DIP Packages

CONCEPT CHECK

CC3.3 Why doesn't the following CMOS transistor configuration yield a buffer?

V_{CC} = +3.4v

Assume that the V_T of the NMOS is small enough that V_{GS} > 0 will turn on the transistor.

In — Out — The output (Out) can only take on values between 0v and +3.4v

The input (In) switches between 0v and +3.4v

Assume that the V_T of the PMOS is small enough that V_{GS} < 0 will turn on the transistor.

GND

A) In order to turn on the NMOS transistor, V_{GS} needs to be greater than zero. In the given configuration, the gate terminal of the NMOS (G) needs to be driven above the source terminal (S). If the source terminal was at +3.4v, then the input (In) would never be able to provide a positive enough voltage to ensure the NMOS is on because "In" doesn't go above +3.4v.

B) There is no way to turn on both transistors in this configuration.

C) The power consumption will damage the device because both transistors will potentially be on.

D) The sources of the two devices can't be connected together without causing a short in the device.

3.4 Driving Loads

At this point we've discussed in depth how proper care must be taken to ensure that not only do the output voltages of the driving gate meet the input specifications of the receiver in order to successfully transmit 1's and 0's, but that the output current of the driver does not exceed the maximum specifications so that the part is not damaged. The output voltage and current for a digital circuit depends greatly on the load that is being driven. The following sections discuss the impact of driving some of the most common digital loads.

3.4.1 Driving Other Gates

Within a logic family, all digital circuits are designed to operate with one another. If there is minimal loss or noise in the interconnect system, then 1's and 0's will be successfully transmitted and no current specifications will be exceeded. Consider the example in Example 3.3 for an inverter driving another inverter from the same logic family.

Example: Determining if Specifications are Violated When Driving Another Gate as a Load

Given: 74HC04 Specifications

I_{I-max} = 1uA
I_q = 20uA
I_{O-max} = 25mA
I_{CC-max} = 50mA

Find: Were I_{O-max} or I_{CC-max} violated?

Solution: The maximum input current of the load (e.g., the receiving inverter) is 1uA. This means that the I_O for the driver will be 1uA because the load sets the output current. This is far below the maximum output current of 25mA so the I_{O-max} specification is not violated.

The driver will draw I_q through its V_{CC} pin to power its functional operation. In addition to I_q, the driver will also pull a current equal to I_O through the V_{CC} pin while driving a logic HIGH. This means the maximum current pulled through the V_{CC} pin is $I_q + I_O$ = 20uA + 1uA = 21uA. Again, this is well below the specification for the maximum amount of current that can flow through the V_{CC} pin (50mA) so the I_{CC}-max specification is also not violated.

Example 3.3
Determining if Specifications are Violated when Driving Another Gate as a Load

From this example, it is clear that there are no issues when a gate is driving another gate from the same family. This is as expected because that is the point of a logic family. In fact, gates are designed to drive multiple gates from within their own family. Based solely on the DC specifications for input and output current, it could be assumed that the number of other gates that can be driven is simply I_{O-max} / I_{I-max}. For the example in Example 3.3, this would result in a 74HC gate being able to drive 25,000 other gates (i.e., 25mA / 1uA = 25,000). In reality, the maximum number of gates that can be driven is dictated by the switching characteristics. This limit is called the **fan-out** specification. The fan-out specification states the maximum number of other gates from within the same family that can be driven. As discussed earlier, the output signal needs to transition quickly through the uncertainty region so that the receiver does not have time to react and go to an unknown state. As more and more gates are driven, this transition time is slowed down. The fan-out specification provides a limit to the maximum number of gates from the same family that can be driven while still ensuring that the output signal transitions between states fast enough to avoid the receivers from going to an unknown state. Example 3.4 shows the process of determining the maximum output current that a driver will need to provide when driving the maximum number of gates allowed by the fan-out specification.

Example: Determining the Output Current When Driving Multiple Gates as the Load

Given: 74HC04 Specifications

Fan-out = 3
I_{I-max}=1uA
Driving the maximum gates allowed by fan-out.

Find: I_O

Solution: The fan-out specification is 3, which means that the transmitting inverter can drive up to 3 other gates from its own logic family. Each of the receivers will draw their input current of I_I=1uA, which will be provided by the driver. The total amount of output current from the driver is 3·1uA = 3uA.

Example 3.4
Determining the Output Current when Driving Multiple Gates as the Load

3.4.2 Driving Resistive Loads

There are many situations where a resistor is the load in a digital circuit. A resistive load can be an actual resistor that is present for some other purpose such as a pull-up, pull-down, or for impedance matching. More complex loads such as buzzers, relays or other electronics can also be modeled as a resistor. When a resistor is the load in a digital circuit, care must be taken to avoid violating the output current specifications of the driver. The electrical circuit analysis technique that is used to evaluate how a resistive load impacts a digital circuit is **Ohm's Law**. Ohm's Law is a very simple relationship between the current and voltage in a resistor. Figure 3.34 gives a primer on Ohm's Law. For use in digital circuits, there are only a select few cases that this technique will be applied to, so no prior experience with Ohm's Law is required at this point.

A Primer on Ohm's Law

Ohm's Law describes the relationship between current and voltage in a resistor. This simple equation is used in nearly all electrical circuit analysis. The equation is as follows:

$$V = I \cdot R$$

A resistor is characterized by its *resistance*, which describes how much current will flow when a voltage is present across its two terminals. The units for resistance are Ohms (Ω = Volts / Amp). The current in Ohm's Law is defined to flow from the + to − of the voltage.

Example: Use Ohm's Law to find the current flowing through the following resistor.

V=+3.4   R = 1kΩ

Solution: Plugging the parameters directly into Ohm's Law we find:

$$V = I \cdot R$$
$$3.4 = I \cdot (1k)$$
$$I = 0.0034 \text{ A} = 3.4 \text{ mA}$$

Figure 3.34
A Primer on Ohm's Law

Let's see how we can use Ohm's Law to analyze the impact of a resistive load in a digital circuit. Consider the circuit configuration in Example 3.5 and how we can use Ohm's Law to determine the output current of the driver. The load in this case is a resistor connected between the output of the driver and the power supply (+5v). When driving a logic HIGH, the output level will be approximately equal to the power supply (i.e., +5v). Since in this situation both terminals of the resistor are at +5v, there is no voltage difference present. That means when plugging into Ohm's Law, the voltage component is 0v, which gives 0 amps of current. In the case where the driver is outputting a logic LOW, the output will be approximately GND. In this case, there is a voltage drop of +5v across the resistor (5v-0v). Plugging this into Ohm's Law yields a current of 50mA flowing through the resistor. This can become problematic because the current flows through the resistor and then into the output of the driver. For the 74HC logic family, this would exceed the I_o max specification of 25mA and damage the part. Additionally, as more current is drawn through the output, the output voltage becomes less and less ideal. In this example, the first order analysis uses V_o=GND. In reality, as the output current increases, the output voltage will move further away from its ideal value and may eventually reach a value within the uncertainty region.

Example 3.5
Determining the Output Current When Driving a Pull-Up Resistor as the Load

   A similar process can be used to determine the output current when driving a resistive load between the output and GND. This process is shown in Example 3.6.

Example 3.6
Determining the Output Current When Driving a Pull-Down Resistor as the Load

3.4.3 Driving LEDs

A light emitting diode (LED) is a very common type of load that is driven using a digital circuit. The behavior of diodes is typically covered in an analog electronics class. Since it is assumed that the reader has not been exposed to the operation of diodes, the behavior of the LED will be described using a highly simplified model. A diode has two terminals, the anode and cathode. Current that flows from the anode to the cathode is called the *forward current*. A voltage that is developed across a diode from its anode to cathode is called the *forward voltage*. A diode has a unique characteristic that when a forward voltage is supplied across its terminal, it will only increase up to a certain point. The amount is specified as the LED's forward voltage (v_f) and is typically between 1.5v – 2v in modern LEDs. When a power supply circuit is connected to the LED, no current will flow until this forward voltage has been reached. Once it has been reached, current will begin to flow and the LED will prevent any further voltage from developing across it. Once current flows, the LED will begin emitting light. The more current that flows, the more light that will be emitted up until the point that the maximum allowable current through the LED is reached and then the device will be damaged. When using an LED, there are two specifications of interest: the forward voltage and the recommended forward current. The symbols for a diode and an LED are given in Figure 3.35.

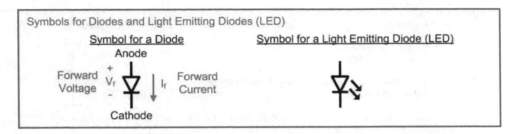

Figure 3.35
Symbols for a Diode and a Light Emitting Diode

When designing an LED driver circuit, a voltage must be supplied in order to develop the forward voltage across the LED so that current will flow. A resistor is included in series with the LED for two reasons. The first reason is to provide a place for any additional voltage provided by the driver to develop in the situation that $V_o > V_f$, which is most often the case. The second reason for the resistor is to set the output current. Since the voltage across the resistor will be a fixed amount (i.e., $V_o - V_f$), then the value of the resistor can be chosen to set the current. This current is typically set to an optimum value that turns on the LED to a desired luminosity while also ensuring that the maximum output current of the driver is not violated. Consider the LED driver configuration shown in Example 3.7 where the LED will be turned on when the driver outputs a HIGH.

Example 3.7
Determining the Output Current When Driving an LED where HIGH=ON

Example 3.8 shows another example of driving an LED, but this time using a different configuration where the LED will be on when the driver outputs a logic LOW.

Example: Determining the Output Current When Driving an LED where LOW=ON

Given: V_f = +1.8v
$I_{f\,(rec)}$ = 4mA

Find: R to achieve the recommended forward current of 4mA through the LED.

Solution: When the driver outputs a logic HIGH, it will provide V_O=+3.4v. This means there will be no voltage that develops across the series combination of the resistor and LED since the other end of the combination is also at +3.4. This means when driving a logic HIGH, the LED will be OFF.

When the driver outputs a logic LOW, it will provide V_O=0v. Since the resistor is tied to +3.4v, this voltage will develop across the series combination of the resistor and LED. The LED will increase up to its forward voltage of +1.8v and then remain there. The rest of the output voltage will develop across the resistor (e.g., +1.6v). We can choose the value of the resistor to set the current that will flow through the series combination using Ohm's Law since we know the voltage across the resistor and the desired current. In this case, the LED will be ON when the driver outputs a logic LOW.

$V = I \cdot R$
$1.6 = (4mA) \cdot R$
$R = 400\ \Omega$

Example 3.8
Determining the Output Current When Driving an LED where HIGH=OFF

CONCEPT CHECK

CC3.4 A fan-out specification is typically around 6-12. If a logic family has a maximum output current specification of $I_{O\text{-}max}$=25mA and a maximum input current specification of only $I_{I\text{-}max}$=1uA, a driver could conceivably source up to 25,000 gates ($I_{O\text{-}max}/I_{I\text{-}max}$ = 25mA/1uA = 25,000) without violating its maximum output current specification. Why isn't the fan-out specification then closer to 25,000?

A) The fan-out specification has significant margin built into it in order to protect the driver.

B) Connecting 25,000 loads to the driver would cause significant wiring congestion and would be impractical.

C) The fan-out specification is in place to reduce power, so keeping it small is desirable.

D) The fan-out specification is in place for AC behavior. It ensures that the AC loading on the driver doesn't slow down its output rise and fall times. If too many loads are connected, the output transition will be too slow and it will reside in the uncertainty region for too long leading to unwanted switching on the receivers.

Summary

- The operation of a logic circuit can be described using either a logic symbol, a truth table, a logic expression, or a logic waveform.

- Logic *gates* represent the most basic operations that can be performed on binary numbers. They are BUF, INV, AND, NAND, OR, NOR, XOR, and XNOR.

- XOR gates that have a number of inputs greater than two are created using a cascade of 2-input XOR gates. This implementation has more practical applications such as arithmetic and error detection codes.

- The logic *level* describes whether the electrical signal representing one of two states is above or below a switching threshold region. The two possible values that a logic level can be are HIGH or LOW.

- The logic *value* describes how the logic levels are mapped into the two binary codes 0 and 1. In positive logic a HIGH=1 and a LOW=0. In negative logic a HIGH=0 and a LOW=1.

- Logic circuits have DC specifications that describe how input voltage levels are interpreted as either HIGHs or LOWs (V_{IH-max}, V_{IH-min}, V_{IL-max}, and V_{IL-min}). Specifications are also given on what output voltages will be produced when driving a HIGH or LOW (V_{OH-max}, V_{OH-min}, V_{OL-max}, and V_{OL-min}).

- In order to successfully transmit digital information, the output voltages of the driver that represent a HIGH and LOW must arrive at the receiver within the voltage ranges that are *interpreted* as a HIGH and LOW. If the voltage arrives at the receiver outside of these specified input ranges, the receiver will not know whether a HIGH or LOW is being transmitted.

- Logic circuits also specify maximum current levels on the power supplies (I_{VCC}, I_{gnd}), inputs (I_{I-max}), and outputs (I_{O-max}) that may not be exceeded. If these levels are exceeded, the circuit may not operate properly or be damaged.

- The current exiting a logic circuit is equal to the current entering.

- When a logic circuit *sources* current to a load, an equivalent current is drawn *into* the circuit through its power supply pin.

- When a logic circuit *sinks* current from a load, an equivalent current flows *out of* the circuit through its ground pin.

- The type of load that is connected to the output of a logic circuit dictates how much current will be drawn from the driver.

- The *quiescent current* (I_q or I_{cc}) is the current that the circuit always draws independent of the input/output currents.

- Logic circuits have AC specifications that describe the delay from the input to the output (t_{PLH}, t_{PHL}) and also how fast the outputs transition between the HIGH and LOW levels (t_r, t_f).

- A *logic family* is a set of logic circuits that are designed to operate with each other.

- The *fan-in* of a logic family describes the maximum number of inputs that a gate may have.

- The *fan-out* of a logic family describes the maximum number of other gates from within the same family that can be driven simultaneously by one gate.

- Complementary Metal Oxide Semiconductor (CMOS) logic is the most popular family series in use today. CMOS logic use two transistors (NMOS and PMOS) that act as complementary switches. CMOS transistors draw very low quiescent current and can be fabricated with extremely small feature sizes.

- In CMOS, only inverters, NAND gates, and NOR gates can be created directly. If it is desired to create a buffer, AND gate, or OR gate, an inverter is placed on the output of the original inverter, NAND, or NOR gate.

Exercise Problems

Section 3.1 – Basic Gates

3.1.1 Give the truth table for a 3-input AND gate with the input variables A, B, C and output F.

3.1.2 Give the truth table for a 3-input OR gate with the input variables A, B, C and output F.

3.1.3 Give the truth table for a 3-input XNOR gate with the input variables A, B, C and output F.

3.1.4 Give the logic expression for a 3-input AND gate with the input variables A, B, C and output F.

3.1.5 Give the logic expression for a 3-input OR gate with the input variables A, B, C and output F.

3.1.6 Give the logic expression for a 3-input XNOR gate with the input variables A, B, C and output F.

3.1.7 Give the logic waveform for a 3-input AND gate with the input variables A, B, C and output F.

3.1.8 Give the logic waveform for a 3-input OR gate with the input variables A, B, C and output F.

3.1.9 Give the logic waveform for a 3-input XNOR gate with the input variables A, B, C and output F.

Section 3.2 – Digital Circuit Operation

3.2.1 Using the DC operating conditions from Table 3.2, give the noise margin HIGH (NM_H) for the 74LS logic family.

3.2.2 Using the DC operating conditions from Table 3.2, give the noise margin LOW (NM_L) for the 74LS logic family.

3.2.3 Using the DC operating conditions from Table 3.2, give the noise margin HIGH (NM_H) for the 74HC logic family with V_{cc}=+5v.

3.2.4 Using the DC operating conditions from Table 3.2, give the noise margin LOW (NM_L) for the 74HC logic family with V_{CC}=+5v.

3.2.5 Using the DC operating conditions from Table 3.2, give the noise margin HIGH (NM_H) for the 74HC logic family with V_{CC}=+3.4v.

3.2.6 Using the DC operating conditions from Table 3.2, give the noise margin LOW (NM_L) for the 74HC logic family with V_{CC}=+3.4v.

3.2.7 For the driver configuration in Figure 3.36, give the current flowing through the Vcc pin.

Figure 3.36

3.2.8 For the driver configuration in Figure 3.36, give the current flowing through the GND pin.

3.2.9 For the driver configuration in Figure 3.37, give the current flowing through the Vcc pin.

Figure 3.37

3.2.10 For the driver configuration in Figure 3.37, give the current flowing through the GND pin.

3.2.11 Using the data sheet excerpt from Figure 3.20, give the maximum propagation delay (t_{pd}) for the 74HC04 inverter when powered with V_{CC}=+2v.

3.2.12 Using the data sheet excerpt from Figure 3.20, give the maximum propagation delay from low to high (t_{PLH}) for the 74HC04 inverter when powered with V_{CC}=+2v.

3.2.13 Using the data sheet excerpt from Figure 3.20, give the maximum propagation delay from high to low (t_{PHL}) for the 74HC04 inverter when powered with V_{CC}=+2v.

3.2.14 Using the data sheet excerpt from Figure 3.20, give the maximum transition time (t_t) for the 74HC04 inverter when powered with V_{CC}=+2v.

3.2.15 Using the data sheet excerpt from Figure 3.20, give the maximum rise time (t_r) for the 74HC04 inverter when powered with V_{CC}=+2v.

3.2.16 Using the data sheet excerpt from Figure 3.20, give the maximum fall time (t_f) for the 74HC04 inverter when powered with V_{CC}=+2v.

Section 3.3 – Logic Families

3.3.1 Provide the transistor-level schematic for a 4-Input NAND gate.

3.3.2 Provide the transistor-level schematic for a 4-Input NOR gate.

3.3.3 Provide the transistor-level schematic for a 2-Input AND gate.

3.3.4 Provide the transistor-level schematic for a 2-Input OR gate.

3.3.5 Provide the transistor-level schematic for a buffer.

Section 3.4 – Driving Loads

3.4.1 In the driver configuration shown in Figure 3.38, the buffer is driving its maximum fan-out specification of 6. The maximum input current for this logic family is I_I=1nA. What is the maximum output current (I_O) that the driver will need to source?

Figure 3.38

3.4.2 For the pull-down driver configuration shown in Figure 3.39, calculate the value of the pull-down resistor (R) in order to ensure that the output current does not exceed 20mA.

Figure 3.39

Figure 3.41

3.4.3 For the pull-up driver configuration shown in Figure 3.40, calculate the value of the pull-up resistor (R) in order to ensure that the output current does not exceed 20 mA.

Figure 3.40

3.4.5 For the LED driver configuration shown in Figure 3.42 where an output of LOW on the driver will turn on the LED, calculate the value of the resistor (R) in order to set the LED forward current to 5mA. The LED has a forward voltage of 1.9v.

Figure 3.42

3.4.4 For the LED driver configuration shown in Figure 3.41 where an output of HIGH on the driver will turn on the LED, calculate the value of the resistor (R) in order to set the LED forward current to 5mA. The LED has a forward voltage of 1.9v.

Chapter 4: Combinational Logic Design

In this chapter we cover the techniques to synthesize, analyze, and manipulate logic functions. The goal of these techniques is to ultimately create a logic circuit using the basic gates described in Chapter 3 from a truth table or word description. This process is called *combinational logic design*. Combinational logic refers to circuits where the output depends on the present value of the inputs. This simple definition implies that there is no storage capability in the circuitry and a change on the input immediately impacts the output. To begin, we first define the rules of Boolean algebra, which provide the framework for the legal operations and manipulations that can be taken on a two-valued number system (i.e., a binary system). We then explore a variety of logic design and manipulation techniques. These techniques allow us to directly create a logic circuit from a truth table and then to manipulate it to either reduce the number of gates necessary in the circuit or to convert the logic circuit into equivalent forms using alternate gates.

Learning Outcomes – After completing this chapter, you will be able to:

4.1   Describe the fundamental principles of Boolean algebra.
4.2   Prove Boolean algebra theorems using proof by exhaustion.
4.3   Determine the logic expression for a combinational logic circuit from its logic diagram.
4.4   Determine the truth table for a combinational logic circuit from its logic diagram.
4.5   Determine the delay of a combinational logic circuit from its logic diagram.
4.6   Describe the functional operation of a logic circuit using a truth table.
4.7   Describe the functional operation of a logic circuit using a canonical sum of products (SOP) form.
4.8   Describe the functional operation of a logic circuit using a minterm list.
4.9   Describe the functional operation of a logic circuit using a canonical product of sums (POS) form.
4.10   Describe the functional operation of a logic circuit using a maxterm list.
4.11   Minimize a logic expression using a Karnaugh Map.
4.12   Find the minimal logic expression from a Karnaugh Map.
4.13   Eliminate timing hazards in a minimal logic expression.
4.14   Exploit "don't cares" to form a minimal logic expression.

4.1 Boolean Algebra

The term *Algebra* refers to the rules of a number system. In Chapter 2 we discussed the number of symbols and relative values of some of the common number systems. Algebra defines the operations that are legal to perform on that system. Once we have defined the rules for a system, we can then use the system for more powerful mathematics such as solving for unknowns and manipulating into equivalent forms. The ability to manipulate into equivalent forms allows us to minimize the number of logic operations necessary and also put into a form that can be directly synthesized using modern logic circuits.

In 1854, English mathematician George Boole presented an abstract algebraic framework for a system that contained only two states, true and false. This framework essentially launched the field of computer science even before the existence of the modern integrated circuits that are used to implement digital logic today. In 1930, American mathematician Claude Shannon applied Boole's algebraic framework to his work on switching circuits at Bell Labs, thus launching the field of digital circuit design and information theory. Boole's original framework is still used extensively in modern digital circuit design and thus bears the name *Boolean algebra*. Today, the term Boolean algebra is often used to describe not only George Boole's original work, but all of those that contributed to the field after him.

4.1.1 Operations

In Boolean algebra there are two valid states (true and false) and three core operations. The operations are conjunction ($\wedge$, equivalent to the AND operation), disjunction ($\vee$, equivalent to the OR operation), and negation ($\neg$, equivalent to the NOT operation). From these three operations, more sophisticated operations can be created including other logic functions (i.e., BUF, NAND, NOR, XOR, XNOR, etc.) and arithmetic. Engineers primarily use the terms AND, OR and NOT instead of conjunction, disjunction and negation. Similarly, engineers primarily use the symbols for these operators described in Chapter 3 (e.g, $\cdot$, + and ') instead of $\wedge$, $\vee$, and $\neg$.

4.1.2 Axioms

An *axiom* is a statement of truth about a system that is accepted by the user. Axioms are very simple statements about a system, but need to be established before more complicated theorems can be proposed. Axioms are so basic that they do not need to be proved in order to be accepted. Axioms can be thought of as the basic *laws* of the algebraic framework. The terms *axiom* and *postulate* are synonymous and used interchangeably. In Boolean algebra there are five main axioms. These axioms will appear redundant with the description of basic gates from Chapter 3, but must be defined in this algebraic context so that more powerful theorems can be proposed.

4.1.2.1 Axiom #1 – Logical Values

This axiom states that in Boolean algebra, a variable A can only take on one of two values, 0 or 1. If the variable A is not 0, then it must be a 1, and conversely, if it is not a 1, then it must be a 0.

Axiom #1 – Boolean Values: A=0 if A≠1, conversely A=1 if A≠0.

4.1.2.2 Axiom #2 – Definition of Logical Negation

This axiom defines logical negation. Negation is also called the NOT operation or taking the *complement*. The negation operation is denoted using either a prime ('), an inversion bar or the negation symbol (¬). If the complement is taken on a 0, it becomes a 1. If the complement is taken on a 1, it becomes a 0.

Axiom #2 – Definition of Logical Negation: if A=0 then A'=1, conversely, if A=1 then A'=0.

4.1.2.3 Axiom #3 – Definition of a Logical Product

This axiom defines a logical product or multiplication. Logical multiplication is denoted using either a dot (·), an ampersand (&) or the conjunction symbol (∧). The result of logical multiplication is true when *both* inputs are true and false otherwise.

Axiom #3 – Definition of a Logical Product: A·B=1 if A=B=1 and A·B=0 otherwise.

4.1.2.4 Axiom #4 – Definition of a Logical Sum

This axiom defines a logical sum or addition. Logical addition is denoted using either a plus sign (+) or the disjunction symbol (∨). The result of logical addition is true when *any* of the inputs are true and false otherwise.

Axiom #4 – Definition of a Logical Sum: A+B=1 if A=1 or B=1 and A+B=0 otherwise.

4.1.2.5 Axiom #5 – Logical Precedence

This axiom defines the order of precedence for the three operators. Unless the precedence is explicitly stated using parentheses, negation takes precedence over a logical product and a logical product takes precedence over a logical sum.

Axiom #5 – Definition of Logical Precedence: *NOT precedes AND, AND precedes OR.*

To illustrate Axiom #5, consider the logic function F=A'·B+C. In this function, the first operation that would take place is the NOT operation on A. This would be followed by the AND operation of A' with B. Finally, the result would be OR'd with C. The precedence of any function can also be explicitly stated using parentheses such as F= (((A') · B) + C).

4.1.3 Theorems

A theorem is a more sophisticated truth about a system that is not intuitively obvious. Theorems are proposed and then must be proved. Once proved, they can be accepted as a truth about the system going forward. Proving a theorem in Boolean algebra is much simpler than in our traditional decimal system due to the fact that variables can only take on one of two values, true or false. Since the number of input possibilities is bounded, Boolean algebra theorems can be proved by simply testing the theorem using every possible input code. This is called **proof by**

exhaustion. The following theorems are used widely in the manipulation of logic expressions and reduction of terms within an expression.

4.1.3.1 DeMorgan's Theorem of Duality

Augustus DeMorgan was a British mathematician and logician who lived during the time of George Boole. DeMorgan is best known for his contribution to the field of logic through the creation of what have been later called the *DeMorgan's Theorems* (often called DeMorgan's Laws). There are two major theorems that DeMorgan proposed that expanded Boolean algebra. The first theorem is named *duality*. Duality states that an algebraic equality will remain true if all 0's and 1's are interchanged and all AND and OR operations are interchanged. The new expression is called the *dual* of the original expression. Example 4.1 shows the process of proving duality using proof by exhaustion.

Example 4.1
Proving DeMorgan's Theorem of Duality using Proof by Exhaustion

Duality is important for two reasons. First, it doubles the impact of a theorem. If a theorem is proved to be true, then the dual of that theorem is also proved to be true. This, in essence, gives twice the theorem with the same amount of proving. Boolean algebra theorems are almost always given in pairs, the original and the dual. That is why duality is covered as the first theorem.

The second reason that duality is important is because it can be used to convert between positive and negative logic. Until now, we have used positive logic for all of our examples (i.e., a logic HIGH = true = 1 and a logic LOW = false = 0). As mentioned earlier, this convention is arbitrary and we could have easily chosen a HIGH to be false and a LOW to be true (i.e., negative logic). Duality allows us to take a logic expression that has been created using positive logic (F) and then convert it into an equivalent expression that is valid for negative logic (F_D). Example 4.2 shows the process for how this works.

Example: Converting Between Positive and Negative Logic Using Duality

Let's start with a logic expression that originates in positive logic convention.

$$F = A \cdot B$$

Positive Logic means that a HIGH=1 and a LOW=0. If we want to implement the equivalent function using negative logic, we instead assign a HIGH=0 and a LOW=1.

The Logic We Want

A	B	F
L	L	L
L	H	L
H	L	L
H	H	H

Mapping with Positive Logic

A	B	F
0	0	0
0	1	0
1	0	0
1	1	1

Mapping with Negative Logic

A	B	F
1	1	1
1	0	1
0	1	1
0	0	0

Let's use Duality to come up with the equivalent logic expression using negative logic.

$$F_D = A+B$$

The dual is found by interchanging all AND/OR operations and all 0's and 1's.

Does this give us what we want for a negative logic convention? Let's take the truth table of the "Mapping with Negative Logic" and rearrange the input codes into a more traditional format:

Mapping with Negative Logic

A	B	F
1	1	1
1	0	1
0	1	1
0	0	0

A	B	F
0	0	0
0	1	1
1	0	1
1	1	1

$$\equiv \quad F = A+B$$

Yes, this truth table is the definition of a Logical Sum per our axioms (e.g., F=A+B). This means that the logic expression created using duality (F_D) created an equivalent function using negative logic.

Example 4.2
Converting Between Positive and Negative Logic Using Duality

One consideration when using duality is that the order of precedence follows the original function. This means that in the original function, the axiom for precedence states the order as NOT-AND-OR; however, this is not necessarily the correct precedence order in the dual. For example, if the original function was $F=A \cdot B+C$, the AND operation of A and B would take place first, and then the result would be OR'd with C. The dual of this expression is $F_D=A+B \cdot C$. If the expression for F_D was evaluated using traditional Boolean precedence, it would show that F_D does NOT give the correct result per the definition of a dual function (i.e., converting a function from positive to negative logic). The order of precedence for F_D must correlate to the precedence in the original function. Since in the original function A and B were operated on first, they must also be operated on first in the dual. In order to easily manage this issue, parentheses can be used to track the order of operations from the original function to the dual. If we put parentheses in the original function to explicitly state the precedence of the operations, it would take the form $F=(A \cdot B)+C$. These parentheses can be mapped directly to the dual yielding $F_D=(A+B) \cdot C$. This order of precedence in the dual is now correct.

Now that we have covered the duality operation, its usefulness and its pitfalls, we can formally define this theorem as:

DeMorgan's Duality: An algebraic equality will remain true if all 0's and 1's are interchanged and all AND and OR operations are interchanged. Furthermore, taking the dual of a positive logic function will produce the equivalent function using negative logic if the original order of precedence is maintained.

4.1.3.2 Identity

An identity operation is one that when performed on a variable will yield itself regardless of the variable's value. The following is the formal definition of identity theorem. Figure 4.1 shows the gate level depiction of this theorem.

Identity: OR'ing any variable with a logic 0 will yield the original variable. The dual: AND'ing any variable with a logic 1 will yield the original variable.

Original   Dual

$A+0 = A$ $A·1 = A$

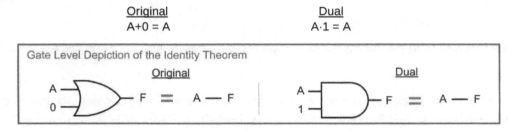

Figure 4.1
Gate Level Depiction of the Identity Theorem

The identity theorem is useful for reducing circuitry when it is discovered that a particular input will never change values. When this is the case, the static input variable can simply be removed from the logic expression making the entire circuit a simple wire from the remaining input variable to the output.

4.1.3.3 Null Element

A null element operation is one that, when performed on a constant value, will yield that same constant value regardless of the values of any variables within the same operation. The following is the formal definition of null element. Figure 4.2 shows the gate level depiction of this theorem.

Null Element: OR'ing any variable with a logic 1 will yield a logic 1 regardless of the value of the input variable. The dual: AND'ing any variable with a logic 0 will yield a logic 0 regardless of the value of the input variable.

Original   Dual

$A+1 = 1$ $A·0 = 0$

Figure 4.2
Gate Level Depiction of the Null Element Theorem

The null element theorem is also useful for reducing circuitry when it is discovered that a particular input will never change values. It is also widely used in computer systems in order to set (i.e., force to a logic 1) or clear (i.e., force to a logic 0) the value of a storage element.

4.1.3.4 Idempotent

An idempotent operation is one that has no effect on the input, regardless of the number of times the operation is applied. The following is the formal definition of idempotence. Figure 4.3 shows the gate level depiction of this theorem.

Idempotent: OR'ing a variable with itself results in itself. The dual: AND'ing a variable with itself results in itself.

Original   Dual

$A+A = A$ $A·A = A$

Figure 4.3
Gate Level Depiction of the Idempotent Theorem

This theorem also holds true for any number of operations such as A+A+A+.....+A=A and A·A·A·......·A=A.

4.1.3.5 Complements

This theorem describes an operation of a variable with the variable's own complement. The following is the formal definition of complements. Figure 4.4 shows the gate level depiction of this theorem.

Complements: OR'ing a variable with its complement will produce a logic 1. The dual: AND'ing a variable with its complement will produce a logic 0.

Original
A+A' = 1

Dual
A·A' = 0

Figure 4.4
Gate Level Depiction of the Complements Theorem

The complement theorem is again useful for reducing circuitry when these types of logic expressions are discovered.

4.1.3.6 Involution

An involution operation describes the result of double negation. The following is the formal definition of involution. Figure 4.5 shows the gate level depiction of this theorem.

Involution: Taking the double complement of a variable will result in the original variable.

Original
A" = A

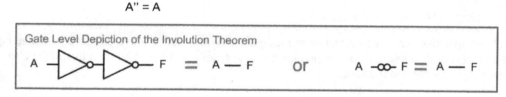

Figure 4.5
Gate Level Depiction of the Involution Theorem

This theorem is not only used to eliminate inverters but also provides us a powerful tool for *inserting* inverters in a circuit. We will see that this is used widely with the second of DeMorgan's Laws that will be introduced at the end of this section.

4.1.3.7 Commutative Property

The term commutative is used to describe an operation in which the order of the quantities or variables in the operation have no impact on the result. The following is the formal definition of the commutative property. Figure 4.6 shows the gate level depiction of this theorem.

Commutative Property: Changing the order of variables in an OR operation does not change the end result. The dual: Changing the order of variables in an AND operation does not change the end result.

Original   Dual

A+B = B+A   A·B = B·A

Figure 4.6
Gate Level Depiction of Commutative Property

One practical use of the commutative property is when wiring or routing logic circuitry together. Example 4.3 shows how the commutative property can be used to untangle crossed wires when implementing a digital system.

Example 4.3
Using the Commutative Property to untangle Crossed Wires

4.1.3.8 Associative Property

The term associative is used to describe an operation in which the grouping of the quantities or variables in the operation have no impact on the result. The following is the formal definition of the associative property. Figure 4.7 shows the gate level depiction of this theorem.

Associative Property: The grouping of variables doesn't impact the result of an OR operation. The dual: The grouping of variables doesn't impact the result of an AND operation.

Original
(A+B)+C = A+(B+C)

Dual
(A·B)·C = A·(B·C)

Figure 4.7
Gate Level Depiction of the Associative Property

One practical use of the associative property is addressing fan-in limitations of a logic family. Since the grouping of the input variables does not impact the result, we can accomplish operations with large numbers of inputs using multiple gates with fewer inputs. Example 4.4 shows the process of using the associative property to address a fan-in limitation.

Example: Using the Associative Property to Address Fan-In Limitations
You are designing a system that calls for a 4-Input OR gate.

F = A+B+C+D

However, upon looking at the data sheets for your logic family, you discover that there is no 4-Input OR gate available. You decide to use the associative property to manipulate the expression to instead use a combination of 2-Input OR gates. This new configuration yields the same logical result but with parts that exist within the logic family you chose.

F = A+B+C+D = (A+B)+(C+D)

Example 4.4
Using the Associative Property to Address Fan-In Limitations

4.1.3.9 Distributive Property

The term distributive describes how an operation on a parenthesized group of operations (or higher precedence operations) can be distributed through each term. The following is the formal definition of the distributive property. Figure 4.8 shows the gate level depiction of this theorem.

Distributive Property: An operation on a parenthesized operation(s), or higher precedence operator, will distribute through each term.

Original
A·(B+C) = A·B + A·C

Dual
A+(B·C) = (A+B)·(A+C)

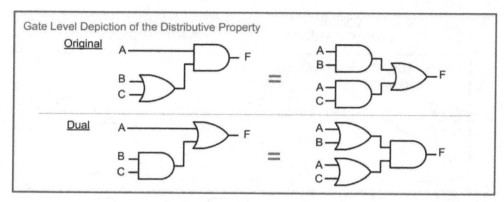

Figure 4.8
Gate Level Depiction of the Distributive Property

The distributive property is used as a logic manipulation technique. It can be used to put a logic expression into a form more suitable for direct circuit synthesis, or to reduce the number of logic gates necessary. Example 4.5 shows how to use the distributive property to reduce the number of gates in a logic circuit.

Example 4.5
Using The Distributive Property to Reduce the Number of Logic Gates in a Circuit

4.1.3.10 Absorption

The term absorption refers to when multiple logic terms within an expression produce the same results. This allows one of the terms to be eliminated from the expression, thus reducing the number of logic operations. The remaining terms essentially *absorb* the functionality of the eliminated term. This theorem is also called *covering* because the remaining term essentially covers the functionality of both itself and the eliminated term. The following is the formal definition of the absorption theorem. Figure 4.9 shows the gate level depiction of this theorem.

Absorption: When a term within a logic expression produces the same output(s) as another term, the second term can be removed without affecting the result.

Original   Dual

$A + A \cdot B = A$ $A \cdot (A + B) = A$

Figure 4.9
Gate Level Depiction of Absorption

This theorem is better understood by looking at the evaluation of each term with respect to the original expression. Example 4.6 shows how the absorption theorem can be proven through proof by exhaustion by evaluating each term in a logic expression.

Example 4.6
Proving the Absorption Theorem using Proof by Exhaustion

4.1.3.11 Uniting

The uniting theorem, also called *combining* or *minimization*, provides a way to remove variables from an expression when they have no impact on the outcome. This theorem is one of the most widely used techniques for the reduction of the number of gates needed in a combinational logic circuit. The following is the formal definition of the uniting theorem. Figure 4.10 shows the gate level depiction of this theorem.

Uniting: When a variable (B) and its complement (B') appear in multiple product terms with a common variable (A) within a logical OR operation, the variable B does not have any effect on the result and can be removed.

$$\text{Original} \qquad\qquad \text{Dual}$$
$$A{\cdot}B + A{\cdot}B' = A \qquad\qquad (A+B){\cdot}(A+B') = A$$

Figure 4.10
Gate Level Depiction of Uniting

This theorem can be proved using prior theorems. Example 4.7 shows how the uniting theorem can be proved using a combination of the distributive property, the complements theorem, and the identity theorem.

Example: Proving the Uniting Theorem

Uniting theorem states that A·B + A·B' = A. Let's use the other Boolean algebra theorems to manipulate the original expression in order to prove this theorem.

The original expression: ──────────────────────→ F = A·B + A·B'

Using the distributive property, we can rewrite the expression as: ──────────→ F = A·(B + B')

The "complements theorem" states that B+B'=1, so we can now rewrite the expression as: ──→ F = A·1

The identity theorem states that A·1=A, so the expression can be written in its final form. ──→ F = A

This proves that the uniting theorem holds true. Uniting theorem is also called *minimization* or *combining*.

Example 4.7
Proving of the Uniting Theorem

4.1.3.12 DeMorgan's Theorem

Now we look at the second of DeMorgan's Laws. This second theorem is simply known as *DeMorgan's Theorem*. This theorem provides a technique to manipulate a logic expression that uses AND gates into one that uses OR gates and vice-versa. It can also be used to manipulate traditional Boolean logic expressions that use AND-OR-NOT operators, into equivalent forms that uses NAND and NOR gates. The following is the formal definition of DeMorgan's theorem. Figure 4.11 shows the gate level depiction of this theorem.

DeMorgan's Theorem: An OR operation with both inputs inverted is equivalent to an AND operation with the output inverted. The dual: An AND operation with both inputs inverted is equivalent to an OR operation with the output inverted.

Original
A' + B' = (A·B)'

Dual
A' · B' = (A + B)'

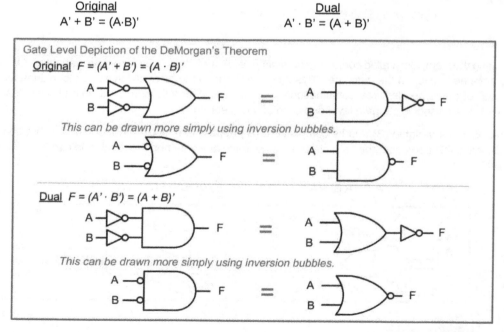

Figure 4.11
Gate Level Depiction of DeMorgan's Theorem

This theorem is used widely in modern logic design because it bridges the gap between the design of logic circuitry using Boolean algebra and the physical implementation of the circuitry using CMOS. Recall that Boolean algebra is defined for only three operations, the AND, the OR and inversion. CMOS, on the other hand, can only directly implement negative-type gates such as NAND, NOR and NOT. DeMorgan's Theorem allows us to design logic circuitry using Boolean algebra and synthesize logic diagrams with AND, OR, and NOT gates, and then directly convert the logic diagrams into an equivalent form using NAND, NOR and NOT gates. As we'll see in the next section, Boolean algebra produces logic expressions in two common forms. These are the **sum of products (SOP)** and the **product of sums (POS)** forms. Using a combination of involution and DeMorgan's Theorem, SOP and POS forms can be converted into equivalent logic circuits that use only NAND and NOR gates. Example 4.8 shows a process to convert a sum of products form into one that uses only NAND gates.

Example 4.8
Converting a Sum of Products Form into One That Uses Only NAND Gates

Example 4.9 shows a process to convert a product of sums form into one that uses only NOR gates.

Example: Converting a Product of Sums Form into One That Uses Only NOR Gates

You are designing a combinational logic circuit that will be implemented in CMOS. You use Boolean algebra to create a circuit in the form of a **product of sums (POS)**.

$$F = \underline{(A+B)} \cdot \underline{(C+D)}$$

These two logical sums (e.g., OR operations) are multiplied together (e.g., AND operation) to form a Product of Sums form.

A Product of Sums at the gate level always has a stage of OR gates feeding into a single AND gate.

Since this logic needs to be implemented in CMOS, you need to convert it into a form that uses only NAND, NOR or NOT gates. You know that DeMorgan's Theorem allows an AND gate with its inputs inverted to be converted to an OR gate with its output inverted (e.g., a NOR gate). To prepare for this manipulation, you take advantage of the theory of involution, which allows you to put double inversions on any net without affecting the result.

Double inverters are placed on these nodes in order to create an AND gate with its inputs inverted.

These inverters can also be denoted using inversion bubbles (e.g., double bubbles).

Moving the inversion bubbles to these locations on the wires highlights that the first stage of OR gates can be directly replaced with NOR gates and the AND gate is ready for DeMorgan's.

The final step is to convert the AND gate with its inputs inverted to an OR gate with its output inverted, which is a NOR gate.

The original Product of Sums that was implemented with only OR/AND operations was replaced with an equivalent circuit that used only NOR gates. This replacement can be made directly anytime a Product of Sums form is present.

Example 4.9
Converting a Product of Sums Form into One That Uses Only NOR Gates

DeMorgan's Theorem can also be accomplished algebraically using a process known as *breaking the bar and flipping the operator*. This process again takes advantage of the Involution Theorem, which allows double negation without impacting the result. When using this technique in algebraic form, involution takes the form of a double inversion bar. If an inversion bar is *broken*, the expression will remain true as long as the operator directly below the break is flipped (AND to OR, OR to AND). Example 4.10 shows how to use this technique when converting an OR gate with its inputs inverted into an AND gate with its output inverted.

Example: Using DeMorgan's Theorem Algebraically, Breaking the Bar and Flipping the Sign (1)

DeMorgan's Theorem can be accomplished algebraically using a process called "breaking the bar and flipping the operator". Let's see if this approach works on an OR gate with its inputs inverted.

$F = \overline{A} + \overline{B}$ ← The original algebraic expression for an OR gate with both inputs inverted.

$F = \overline{\overline{\overline{A} + \overline{B}}}$ ← Involution allows double negation without impacting the result. This is accomplished with two inversion bars.

$F = \overline{\overline{\overline{A} + \overline{B}}}$ ← An inversion bar can be "broken", but in order for the expression to remain true, the OR operator beneath the break must be flipped to an AND.

(+ to ·)

$F = \overline{\overline{A} \cdot \overline{B}}$ ← Involution can be used again to remove the double negations above A and B.

$F = \overline{A \cdot B}$ ← The resulting expression is an AND gate with its output inverted.

This technique upheld DeMorgan's Theorem that an OR gate with its inputs inverted is equivalent to an AND gate with its output inverted.

$$F = \overline{A} + \overline{B} = \overline{A \cdot B}$$

Example 4.10
Using DeMorgan's Theorem in Algebraic Form (1)

Example 4.11 shows how to use this technique when converting an AND gate with its inputs inverted into an OR gate with its output inverted.

Example: Using DeMorgan's Theorem Algebraically, Breaking the Bar and Flipping the Sign (2)

Let's see if the "breaking the bar and flipping the operator" approach works on an AND gate with its inputs inverted.

$F = \overline{A} \cdot \overline{B}$ ← The original algebraic expression for an AND gate with both inputs inverted.

$F = \overline{\overline{\overline{A} \cdot \overline{B}}}$ ← Involution allows double negation without impacting the result. This is accomplished with two inversion bars.

$F = \overline{\overline{\overline{A} \cdot \overline{B}}}$ ← An inversion bar can be "broken", but in order for the expression to remain true, the AND operator beneath the break must be flipped to an OR.

(· to +)

$F = \overline{\overline{A} + \overline{B}}$ ← Involution can be used again to remove the double negations above A and B.

$F = \overline{A + B}$ ← The resulting expression is an OR gate with its output inverted.

This technique upheld DeMorgan's Theorem that an AND gate with its inputs inverted is equivalent to an OR gate with its output inverted.

$$F = \overline{A} \cdot \overline{B} = \overline{A + B}$$

Example 4.11
Using DeMorgan's Theorem in Algebraic Form (2)

Table 4.1 gives a summary of all the Boolean algebra theorems just covered. The theorems are grouped in this table with respect to the number of variables that they contain. This grouping is the most common way these theorems are presented.

Summary of Boolean Algebra Theorems		
Single Variable Theorems	Original	Dual
Identity	$A+0 = A$	$A \cdot 1 = A$
Null Element	$A+1 = 1$	$A \cdot 0 = 0$
Idempotency	$A+A = A$	$A \cdot A = A$
Complements	$A+A' = 1$	$A \cdot A' = 0$
Involution	$A'' = A$	
Multiple Variable Theorems		
Commutative	$A+B = B+A$	$A \cdot B = B \cdot A$
Associative	$(A+B)+C = A+(B+C)$	$(A \cdot B) \cdot C = A \cdot (B \cdot C)$
Distributive	$A \cdot (B+C) = A \cdot B + A \cdot C$	$A+(B \cdot C) = (A+B) \cdot (A+C)$
Absorption (or Covering)	$A+A \cdot B = A$	$A \cdot (A+B) = A$
Uniting (or Combining)	$A \cdot B + A \cdot B' = A$	$(A+B) \cdot (A+B') = A$
DeMorgan's	$A' \cdot B' = (A + B)'$	$A'+B' = (A \cdot B)'$

Table 4.1
Summary of Boolean Algebra Theorems

4.1.4 Functionally Complete Operation Sets

A set of Boolean operators is said to be *functionally complete* when the set can implement all possible logic functions. The set of operators {AND, OR, NOT} is functionally complete because every other operation can be implemented using these three operators (i.e., NAND, NOR, BUF, XOR, XNOR). The DeMorgan's Theorem showed us that all AND and OR operations can be replaced with NAND and NOR operators. This means that NAND and NOR operations could be by themselves functionally complete if they could perform a NOT operation. Figure 4.12 shows how a NAND gate can be configured to perform a NOT operation. This configuration allows a NAND gate to be considered functionally complete because all other operations can be implemented.

Figure 4.12
Configuration to Use a NAND Gate as an Inverter

This approach can also be used on a NOR gate to implement an inverter. Figure 4.13 shows how a NOR gate can be configured to perform a NOT operation, thus also making it functionally complete.

Configuration to use a NOR Gate as an Inverter

The truth table for a NOR gate is as follows:

A	B	F
0	0	1
0	1	0
1	0	0
1	1	0

Consider the operation of this device if both of its inputs are tied together:

A	B	F
0	0	1
0	1	0
1	0	0
1	1	0

The only two input codes that are possible are when A=B. This leads to a new truth table of:

In	F
0	1
1	0

This is the functionality of an inverter. A NOR gate with its inputs tied together is equivalent to an inverter.

Figure 4.13
Configuration to Use a NOR Gate as an Inverter

CONCEPT CHECK

CC4.1   If the logic expression F=A·B·C·D·E·F·G·H is implemented with only 2-input AND gates, how many levels of logic will the final implementation have? Hint: Consider using the associative property to manipulate the logic expression to use only 2-input AND operations.

A) 2   B) 3   C) 4   D) 5

4.2 Combinational Logic Analysis

Combinational logic analysis refers to the act of deciphering the operation of a circuit from its final logic diagram. This is a useful skill that can aid designers when debugging their circuits. This can also be used to understand the timing performance of a circuit and to reverse-engineer an unknown design.

4.2.1 Finding the Logic Expression from a Logic Diagram

Combinational logic diagrams are typically written with their inputs on the left and their output on the right. As the inputs change, the intermediate *nodes*, or connections, within the diagram hold the interim computations that contribute to the ultimate circuit output. These computations propagate from left to right until ultimately the final output of the system reaches its final steady state value. When analyzing the behavior of a combinational logic circuit a similar *left-to-right* approach is used. The first step is to label each intermediate node in the system. The second step is to write in the logic expression for each node based on the preceding logic operation(s). The logic expressions are written working left-to-right until the output of the system is reached and the final logic expression of the circuit has been found. Consider the example of this analysis in Example 4.12.

Example: Determining the Logic Expression from a Logic Diagram

Given: The following combinational logic diagram.

Find: The logic expression for the output F.

Solution: First, let's label each of the internal nodes of the circuit. We'll call these nodes n1, n2, and n3. Next, let's insert the logic expression for each node working from the left to the right. Finally, we can write the final output logic expression for F based on all of the prior internal node expressions. Substitutions can be made within each expression to put the logic in terms of only the input variable names (i.e., A, B, and C).

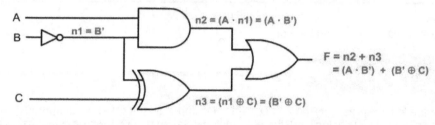

Example 4.12
Determining the Logic Expression from a Logic Diagram

4.2.2 Finding the Truth Table from a Logic Diagram

The final truth table of a circuit can also be found in a similar manner as the logic expression. Each internal node within the logic diagram can be evaluated working from the left to the right for each possible input code. Each subsequent node can then be evaluated using the values of the preceding nodes. Consider the example of this analysis is Example 4.13.

Example: Determining the Truth Table from a Logic Diagram

Given: The following combinational logic diagram.

Find: The truth table for the output F.

Solution: First, we label each internal node and record the intermediate logic expressions.

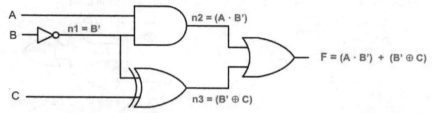

Next, we evaluate each node for all possible input codes working from the left to the right. This allows us to keep a record of the values of each intermediate node that can be used in the subsequent evaluations. We continue this process until we reach the final output F.

A	B	C	n1 = B'	n2 = A·B'	n3 = B'⊕C	F = (A·B') + (B'⊕C)
0	0	0	1	0	1	1
0	0	1	1	0	0	0
0	1	0	0	0	0	0
0	1	1	0	0	1	1
1	0	0	1	1	1	1
1	0	1	1	1	0	1
1	1	0	0	0	0	0
1	1	1	0	0	1	1

Notice that the intermediate computations can be used in the subsequent evaluations.

Example 4.13
Determining the Truth Table from a Logic Diagram

4.2.3 Timing Analysis of a Combinational Logic Circuit

Real logic gates have a propagation delay (t_{pd}, t_{PHL}, or t_{PLH}) as presented in Chapter 3. Performing a timing analysis on a combinational logic circuit refers to observing how long it takes for a change in the inputs to propagate to the output. Different paths through the combinational logic circuit will take different times to compute since they may use gates with different delays. When determining the delay of the entire combinational logic circuit we always consider the longest delay path. This is because this delay represents the worst case scenario. As long as we wait for the longest path to propagate through the circuit, then we are ensured that the output will always be valid after this time. To determine which signal path has the longest delay, we map out each and every path the inputs can take to the output of the circuit. We then sum up the gate delay along each path. The path with the longest delay dictates the delay of the entire combinational logic circuit. Consider this analysis shown in Example 4.14.

Example: Determining the Delay of a Combinational Logic Circuit

Given: The following combinational logic diagram with the associated gate delays.

Find: The delay of the combinational logic circuit.

Solution: We begin by mapping the route of each and every path from the inputs to the output. For each path, we sum the delay through each gate that is used.

$t_{delay-1}$ = 2ns + 3ns = 5ns

$t_{delay-2}$ = 1ns + 2ns + 3ns = 6ns

$t_{delay-3}$ = 1ns + 4ns + 3ns = 8ns

$t_{delay-4}$ = 4ns + 3ns = 7ns

The longest delay path through this circuit is from B to F in which the signal traverses the inverter, XOR gate, and OR gate ($t_{delay-3}$). This path takes 8ns to compute. Since we must always consider the longest delay path when calculating how fast this circuit can operate, we can say that the delay of this combinational logic circuit is 8ns.

Example 4.14
Determining the Delay of a Combinational Logic Circuit

CONCEPT CHECK

CC4.2 Does the delay specification of a combinational logic circuit change based on the input values that the circuit is evaluating?

    A) Yes. There are times when the inputs switch between inputs codes that use paths through the circuit with different delays.

    B) No. The delay is always specified as the longest delay path.

    C) Yes. The delay can vary between the longest delay path and zero. A delay of zero occurs when the inputs switch between two inputs codes that produce the same output.

    D) No. The output is always produced at a time equal to the longest delay path.

4.3 Combinational Logic Synthesis

4.3.1 Canonical Sum of Products

One technique to directly synthesize a logic circuit from a truth table is to use a canonical sum of products topology based on **minterms**. The term *canonical* refers to this topology yielding potentially unminimized logic. A minterm is a product term (i.e., an AND operation) that will be true for one and only one input code. The minterm must contain every input variable in its expression. Complements are applied to the input variables as necessary in order to produce a true output for the individual input code. We define the word *literal* to describe an input variable which may or may not be complemented. This is a more useful word because if we say that a minterm "must include all variables", it implies that all variables are included in the term uncomplemented. A more useful statement is that a minterm "must include all literals". This now implies that each variable must be included, but it can be in the form of itself or its complement (e.g., A or A'). Figure 4.14 shows the definition and gate level depiction of a minterm expression. Each minterm can be denoted using the lower case "m" with the row number as a subscript.

Figure 4.14
Definition and Gate Level Depiction of a Minterm

For an arbitrary truth table, a minterm can be used for each row corresponding to a true output. If each of these minterms' outputs are fed into a single OR gate, then a sum of products logic circuit is formed that will produce the logic listed in the truth table. In this topology, any input code that corresponds to an output of 1 will cause its corresponding minterm to output a 1. Since a 1 on any input of an OR gate will cause the output to go to a 1, the output of the minterm is passed to the final result. Example 4.15 shows this process. One important consideration of this approach is that no effort has been taken to minimize the logic expression. This unminimized logic expression is also called the **canonical sum**. The canonical sum is logically correct but uses the most amount of circuitry possible for a given truth table. This canonical sum can be the starting point for minimization using Boolean algebra.

Example: Creating a Canonical Sum of Products Logic Circuit using Minterms

Given: The following truth table.

A	B	F
0	0	0
0	1	1
1	0	1
1	1	0

Find: The Canonical SOP

Solution: Let's first start by writing the minterms for the rows that correspond to a 1 on the output. These can then be implemented using inverters and AND gates. The final step is to feed the outputs of each minterm circuit into a single OR gate.

row	A	B	minterm
0	0	0	-
1	0	1	$m_1 = A' \cdot B$
2	1	0	$m_2 = A \cdot B'$
3	1	1	-

$$F = A' \cdot B + A \cdot B'$$

Let's now check that this circuit performs as intended by testing it under each input code for A and B and observing the output F.

A=0, B=0

A=0, B=1

Notice that m_1 is producing a 1

A=1, B=0

Notice that m_2 is producing a 1

A=1, B=1

This circuit operates as intended.

Example 4.15
Creating a Canonical Sum of Products Logic Circuit Using Minterms

4.3.2 The Minterm List (Σ)

A *minterm list* is a compact way to describe the functionality of a logic circuit by simply listing the row numbers that correspond to an output of 1 in the truth table. The Σ symbol is used to denote a minterm list. All input variables must be listed in the order they appear in the truth table. This is necessary because since a minterm list uses only the row numbers to indicate which input codes result in an output of 1, the minterm list must indicate how many variables comprise the row number, which variable is in the most significant position and which is in the least significant position. After the Σ symbol, the row numbers corresponding to a true output are listed in a comma-delimited format within parentheses. Example 4.16 shows the process for creating a minterm list from a truth table.

Example: Creating a Minterm List from a Truth Table

Given: The following truth table.

row	A	B	F
0	0	0	0
1	0	1	1
2	1	0	1
3	1	1	0

Find: The minterm list.

Solution:

$$F = \sum_{A,B}(1,2)$$

This symbol indicates that it is a minterm list and will provide the row numbers corresponding to an output of 1.

The row numbers for each input code that produces an output of 1 is listed between the parenthesis separated by a comma.

The input variables are listed as a subscript. Since there are two variables listed (A,B), this means the row numbers go from 0 to 3 with A being in the most significant position and B being in the least. A comma is necessary to separate the variables, otherwise "AB" could have been interpreted as a unique variable name.

An alternative form of a minterm list is shown below that does not use subscripts. This form is sometimes used when a text editor does not support subscripts.

$$F(A,B) = \sum(1,2)$$

Example 4.16
Creating a Minterm List from a Truth Table

A minterm list contains the same information as the truth table, the canonical sum and the canonical sum of products logic diagram. Since the minterms themselves are formally defined for an input code, it is trivial to go back and forth between the minterm list and these other forms. Example 4.17 shows how a minterm list can be used to generate an equivalent truth table, canonical sum and canonical sum of products logic diagram.

Example: Creating Equivalent Functional Representations from a Minterm List

Given: The following minterm list. $F = \Sigma_{A,B,C}(0,3,7)$

Find: The truth table, canonical sum logic expression and the canonical sum of products logic diagram.

Solution: First, let's generate the **truth table**. From the minterm list subscripts, we know that there are three input variables named A, B and C. These will be listed in the truth table with A in the most significant position and C in the least significant position. We can fill in the input codes as a binary count and insert the row numbers. We can then list the output values that are true. From the minterm list we know that the true outputs are on rows 0, 3 and 7. Since we know we will need the minterm expressions for these rows in the canonical sum, we can also list them in the truth table.

row	A	B	C	F	minterm
0	0	0	0	1	$m_0 = A'{\cdot}B'{\cdot}C'$
1	0	0	1	0	-
2	0	1	0	0	-
3	0	1	1	1	$m_3 = A'{\cdot}B{\cdot}C$
4	1	0	0	0	-
5	1	0	1	0	-
6	1	1	0	0	-
7	1	1	1	1	$m_7 = A{\cdot}B{\cdot}C$

The **canonical sum** is simply the minterm expressions corresponding to a true output OR'd together. Since we already wrote the minterm expressions for rows 0, 3 and 7 (e.g., m_0, m_3 and m_7) in the truth table, we can write the canonical sum directly.

$$F = A'{\cdot}B'{\cdot}C' + A'{\cdot}B{\cdot}C + A{\cdot}B{\cdot}C$$

The **canonical sum of products logic diagram** is simply the gate level depiction of the canonical sum. When logic diagrams get larger, it is acceptable to indicate a variable's complement as a prime instead of placing individual inverters and drawing connection wires that cross each other. It is implied that multiple listings of a variable's complement (e.g., A' in m_0 and m_3) will come from the same inverter.

Example 4.17
Creating Equivalent Functional Representations from a Minterm List

4.3.3 Canonical Product of Sums (POS)

Another technique to directly synthesize a logic circuit from a truth table is to use a canonical product of sums topology based on **maxterms**. A maxterm is a sum term (i.e., an OR operation) that will be false for one and only one input code. The maxterm must contain every literal in its expression. Complements are applied to the input variables as necessary in order to produce a false output for the individual input code. Figure 4.15 shows the definition and gate level depiction of a maxterm expression. Each maxterm can be denoted using the upper case "M" with the row number as a subscript.

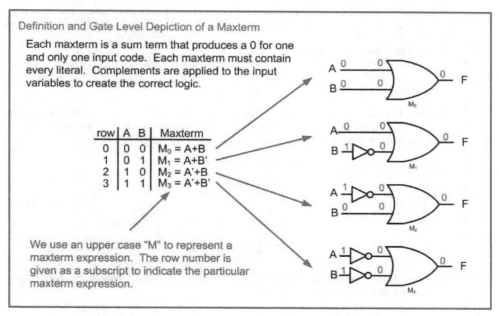

Figure 4.15
Definition and Gate Level Depiction of a Maxterm

For an arbitrary truth table, a maxterm can be used for each row corresponding to a false output. If each of these maxterms outputs are fed into a single AND gate, then a product of sums logic circuit is formed that will produce the logic listed in the truth table. In this topology, any input code that corresponds to an output of 0 will cause its corresponding maxterm to output a 0. Since a 0 on any input of an AND gate will cause the output to go to a 0, the output of the maxterm is passed to the final result. Example 4.18 shows this process. This approach is complementary to the sum of products approach. In the sum of products approach based on minterms, the circuit operates by producing 1's that are passed to the output for the rows that require a true output. For all other rows, the output is false. A product of sums approach based on maxterms operates by producing 0's that are passed to the output for the rows that require a false output. For all other rows, the output is true. These two approaches produce the equivalent logic functionality. Again, at this point no effort has been taken to minimize the logic expression. This unminimized form is called a **canonical product**. The canonical product is logically correct, but uses the most amount of circuitry possible for a given truth table. This canonical product can be the starting point for minimization using the Boolean algebra theorems.

Example: Creating a Canonical Product of Sums Logic Circuit using Maxterms

Given: The following truth table.

A	B	F
0	0	0
0	1	1
1	0	1
1	1	0

Find: The Canonical POS.

Solution: Let's first start by writing the maxterms for the rows that correspond to a 0 on the output. These can then be implemented using inverters and OR gates. The final step is to feed the outputs of each maxterm circuit into a single AND gate.

row	A	B	Maxterm
0	0	0	$M_0 = A+B$
1	0	1	-
2	1	0	-
3	1	1	$M_3 = A'+B'$

$$F = (A+B) \cdot (A'+B')$$

Let's now check that this circuit performs as intended by testing it under each input code for A and B and observing the output F.

This circuit operates as intended.

Example 4.18
Creating a Product of Sums Logic Circuit Using Maxterms

4.3.4 The Maxterm List (Π)

A maxterm list is a compact way to describe the functionality of a logic circuit by simply listing the row numbers that correspond to an output of 0 in the truth table. The Π symbol is used to denote a maxterm list. All literals used in the logic expression must be listed in the order they appear in the truth table. After the Π symbol, the row numbers corresponding to a false output are listed in a comma-delimited format within parentheses. Example 4.19 shows the process for creating a maxterm list from a truth table.

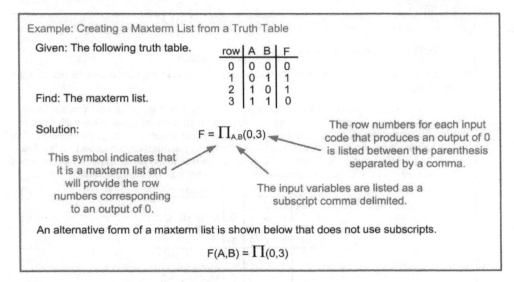

Example 4.19
Creating a Maxterm List from a Truth Table

A maxterm list contains the same information as the truth table, the canonical product and the canonical product of sums logic diagram. Example 4.20 shows how a maxterm list can be used to generate these equivalent forms.

Example: Creating Equivalent Functional Representations from a Maxterm List

Given: The following maxterm list. $F = \prod_{A,B,C}(1,2,4,5,6)$

Find: The truth table, canonical product logic expression and the canonical product of sums logic diagram.

Solution: First, let's generate the **truth table**. From the maxterm list subscripts, we know that there are three input variables named A, B and C that will be used in the truth table in that order. We can fill in the input codes as a binary count and insert the row numbers. We then can list the output values that are false. From the maxterm list we know that the false outputs are on rows 1, 2, 4, 5 and 6. Since we know we will need the maxterm expressions for these rows in the canonical product, we can also list them in the truth table.

row	A	B	C	F	Maxterm
0	0	0	0	1	-
1	0	0	1	0	$M_1 = A+B+C'$
2	0	1	0	0	$M_2 = A+B'+C$
3	0	1	1	1	-
4	1	0	0	0	$M_4 = A'+B+C$
5	1	0	1	0	$M_5 = A'+B+C'$
6	1	1	0	0	$M_6 = A'+B'+C$
7	1	1	1	1	-

The **canonical product** is simply the maxterm expressions corresponding to a false output AND'd together. Since we already wrote these maxterm expressions in the truth table (M_1, M_2, M_4, M_5 and M_6) we can write the canonical product directly.

$$F = (A+B+C') \cdot (A+B'+C) \cdot (A'+B+C) \cdot (A'+B+C') \cdot (A'+B'+C)$$

The **canonical product of sums logic diagram** is simply the gate level depiction of the canonical product.

Example 4.20
Creating Equivalent Functional Representations from a Maxterm List

4.3.5 Minterm and Maxterm List Equivalence

The examples in Example 4.17 and Example 4.20 illustrate how minterm and maxterm lists produce the exact same logic functionality but in a complementary fashion. It is trivial to switch back and forth between minterm lists and maxterm lists. This is accomplished by simply changing the list type (i.e., min to max, max to min) and then switching the row numbers between those listed and those not listed. Example 4.21 shows multiple techniques for representing equivalent logic functionality as a truth table.

Example: Creating Equivalent Forms to Represent Logic Functionality

Given: The following minterm list.

row	A	B	F
0	0	0	1
1	0	1	0
2	1	0	0
3	1	1	1

Find: All equivalent forms to describe the same functionality as the truth table.

Solution: Let's start by writing the **minterm list** and the **maxterm list**. These two lists are equivalent to each other. Remember that the minterm list provides the row numbers corresponding to an output of true while the maxterm list provides the row numbers corresponding to an output of false.

$$F = \sum_{A,B}(0,3) = \prod_{A,B}(1,2)$$

Let's write the minterm and maxterm expressions in the truth table. These will be used when creating the canonical sum and product expressions.

row	A	B	F	minterm	maxterm
0	0	0	1	$m_0 = A' \cdot B'$	-
1	0	1	0	-	$M_1 = A + B'$
2	1	0	0	-	$M_2 = A' + B$
3	1	1	1	$m_3 = A \cdot B$	-

Now let's write the **canonical sum** and **canonical product** logic expressions using these minterms and maxterms. Remember that a canonical sum is simply all of the minterms corresponding to an output of true OR'd together, and a canonical product is simply all of the maxterms corresponding to an output of false AND'd together.

$$F = A' \cdot B' + A \cdot B = (A + B') \cdot (A' + B)$$

Finally, let's draw the **canonical sum of products logic diagram** and the **canonical product of sums logic diagram**.

Example 4.21
Creating Equivalent Forms to Represent Logic Functionality

CONCEPT CHECK

CC4.3   All logic functions can be implemented equivalently using either a <u>canonical</u> sum of products (SOP) or <u>canonical</u> product of sums (POS) topology. Which of these statements is true with respect to selecting a topology that requires the least amount of gates.

A)   Since a minterm list and a maxterm list can both be written to describe the same logic functionality, the number of gates in an SOP and POS will always be the same.

B)   If a minterm list has over half of its row numbers listed, an SOP topology will require fewer gates than a POS.

C)   A POS topology always requires more gates because it needs additional logic to convert the inputs from positive to negative logic.

D)   If a minterm list has over half of its row numbers listed, a POS topology will require fewer gates than SOP.

4.4 Logic Minimization

We now look at how to reduce the canonical expressions into equivalent forms that use less logic. This minimization is key to reducing the complexity of the logic prior to implementing in real circuitry. This reduces the amount of gates needed, placement area, wiring and power consumption of the logic circuit.

4.4.1 Algebraic Minimization

Canonical expressions can be reduced algebraically by applying the theorems covered in prior sections. This process typically consists of a series of factoring based on the distributive property followed by replacing variables with constants (i.e., 0's and 1's) using the Complements Theorem. Finally, constants are removed using the Identity Theorem. Example 4.22 shows this process.

Example: Minimizing a Logic Expression Algebraically

Given: The following truth table.

row	A	B	C	F	minterm
0	0	0	0	1	$m_0 = A' \cdot B' \cdot C'$
1	0	0	1	0	-
2	0	1	0	1	$m_2 = A' \cdot B \cdot C'$
3	0	1	1	1	$m_3 = A' \cdot B \cdot C$
4	1	0	0	0	-
5	1	0	1	0	-
6	1	1	0	1	$m_6 = A \cdot B \cdot C'$
7	1	1	1	1	$m_7 = A \cdot B \cdot C$

Find: A minimized logic expression using algebraic manipulations.

Solution:

$$F = A' \cdot B' \cdot C' + A' \cdot B \cdot C' + A' \cdot B \cdot C + A \cdot B \cdot C' + A \cdot B \cdot C$$

The first step is to write the canonical sum. The minterms are written in the truth table so this sum can be written directly as:

$$F = A' \cdot B' \cdot C' + (A' \cdot B \cdot C' + A' \cdot B \cdot C + A \cdot B \cdot C' + A \cdot B \cdot C)$$

$$F = A' \cdot B' \cdot C' + B \cdot (A' \cdot C' + A' \cdot C + A \cdot C' + A \cdot C)$$

Next, we notice that B exists in each of these product terms. Let's factor it out using the distributive property.

$$F = A' \cdot B' \cdot C' + B \cdot ((A' \cdot C' + A' \cdot C) + (A \cdot C' + A \cdot C))$$

$$F = A' \cdot B' \cdot C' + B \cdot (A' \cdot (C' + C) + A \cdot (C' + C))$$

Now we notice that A' and A can be factored out of these product terms using the distributive property.

$$F = A' \cdot B' \cdot C' + B \cdot (A' \cdot (C' + C) + A \cdot (C' + C))$$

$$F = A' \cdot B' \cdot C' + B \cdot (A' \cdot 1 + A \cdot 1)$$

The new expression contains terms that can be minimized using the complements theorem.

$$F = A' \cdot B' \cdot C' + B \cdot (A' + A)$$

The identity property will get rid of anything AND'd with a 1.

$$F = A' \cdot B' \cdot C' + B \cdot (A' + A)$$

$$F = A' \cdot B' \cdot C' + B \cdot (1)$$

$$F = A' \cdot B' \cdot C' + B$$

The complements theorem is again used followed by identity to reduce this term entirely to B.

$$F = A' \cdot B' \cdot C' + A' \cdot B \cdot C' + B$$

$$F = A' \cdot C' \cdot (B' + B) + B$$

$$F = A' \cdot C' \cdot 1 + B$$

$$F = A' \cdot C' + B$$

The next step involves recognizing that one of the eliminated product terms could also have been used to reduce $A' \cdot B' \cdot C'$. We can write the term back in the expression without impacting the result. We then apply factoring, complements and identity to reduce the expression.

Example 4.22
Minimizing a Logic Expression Algebraically

The primary drawback of this approach is that it requires recognition of where the theorems can be applied. This can often lead to missed minimizations. Computer automation is often the best mechanism to perform this minimization for large logic expressions.

4.4.2 Minimization using Karnaugh Maps

A Karnaugh map is a graphical way to minimize logic expressions. This technique is named after Maurice Karnaugh, American physicist, who introduced the map in its latest form in 1953 while working at Bell Labs. The Karnaugh map (or K-map) is a way to put a truth table into a form that allows logic minimization through a graphical process. This technique provides a graphical process that accomplishes the same result as factoring variables via the distributive property and removing variables via the Complements and Identity Theorems. K-maps present a truth table in a form that allows variables to be removed from the final logic expression in a graphical manner.

4.4.2.1 Formation of a K-map

A K-map is constructed as a two-dimensional grid. Each *cell* within the map corresponds to the output for a specific input code. The cells are positioned such that neighboring cells only differ by one bit in their input codes. Neighboring cells are defined as cells immediately adjacent horizontally and immediately adjacent vertically. Two cells positioned diagonally next to each other are not considered neighbors. The input codes for each variable are listed along the top and side of the K-map. Consider the construction of a 2-input K-map shown in Figure 4.16.

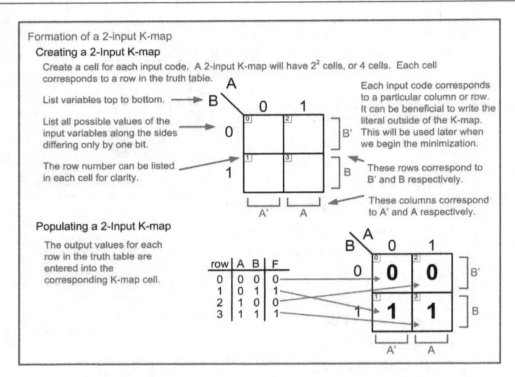

Figure 4.16
Formation of a 2-Input K-map

When constructing a 3-input K-map, it is important to remember that each input code can only differ from its neighbor by one bit. For example, the two codes 01 and 10 differ by two bits (i.e., the MSB is different and the LSB is different), thus they could not be neighbors; however, the codes 01-11 and 11-10 can be neighbors. As such, the input codes along the top of the 3-input K-map must be ordered accordingly (i.e., 00-01-11-10). Consider the construction of a 3-input K-map shown in Figure 4.17. The rows and columns that correspond to the input literals can now span multiple rows and columns. Notice how in this 3-input K-map, the literals A, A', B and B' all correspond to two columns. Also, notice that B' spans two columns, but the columns are on different edges of the K-map. The side edges of the 3-input K-map are still considered neighbors because the input codes for these columns only differ by one bit. This is an important attribute once we get to the minimization of variables because it allows us to examine an input literal's impact not only within the obvious adjacent cells but also when the variables *wrap* around the edges of the K-map.

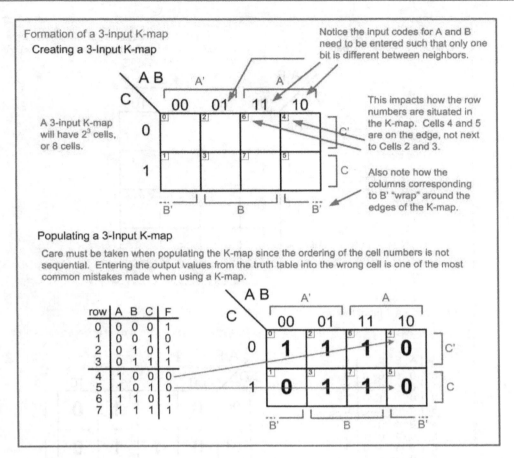

Figure 4.17
Formation of a 3-Input K-map

When constructing a 4-input K-map, the same rules apply that the input codes can only differ from their neighbors by one bit. Consider the construction of a 4-input K-map in Figure 4.18. In a 4-input K-map, neighboring cells can wrap around both the top-to-bottom edges in addition to the side-to-side edges. Notice that all 16 cells are positioned within the map so that their neighbors on the top, bottom and sides only differ by one bit in their input codes.

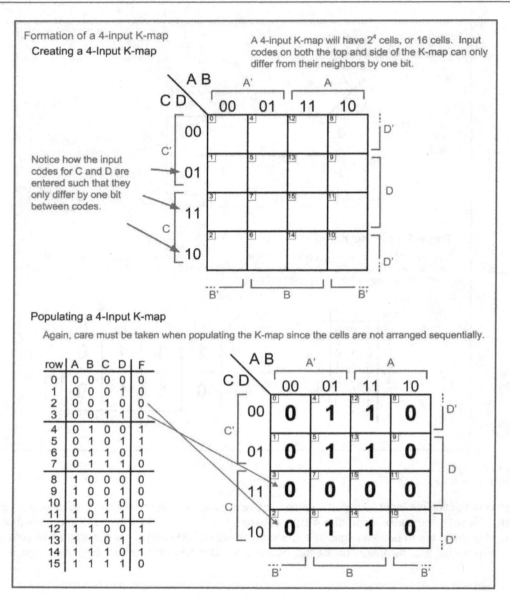

Figure 4.18
Formation of a 4-Input K-map

4.4.2.2 Logic Minimization Using K-maps (Sum of Products)

Now we look at using a K-map to create a minimized logic expression in a SOP form. Remember that each cell with an output of 1 has a minterm associated with it, just as in the truth table. When two neighboring cells have outputs of 1, it graphically indicates that the two minterms can be reduced into a minimized product term that will cover both outputs. Consider the example given in Figure 4.19.

Figure 4.19
Observing how K-Maps Visually Highlight Logic Minimizations

These observations can be put into a formal process to produce a minimized SOP logic expression using a K-map. The steps are as follows:

1) Circle groups of 1's in the K-map following the rules:

- Each circle should contain the largest number of 1's possible.
- The circles encompass only neighboring cells (i.e., side-to-side sides and/or top and bottom).
- The circles must contain a number of 1's that is a power of 2 (i.e., 1, 2, 4, 8 or 16).
- Enter as many circles as possible without having any circles fully cover another circle.
- Each circle is called a *Prime Implicant*.

2) Create a product term for each prime implicant following the rules:

- Each variable in the K-map is evaluated one-by-one.
- If the circle covers a region where the input variable is a 1, then include it in the product term <u>uncomplemented</u>.
- If the circle covers a region where the input variable is a 0, then include it in the product term <u>complemented</u>.
- If the circle covers a region where the input variable is both a 0 and 1, then the variable is <u>excluded</u> from the product term.

3) Sum all of the product terms for each prime implicant.

Let's apply this approach to our 2-input K-map example. Example 4.23 shows the process of finding a minimized sum of products logic expression for a 2-input logic circuit using a K-map. This process yielded the same SOP expression as the algebraic minimization and observations shown in Figure 4.19, but with a formalized process.

Example: Using a K-map to find a Minimized Sum of Products Expression (2-input)

Step 1: Circle groups of 1's in the K-map

We form the largest group of neighboring 1's possible that is a power of 2. In this case, there are two 1's in the group. This circle covers all of the 1's in the K-map so it is the only prime implicant.

Step 1 states that circles should not fully encompass other circles. This is why circles are not included that only cover cell 1 and cell 3 since the larger circle would fully encompass these smaller circles. This is a graphical representation of the absorption theorem.

INCORRECT

Step 2: Create a product term for each prime implicant

We only have one prime implicant that covers cells 1 and 3. We take each variable one-by-one and evaluate how and if it is included in the product term for the prime implicant. This step is where having the literals listed outside of the K-map becomes useful.

Evaluating variable A: The circle covers a region where A is both a 0 and a 1. This means A is excluded from the product term for this prime implicant.

Evaluating variable B: The circle covers a region where B is a 1. This means B is included in the product term uncomplemented.

The product term for this prime implicant is simply B

Step 3: Sum all of the product terms for each prime implicant

There is only one product term since there is only one circle. This means the final minimized SOP expression is:

F=B

Example 4.23
Using a K-map to find a Minimized Sum of Products Expression (2-input)

Let's now apply this process to our 3-input K-map example. Example 4.24 shows the process of finding a minimized sum of products logic expression for a 3-input logic circuit using a K-map. This example shows circles that overlap. This is legal as long as one circle does not fully encompass another. Overlapping circles are common since the K-map process dictates that circles should be drawn that group the largest number of ones possible as long as they are in powers of 2. Forming groups of ones using ones that have already been circled is perfectly legal to accomplish larger groupings. The larger the grouping of ones, the more chance there is for a variable to be excluded from the product term. This results in better minimization of the logic.

Example: Using a K-map to find a Minimized Sum of Products Expression (3-input)

Step 1: Circle groups of 1's in the K-map

The two prime implicants overlap in cell 2, but this is legal because the larger circle does not fully encompass the smaller circle.

Step 2: Create a product term for each prime implicant

Variable A: The circle covers a region where A is a 0 so it is included in the product term complemented.

Variable B: The circle covers a region where B is both a 0 and 1, so it is excluded from the product term.

Variable C: The circle covers a region where C is a 0, so it is included in the product term complemented.

The product term for this prime implicant is: A'·C'

Variable A: The circle covers a region where A is both a 0 and 1, so it is excluded from the product term.

Variable B: The circle covers a region where B is a 1, so it is included in the product term uncomplemented.

Variable C: The circle covers a region where C is both a 0 and 1, so it is excluded from the product term.

The product term for this prime implicant is: B

Step 3: Sum all of the product terms for each prime implicant

There are two product terms, one for each circle. The final minimized SOP expression is:

F = A'·C' + B

Example 4.24
Using a K-map to find a Minimized Sum of Products Expression (3-input)

Let's now apply this process to our 4-input K-map example. Example 4.25 shows the process of finding a minimized sum of products logic expression for a 4-input logic circuit using a K-map.

Example: Using a K-map to find a Minimized Sum of Products Expression (4-input)

Step 1: Circle groups of 1's in the K-map

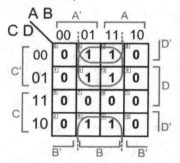

Circles can be drawn that "wrap" around the edges. Notice that the input codes for cells 4 and 12 only differ by 1 bit from cells 6 and 14. This makes them neighbors and grouping these 4 cells together is legal.

Again, circles that overlap are legal as long as one circle does not fully encompass another.

Step 2: Create a product term for each prime implicant

Variable A: The circle covers a region where A is both a 0 and 1, so it is excluded from the product term.

Variable B: The circle covers a region where B is a 1, so it is included in the product term uncomplemented.

Variable C: The circle covers a region where C is a 0, so it is included in the product term complemented.

Variable D: The circle covers a region where D is both a 0 and 1, so it is excluded from the product term.

The product term for this prime implicant is: B·C'

Variable A: The circle covers a region where A is both a 0 and 1, so it is excluded from the product term.

Variable B: The circle covers a region where B is a 1, so it is included in the product term uncomplemented.

Variable C: The circle covers a region where C is both a 0 and 1, so it is excluded from the product term.

Variable D: The circle covers a region where D is a 0, so it is included in the product term complemented.

The product term for this prime implicant is: B·D'

Step 3: Sum all of the product terms for each prime implicant

There are two product terms, one for each circle. The final minimized SOP expression is:

$$F = B \cdot C' + B \cdot D'$$

This expression could be further factored using the distributive property to F = B·(C' + D') to eliminate one more logic operation; however, since the problem asked for an SOP form, this last step was not necessary. Also, leaving a logic expression in an SOP form allows it to be directly converted into a NAND gate only implementation using DeMorgan's Theorem if the target logic family is CMOS.

Example 4.25
Using a K-map to find a Minimized Sum of Products Expression (4-input)

4.4.2.3 Logic Minimization Using K-maps (Product of Sums)

K-maps can also be used to create minimized product of sums logic expressions. This is the same concept as how a minterm list and maxterm list each produce the same logic function, but in complementary fashions. When creating a product of sums expression from a K-map, groups of 0's are circled. For each circle, a sum term is derived with a negation of variables similar to when forming a maxterm (i.e., in the input variable is a 0, then it is included uncomplemented in the sum term and vice versa). The final step in forming the minimized POS expression is to AND all of the sum terms together. The formal process is as follows:

1) Circle groups of 0's in the K-map following the rules:

- Each circle should contain the largest number of 0's possible.
- The circles encompass only neighboring cells (i.e., side-to-side sides and/or top and bottom).
- The circles must contain a number of 0's that is a power of 2 (i.e., 1, 2, 4, 8 or 16).
- Enter as many circles as possible without having any circles fully cover another circle.
- Each circle is called a *Prime Implicant*.

2) Create a sum term for each prime implicant following the rules:

- Each variable in the K-map is evaluated one-by-one.
- If the circle covers a region where the input variable is a 1, then include it in the sum term <u>complemented</u>.
- If the circle covers a region where the input variable is a 0, then include it in the sum term <u>uncomplemented</u>.
- If the circles cover a region where the input variable is both a 0 and 1, then the variable is <u>excluded</u> from the sum term.

3) Multiply all of the sum terms for each prime implicant.

Let's apply this approach to our 2-input K-map example. Example 4.26 shows the process of finding a minimized product of sums logic expression for a 2-input logic circuit using a K-map. Notice that this process yielded the same logic expression as the SOP approach shown in Example 4.23. This illustrates that both the POS and SOP expressions produce the correct logic for the circuit.

Example 4.26
Using a K-map to find a Minimized Product of Sums Expression (2-input)

Let's now apply this process to our 3-input K-map example. Example 4.27 shows the process of finding a minimized product of sums logic expression for a 3-input logic circuit using a K-map. Notice that the logic expression in POS form is not identical to the SOP expression found in Example 4.24; however, using a few steps of algebraic manipulation shows that the POS expression can be put into a form that *is* identical to the prior SOP expression. This illustrates that both the POS and SOP produce equivalent functionality for the circuit.

Example: Using a K-map to find a Minimized Product of Sums Expression (3-input)

Step 1: Circle groups of 0's in the K-map

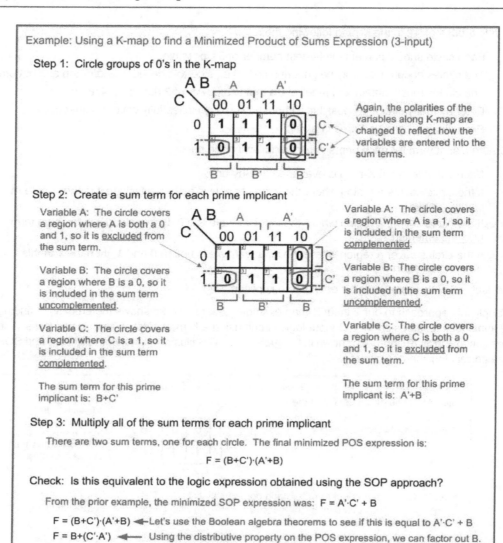

Again, the polarities of the variables along K-map are changed to reflect how the variables are entered into the sum terms.

Step 2: Create a sum term for each prime implicant

Variable A: The circle covers a region where A is both a 0 and 1, so it is <u>excluded</u> from the sum term.

Variable B: The circle covers a region where B is a 0, so it is included in the sum term <u>uncomplemented</u>.

Variable C: The circle covers a region where C is a 1, so it is included in the sum term <u>complemented</u>.

The sum term for this prime implicant is: B+C'

Variable A: The circle covers a region where A is a 1, so it is included in the sum term <u>complemented</u>.

Variable B: The circle covers a region where B is a 0, so it is included in the sum term <u>uncomplemented</u>.

Variable C: The circle covers a region where C is both a 0 and 1, so it is <u>excluded</u> from the sum term.

The sum term for this prime implicant is: A'+B

Step 3: Multiply all of the sum terms for each prime implicant

There are two sum terms, one for each circle. The final minimized POS expression is:

$$F = (B+C') \cdot (A'+B)$$

Check: Is this equivalent to the logic expression obtained using the SOP approach?

From the prior example, the minimized SOP expression was: F = A'·C' + B

$F = (B+C') \cdot (A'+B)$ ◄— Let's use the Boolean algebra theorems to see if this is equal to A'·C' + B

$F = B+(C' \cdot A')$ ◄—— Using the distributive property on the POS expression, we can factor out B.

$F = A' \cdot C' + B$ ◄—— The commutative property allows us to rearrange terms to match the SOP expression exactly.

Yes, its POS expression is equivalent to the SOP expression.

Example 4.27
Using a K-map to find a Minimized Product of Sums Expression (3-input)

Let's now apply this process to our 4-input K-map example. Example 4.28 shows the process of finding a minimized product of sums logic expression for a 4-input logic circuit using a K-map.

Example: Using a K-map to find a Minimized Product of Sums Expression (4-input)

Step 1: Circle groups of 0's in the K-map

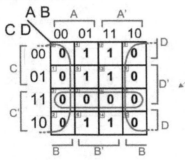

Again, the polarities of the variables along K-map are changed to reflect how the variables are entered into the sum terms.

Step 2: Create a sum term for each prime implicant

Variable A: The circle covers a region where A is both a 0 and 1, so it is excluded from the sum term.

Variable B: The circle covers a region where B is a 0, so it is included in the sum term uncomplemented.

Variable C: The circle covers a region where C is both a 0 and 1, so it is excluded from the sum term.

Variable D: The circle covers a region where D is both a 0 and 1, so it is excluded from the sum term.

The sum term for this prime implicant is: B

Variable A: The circle covers a region where A is both a 0 and 1, so it is excluded from the sum term.

Variable B: The circle covers a region where B is both a 0 and 1, so it is excluded from the sum term.

Variable C: The circle covers a region where C is a 1, so it is included in the sum term complemented.

Variable D: The circle covers a region where D is a 1, so it is included in the sum term complemented.

The sum term for this prime implicant is: C'+D'

Step 3: Multiply all of the sum terms for each prime implicant

There are two sum terms, one for each circle. The final minimized POS expression is:

$$F = (B) \cdot (C'+D')$$

Check: Is this equivalent to the logic expression obtained using the SOP approach?

From the prior example, the minimized SOP expression was: F = B·C' + B·D'

$F = (B) \cdot (C'+D')$ ◀— Let's use the Boolean algebra theorems to see if this is equal to B·C' + B·D'

$F = B \cdot C' + B \cdot D'$ ◀— Using the distributive property on the POS expression shows that this is equal to the minimized SOP expression.

Example 4.28
Using a K-map to find a Minimized Product of Sums Expression (4-input)

4.4.2.4 Minimal Sum

One situation that arises when minimizing logic using a K-map is that some of the prime implicants may be redundant. Consider the example in Figure 4.20.

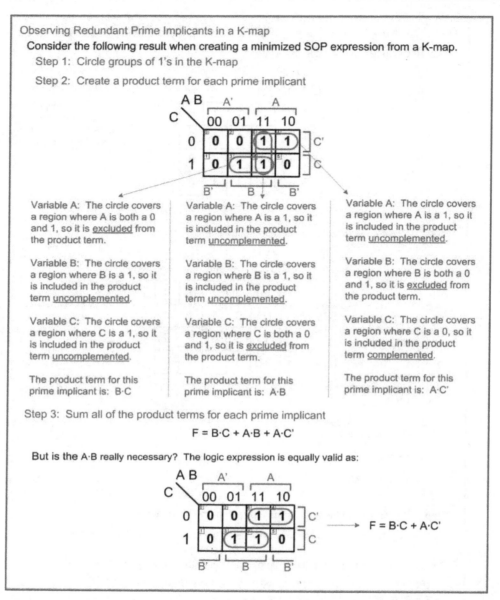

Figure 4.20
Observing Redundant Prime Implicants in a K-map

We need to define a formal process for identifying redundant prime implicants that can be removed without impacting the result of the logic expression. Let's start with examining the sum of products form. First, we define the term **essential prime implicant** as a prime implicant that *cannot* be removed from the logic expression without impacting its result. We then define the term **minimal sum** as a logic expression that represents the most minimal set of logic operations to accomplish a sum of products form. There may be multiple minimal sums for a given truth table, but each would have the same number of logic operations. In order to determine if a prime implicant is essential, we first put in each and every possible prime implicant into the K-map. This gives a logic expression known as the **complete sum**. From this point we identify any cells that have only one prime implicant covering them. These cells are called **distinguished one cells**. Any prime implicant that covers a distinguished one cell is defined as an essential prime implicant. All prime implicants that are not essential are removed from the K-map. A minimal sum is then simply the sum of all remaining product terms associated with the essential prime implicants. Example 4.29 shows how to use this process.

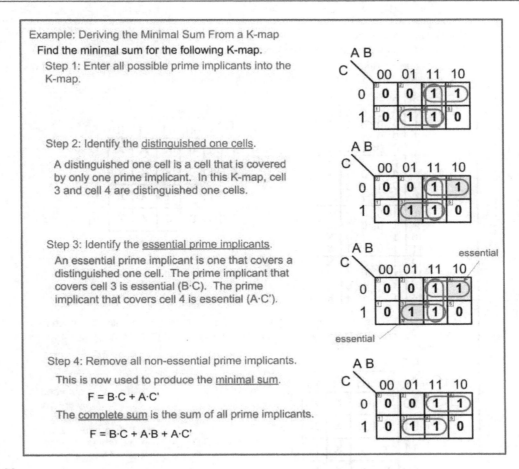

Example: Deriving the Minimal Sum From a K-map

Find the minimal sum for the following K-map.

Step 1: Enter all possible prime implicants into the K-map.

Step 2: Identify the distinguished one cells.

A distinguished one cell is a cell that is covered by only one prime implicant. In this K-map, cell 3 and cell 4 are distinguished one cells.

Step 3: Identify the essential prime implicants.

An essential prime implicant is one that covers a distinguished one cell. The prime implicant that covers cell 3 is essential (B·C). The prime implicant that covers cell 4 is essential (A·C').

Step 4: Remove all non-essential prime implicants.

This is now used to produce the minimal sum.

$$F = B·C + A·C'$$

The complete sum is the sum of all prime implicants.

$$F = B·C + A·B + A·C'$$

Example 4.29
Deriving the Minimal Sum From a K-map

This process is identical for the product of sums form to produce the **minimal product**.

4.4.3 Don't Cares

There are often times when framing a design problem that there are specific input codes that require exact output values, but there are other codes where the output value doesn't matter. This can occur for a variety of reasons, such as knowing that certain input codes will never occur due to the nature of the problem or that the output of the circuit will only be used under certain input codes. We can take advantage of this situation to produce a more minimal logic circuit. We define an output as a **don't care** when it doesn't matter whether it is a 1 or 0 for the particular input code. The symbol for a don't care is "X". We take advantage of don't cares when performing logic minimization by treating them as whatever output value will produce a minimal logic expression. Example 4.30 shows how to use this process.

Example: Using Don't Cares to Produce a Minimal SOP Logic Expression

Let's create a minimized sum of products expression by taking advantage of don't cares.

Don't cares are indicated using the symbol "X". These go directly into the K-map. If we initially just circle 1's, we get the following logic expression:

However, we can take advantage of the don't cares that are in cells 5 and 11. If we treat them as 1's, we can include them in the prime implicant giving a more minimal logic expression.

Example 4.30
Using Don't Cares to Produce a Minimal SOP Logic Expression

4.4.4 Using XOR Gates

While Boolean algebra does not include the exclusive-OR and exclusive-NOR operations, XOR and XNOR gates do indeed exist in modern electronics. They can be a useful tool to provide logic circuitry with less operations, sometimes even compared to a minimal sum or product synthesized using the techniques just described. An XOR/XNOR operation can be identified by putting the values from a truth table into a K-map. The XOR/XNOR operations will result in a characteristic checkerboard pattern in the K-map. Consider the following patterns for XOR and XNOR gates in Figure 4.21, Figure 4.22 and Figure 4.23. Anytime these patterns are observed, it indicates an XOR/XNOR gate.

Figure 4.21
XOR and XNOR Checkerboard Patterns Observed in K-maps (2-Input)

Figure 4.22
XOR and XNOR Checkerboard Patterns Observed in K-maps (3-Input)

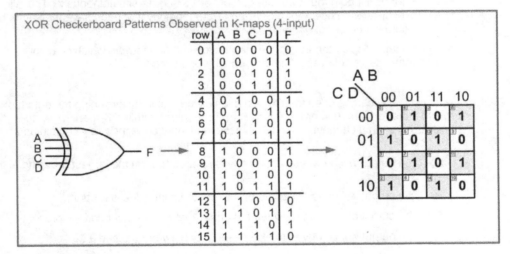

Figure 4.23
XOR Checkerboard Pattern Observed in K-maps (4-Input)

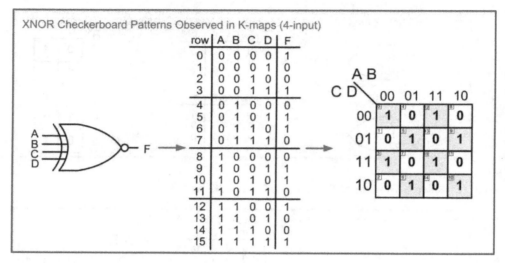

Figure 4.24
XNOR Checkerboard Pattern Observed in K-maps (4-Input)

CONCEPT CHECK

CC4.4(a) Logic minimization is accomplished by removing variables from the original canonical logic expression that don't impact the result. How does a Karnaugh map graphically show what variables can be removed?

- A) K-maps contain the same information as a truth table but the data is formatted as a grid. This allows variables to be removed by inspection.

- B) K-maps rearrange a truth table so that adjacent cells have one and only one input variable changing at a time. If adjacent cells have the same output value when an input variable is both a 0 and a 1, that variable has no impact on the interim result and can be eliminated.

- C) K-maps list both the rows with outputs of 1's and 0's simultaneously. This allows minimization to occur for a SOP and POS topology that each have the same, but minimal, number of gates.

- D) K-maps display the truth table information in a grid format, which is a more compact way of presenting the behavior of a circuit.

CC4.4(b) A "Don't Care" can be used to minimize a logic expression by assigning the output of a row to either a 1 or a 0 in order to form larger groupings within a K-map. How does the output of the circuit behave when it processes the input code for a row containing a don't care?

- A) The output will be whatever value was needed to form the largest grouping in the K-map.

- B) The output will go to either a 0 or a 1, but the final value is random.

- C) The output can toggle between a 0 and a 1 when this input code is present.

- D) The output will be driven to exactly halfway between a 0 and a 1.

4.5 Timing Hazards & Glitches

Timing hazards, or glitches, refer to unwanted transitions on the output of a combinational logic circuit. These are most commonly due to different delay paths through the gates in the circuit. In real circuitry there is always a finite propagation delay through each gate. Consider the circuit shown in Figure 4.25 where gate delays are included and how they can produce unwanted transitions.

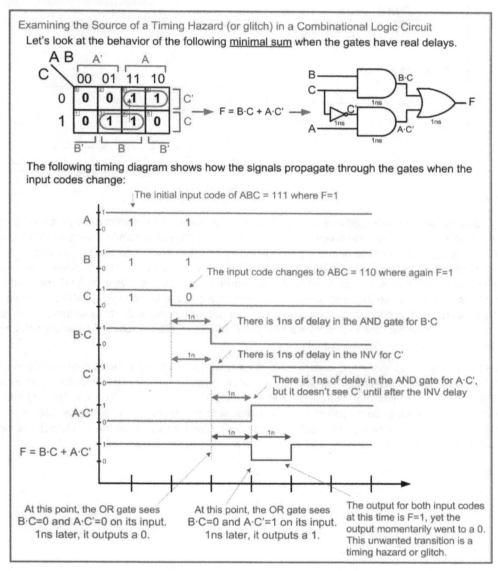

Figure 4.25
Examining the Source of a Timing Hazard (or glitch) in a Combinational Logic Circuit

These timing hazards are given unique names based on the type of transition that occurs. A **static 0** timing hazard is when the input switches between two input codes that both yield an output of 0 but the output momentarily switches to a 1. A **static 1** timing hazard is when the input switches between two input codes that both yield an output of 1 but the output momentarily switches to a 0. A **dynamic hazard** is when the input switches between two input codes that result in a real transition on the output (i.e., 0 to 1 or 1 to 0), but the output has a momentary glitch before reaching its final value. These definitions are shown in Figure 4.26.

Figure 4.26
Timing Hazard Definitions

Timing hazards can be addressed in a variety of ways. One way is to try to match the propagation delays through each path of the logic circuit. This can be difficult, particularly in modern logic families such as CMOS. In the example in Figure 4.25, the root cause of the different propagation delays was due to an inverter on one of the variables. It seems obvious that this could be addressed by putting buffers on the other inputs with equal delays as the inverter. This would create a situation where all input codes would arrive at the first stage of AND gates at the same time regardless of whether they were inverted or not and eliminate the hazards; however, CMOS implements a buffer as two inverters in series, so it is difficult to insert a buffer in a circuit with an equal delay to an inverter. Addressing timing hazards in this way is possible, but it involves a time-consuming and tedious process of adjusting the transistors used to create the buffer and inverter to have equal delays.

Another technique to address timing hazards is to place additional circuitry in the system that will ensure the correct output while the input codes switch. Consider how including a non-essential prime implicant can eliminate a timing hazard in Example 4.31. In this approach, the minimal sum from Figure 4.25 is instead replaced with the complete sum. The use of the complete sum instead of the minimal sum can be shown to eliminate both static and dynamic timing hazards. The drawback of this approach is the addition of extra circuitry in the combinational logic circuit (i.e., non-essential prime implicants).

Example 4.31
Eliminating a Timing Hazard by Including Non-Essential Product Terms

CONCEPT CHECK

CC4.5 How long do you need to wait for all hazards to settle out?

A) The time equal to the delay through the non-essential prime implicants.

B) The time equal to the delay through the essential prime implicants.

C) The time equal to the shortest delay path in the circuit.

D) The time equal to the longest delay path in the circuit.

Summary

❖ Boolean algebra defines the axioms and theorems that guide the operations that can be performed on a two-valued number system.

❖ Boolean algebra theorems allow logic expressions to be manipulated to make circuit synthesis simpler. They also allow logic expressions to be minimized.

❖ The delay of a combinational logic circuit is always dictated by the longest delay path from the inputs to the output.

❖ The *canonical form* of a logic expression is one that has not been minimized.

❖ A *canonical sum of products* form is a logic synthesis technique based on *minterms*. A minterm is a product term that will output a <u>one</u> for only one unique input code. A minterm is used for each row of a truth table corresponding to an output of a <u>one</u>. Each of the minterms are then summed together to create the final system output.

❖ A *minterm list* is a shorthand way of describing the information in a truth table. The symbol "Σ" is used to denote a minterm list. Each of the input variables are added to this symbol as comma delimited subscripts. The row number is then listed for each row corresponding to an output of a <u>one</u>.

❖ A *canonical product of sums* form is a logic synthesis technique based on *maxterms*. A maxterm is a sum term that will output a <u>zero</u> for only one unique input code. A maxterm is used for each row of a truth table corresponding to an output of a <u>zero</u>. Each of the maxterms are then multiplied together to create the final system output.

❖ A *maxterm list* is a shorthand way of describing the information in a truth table. The symbol "Π" is used to denote a maxterm list. Each of the input variables are added to this symbol as comma delimited subscripts. The row number is then listed for each row corresponding to an output of a <u>zero</u>.

❖ Canonical logic expressions can be minimized through a repetitive process of factoring common variables using the *distributive* property and then eliminating remaining variables using a combination of the *complements* and *identity* theorems.

❖ A *Karnaugh map* (K-map) is a graphical approach to minimizing logic expressions. A K-map arranges a truth table into a grid in which the neighboring cells have input codes that differ by only one bit. This allows the impact of an input variable on a group of outputs to be quickly identified.

❖ A *minimized sum of products* expression can be found from a K-map by circling neighboring <u>ones</u> to form groups that can be produced by a single product term. Each product term (aka *prime implicant*) is then summed together to form the circuit output.

❖ A *minimized product of sums* expression can be found from a K-map by circling neighboring <u>zeros</u> to form groups that can be produced by a single sum term. Each sum term (aka *prime implicant*) is then multiplied together to form the circuit output.

❖ A *minimal sum* or *minimal product* is a logic expression that contains only essential prime implicants and represents the smallest number of logic operations possible to produce the desired output.

❖ A *don't care* (X) can be used when the output of a truth table row can be either a zero or a one without affecting the system behavior. This typically occurs when some of the input codes of a truth table will never occur. The value for the row of a truth table containing a don't care output can be chosen to give the most minimal logic expression. In a K-map, don't cares can be included to form the largest groupings in order to give the least amount of logic.

❖ While exclusive-OR gates are not used in Boolean algebra, they can be visually identified in K-maps by looking for checkerboard patterns.

❖ Timing hazards are temporary glitches that occur on the output of a combinational logic circuit due to timing mismatches through different paths in the circuit. Hazards can be minimized by including additional circuitry in the system or by matching the delay of all signal paths.

Exercise Problems

Section 4.1 – Boolean Algebra

4.1.1　Which Boolean algebra theorem describes the situation where *any variable OR'd with itself will yield itself*?

4.1.2　Which Boolean algebra theorem describes the situation where *any variable that is double complemented will yield itself*?

4.1.3　Which Boolean algebra theorem describes the situation where *any variable OR'd with a 1 will yield a 1*?

4.1.4　Which Boolean algebra theorem describes the situation where a variable that exists in multiple product terms can be factored out?

4.1.5　Which Boolean algebra theorem describes the situation where when output(s) corresponding to a term within an expression are handled by another term the original term can be removed?

4.1.6　Which Boolean algebra theorem describes the situation where *any variable AND'd with its complement will yield a 0*?

4.1.7 Which Boolean algebra theorem describes the situation where *any variable AND'd with a 0 will yield a 0*?

4.1.8 Which Boolean algebra theorem describes the situation where an AND gate with its inputs inverted is equivalent to an OR gate with its outputs inverted?

4.1.9 Which Boolean algebra theorem describes the situation where *a variable that exists in multiple sum terms can be factored out*?

4.1.10 Which Boolean algebra theorem describes the situation where an OR gate with its inputs inverted is equivalent to an AND gate with its outputs inverted?

4.1.11 Which Boolean algebra theorem describes the situation where the grouping of variables in an OR operation does not affect the result?

4.1.12 Which Boolean algebra theorem describes the situation where *any variable AND'd with itself will yield itself*?

4.1.13 Which Boolean algebra theorem describes the situation where the order of variables in an OR operation does not affect the result?

4.1.14 Which Boolean algebra theorem describes the situation where *any variable AND'd with a 1 will yield itself*?

4.1.15 Which Boolean algebra theorem describes the situation where the grouping of variables in an AND operation does not affect the result?

4.1.16 Which Boolean algebra theorem describes the situation where *any variable OR'd with its complement will yield a 1*?

4.1.17 Which Boolean algebra theorem describes the situation where the order of variables in an AND operation does not affect the result?

4.1.18 Which Boolean algebra theorem describes the situation where *a variable OR'd with a 0 will yield itself*?

4.1.19 Use <u>proof by exhaustion</u> to prove that an OR gate with its inputs inverted is equivalent to an AND gate with its outputs inverted.

4.1.20 Use <u>proof by exhaustion</u> to prove that an AND gate with its inputs inverted is equivalent to an OR gate with its outputs inverted.

Section 4.2 – Combinational Logic Analysis

4.2.1 For the logic diagram given in Figure 4.27, give the logic expression for the output F.

Figure 4.27

4.2.2 For the logic diagram given in Figure 4.27, give the truth table for the output F.

4.2.3 For the logic diagram given in Figure 4.27, give the delay.

4.2.4 For the logic diagram given in Figure 4.28, give the logic expression for the output F.

Figure 4.28

4.2.5 For the logic diagram given in Figure 4.28, give the truth table for the output F.

4.2.6 For the logic diagram given in Figure 4.28, give the delay.

4.2.7 For the logic diagram given in Figure 4.29, give the logic expression for the output F.

Figure 4.29

4.2.8 For the logic diagram given in Figure 4.29, give the truth table for the output F.

4.2.9 For the logic diagram given in Figure 4.29, give the delay.

Section 4.3 – Combinational Logic Synthesis

4.3.1 For the 2-input truth table in Figure 4.30, give the <u>canonical sum of products (SOP) logic expression</u>.

A	B	F
0	0	0
0	1	1
1	0	0
1	1	1

Figure 4.30

4.3.2 For the 2-input truth table in Figure 4.30, give the <u>canonical sum of products (SOP) logic diagram</u>.

4.3.3 For the 2-input truth table in Figure 4.30, give the <u>minterm list</u>.

4.3.4 For the 2-input truth table in Figure 4.30, give the <u>canonical product of sums (POS) logic expression</u>.

4.3.5 For the 2-input truth table in Figure 4.30, give the <u>canonical product of sums (POS) logic diagram</u>.

4.3.6 For the 2-input truth table in Figure 4.30, give the <u>maxterm list</u>.

4.3.7 For the 2-input minterm list in Figure 4.31, give the <u>canonical sum of products (SOP) logic expression</u>.

$$F = \sum_{A,B}(1,2,3)$$

Figure 4.31

4.3.8 For the 2-input minterm list in Figure 4.31, give the <u>canonical sum of products (SOP) logic diagram</u>.

4.3.9 For the 2-input minterm list in Figure 4.31, give the <u>truth table</u>.

4.3.10 For the 2-input minterm list in Figure 4.31, give the <u>canonical product of sums (POS) logic expression</u>.

4.3.11 For the 2-input minterm list in Figure 4.31, give the <u>canonical product of sums (POS) logic diagram</u>.

4.3.12 For the 2-input minterm list in Figure 4.31, give the <u>maxterm list</u>.

4.3.13 For the 2-input maxterm list in Figure 4.32, give the <u>canonical sum of products (SOP) logic expression</u>.

$$F = \prod_{A,B}(1,2,3)$$

Figure 4.32

4.3.14 For the 2-input maxterm list in Figure 4.32, give the <u>canonical sum of products (SOP) logic diagram</u>.

4.3.15 For the 2-input maxterm list in Figure 4.32, give the <u>minterm list</u>.

4.3.16 For the 2-input maxterm list in Figure 4.32, give the <u>canonical product of sums (POS) logic expression</u>.

4.3.17 For the 2-input maxterm list in Figure 4.32, give the <u>canonical product of sums (POS) logic diagram</u>.

4.3.18 For the 2-input maxterm list in Figure 4.32, give the <u>truth table</u>.

4.3.19 For the 3-input truth table in Figure 4.33, give the <u>canonical sum of products (SOP) logic expression</u>.

A	B	C	F
0	0	0	0
0	0	1	1
0	1	0	0
0	1	1	1
1	0	0	1
1	0	1	0
1	1	0	1
1	1	1	0

Figure 4.33

4.3.20 For the 3-input truth table in Figure 4.33, give the <u>canonical sum of products (SOP) logic diagram</u>.

4.3.21 For the 3-input truth table in Figure 4.33, give the <u>minterm list</u>.

4.3.22 For the 3-input truth table in Figure 4.33, give the <u>canonical product of sums (POS) logic expression</u>.

4.3.23 For the 3-input truth table in Figure 4.33, give the <u>canonical product of sums (POS) logic diagram</u>.

4.3.24 For the 3-input truth table in Figure 4.33, give the <u>maxterm list</u>.

4.3.25 For the 3-input minterm list in Figure 4.34, give the <u>canonical sum of products (SOP) logic expression</u>.

$$F = \sum_{A,B,C}(2,4,6)$$

Figure 4.34

4.3.26 For the 3-input minterm list in Figure 4.34, give the <u>canonical sum of products (SOP) logic diagram</u>.

4.3.27 For the 3-input minterm list in Figure 4.34, give the <u>truth table</u>.

4.3.28 For the 3-input minterm list in Figure 4.34, give the <u>canonical product of sums (POS) logic expression</u>.

4.3.29 For the 3-input minterm list in Figure 4.34, give the <u>canonical product of sums (POS) logic diagram</u>.

4.3.30 For the 3-input minterm list in Figure 4.34, give the <u>maxterm list</u>.

4.3.31 For the 3-input maxterm list in Figure 4.35, give the <u>canonical sum of products (SOP) logic expression</u>.

$$F = \prod_{A,B,C}(2,3,5,6,7)$$

Figure 4.35

4.3.32 For the 3-input maxterm list in Figure 4.35, give the <u>canonical sum of products (SOP) logic diagram</u>.

4.3.33 For the 3-input maxterm list in Figure 4.35, give the <u>minterm list</u>.

4.3.34 For the 3-input maxterm list in Figure 4.35, give the <u>canonical product of sums (POS) logic expression</u>.

4.3.35 For the 3-input maxterm list in Figure 4.35, give the <u>canonical product of sums (POS) logic diagram</u>.

4.3.36 For the 3-input maxterm list in Figure 4.35, give the <u>truth table</u>.

4.3.37 For the 4-input truth table in Figure 4.36, give the <u>canonical sum of products (SOP) logic expression</u>.

A	B	C	D	F
0	0	0	0	0
0	0	0	1	1
0	0	1	0	0
0	0	1	1	1
0	1	0	0	0
0	1	0	1	0
0	1	1	0	0
0	1	1	1	0
1	0	0	0	0
1	0	0	1	1
1	0	1	0	0
1	0	1	1	1
1	1	0	0	0
1	1	0	1	0
1	1	1	0	0
1	1	1	1	0

Figure 4.36

4.3.38 For the 4-input truth table in Figure 4.36, give the <u>canonical sum of products (SOP) logic diagram</u>.

4.3.39 For the 4-input truth table in Figure 4.36, give the <u>minterm list</u>.

4.3.40 For the 4-input truth table in Figure 4.36, give the <u>canonical product of sums (POS) logic expression</u>.

4.3.41 For the 4-input truth table in Figure 4.36, give the <u>canonical product of sums (POS) logic diagram</u>.

4.3.42 For the 4-input truth table in Figure 4.36, give the <u>maxterm list</u>.

4.3.43 For the 4-input minterm list in Figure 4.37, give the <u>canonical sum of products (SOP) logic expression</u>.

$$F = \sum_{A,B,C,D}(4,5,7,12,13,15)$$

Figure 4.37

4.3.44 For the 4-input minterm list in Figure 4.37, give the <u>canonical sum of products (SOP) logic diagram</u>.

4.3.45 For the 4-input minterm list in Figure 4.37, give the truth table.

4.3.46 For the 4-input minterm list in Figure 4.37, give the canonical product of sums (POS) logic expression.

4.3.47 For the 4-input minterm list in Figure 4.37, give the canonical product of sums (POS) logic diagram.

4.3.48 For the 4-input minterm list in Figure 4.37, give the maxterm list.

4.3.49 For the 4-input maxterm list in Figure 4.38, give the canonical sum of products (SOP) logic expression.

$$F = \prod_{A,B,C,D}(3,7,11,15)$$

Figure 4.38

4.3.50 For the 4-input maxterm list in Figure 4.38, give the canonical sum of products (SOP) logic diagram.

4.3.51 For the 4-input maxterm list in Figure 4.38, give the minterm list.

4.3.52 For the 4-input maxterm list in Figure 4.38, give the canonical product of sums (POS) logic expression.

4.3.53 For the 4-input maxterm list in Figure 4.38, give the canonical product of sums (POS) logic diagram.

4.3.54 For the 4-input maxterm list in Figure 4.38, give the truth table.

Section 4.4 –Logic Minimization

4.4.1 For the 2-input truth table in Figure 4.39, use a K-map to derive a minimized sum of products (SOP) logic expression.

A	B	F
0	0	0
0	1	1
1	0	0
1	1	1

Figure 4.39

4.4.2 For the 2-input truth table in Figure 4.39, use a K-map to derive a minimized product of sums (POS) logic expression.

4.4.3 For the 2-input truth table in Figure 3.39, use a K-map to derive a minimized sum of products (SOP) logic expression.

A	B	F
0	0	0
0	1	1
1	0	1
1	1	1

Figure 4.40

4.4.4 For the 2-input truth table in Figure 3.39, use a K-map to derive a minimized product of sums (POS) logic expression.

4.4.5 For the 2-input truth table in Figure 4.41, use a K-map to derive a minimized sum of products (SOP) logic expression.

A	B	F
0	0	1
0	1	0
1	0	0
1	1	0

Figure 4.41

4.4.6 For the 2-input truth table in Figure 4.41, use a K-map to derive a minimized product of sums (POS) logic expression.

4.4.7 For the 2-input truth table in Figure 4.42, use a K-map to derive a minimized sum of products (SOP) logic expression.

A	B	F
0	0	1
0	1	1
1	0	0
1	1	0

Figure 4.42

4.4.8 For the 2-input truth table in Figure 4.42, use a K-map to derive a minimized product of sums (POS) logic expression.

4.4.9 For the 3-input truth table in Figure 4.43, use a K-map to derive a minimized sum of products (SOP) logic expression.

A	B	C	F
0	0	0	0
0	0	1	1
0	1	0	0
0	1	1	1
1	0	0	1
1	0	1	0
1	1	0	1
1	1	1	0

Figure 4.43

4.4.10 For the 3-input truth table in Figure 4.43, use a K-map to derive a minimized product of sums (POS) logic expression.

4.4.11 For the 3-input truth table in Figure 4.44, use a K-map to derive a minimized sum of products (SOP) logic expression.

A	B	C	F
0	0	0	0
0	0	1	0
0	1	0	1
0	1	1	0
1	0	0	1
1	0	1	0
1	1	0	1
1	1	1	0

Figure 4.44

4.4.12 For the 3-input truth table in Figure 4.44, use a K-map to derive a minimized product of sums (POS) logic expression.

4.4.13 For the 3-input truth table in Figure 4.45, use a K-map to derive a minimized sum of products (SOP) logic expression.

A	B	C	F
0	0	0	1
0	0	1	1
0	1	0	0
0	1	1	0
1	0	0	1
1	0	1	0
1	1	0	0
1	1	1	0

Figure 4.45

4.4.14 For the 3-input truth table in Figure 4.45, use a K-map to derive a <u>minimized product of sums (POS) logic expression</u>.

4.4.15 For the 3-input truth table in Figure 4.46, use a K-map to derive a <u>minimized sum of products (SOP) logic expression</u>.

A	B	C	F
0	0	0	1
0	0	1	1
0	1	0	0
0	1	1	0
1	0	0	1
1	0	1	1
1	1	0	0
1	1	1	1

Figure 4.46

4.4.16 For the 3-input truth table in Figure 4.46, use a K-map to derive a <u>minimized product of sums (POS) logic expression</u>.

4.4.17 For the 4-input truth table in Figure 4.47, use a K-map to derive a <u>minimized sum of products (SOP) logic expression</u>.

A	B	C	D	F
0	0	0	0	0
0	0	0	1	1
0	0	1	0	0
0	0	1	1	1
0	1	0	0	0
0	1	0	1	0
0	1	1	0	0
0	1	1	1	0
1	0	0	0	0
1	0	0	1	1
1	0	1	0	0
1	0	1	1	1
1	1	0	0	0
1	1	0	1	0
1	1	1	0	0
1	1	1	1	0

Figure 4.47

4.4.18 For the 4-input truth table in Figure 4.47, use a K-map to derive a <u>minimized product of sums (POS) logic expression</u>.

4.4.19 For the 4-input truth table in Figure 4.48, use a K-map to derive a <u>minimized sum of products (SOP) logic expression</u>.

A	B	C	D	F
0	0	0	0	0
0	0	0	1	0
0	0	1	0	0
0	0	1	1	0
0	1	0	0	1
0	1	0	1	1
0	1	1	0	0
0	1	1	1	1
1	0	0	0	0
1	0	0	1	0
1	0	1	0	0
1	0	1	1	0
1	1	0	0	1
1	1	0	1	1
1	1	1	0	0
1	1	1	1	1

Figure 4.48

4.4.20 For the 4-input truth table in Figure 4.48, use a K-map to derive a <u>minimized product of sums (POS) logic expression</u>.

4.4.21 For the 4-input truth table in Figure 4.49, use a K-map to derive a <u>minimized sum of products (SOP) logic expression</u>.

A	B	C	D	F
0	0	0	0	1
0	0	0	1	1
0	0	1	0	1
0	0	1	1	0
0	1	0	0	1
0	1	0	1	1
0	1	1	0	1
0	1	1	1	0
1	0	0	0	1
1	0	0	1	1
1	0	1	0	1
1	0	1	1	0
1	1	0	0	1
1	1	0	1	1
1	1	1	0	1
1	1	1	1	0

Figure 4.49

4.4.22 For the 4-input truth table in Figure 4.49, use a K-map to derive a <u>minimized product of sums (POS) logic expression</u>.

4.4.23 For the 4-input truth table in Figure 4.50, use a K-map to derive a <u>minimized sum of products (SOP) logic expression</u>.

A	B	C	D	F
0	0	0	0	1
0	0	0	1	0
0	0	1	0	1
0	0	1	1	1
0	1	0	0	1
0	1	0	1	1
0	1	1	0	1
0	1	1	1	1
1	0	0	0	1
1	0	0	1	0
1	0	1	0	1
1	0	1	1	0
1	1	0	0	1
1	1	0	1	0
1	1	1	0	1
1	1	1	1	1

Figure 4.50

4.4.24 For the 4-input truth table in Figure 4.50, use a K-map to derive a <u>minimized product of sums (POS) logic expression</u>.

4.4.25 For the 3-input truth table and K-map in Figure 4.51, provide the row number(s) of any <u>distinguished one-cells</u>.

A	B	C	F
0	0	0	0
0	0	1	0
0	1	0	1
0	1	1	1
1	0	0	1
1	0	1	0
1	1	0	1
1	1	1	0

Figure 4.51

4.4.26 For the 3-input truth table and K-map in Figure 4.51, give the product terms for the <u>essential prime implicants</u>.

4.4.27 For the 3-input truth table and K-map in Figure 4.51, give the <u>minimal sum of products logic expression</u>.

4.4.28 For the 3-input truth table and K-map in Figure 4.51, give the <u>complete sum of products logic expression</u>.

4.4.29 For the 4-input truth table and K-map in Figure 4.52, provide the row number(s) of any <u>distinguished one-cells</u>.

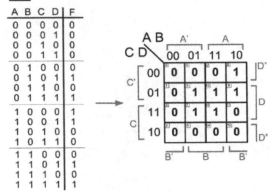

Figure 4.52

4.4.30 For the 4-input truth table and K-map in Figure 4.52, give the product terms for the <u>essential prime implicants</u>.

4.4.31 For the 4-input truth table and K-map in Figure 4.52, give the <u>minimal sum of products (SOP) logic expression</u>.

4.4.32 For the 4-input truth table and K-map in Figure 4.52, give the <u>complete sum of products (SOP) logic expression</u>.

4.4.33 For the 4-input truth table and K-map in Figure 4.53, give the <u>minimal sum of products (SOP)</u> logic expression by <u>exploiting "don't cares"</u>.

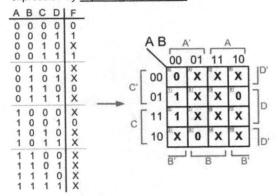

Figure 4.53

4.4.34 For the 4-input truth table and K-map in Figure 4.54, give the <u>minimal product of sums (POS)</u> logic expression by <u>exploiting "don't cares"</u>.

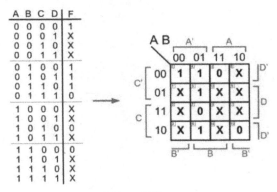

Figure 4.54

4.5 –Timing Hazards & Glitches

4.5.1 Describe the situation in which a static-1 timing hazard may occur.

4.5.2 Describe the situation in which a static-0 timing hazard may occur.

4.5.3 In which topology will a static-1 timing hazard occur (SOP, POS, or both)?

4.5.4 In which topology will a static-0 timing hazard occur (SOP, POS, or both)?

4.5.5 For the 3-input truth table and K-map in Figure 4.51, give the product term that helps <u>eliminate timing hazards</u> in this circuit.

4.5.6 For the 4-input truth table and K-map in Figure 4.52, give the product term that helps <u>eliminate timing hazards</u> in this circuit.

Chapter 5: VHDL (Part 1)

Based on the material presented in Chapter 4, there are a few observations about logic design that are apparent. First, the size of logic circuitry can scale quickly to the point where it is difficult to design by hand. Second, the process of moving from a high level description of how a circuit works (e.g., a truth table) to a form that is ready to be implemented with real circuitry (e.g., a minimized logic diagram) is straightforward and well-defined. Both of these observations motivate the use of computer aided design (CAD) tools to accomplish logic design. This chapter introduces hardware description languages (HDLs) as a means to describe digital circuitry using a text-based language. HDLs provide a means to describe large digital systems without the need for schematics, which can become impractical in very large designs. HDLs have evolved to support logic simulation at different levels of abstraction. This provides designers the ability to begin designing and verifying functionality of large systems at a high level of abstraction and postpone the details of the circuit implementation until later in the design cycle. This enables a top-down design approach that is scalable across different logic families. HDLs have also evolved to support automated *synthesis*, which allows the CAD tools to take a functional description of a system (e.g., a truth table) and automatically create the gate level circuitry to be implemented in real hardware. This allows designers to focus their attention on designing the behavior of a system and not spend as much time performing the formal logic synthesis steps that were presented in Chapter 4. The intent of this chapter is to introduce HDLs and their use in the modern digital design flow. This chapter will cover the basics of designing combinational logic in an HDL and also hierarchical design. The more advanced concepts of HDLs such as sequential logic design, high level abstraction and adding functionality to an HDL through additional libraries and packages are covered later so that the reader can get started quickly using HDLs to gain experience with the languages and design flow.

There are two dominant hardware description languages in use today. They are VHDL and Verilog. VHDL stands for *very high speed integrated circuit hardware description language*. This is also written as *VHSIC hardware description language*. Verilog is not an acronym but rather a trade name. The use of these two HDLs is split equally within the digital design industry. Once one language is learned it is simple to learn the other language, so the choice of the HDL to learn first is somewhat arbitrary. In this text we will use VHDL to learn the concepts of an HDL. VHDL is stricter in its syntax and typecasting than Verilog, so it is a good platform for beginners as it provides more of a scaffold for the description of circuits. This helps avoid some of the common pitfalls that beginners typically encounter.

Learning Outcomes – After completing this chapter, you will be able to:

5.1	Describe the role of hardware description languages in modern digital design.
5.2	Describe the fundamentals of design abstraction in modern digital design.
5.3	Describe the modern digital design flow based on hardware description languages.
5.4	Describe the fundamental constructs of VHDL.
5.5	Design a VHDL model for a combinational logic circuit using concurrent signal assignments and logical operators.
5.6	Design a VHDL model for a combinational logic circuit using conditional signal assignments.
5.7	Design a VHDL model for a combinational logic circuit using selected signal assignments.
5.8	Design a VHDL model for a combinational logic circuit using a structural design approach.

5.1 History of Hardware Description Languages

The invention of the integrated circuit is most commonly credited to two individuals who filed patents on different variations of the same basic concept within six months of each other in 1959. Jack Kilby filed the first patent on the integrated circuit in February of 1959 titled "Miniaturized Electronic Circuits" while working for *Texas Instruments*. Robert Noyce was the second to file a patent on the integrated circuit in July of 1959 titled "Semiconductor Device and Lead Structure" while at a company he cofounded called *Fairchild Semiconductor*. Kilby went on to win the Nobel Prize in Physics in 2000 for his invention, while Noyce went on to cofound *Intel Corporation* in 1968 with Gordon Moore. In 1971, Intel introduced the first single-chip microprocessor using integrated circuit technology, the *Intel 4004*. This microprocessor IC contained 2300 transistors. This series of inventions launched the semiconductor industry, which was the driving force behind the growth of Silicon Valley, and led to 40 years of unprecedented advancement in technology that has impacted every aspect of the modern world.

Gordon Moore, cofounder of Intel, predicted in 1965 that the number of transistors on an integrated circuit would double every two years. This prediction, now known as *Moore's Law*, has held true since the invention of the integrated circuit. As the number of transistors on an integrated circuit grew, so did the size of the design and the functionality that could be implemented. Once the first microprocessor was invented in 1971, the capability of CAD tools increased rapidly enabling larger designs to be accomplished. These larger designs, including newer microprocessors, enabled the CAD tools to become even more sophisticated and, in turn, yield even larger designs. The rapid expansion of electronic systems based on digital integrated circuits required that different manufacturers needed to produce designs that were compatible with each other. The adoption of logic family standards helped manufacturers ensure their parts would be compatible with other manufacturers at the physical layer (e.g., voltage and current); however, one challenge that was encountered by the industry was a way to document the complex behavior of larger systems. The use of schematics to document large digital designs became too cumbersome and difficult to understand by anyone besides the designer. Word descriptions of the behavior were easier to understand, but even this form of documentation became too voluminous to be effective for the size of designs that were emerging.

In 1983, the US Department of Defense (DoD) sponsored a program to create a means to document the behavior of digital systems that could be used across all of its suppliers. This program was motivated by a lack of adequate documentation for the functionality of application specific integrated circuits (ASICs) that were being supplied to the DoD. This lack of documentation was becoming a critical issue as ASICs would come to the end of their life cycle and need to be replaced. With the lack of a standardized documentation approach, suppliers had difficulty reproducing equivalent parts to those that had become obsolete. The DoD contracted three companies (Texas Instruments, IBM, and Intermetrics) to develop a standardized documentation tool that provided detailed information about both the interface (i.e., inputs and outputs) and the behavior of digital systems. The new tool was to be implemented in a format similar to a programming language. Due to the nature of this type of language-based tool, it was a natural extension of the original project scope to include the ability to *simulate* the behavior of a digital system. The simulation capability was desired to span multiple levels of abstraction to provide maximum flexibility. In 1985, the first version of this tool, called VHDL, was released. In order to gain widespread adoption and ensure consistency of use across the industry, VHDL was turned over to the *Institute of Electrical and Electronic Engineers* (IEEE) for standardization. IEEE is a professional association that defines a broad range of open technology standards. In 1987, IEEE released the first industry standard version of VHDL. The release was titled IEEE 1076-1987. Feedback from the initial version resulted in a major revision of the standard in 1993 titled IEEE 1076-1993. While many minor revisions have been made to the 1993 release, the 1076-1993 standard contains the vast majority of VHDL functionality in use today. The most recent VHDL standard is IEEE 1076-2008.

Also in 1983, the Verilog HDL was developed by *Automated Integrated Design Systems* as a logic simulation language. The development of Verilog took place completely independent from the VHDL project. Automated Integrated Design Systems (renamed *Gateway Design Automation* in 1985) was acquired by CAD tool vendor *Cadence Design Systems* in 1990. In response to the rapid adoption of the open VHDL standard, Cadence made the Verilog HDL open to the public in order to stay competitive. IEEE once again developed the open standard for this HDL, and in 1995 released the Verilog standard titled IEEE 1364.

The development of CAD tools to accomplish automated logic synthesis can be dated back to the 1970's when IBM began developing a series of practical synthesis engines that were used in the design of their mainframe computers; however, the main advancement in logic synthesis came with the founding of a company called *Synopsis* in 1986. Synopsis was the first company to focus on logic synthesis directly from HDLs. This was a major contribution because designers were already using HDLs to describe and simulate their digital systems, and now logic synthesis became integrated in the same design flow. Due to the complexity of synthesizing highly abstract functional descriptions, only lower-levels of abstraction that were thoroughly elaborated were initially able to be synthesized. As CAD tool capability evolved, synthesis of higher levels of abstraction became possible, but even today not all functionality that can be described in an HDL can be synthesized.

The history of HDLs, their standardization and the creation of the associated logic synthesis tools is key to understanding the use and limitations of HDLs. HDLs were originally designed for documentation and behavioral simulation. Logic synthesis tools were developed independently and modified later to work with HDLs. This history provides some background into the most common pitfalls that beginning digital designers encounter, that being that most any type of behavior can be described and simulated in an HDL, but only a subset of well-described functionality can be synthesized. Beginning digital designers are often plagued by issues related to designs that simulate perfectly but that will not synthesize correctly. In this book, an effort is made to introduce VHDL at a level that provides a reasonable amount of abstraction while preserving the ability to be synthesized. Figure 5.1 shows a timeline of some of the major technology milestones that have occurred in the past 150 years in the field of digital logic and HDLs.

Figure 5.1
Major Milestones in the Advancement of Digital Logic and HDLs

CONCEPT CHECK

CC5.1 Why does VHDL support modeling techniques that *aren't* synthesizable?

A) Since synthesis wasn't within the original scope of the VHDL project, there wasn't sufficient time to make everything synthesizable.

B) At the time VHDL was created, synthesis was deemed too difficult to implement.

C) To allow VHDL to be used as a generic programming language.

D) VHDL needs to support all steps in the modern digital design flow, some of which are unsynthesizable such as test pattern generation and timing verification.

5.2 HDL Abstraction

HDLs were originally defined to be able to model behavior at multiple levels of abstraction. Abstraction is an important concept in engineering design because it allows us to specify how systems will operate without getting consumed prematurely with implementation details. Also, by removing the details of the lower level implementation, simulations can be conducted in reasonable amounts of time to model the higher level functionality. If a full computer system was simulated using detailed models for every MOSFET, it would take an impracticable amount of time to complete. Figure 5.2 shows a graphical depiction of the different layers of abstraction in digital system design.

Figure 5.2
Levels of Design Abstraction

The highest level of abstraction is the *system level*. At this level, behavior of a system is described by stating a set of broad specifications. An example of a design at this level is a specification such as "the computer system will perform 10 Tera Floating Point Operations per Second (10 TFLOPS) on double precision data and consume no more than 100 Watts of power". Notice that these specifications do not dictate the lower level details such as the type of logic family or the type of computer architecture to use. One level down from the system level is the *algorithmic level*. At this level, the specifications begin to be broken down into sub-systems, each with an associated behavior that will accomplish a part of the primary task. At this level, the example computer specifications might be broken down into sub-systems such as a central processing unit (CPU) to perform the computation and random access memory (RAM) to hold the inputs and outputs of the computation. One level down from the algorithmic level is the *register transfer level (RTL)*. At this level, the details of how data is moved between and within sub-systems are described in addition to how the data is manipulated based on system inputs. One level down from the RTL level is the *gate level*. At this level, the design is described using basic gates and registers (or storage elements). The gate level is essentially a schematic (either graphically or text-based) that contains the components and connections that will implement the functionality from the above levels of abstraction. One level down from the gate level is the *circuit level*. The circuit level describes the operation of the basic gates and registers using transistors, wires and other electrical components such as resistors and capacitors. Finally, the lowest level of design abstraction is the *material level*. This level describes how different materials are combined and shaped in order to implement the transistors, devices and wires from the circuit level.

HDLs are designed to model behavior at all of these levels with the exception of the material level. While there is some capability to model circuit level behavior such as MOSFETs as ideal switches and pull-up/pull-down resistors, HDLs are not typically used at the circuit level. Another graphical depiction of design abstraction is known as the **Gajski and Kuhn's Y-chart**. A Y-chart depicts abstraction across three different design domains: behavioral, structural and physical. Each of these design domains contains levels of abstraction (i.e., system, algorithm, RTL, gate, and circuit). An example Y-chart is shown in Figure 5.3.

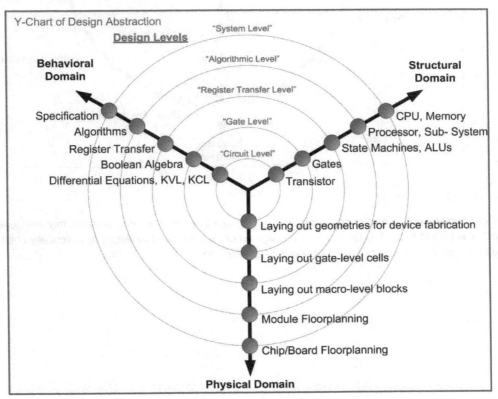

Figure 5.3
Y-Chart of Design Abstraction

A Y-chart also depicts how the abstraction levels of different design domains are related to each other. A top-down design flow can be visualized in a Y-chart by spiraling inward in a clockwise direction. Moving from the behavioral domain to the structural domain is the process of *synthesis*. Whenever synthesis is performed, the resulting system should be compared with the prior behavioral description. This checking is called *verification*. The process of creating the physical circuitry corresponding to the structural description is called *implementation*. The spiral continues down through the levels of abstraction until the design is implemented at a level that the geometries representing circuit elements (transistors, wires, etc.) are ready to be fabricated in silicon. Figure 5.4 shows the top-down design process depicted as an inward spiral on the Y-chart.

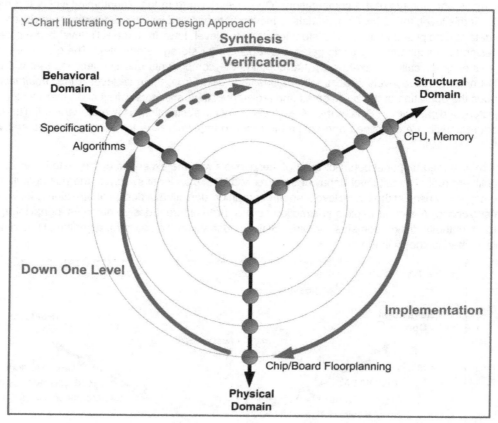

Figure 5.4
Y-Chart Illustrating Top-Down Design Approach

The Y-chart represents a formal approach for large digital systems. For large systems that are designed by teams of engineers, it is critical that a formal, top-down design process is followed to eliminate potentially costly design errors as the implementation is carried out at lower levels of abstraction.

CONCEPT CHECK

CC5.2 Why is abstraction an essential part of engineering design?

A) Without abstraction all schematics would be drawn at the transistor-level.

B) Abstraction allows computer programs to aid in the design process.

C) Abstraction allows the details of the implementation to be hidden while the higher-level systems are designed. Without abstraction, the details of the implementation would overwhelm the designer.

D) Abstraction allows analog circuit designers to include digital blocks in their systems.

5.3 The Modern Digital Design Flow

When performing a smaller design or the design of fully-contained sub-systems, the process can be broken down into individual steps. These steps are shown in Figure 5.5. This process is given generically and applies to both *classical* and *modern* digital design. The distinction between classical and modern is that modern digital design uses HDLs and automated CAD tools for simulation, synthesis, place and route, and verification.

Figure 5.5
Generic Digital Design Flow

This generic design process flow can be used across classical and modern digital design, although modern digital design allows additional verification at each step using automated CAD tools. Figure 5.6 shows how this flow is used in the classical design approach of a combinational logic circuit.

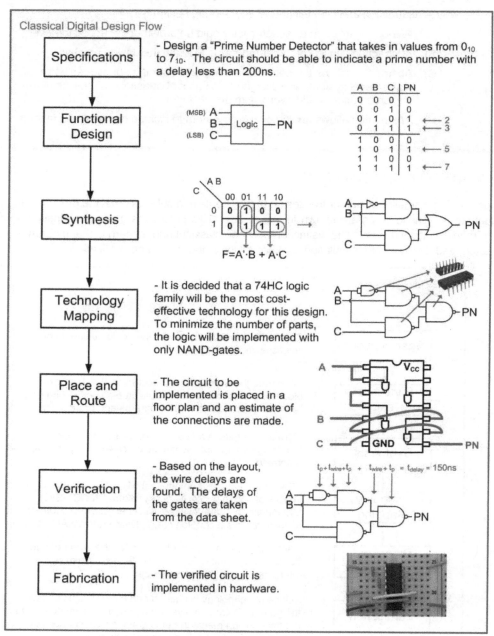

Figure 5.6
Classical Digital Design Flow

The modern design flow based on HDLs includes the ability to simulate functionality at each step of the process. Functional simulations can be performed on the initial behavioral description of the system. At each step of the design process the functionality is described in more detail, ultimately moving toward the fabrication step. At each level, the detailed information can be included in the simulation to verify that the functionality is still correct and that the design is still meeting the original specifications. Figure 5.7 shows the modern digital design flow with the inclusion of simulation capability at each step.

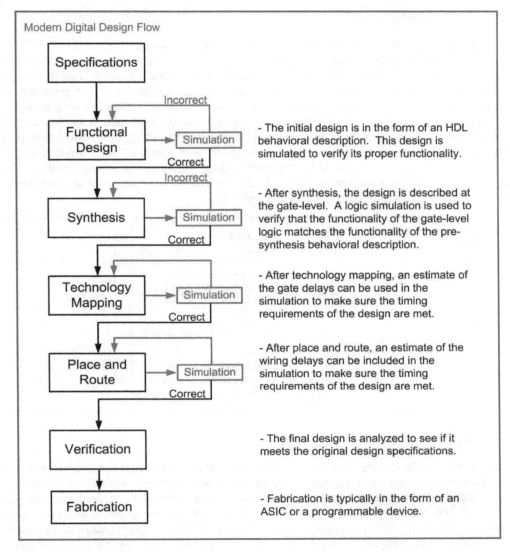

Figure 5.7
Modern Digital Design Flow

CONCEPT CHECK

CC5.3 Why did digital designs move from schematic-entry to text-based HDLs?

    A) HDL models could be much larger by describing functionality in text similar to traditional programming language.

    B) Schematics required sophisticated graphics hardware to display correctly.

    C) Schematics symbols became too small as designs became larger.

    D) Text was easier to understand by a broader range of engineers.

5.4 VHDL Constructs

Now we begin looking at the details of VHDL. A VHDL design describes a single system in a single file. The file has the suffix *.vhd. Within the file, there are two parts that describe the system: the **entity** and the **architecture**. The entity describes the interface to the system (i.e., the inputs and outputs) and the architecture describes the behavior. The functionality of VHDL (e.g., operators, signal types, functions, etc.) is defined in the **package**. Packages are grouped within a **library**. IEEE defines the base set of functionality for VHDL in the *standard* package. This package is contained within a library called *IEEE*. The library and package inclusion is stated at the beginning of a VHDL file before the entity and architecture. Additional functionality can be added to VHDL by including other packages, but all packages are based on the core functionality defined in the standard package. As a result, it is not necessary to explicitly state that a design is using the IEEE standard package because it is inherent in the use of VHDL. All functionality described in this chapter is for the IEEE standard package while other common packages are covered in Chapter 8. Figure 5.8 shows a graphical depiction of a VHDL file.

Figure 5.8
The Anatomy of a VHDL File

VHDL is not case sensitive. Also, each VHDL assignment, definition or declaration is terminated with a semicolon (;). As such, line wraps are allowed and do not signify the end of an assignment, definition or declaration. Line wraps can be used to make the VHDL more readable. Comments in VHDL are preceded with two dashes (i.e., --) and continue until the end of the line. All user-defined names in VHDL must start with an alphabetic letter, not a number. User-defined names are not allowed to be the same as any VHDL keyword. This chapter contains many definitions of syntax in VHDL. The following notations will be used throughout the chapter when introducing new constructs.

bold = VHDL keyword, use as is
italics = User-defined name
<> = A required characteristic such as a data type, input/output, etc.

5.4.1 Data Types

In VHDL, every signal, constant, variable and function must be assigned a *data type*. The IEEE standard package provides a variety of pre-defined data types. Some data types are synthesizable, while others are only for modeling abstract behavior. The following are the most commonly used data types in the VHDL standard package.

5.4.1.1 Enumerated Types

An *enumerated type* is one in which the exact values that the type can take on are defined.

Type	Values that the type can take on
bit	{0, 1}
boolean	{false, true}
character	{"any of the 256 ASCII characters defined in ISO 8859-1"}

The type bit is synthesizable while boolean and character are not. The individual scalar values are indicated by putting them inside single quotes (e.g., '0', 'a', 'true').

5.4.1.2 Range Types

A *range type* is one that can take on any value within a range.

Type	Values that the type can take on
integer	Whole numbers between -2,147,483,648 to +2,147,483,647
real	Fractional numbers between $-1.7e^{38}$ to $+1.7e^{38}$

The integer type is a 32-bit, signed, two's complement number and is synthesizable. If the full range of integer values is not desired, this type can be bounded by including *range <min> to <max>*. The real type is a 32-bit, floating point value and is not directly synthesizable unless an additional package is included that defines the floating point format. The values of these types are indicated by simply using the number without quotes (e.g., 33, 3.14).

5.4.1.3 Physical Types

A *physical type* is one that contains both a value and units. In VHDL, *time* is the primary supported physical type.

Type	Values that the type can take on
time	Whole numbers between -2,147,483,648 to +2,147,483,647

(unit relationships)		
	fs	(femtosecond, 10^{-15}), base unit
	ps = 1000 fs	(picosecond, 10^{-12})
	ns = 1000 ps	(nanosecond, 10^{-9})
	us = 1000 ns	(microsecond, 10^{-6})
	ms = 1000 us	(millisecond, 10^{-3})
	sec = 1000 ms	(second)
	min = 60 sec	(minute)
	hr = 60 min	(hour)

The base unit for time is fs, meaning that if no units are provided, the value is assumed to be in femtoseconds. The value of time is held as a 32-bit, signed number and is not synthesizable.

5.4.1.4 Vector Types

A *vector type* is one that consists of a linear array of scalar types.

Type	Construction
bit_vector	A linear array of type bit
string	A linear array of type character

The size of a vector type is defined by including the maximum index, the keyword **downto**, and the minimum index. For example, if a signal called *BUS_A* was given the type bit_vector(7 downto 0), it would create a vector of 8 scalars, each of type bit. The leftmost scalar would have an index of 7 and the rightmost scalar would have an index of 0. Each of the individual scalars within the vector can be accessed by providing the index number in parentheses. For example, BUS_A(0) would access the scalar in the rightmost position. The indices do not always need to have a minimum value of 0, but this is the most common indexing approach in logic design. The type bit_vector is synthesizable while string is not. The values of these types are indicated by enclosing them inside double quotes (e.g., "0011", "abcd").

5.4.1.5 User-Defined Enumerated Types

A *user-defined enumerated type* is one in which the name of the type is specified by the user in addition to all of the possible values that the type can assume. The creation of a user-defined enumerated type is shown below.

```
type name is (value1, value2, …);
```

Example:

```
type traffic_light is (red, yellow, green);
```

In this example, a new type is created called *traffic_light*. If we declared a new signal called Sig1 and assigned it the type traffic_light, the signal could only take on values of red, yellow and green. User-defined enumerated types are synthesizable in specific applications.

5.4.1.6 Array Type

An *array* contains multiple elements of the same type. Elements within an array can be scalar or vectors. In order to use an array, a new type must be declared that defines the configuration of the array. Once the new type is created, signals may be declared of that type. The *range* of the array must be defined in the array type declaration. The range is specified with integers (min and max) and either the keywords *downto* or *to*. The creation of an array type is shown below.

```
type name is array (<range>) of <element_type>;
```

Example:

```
type block_8x16 is array (0 to 7) bit_vector(15 downto 0);
signal my_array : block_8x16;
```

In this example, the new array type is declared with 8 elements. The beginning index of the array is 0 and the ending index is 7. Each element in the array is a 16-bit vector of type bit_vector.

5.4.1.7 Subtypes

A *subtype* is a constrained version, or subset of another type. Subtypes are user-defined, although a few commonly used subtypes are pre-defined in the standard package. The following is the syntax for declaring a subtype and two examples of commonly used subtypes (NATURAL and POSTIVE) that are defined in the standard package.

```
subtype name is <type> range <min> to <max>;
```

Example:

```
subtype NATURAL is integer range 0 to 255;
subtype POSTIVE is integer range 1 to 256;
```

5.4.2 Libraries and Packages

As mentioned earlier, the IEEE standard package is implied when using VHDL; however, we can use it as an example of how to include packages in VHDL. The keyword **library** is used to signify that packages are going to be added to the VHDL design from the specified library. The name of the library follows this keyword. To include a specific package from the library, a new line is used with the keyword **use** followed by the package details. The package syntax has three fields separated with a period. The first field is the library name. The second field is the package name. The third field is the specific functionality of the package to be included. If all functionality of a package is to be used, then the keyword **all** is used in the third field. Examples of how to include some of the commonly-used packages from the IEEE library are shown below.

```
library IEEE;
use IEEE.std_logic_1164.all;
use IEEE.numeric_std.all;
use IEEE.std_logic_textio.all;
```

5.4.3 The Entity

The entity in VHDL describes the inputs and outputs of the system. These are called **ports**. Each port needs to have its name, mode and type specified. The name is user-defined. The mode describes the direction data is transferred through the port and can take on values of **in**, **out**, **inout** and **buffer**. The type is one of the legal data types described above. Port names with the same mode and type can be listed on the same line separated by commas. The definition of an entity is given below.

```
entity entity_name is
   port (port_name   : <mode> <type>;
         port_name   : <mode> <type>);
end entity;
```

Example 5.1 shows multiple approaches for defining an entity.

Example 5.1
Defining VHDL Entities

5.4.4 The Architecture

The architecture in VHDL describes the behavior of a system. There are numerous techniques to describe behavior in VHDL that span multiple levels of abstraction. The architecture is where the majority of the design work is conducted. The form of a generic architecture is given below.

```
architecture architecture_name of <entity associated with> is

   -- user-defined enumerated type declarations      (optional)
   -- signal declarations                            (optional)
   -- constant declarations                          (optional)
   -- component declarations                         (optional)


   begin

   -- behavioral description of the system goes here

   end architecture;
```

5.4.4.1 Signal Declarations

A signal that is used for internal connections within a system is declared in the architecture. Each signal must be declared with a type. The signal can only be used to make connections of like types. A signal is declared with the keyword **signal** followed by a user-defined name, colon and the type. Signals of like type can be declared on the same line separated with a comma. All of the legal data types described above can be used for signals. Signals represent wires within the system so they do not have a direction or mode. Signals cannot have the same name as a port in the system in which they reside. The syntax for a signal declaration is as follows:

```
signal name : <type>;
```

Example:

```
signal node1  : bit;
signal a1, b1 : integer;
signal Bus3   : bit_vector (15 downto 0);
signal C_int  : integer range 0 to 255;
```

VHDL supports a hierarchical design approach. Signal names can be the same within a sub-system as those at a higher level without conflict. Figure 5.9 shows an example of legal signal naming in a hierarchical design.

Figure 5.9
VHDL Signals and Systems

5.4.4.2 Constant Declarations

A constant is useful for representing a quantity that will be used multiple times in the architecture. The syntax for declaring a constant is as follows:

```
constant constant_name : <type> := <value>;
```

Example:

```
constant BUS_WIDTH : integer := 32;
```

Once declared, the constant name can now be used throughout the architecture. The following example illustrates how we can use a constant to define the size of a vector. Notice that since we defined the constant to be the actual width of the vector (i.e., 32-bits), we need to subtract one from its value when defining the indices (i.e., 31 downto 0).

Example:

```
signal BUS_A : bit_vector (BUS_WIDTH-1 downto 0);
```

5.4.4.3 Component Declarations

A **component** is the term used for a VHDL sub-system that is instantiated within a higher level system. If a component is going to be used within a system, it must be declared in the architecture before the begin statement. The syntax for a component declaration is as follows.

```
component component_name
    port (port_name   : <mode> <type>;
          port_name   : <mode> <type>);
end component;
```

The port definitions of the component must match the port definitions of the sub-system's entity exactly. As such, these lines are typically copied directly from the lower level systems VHDL entity description. Once declared, a component can be instantiated after the begin statement in the architecture as many times as needed.

CONCEPT CHECK

CC5.4(a) Why don't we need to explicitly include the STANDARD package when creating a VHDL design?

    A) It defines the base functionality of VHDL so its use is implied.

    B) The simulator will automatically add it to the .vhd file upon compile.

    C) It isn't recognized by synthesizers so it shouldn't be included.

    D) It is a historical artifact that that isn't used anymore.

CC5.4(b) What is the difference between types Boolean {TRUE, FALSE} and bit {0, 1}?

    A) They are the same.

    B) Boolean is used for decision making constructs (when, else) while bit is used to model real digital signals.

    C) Logical operators work with type Boolean but not for type bit.

    D) Only type bit is synthesizable.

5.5 Modeling Concurrent Functionality in VHDL

It is important to remember that VHDL is a hardware description language, not a programming language. In a programming language, the lines of code are executed sequentially as they appear in the source file. In VHDL, the lines of code represent the behavior of real hardware. As a result, all signal assignments are by default executed concurrently unless specifically noted otherwise. All operations in VHDL must be on like types and the result must be assigned to the same type as the operation inputs.

5.5.1 VHDL Operators

There are a variety of pre-defined operators in the IEEE standard package. It is important to note that operators are defined to work on specific data types and that not all operators are synthesizable.

5.5.1.1 Assignment Operator

VHDL uses **<=** for all signal assignments and **:=** for all variable and initialization assignments. These assignment operators work on all data types. The target of the assignment goes on the left of these operators and the input arguments go on the right.

Example:

```
F1 <= A;        -- F1 and A must be the same size and type
F2 <= '0';      -- F2 is type bit in this example
F3 <= "0000";   -- F3 is type bit_vector(3 downto 0) in this example
F4 <= "hello";  -- F4 is type string in this example
F5 <= 3.14;     -- F5 is type real in this example
F6 <= x"1A";    -- F6 is type bit_vector(7 downto 0), x"1A" is in HEX
```

5.5.1.2 Logical Operators

VHDL contains the following logical operators:

Operator	Operation
not	logical negation
and	logical AND
nand	logical NAND
or	logical OR

nor	logical NOR
xor	logical Exclusive-OR
xnor	logical Exclusive-NOR

These operators work on types bit, bit_vector and boolean. For operations on the type bit_vector, the input vectors must be the same size and will take place in a bit-wise fashion. For example, if two 8-bit buses called BusA and BusB were AND'd together, BusA(0) would be individually AND'd with BusB(0), BusA(1) would be individually AND'd with BusB(1), etc. The not operator is a unary operation (i.e., it operates on a single input), and the keyword is put before the signal being operated on. All other operators have two or more inputs and are placed in-between the input names.

Example:

```
F1 <= not A;
F2 <= B and C;
```

The order of precedence in VHDL is different from in Boolean algebra. The NOT operator is a higher priority than all other operators. All other logical operators have the same priority and have no inherent precedence. This means that in VHDL, the AND operator will *not* precede the OR operation as it does in Boolean algebra. Parentheses are used to explicitly describe precedence. If operators are used that have the same priority and parentheses are not provided, then the operations will take place on the signals listed first moving left to right in the signal assignment. The following are examples on how to use these operators.

Example:

```
F3 <= not D nand E;        -- D will be complemented first, the result
                           -- will then be NAND'd with E, then the
                           -- result will be assigned to F3
F4 <= not (F or G);        -- the parentheses take precedence so
                           -- F will be OR'd with G first, then
                   -- complemented, and then assigned to F4.

F5 <= H nor I nor J;    -- logic operations can have any number of
                           -- inputs.

F6 <= K xor L xnor M;   -- XOR and XNOR have the same priority so with
                           -- no parentheses given, the logic operations
                           -- will take place on the signals from
                           -- left to right. K will be XOR'd with L first,
                           -- then the result will be XNOR'd with M.
```

5.5.1.3 Numerical Operators

VHDL contains the following numerical operators:

Operator	Operation
+	addition
-	subtraction
*	multiplication
/	division
mod	modulus
rem	remainder
abs	absolute value
**	exponential

These operators work on types integer and real. Note that the default VHDL standard does not support numerical operators on types bit and bit_vector.

5.5.1.4 Relational Operators

VHDL contains the following relational operators. These operators compare two inputs of the same type and returns the type boolean (i.e., true or false).

Operator	Returns true if the comparison is:
=	equal
/=	not equal
<	less than
<=	less than or equal
>	greater than
>=	greater than or equal

5.5.1.5 Shift Operators

VHDL contains the following shift operators. These operators work on vector types bit_vector and string.

Operator	Operation
sll	shift left logical
srl	shift right logical
sla	shift left arithmetic
sra	shift right arithmetic
rol	rotate left
ror	rotate right

The syntax for using a shift operation is to provide the name of the vector followed by the desired shift operator, followed by an integer indicating how many shift operations to perform. The target of the assignment must be the same type and size as the input.

Example:

```
A <= B srl 3;          -- A is assigned the result of a logical shift
                       -- right 3 times on B.
```

5.5.1.6 Concatenation Operator

In VHDL the **&** is used to concatenate multiple signals. The target of this operation must be the same size of the sum of the sizes of the input arguments.

Example:

```
Bus1 <= "11" & "00";   -- Bus1 must be 4-bits and will be assigned
            -- the value "1100"

Bus2 <= BusA & BusB;   -- If BusA and BusB are 4-bits, then Bus2
                            -- must be 8-bits.

Bus3 <= '0' & BusA;    -- This attaches a leading '0' to BusA.  Bus3
                            -- must be 5-bits
```

5.5.2 Concurrent Signal Assignments

Concurrent signal assignments are accomplished by simply using the <= operator after the begin statement in the architecture. Each individual assignment will be executed concurrently and synthesized as separate logic circuits. Consider the following example.

Example:

```
X <= A;
Y <= B;
Z <= C;
```

When simulated, these three lines of VHDL will make three separate signal assignments at the exact same time. This is different from a programming language that will first assign A to X, then B to Y and finally C to Z. In VHDL this functionality is identical to three separate wires. This description will be directly synthesized into three separate wires.

Below is another example of how concurrent signal assignments in VHDL differ from a sequentially executed programming language.

Example:

```
A <= B;
B <= C;
```

In a VHDL simulation, the signal assignments of C to B and B to A will take place at the same time; however, during synthesis, the signal B will be eliminated from the design since this functionality describes two wires in series. Automated synthesis tools will eliminate this unnecessary signal name. This is not the same functionality that would result if this example was implemented as a sequentially executed computer program. A computer program would execute the assignment of B to A first, then assign the value of C to B second. In this way, B represents a storage element that is passed to A before it is updated with C.

5.5.3 Concurrent Signal Assignments with Logical Operators

Each of the logical operators described in Section 5.5.1.2 can be used in conjunction with concurrent signal assignments to create individual combinational logic circuits. Example 5.2 shows how to design a VHDL model of a combinational logic circuit using this approach.

Example: Modeling Logic using Concurrent Signal Assignments and Logical Operators

Implement the following truth table using <u>concurrent signal assignments with logical operators</u>.

A	B	C	F
0	0	0	1
0	0	1	0
0	1	0	1
0	1	1	0
1	0	0	0
1	0	1	0
1	1	0	1
1	1	1	0

First, let's design the entity. Let's call the entity *SystemX*. The entity will have three inputs (A, B, C) and one output (F). We'll use the type bit for all inputs/outputs so that this will synthesize directly into real circuitry.

```
entity SystemX is
    port (A, B, C  :  in  bit;
              F     :  out bit);
end entity;
```

Now we design the architecture. We can create a canonical sum of products logic expression for this truth table using minterms.

$$F = \Sigma_{A,B,C}(0,2,6) = A' \cdot B' \cdot C' + A' \cdot B \cdot C' + A \cdot B \cdot C'$$

Drawing out the logic diagram will help us understand which internal signals need to be declared for the interim connections. Since there is a need for the complement of each of the inputs, the first set of logic will be three inverters. We'll need to create three signals to hold the inverted versions of the inputs. Let's call them An, Bn and Cn. We'll also need three signal to hold the outputs of the AND gates. Let's call them m0, m2 and m6. Using these internal signals, the port names from the entity, and logical operators, we can describe the behavior of the logic expression above.

```
architecture SystemX_arch of SystemX is

    signal  An, Bn, Cn : bit;
    signal  m0, m2, m6 : bit;

begin

    An <= not A;              -- NOT's
    Bn <= not B;
    Cn <= not C;

    m0 <= An and Bn and Cn; -- AND's
    m2 <= An and B  and Cn;
    m6 <= A  and B  and Cn;

    F  <= m0 or m2 or m6;    -- OR

end architecture;
```

Example 5.2
Modeling Logic using Concurrent Signal Assignments and Logical Operators

5.5.4 Conditional Signal Assignments

Logical operators are good for describing the behavior of small circuits; however, in the prior example we still needed to create the canonical sum of products logic expression by hand before describing the functionality in VHDL. The true power of an HDL is when the behavior of the system can be described fully without requiring any hand design. A conditional signal assignment allows us to describe a concurrent signal assignment using Boolean conditions that effect the values of the result. In a conditional signal assignment, the keyword **when** is used to describe the signal assignment for a particular Boolean condition. The keyword **else** is used to describe the signal assignments for any other conditions. Multiple Boolean conditions can be used to fully describe the output of the circuit under all input conditions. Logical operators can also be used in the Boolean conditions to create more sophisticated conditions. The Boolean conditions can be encompassed within parentheses for readability. The syntax for a conditional signal assignment is shown below.

```
signal_name <= expression_1 when condition_1 else
               expression_2 when condition_2 else
                          :
               expression_n;
```

Example:

```
F1 <= '0' when A='0' else '1';
F2 <= '1' when (A='0' and B='1') else '0';
F3 <= A when (C = D) else B;
```

An important consideration of conditional signal assignments is that they are still executed concurrently. Each assignment represents a separate, combinational logic circuit. In the above example, F1, F2 and F3 will be implemented as three separate circuits. Example 5.3 shows how to design a VHDL model of a combinational logic circuit using conditional signal assignments. Note that this example uses the same truth table as in Example 5.2 to illustrate a comparison between approaches.

Example: Modeling Logic using Conditional Signal Assignments
Implement the following truth table using a <u>conditional signal assignment</u>.

A	B	C	F
0	0	0	1
0	0	1	0
0	1	0	1
0	1	1	0
1	0	0	0
1	0	1	0
1	1	0	1
1	1	1	0

```
entity SystemX is
    port (A, B, C  :  in  bit;
          F        :  out bit);
end entity;
```

We can implement the entire truth table in its current form using a conditional signal assignment. While this is a verbose approach, it is sometimes more readable.

```
architecture SystemX_arch of SystemX is

begin

    F <= '1' when (A='0' and B='0' and C='0') else
         '0' when (A='0' and B='0' and C='1') else
         '1' when (A='0' and B='1' and C='0') else
         '0' when (A='0' and B='1' and C='1') else
         '0' when (A='1' and B='0' and C='0') else
         '0' when (A='1' and B='0' and C='1') else
         '1' when (A='1' and B='1' and C='0') else
         '0' when (A='1' and B='1' and C='1');

end architecture;
```

We can also reduce this into a more compressed form by only stating the input conditions that correspond to an output of '1' and using the "else" statement to produce an output of '0' for all other input codes.

```
architecture SystemX_arch of SystemX is

begin

    F <= '1' when (A='0' and B='0' and C='0') else
         '1' when (A='0' and B='1' and C='0') else
         '1' when (A='1' and B='1' and C='0') else
         '0';

end architecture;
```

Example 5.3
Modeling Logic using Conditional Signal Assignments

5.5.5 Selected Signal Assignments

A selected signal assignment provides another technique to implement concurrent signal assignments. In this approach, the signal assignment is based on a specific value on the input signal. The keyword **with** is used to begin the selected signal assignment. It is then followed by the name of the input that will be used to dictate the value of the output. Only a single variable name can be listed as the input. This means that if the assignment is going to be based on multiple variables, they must first be concatenated into a single vector name before starting the selected signal assignment. After the input is listed, the keyword **select** signifies the beginning of the signal assignments. An assignment is made to a signal based on a list of possible input values that follow the keyword **when**. Multiple values of the input codes can be used and are separated by commas. The keyword **others** is used to cover any input values that are not explicitly stated. The syntax for a selected signal assignment is as follows:

```
with input_name select
    signal_name <= expression_1 when condition_1,
                   expression_2 when condition_2,
                          :
                   expression_n when others;
```

Example:

```
with A select
  F1 <= '1' when '0', -- F1 will be assigned '1' when A='0'
        '0' when '1'; -- F1 will be assigned '0' when A='1'


AB <= A&B; -- concatenate A and B so that they can be used as a vector
with AB select
  F2 <= '0' when "00", -- F2 will be assigned '0' when AB="00"
        '1' when "01",
        '1' when "10",
        '0' when "11";


with AB select
  F3 <= '1' when "01",
        '1' when "10",
        '0' when others;
```

One feature of selected signal assignments that makes its form even more compact is that multiple input codes that correspond to the same output assignment can be listed on the same line pipe (|)-delimited. The example for F3 can be equivalently described as:

```
with AB select
  F3 <= '1' when "01" | "10",
        '0' when others;
```

Example 5.4 shows how to design a VHDL model of a combinational logic circuit using selected signal assignments. Note that this example again uses the same truth table as in Example 5.2 and Example 5.3 to illustrate a comparison between approaches.

Example: Modeling Logic using Selected Signal Assignments

Implement the following truth table using a <u>selected signal assignment</u>.

```
A B C | F
0 0 0 | 1
0 0 1 | 0
0 1 0 | 1
0 1 1 | 0
1 0 0 | 0
1 0 1 | 0
1 1 0 | 1
1 1 1 | 0
```

```
entity SystemX is
    port (A, B, C  :  in  bit;
          F        :  out bit);
end entity;
```

We can implement the entire truth table in its current form using a selected signal assignment. Since we are basing our output values on three separate scalar inputs, we need to concatenate them into a vector so that the new vector name can be used as the input in the selected signal assignment. We'll first declare a new signal called "ABC" of type bit_vector(2 downto 0). After the begin statement, we'll assign the concatenation of A, B and C to this vector. The new vector name can now be used as an input.

```
architecture SystemX_arch of SystemX is

  signal ABC : bit_vector(2 downto 0);

begin

  ABC <= A & B & C;

  with (ABC) select
    F <= '1' when "000",
         '0' when "001",
         '1' when "010",
         '0' when "011",
         '0' when "100",
         '0' when "101",
         '1' when "110",
         '0' when "111";

end architecture;
```

We can reduce the size of the selected signal assignment by only listing the input codes corresponding to an output of '1' and use the "others" keyword to handle all input codes corresponding to an output of '0'.

```
architecture SystemX_arch of SystemX is

  signal ABC : bit_vector(2 downto 0);

begin

  ABC <= A & B & C;

  with (ABC) select
    F <= '1' when "000",
         '1' when "010",
         '1' when "110",
         '0' when others;

end architecture;
```

We can further reduce the size of the selected signal assignment by pipe delimiting the input codes corresponding to an output of '1'.

```
architecture SystemX_arch of SystemX is

  signal ABC : bit_vector(2 downto 0);

begin

  ABC <= A & B & C;

  with (ABC) select
    F <= '1' when "000"|"010"|"110",
         '0' when others;

end architecture;
```

Example 5.4
Modeling Logic using Selected Signal Assignments

5.5.6 Delayed Signal Assignments

VHDL provides the ability to delay a concurrent signal assignment in order to more accurately model the behavior of real gates. The keyword **after** is used to delay an assignment by a certain amount of time. The magnitude of the delay is provided as type time. The syntax for delaying an assignment is as follows:

```
signal_name <= <expression> after <time>;
```

Example:

```
A <= B after 3us;
C <= D and E after 10ns;
```

If an input pulse is shorter in duration than the amount of the delay, the input pulse is ignored. This is called the *inertial delay model*. Example 5.5 shows how to design a VHDL model with a delayed signal assignment using the inertial delay model.

Example 5.5
Modeling Logic using Delayed Signal Assignments (Inertial Delay Model)

Ignoring brief input pulses on the input accurately models the behavior of on-chip gates. When the input pulse is faster than the delay of the gate, the output of the gate does not have time to respond. As a result, there will not be a logic change on the output. If it is desired to have all pulses on the inputs show up on the outputs when modeling the behavior of other types of digital logic, the keyword **transport** is used in conjunction with the after statement. This is called the *transport delay model*.

```
signal_name <= transport <expression> after <time>;
```

Example 5.6 shows how to perform a delayed signal assignment using the transport delay model.

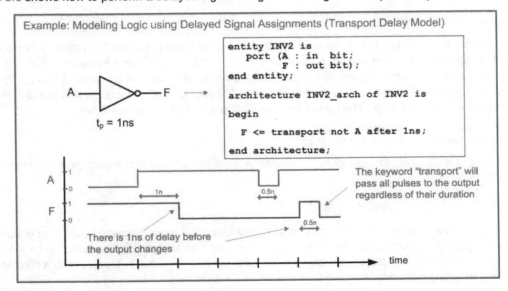

Example 5.6
Modeling Logic using Delayed Signal Assignments (Transport Delay Model)

CONCEPT CHECK

CC5.5(a) Why is concurrency such an important concept in HDLs?

A) Concurrency is a feature of HDLs that can't be modeled using schematics.

B) Concurrency allows automated synthesis to be performed.

C) Concurrency allows logic simulators to display useful system information.

D) Concurrency is necessary to model real systems that operate in parallel.

CC5.5(b) Why does modeling combinational logic in its canonical form with concurrent signal assignments with logical operators defeat the purpose of the modern digital design flow?

A) It requires the designer to first create the circuit using the classical digital design approach and then enter it into the HDL in a form that is essentially a text-based netlist. This doesn't take advantage of the abstraction capabilities and automated synthesis in the modern flow.

B) It cannot be synthesized because the order of precedence of the logical operators in VHDL doesn't match the precedence defined in Boolean algebra.

C) The circuit is in its simplest form so there is no work for the synthesizer to do.

D) It doesn't allow an *else* clause to cover the outputs for any remaining input codes not explicitly listed.

5.6 Structural Design using Components

Structural design in VHDL refers to including lower level sub-systems within a higher level system in order to produce the desired functionality. A purely structural VHDL design would not contain any behavioral modeling in the architecture such as signal assignments, but instead just contain the instantiation and interconnections of other sub-systems. A sub-system is called a **component** in VHDL. For any component that is going to be used in an architecture, it must be declared before the begin statement. Refer to section 5.4.4.3 for the syntax of declaring a component. A specific component only needs to be declared once. After the begin statement it can be used as many times as necessary. Each component is executed concurrently.

5.6.1 Component Instantiation

The term *instantiation* refers to the *use* or *inclusion* of the component in the VHDL system. When a component is instantiated, it needs to be given a unique identifying name. This is called the *instance name*. To instantiate a component, the instance name is given first, followed by a colon and then the component name. The last part of instantiating a component is connecting signals to its ports. The way in which signals are connected to the ports of the component is called the **port map**. The syntax for instantiating a component is as follows:

```
instance_name : <component name>
   port map (<port connections>);
```

There are two techniques to connect signals to the ports of the component, *explicit port mapping* and *positional port mapping*.

5.6.1.1 Explicit Port Mapping

In explicit port mapping the name of each port of the component is given, followed by the connection indicator **=>**, followed by the signal it is connected to. The port connections can be listed in any order since the details of the connection (i.e., port name to signal name) are explicit. Each connection name is separated by a comma. The syntax for explicit port mapping is as follows:

```
instance_name : <component name>
   port map (port1 => signal1, port2 => signal2, ...);
```

Example 5.7 shows how to design a VHDL model of a combinational logic circuit using structural VHDL and explicit port mapping. Note that this example again uses the same truth table as in Example 5.2, Example 5.3, and Example 5.4 to illustrate a comparison between approaches.

Example 5.7
Modeling Logic using Structural VHDL (Explicit Port Mapping)

5.6.1.1 Positional Port Mapping

In positional port mapping the names of the ports of the component are not explicitly listed. Instead, the signals are listed in the same order that the ports of the component were defined. Each signal name is separated by a comma. This approach requires less text to describe but can also lead to misconnections due to mismatches in the order of the signals being connected. The syntax for positional port mapping is as follows:

```
    instance_name : <component name>
        port map (signal1, signal2, ...);
```

Example 5.8 shows how to create the same structural VHDL model as in Example 5.7, but using positional port mapping instead.

```
Example: Modeling Logic using Structural VHDL (Positional Port Mapping)
In positional port mapping the port names are not listed in the component instantiation.
Instead, the signals are simply listed in the same order as the ports were defined.  The signal
listed first will be connected to the port defined first.  The signal listed second will be
connected to the port defined second, etc.
```

Explicit Port Mapping	```begin``` ```U1 : INV1 port map (A=>A, F=>An);``` ```U2 : INV1 port map (A=>B, F=>Bn);``` ```U3 : INV1 port map (A=>C, F=>Cn);``` ```U4 : AND3 port map (A=>An, B=>Bn, C=>Cn, F=>m0);``` ```U5 : AND3 port map (A=>An, B=>B, C=>Cn, F=>m2);``` ```U6 : AND3 port map (A=>A, B=>B, C=>Cn, F=>m6);``` ```U7 : OR3 port map (A=>m0, B=>m2, C=>m6, F=>F);```
Positional Port Mapping of Same System	```begin``` ```U1 : INV1 port map (A, An);``` ```U2 : INV1 port map (B, Bn);``` ```U3 : INV1 port map (C, Cn);``` ```U4 : AND3 port map (An, Bn, Cn, m0);``` ```U5 : AND3 port map (An, B, Cn, m2);``` ```U6 : AND3 port map (A, B, Cn, m6);``` ```U7 : OR3 port map (m0, m2, m6, F);```

Example 5.8
Modeling Logic using Structural VHDL (Positional Port Mapping)

CONCEPT CHECK

CC5.6   Does the use of components model concurrent functionality? Why?

   A)   No. Since the lower level behavior of the component being instantiated may contain non-concurrent behavior, it is not known what functionality will be modeled.

   B)   Yes. The components are treated like independent sub-systems whose behavior runs in parallel just as if separate parts were placed in a design.

5.7 Overview of Simulation Test Benches

One of the essential components of the modern digital design flow is verifying functionality through simulation. This simulation takes place at many levels of abstraction. For a system to be tested, there needs to be a mechanism to generate input patterns to drive the system and then observe the outputs to verify correct operation. The mechanism to do this in VHDL is called a **test bench**. A test bench is a file in VHDL that has no inputs or outputs. The test bench declares the system to be tested as a component and then instantiates it. The test bench generates the input conditions and drives them into the input ports of the system being tested. VHDL contains numerous methods to generate stimulus patterns. Since a test bench will not be synthesized, very abstract behavioral modeling can be used to generate the inputs. The output of the system can be viewed as a waveform in a simulation tool. VHDL also has the ability to check the outputs against the expected results and notify the user if differences occur. Figure 5.10 gives an overview of how test benches are used in VHDL. The techniques to generate the stimulus patterns are covered in Chapter 8.

Overview of VHDL Test Benches

A test bench is used to drive in signals and observe the outputs of a "device under test" or DUT. A test bench has no inputs or outputs. It calls the DUT as a component and then generates the inputs to verify its functionality.

SystemX_TB

The test bench is typically named the same as the DUT but with "_TB" at the end.

Stimulus

SystemX (DUT)

The design to be tested is declared as a component and instantiated in the test bench. Signals are declared to connect to the ports of the DUT.

Stimulus patterns are generated in the test bench and driven into the DUT. The patterns should cover every possible input condition.

The output of the DUT can be viewed as a waveform in a simulation tool. VHDL also has constructs to perform automated checking against a description of the expected outputs.

```
entity SystemX_TB is
end entity;

architecture SystemX_TB_arch of SystemX_TB is

  component SystemX                    -- Component Declaration
    port (A, B, C  : in  bit;
          F        : out bit);
  end component;

  signal   A_TB, B_TB, C_TB : bit;     -- Signal Declaration
  signal   F_TB             : bit;

  begin

  DUT1 : SystemX port map (A => A_TB,   -- DUT Instantiation
                           B => B_TB,
                           C => C_TB,
                           F => F_TB);

  -- Stimulus Generation to Drive A_TB, B_TB and C_TB
  -- (covered in Chapter 8)

  -- Automated Output Checking & Reporting for F_TB
  -- (covered in Chapter 8)

end architecture;
```

Figure 5.10
Overview of VHDL Test Benches

CONCEPT CHECK

CC5.7   How can the output of a DUT be verified when it is connected to a signal that does not go anywhere?

A)   It can't. The output must be routed to an output port on the test bench.

B)   The values of any dangling signal are automatically written to a text file.

C)   It is viewed in the logic simulator as either a waveform or text listing.

D)   It can't. A signal that does not go anywhere will cause an error when the VHDL file is compiled.

Summary

❖ The modern digital design flow relies on computer aided engineering (CAE) and computer aided design (CAD) tools to manage the size and complexity of today's digital designs.

❖ Hardware description languages (HDLs) allow the functionality of digital systems to be entered using text. VHDL and Verilog are the two most common HDLs in use today.

❖ VHDL was originally created to document the behavior of large digital systems and support functional simulations.

❖ The ability to automatically synthesize a logic circuit from a VHDL behavioral description became possible approximately 10 years after the original definition of VHDL. As such, only a sub-set of the behavioral modeling techniques in VHDL can be automatically synthesized.

❖ HDLs can model digital systems at different levels of design abstraction. These include the *system*, *algorithmic*, *RTL*, *gate*, and *circuit* levels. Designing at a higher level of abstraction allows more complex systems to be modeled without worrying about the details of the implementation.

❖ In a VHDL source file there are three main sections. These are the package, the entity, and the architecture. Including a package allows additional functionality to be included in VHDL. The entity is where the inputs and outputs of the system are declared. The architecture is where the behavior of the system is described.

❖ A *port* is an input or output to a system that is declared in the entity. A *signal* is an internal connection within the system that is declared in the architecture. A signal is not visible outside of the system.

❖ A *component* is how a VHDL system uses another sub-system. A component is first *declared*, which defines the name and entity of the sub-system to be used. The component can then be *instantiated* one or more times. The ports of the component can be connected using either *explicit* or *positional port mapping*.

❖ *Concurrency* is the term that describes operations being performed in parallel. This allows real-world system behavior to be modeled.

❖ VHDL contains three direct techniques to model concurrent logic behavior. These are *concurrent signal assignments with logical operators*, *conditional signal assignments*, and *selected signal assignments*.

❖ VHDL components are also treated as concurrent sub-systems.

❖ Delay can be modeled in VHDL using either the *initial* or *transport* model.

❖ A *simulation test bench* is a VHDL file that drives stimulus into a device under test (DUT). Test benches do not have inputs or outputs and are not synthesizable.

Exercise Problems

Section 5.1 – History of HDLs

5.1.1   What was the original purpose of VHDL?

5.1.2   Can all of the functionality that can be described in VHDL be simulated?

5.1.3   Can all of the functionality that can be described in VHDL be synthesized?

Section 5.2 – HDL Abstraction

5.2.1   Give the level of design abstraction that the following statement relates to: *if there is ever an error in the system, it should return to the reset state.*

5.2.2   Give the level of design abstraction that the following statement relates to: *once the design is implemented in a sum of products form, DeMorgan's Theorem will be used to convert it to a NAND-gate only implementation.*

5.2.3   Give the level of design abstraction that the following statement relates to: *the design will be broken down into two sub-systems, one that will handle data collection and the other that will control data flow.*

5.2.4   Give the level of design abstraction that the following statement relates to: *the interconnect on the IC should be changed from aluminum to copper to achieve the performance needed in this design.*

5.2.5   Give the level of design abstraction that the following statement relates to: *the MOSFETs need to be able to drive at least 8 other loads in this design.*

5.2.6   Give the level of design abstraction that the following statement relates to: *this system will contain 1 host computer and support up to 1000 client computers.*

5.2.7   Give the design domain that the following activity relates to: *drawing the physical layout of the CPU will require six months of engineering time.*

5.2.8   Give the design domain that the following activity relates to: *the CPU will be connected to 4 banks of memory.*

5.2.9   Give the design domain that the following activity relates to: *the fan-in specifications for this logic family require excessive logic circuitry to be used.*

5.2.10   Give the design domain that the following activity relates to: *the performance specifications for this system require 1 TFLOP at < 5W.*

Section 5.3 – The Modern Digital Design Flow

5.3.1   Which step in the modern digital design flow does the following statement relate to: *a CAD tool will convert the behavioral model into a gate-level description of functionality.*

5.3.2 Which <u>step in the modern digital design flow</u> does the following statement relate to: after realistic gate and wiring delays are determined, one last simulation should be performed to make sure the design meets the original timing requirements.

5.3.3 Which <u>step in the modern digital design flow</u> does the following statement relate to: if the memory is distributed around the perimeter of the CPU, the wiring density will be minimized.

5.3.4 Which <u>step in the modern digital design flow</u> does the following statement relate to: *the design meets all requirements so now I'm building the hardware that will be shipped.*

5.3.5 Which <u>step in the modern digital design flow</u> does the following statement relate to: *the system will be broken down into three sub-systems with the following behaviors.*

5.3.6 Which <u>step in the modern digital design flow</u> does the following statement relate to: *this system needs to have 10 Gbytes of memory.*

5.3.7 Which <u>step in the modern digital design flow</u> does the following statement relate to: *to meet the power requirements, the gates will be implemented in the 74HC logic family.*

Section 5.4 – VHDL Constructs

5.4.1 In which construct of VHDL are the inputs and outputs of the system defined?

5.4.2 In which construct of VHDL is the behavior of the system described?

5.4.3 Which construct is used to add additional functionality such as data types to VHDL?

5.4.4 What are all the possible values that the type *bit* can take on in VHDL?

5.4.5 What are all the possible values that the type *boolean* can take on in VHDL?

5.4.6 What is the range of decimal numbers that can be represented using the type *integer* in VHDL?

5.4.7 What is the width of the vector defined using the type *bit_vector(63 downto 0)*?

5.4.8 What is the syntax for indexing the most significant bit in the type *bit_vector(31 downto 0)*? Assume the vector is named *example*.

5.4.9 What is the syntax for indexing the least significant bit in the type *bit_vector(31 downto 0)*? Assume the vector is named *example*.

5.4.10 What is the difference between an *enumerated* type and a *range* type?

5.4.11 What scalar type does a *bit_vector* consist of?

5.4.12 What scalar type does a *string* consist of?

Section 5.5 – Modeling Concurrent Functionality in VHDL

5.5.1 Design a VHDL model to implement the behavior described by the 3-input minterm list shown in Figure 5.11. Use <u>concurrent signal assignments and logical operators</u>. Declare your entity to match the block diagram provided. Use the type bit for your ports.

$$F = \sum_{A,B,C}(1,3,4,6)$$

Figure 5.11

5.5.2 Design a VHDL model to implement the behavior described by the 3-input minterm list shown in Figure 5.11. Use <u>conditional signal assignments</u>. Declare your entity to match the block diagram provided. Use the type bit for your ports.

5.5.3 Design a VHDL model to implement the behavior described by the 3-input minterm list shown in Figure 5.11. Use <u>selected signal assignments</u>. Declare your entity to match the block diagram provided. Use the type bit for your ports.

5.5.4 Design a VHDL model to implement the behavior described by the 3-input maxterm list shown in Figure 5.12. Use <u>concurrent signal assignments and logical operators</u>. Declare your entity to match the block diagram provided. Use the type bit for your ports.

$$F = \prod_{A,B,C}(0,1,3,5,7)$$

Figure 5.12

5.5.5 Design a VHDL model to implement the behavior described by the 3-input maxterm list shown in Figure 5.12. Use <u>conditional signal assignments</u>. Declare your entity to match the block diagram provided. Use the type bit for your ports.

5.5.6 Design a VHDL model to implement the behavior described by the 3-input maxterm list shown in Figure 5.12. Use <u>selected signal assignments</u>. Declare your entity to match the block diagram provided. Use the type bit for your ports.

5.5.7 Design a VHDL model to implement the behavior described by the 3-input truth table shown in Figure 5.13. Use <u>concurrent signal assignments and logical operators</u>. Declare your entity to match the block diagram provided. Use the type bit for your ports.

A	B	C	F
0	0	0	1
0	0	1	1
0	1	0	0
0	1	1	0
1	0	0	1
1	0	1	0
1	1	0	0
1	1	1	0

Figure 5.13

5.5.8 Design a VHDL model to implement the behavior described by the 3-input truth table shown in Figure 5.13. Use <u>conditional signal assignments</u>. Declare your entity to match the block diagram provided. Use the type bit for your ports.

5.5.9 Design a VHDL model to implement the behavior described by the 3-input truth table shown in Figure 5.13. Use <u>selected signal assignments</u>. Declare your entity to match the block diagram provided. Use the type bit for your ports.

5.5.10 Design a VHDL model to implement the behavior described by the 4-input minterm list shown in Figure 5.14. Use <u>concurrent signal assignments and logical operators</u>. Declare your entity to match the block diagram provided. Use the type bit for your ports.

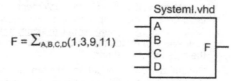

$$F = \Sigma_{A,B,C,D}(1,3,9,11)$$

Figure 5.14

5.5.11 Design a VHDL model to implement the behavior described by the 4-Input minterm list shown in Figure 5.14. Use <u>conditional signal assignments</u>. Declare your entity to match the block diagram provided. Use the type bit for your ports.

5.5.12 Design a VHDL model to implement the behavior described by the 4-input minterm list shown in Figure 5.14. Use <u>selected signal assignments</u>. Declare your entity to match the block diagram provided. Use the type bit for your ports.

5.5.13 Design a VHDL model to implement the behavior described by the 4-input maxterm list shown in Figure 5.15. Use <u>concurrent signal assignments and logical operators</u>. Declare your entity to match the block diagram provided. Use the type bit for your ports.

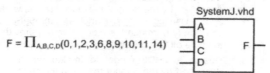

$$F = \Pi_{A,B,C,D}(0,1,2,3,6,8,9,10,11,14)$$

Figure 5.15

5.5.14 Design a VHDL model to implement the behavior described by the 4-input maxterm list shown in Figure 5.15. Use <u>conditional signal assignments</u>. Declare your entity to match the block diagram provided. Use the type bit for your ports.

5.5.15 Design a VHDL model to implement the behavior described by the 4-input maxterm list shown in Figure 5.15. Use <u>selected signal assignments</u>. Declare your entity to match the block diagram provided. Use the type bit for your ports.

5.5.16 Design a VHDL model to implement the behavior described by the 4-input truth table shown in Figure 5.16. Use <u>concurrent signal assignments and logical operators</u>. Declare your entity to match the block diagram provided. Use the type bit for your ports.

A	B	C	D	F
0	0	0	0	1
0	0	0	1	1
0	0	1	0	1
0	0	1	1	0
0	1	0	0	1
0	1	0	1	1
0	1	1	0	1
0	1	1	1	0
1	0	0	0	1
1	0	0	1	1
1	0	1	0	1
1	0	1	1	0
1	1	0	0	1
1	1	0	1	1
1	1	1	0	1
1	1	1	1	0

Figure 5.16

5.5.17 Design a VHDL model to implement the behavior described by the 4-input truth table shown in Figure 5.16. Use <u>conditional signal assignments</u>. Declare your entity to match the block diagram provided. Use the type bit for your ports.

5.5.18 Design a VHDL model to implement the behavior described by the 4-input truth table shown in Figure 5.16. Use <u>selected signal assignments</u>. Declare your entity to match the block diagram provided. Use the type bit for your ports.

Section 5.6 – Structural Design in VHDL

5.6.1 Design a VHDL model to implement the behavior described by the 3-input minterm list shown in Figure 5.11. Use a <u>structural design approach and basic gates</u>. You will need to create whatever basic gates are needed for your design (e.g., INV1, AND2, OR4, etc.) and then instantiate them in your upper level architecture to create the desired functionality. The lower level gates can be implemented with concurrent signal assignments and logical operators (e.g., F<= not A). Declare your entity to match the block diagram provided. Use the type bit for your ports.

5.6.2 Design a VHDL model to implement the behavior described by the 3-input maxterm list shown in Figure 5.12. Use a <u>structural design approach and basic gates</u>. You will need to create whatever basic gates are needed for your design (e.g., INV1, AND2, OR4, etc.) and then instantiate them in your upper level architecture to create the desired functionality. The lower level gates can be implemented with concurrent signal assignments and logical operators (e.g., F<= not A). Declare your entity to match the block diagram provided. Use the type bit for your ports.

5.6.3 Design a VHDL model to implement the behavior described by the 3-input truth table shown in Figure 5.13. Use a <u>structural design approach and basic gates</u>. You will need to create whatever basic gates are needed for your design (e.g., INV1, AND2, OR4, etc.) and then instantiate them in your upper level architecture to create the desired functionality. The lower level gates can be implemented with concurrent signal assignments and logical operators (e.g., F<= not A). Declare your entity to match the block diagram provided. Use the type bit for your ports.

5.6.4 Design a VHDL model to implement the behavior described by the 4-input minterm list shown in Figure

5.14. Use a <u>structural design approach and basic gates</u>. You will need to create whatever basic gates are needed for your design (e.g., INV1, AND2, OR4, etc.) and then instantiate them in your upper level architecture to create the desired functionality. The lower level gates can be implemented with concurrent signal assignments and logical operators (e.g., F<= not A). Declare your entity to match the block diagram provided. Use the type bit for your ports.

5.6.5   Design a VHDL model to implement the behavior described by the 4-input maxterm list shown in Figure 5.15. Use a <u>structural design approach and basic gates</u>. You will need to create whatever basic gates are needed for your design (e.g., INV1, AND2, OR4, etc.) and then instantiate them in your upper level architecture to create the desired functionality. The lower level gates can be implemented with concurrent signal assignments and logical operators (e.g., F<= not A). Declare your entity to match the block diagram provided. Use the type bit for your ports.

5.6.6   Design a VHDL model to implement the behavior described by the 4-input truth table shown in Figure 5.16. Use a <u>structural design approach and basic gates</u>. You will need to create whatever basic gates are needed for your design (e.g., INV1, AND2, OR4, etc.) and then instantiate them in your upper level architecture to create the desired functionality. The lower level gates can be implemented with concurrent signal assignments and logical operators (e.g., F<= not A). Declare your entity to match the block diagram provided. Use the type bit for your ports.

Section 5.7 – Overview of Simulation Test Benches

5.7.1   What is the purpose of a test bench?

5.7.2   Does a test bench have input and output ports?

5.7.3   Can a test bench be simulated?

5.7.4   Can a test bench be synthesized?

Chapter 6: MSI Logic

This chapter introduces a group of combinational logic building blocks that are commonly used in digital design. As we move into systems that are larger than individual gates, there are naming conventions that are used to describe the size of the logic. Table 6.1 gives these naming conventions. In this chapter we will look at *medium scale integrated circuit* (MSI) logic. Each of these building blocks can be implemented using the combinational logic design steps covered in Chapters 4 and 5.

Commonly Used Names to Describe The Size of Digital Logic

Name	Example	# of Transistors
SSI - Small Scale Integrated Circuits	Individual Gates (NAND, INV)	10's
MSI - Medium Scale Integrated Circuits	Decoders, Multiplexers	100's
LSI – Large Scale Integrated Circuits	Arithmetic Circuits, RAM	1k – 10k
VLSI – Very Large Scale Integrated Circuits	Microprocessors	100k – 1M

While there are names for logic sizes above 1M transistor such as ULSI (Ultra), the term "VLSI" is now used to describe all integrated circuits that are so large they require CAD tools for their design, synthesis and implementation.

Table 6.1
Naming Convention for the Size of Digital Systems

Learning Outcomes – After completing this chapter, you will be able to:

6.1   Design a decoder circuit by hand using the classical digital design approach.
6.2   Design a VHDL model of a decoder circuit using concurrent behavior modeling techniques.
6.3   Design an encoder circuit by hand using the classical digital design approach.
6.4   Design a VHDL model of an encoder circuit using concurrent behavior modeling techniques.
6.5   Design a multiplexer circuit by hand using the classical digital design approach.
6.6   Design a VHDL model of a multiplexer circuit using concurrent behavior modeling techniques.
6.7   Design a demultiplexer circuit by hand using the classical digital design approach.
6.8   Design a VHDL model of a demultiplexer circuit using concurrent behavior modeling techniques.

6.1 Decoders

A decoder is a circuit that takes in a binary *code* and has outputs that are asserted for specific values of that code. The code can be of any type or size (e.g., unsigned, two's complement, etc.). Each output will assert for only specific input codes. Since combinational logic circuits only produce a single output, this means that within a decoder, there will be a separate combinational logic circuit for each output.

6.1.1 Example: One-Hot Decoder

A one-hot decoder is a circuit that has n inputs and 2^n outputs. Each output will assert for one and only one input code. Since there are 2^n outputs, there will always be one and only one output asserted at any given time. Example 6.1 shows the process of designing a 2-to-4 one-hot decoder by hand (i.e., using the classical digital design approach).

Example: 2-to-4 One-Hot Decoder - Logic Synthesis by Hand

The block diagram and truth table for this system are as follows:

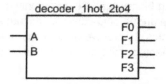

A	B	F3	F2	F1	F0
0	0	0	0	0	1
0	1	0	0	1	0
1	0	0	1	0	0
1	1	1	0	0	0

Each output asserts for a specific input code. This is where the term "one-hot" comes from. Each output is only "hot" for one input code.

When designing this circuit, each output needs to have its own separate combinational logic circuit. This is the same as if there were four separate truth tables. This design could be implemented using 4x, 2-input K-maps to form the logic expressions for these outputs; however, by inspection a minterm list for each output will be the most minimal circuit.

$$F0 = \Sigma_{A,B}(0) = A'\cdot B' \qquad F2 = \Sigma_{A,B}(2) = A\cdot B'$$

$$F1 = \Sigma_{A,B}(1) = A'\cdot B \qquad F3 = \Sigma_{A,B}(3) = A\cdot B$$

When implementing the final decoder, the input inversions for A and B can be shared across all of the AND gates.

Example 6.1
2-to-4 One-Hot Decoder - Logic Synthesis by Hand

As decoders get larger, it is necessary to use hardware description languages to model their behavior. Example 6.2 shows how to model a 3-to-8 one-hot decoder in VHDL with concurrent signal assignments and logic operators.

Example: 3-to-8 One-Hot Decoder – VHDL Modeling using Logical Operators

The block diagram and truth table for this system are as follows:

A	B	C	F7	F6	F5	F4	F3	F2	F1	F0
0	0	0	0	0	0	0	0	0	0	1
0	0	1	0	0	0	0	0	0	1	0
0	1	0	0	0	0	0	0	1	0	0
0	1	1	0	0	0	0	1	0	0	0
1	0	0	0	0	0	1	0	0	0	0
1	0	1	0	0	1	0	0	0	0	0
1	1	0	0	1	0	0	0	0	0	0
1	1	1	1	0	0	0	0	0	0	0

To implement this in VHDL using logical operators, we must first determine the logic that will be used in the concurrent signal assignments. Again, since each logic function only has one input code corresponding to an output of '1', the minterm can be used to implement the logic.

$$F0 = \sum_{A,B,C}(0) = A' \cdot B' \cdot C' \qquad F4 = \sum_{A,B,C}(4) = A \cdot B' \cdot C'$$

$$F1 = \sum_{A,B,C}(1) = A' \cdot B' \cdot C \qquad F5 = \sum_{A,B,C}(5) = A \cdot B' \cdot C$$

$$F2 = \sum_{A,B,C}(2) = A' \cdot B \cdot C' \qquad F6 = \sum_{A,B,C}(6) = A \cdot B \cdot C'$$

$$F3 = \sum_{A,B,C}(3) = A' \cdot B \cdot C \qquad F7 = \sum_{A,B,C}(7) = A \cdot B \cdot C$$

In VHDL, each of the outputs requires a separate signal assignment.

```
entity decoder_1hot_3to8 is
   port (A,B,C                       : in  bit;
         F0,F1,F2,F3,F4,F5,F6,F7 : out bit);
end entity;

architecture decoder_1hot_3to8_arch of decoder_1hot_3to8 is

 begin

   F0 <= (not A) and (not B) and (not C);
   F1 <= (not A) and (not B) and (C);
   F2 <= (not A) and (B)     and (not C);
   F3 <= (not A) and (B)     and (C);
   F4 <= (A)     and (not B) and (not C);
   F5 <= (A)     and (not B) and (C);
   F6 <= (A)     and (B)     and (not C);
   F7 <= (A)     and (B)     and (C);

end architecture;
```

Example 6.2
3-to-8 One-Hot Decoder - VHDL Modeling using Logical Operators

This description can be further simplified by using vector notation for the ports and describing the functionality using either conditional or select signal assignment. Example 6.3 shows how to model the 3-to-8 one-hot decoder in VHDL with conditional and select signal assignments.

Example: 3-to-8 One-Hot Decoder – VHDL Modeling – Conditional/Select Signal Assignments

The block diagram and truth table for this system are as follows. Notice that the input and output ports now use type bit_vector in order to create a more compact description.

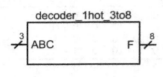

ABC	F(7)	F(6)	F(5)	F(4)	F(3)	F(2)	F(1)	F(0)
"000"	0	0	0	0	0	0	0	1
"001"	0	0	0	0	0	0	1	0
"010"	0	0	0	0	0	1	0	0
"011"	0	0	0	0	1	0	0	0
"100"	0	0	0	1	0	0	0	0
"101"	0	0	1	0	0	0	0	0
"110"	0	1	0	0	0	0	0	0
"111"	1	0	0	0	0	0	0	0

The following is the entity for this design that uses bit_vectors for the inputs and outputs.

```
entity decoder_1hot_3to8 is
    port (ABC  : in  bit_vector(2 downto 0);
          F    : out bit_vector(7 downto 0));
end entity;
```

The following are two different ways to implement the behavior of the decoder: (1) conditional signal assignments and (2) selected signal assignments. In these techniques the signal assignment can be made to the entire F vector instead of to the individual scalar outputs. This creates a compact VHDL model but will still synthesis into eight separate combinational logic circuits.

(1)
```
architecture decoder_1hot_3to8_arch of decoder_1hot_3to8 is

begin

  F <= "00000001" when (ABC = "000") else
       "00000010" when (ABC = "001") else
       "00000100" when (ABC = "010") else
       "00001000" when (ABC = "011") else
       "00010000" when (ABC = "100") else
       "00100000" when (ABC = "101") else
       "01000000" when (ABC = "110") else
       "10000000" when (ABC = "111");

end architecture;
```

(2)
```
architecture decoder_1hot_3to8_arch of decoder_1hot_3to8 is

begin

  with (ABC) select
    F <= "00000001" when "000",
         "00000010" when "001",
         "00000100" when "010",
         "00001000" when "011",
         "00010000" when "100",
         "00100000" when "101",
         "01000000" when "110",
         "10000000" when "111";

end architecture;
```

Example 6.3
3-to-8 One-Hot Decoder - VHDL Modeling using Conditional and Select Signal Assignments

6.1.2 Example: 7-Segment Display Decoder

A 7-segment display decoder is a circuit used to drive character displays that are commonly found in applications such as digital clocks and household appliances. A character display is made up of 7 individual LEDs, typically labeled a-g. The input to the decoder is the binary equivalent of the decimal or Hex character that is to be displayed. The output of the decoder is the arrangement of LEDs that will form the character. Decoders with 2-inputs can drive characters "0" to "3". Decoders with 3-inputs can drive characters "0" to "7". Decoders with 4-inputs can drive characters "0" to "F" with the case of the Hex characters being "A, b, c or C, d, E and F".

Let's look at an example of how to design a 3-input, 7-segment decoder by hand. The first step in the process is to create the truth table for the outputs that will drive the LEDs in the display. We'll call these outputs F_a, F_b, ..., F_g. Example 6.4 shows how to construct the truth table for the 7-segment display decoder. In this table, a logic 1 corresponds to the LED being ON.

Example: 7-Segment Display Decoder - Truth Table

LED Labels

A	B	C		F_a	F_b	F_c	F_d	F_e	F_f	F_g
0	0	0		1	1	1	1	1	1	0
0	0	1		0	1	1	0	0	0	0
0	1	0		1	1	0	1	1	0	1
0	1	1		1	1	1	1	0	0	1
1	0	0		0	1	1	0	0	1	1
1	0	1		1	0	1	1	0	1	1
1	1	0		1	0	1	1	1	1	1
1	1	1		1	1	1	0	0	0	0

Example 6.4
7-Segment Display Decoder - Truth Table

If we wish to design this decoder by hand we need to create seven separate combinational logic circuits. Each of the outputs ($F_a - F_g$) can be put into a 3-input K-map to find the minimized logic expression. Example 6.5 shows the design of the decoder from the truth table in Example 6.4 by hand.

Example: 7-Segment Display Decoder – Logic Synthesis by Hand

The block diagram and truth table for this system are as follows:

A	B	C	Fa	Fb	Fc	Fd	Fe	Ff	Fg
0	0	0	1	1	1	1	1	1	0
0	0	1	0	1	1	0	0	0	0
0	1	0	1	1	0	1	1	0	1
0	1	1	1	1	1	1	0	0	1
1	0	0	0	1	1	0	0	1	1
1	0	1	1	0	1	1	0	1	1
1	1	0	1	0	1	1	1	1	1
1	1	1	1	1	1	0	0	0	0

Each output of the decoder needs its own logic expression.

$Fa = A' \cdot C' + B + A \cdot C$

$Fb = B' \cdot C' + A' + B \cdot C$

$Fc = A + B' + C$

$Fd = A' \cdot C' + A' \cdot B + B \cdot C' + A \cdot B' \cdot C$

$Fe = A' \cdot C' + B \cdot C'$

$Ff = B' \cdot C' + A \cdot C' + A \cdot B'$

$Fg = A' \cdot B + A \cdot C' + A \cdot B'$

Example 6.5
7-Segment Display Decoder - Logic Synthesis by Hand

This same functionality can be modeled in VHDL using concurrent signal assignments with logical operators. Example 6.6 shows how to model the 7-segment decoder in VHDL using concurrent signal assignments with logic operators.

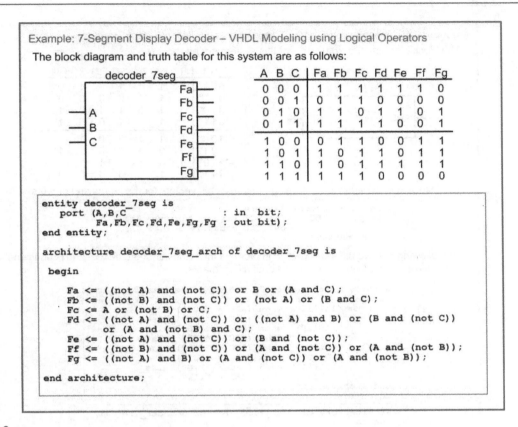

Example: 7-Segment Display Decoder – VHDL Modeling using Logical Operators

The block diagram and truth table for this system are as follows:

A	B	C	Fa	Fb	Fc	Fd	Fe	Ff	Fg
0	0	0	1	1	1	1	1	1	0
0	0	1	0	1	1	0	0	0	0
0	1	0	1	1	0	1	1	0	1
0	1	1	1	1	1	1	0	0	1
1	0	0	0	1	1	0	0	1	1
1	0	1	1	0	1	1	0	1	1
1	1	0	1	0	1	1	1	1	1
1	1	1	1	1	1	0	0	0	0

```
entity decoder_7seg is
   port (A,B,C                   : in  bit;
         Fa,Fb,Fc,Fd,Fe,Fg,Fg : out bit);
end entity;

architecture decoder_7seg_arch of decoder_7seg is

 begin

    Fa <= ((not A) and (not C)) or B or (A and C);
    Fb <= ((not B) and (not C)) or (not A) or (B and C);
    Fc <= A or (not B) or C;
    Fd <= ((not A) and (not C)) or ((not A) and B) or (B and (not C))
          or (A and (not B) and C);
    Fe <= ((not A) and (not C)) or (B and (not C));
    Ff <= ((not B) and (not C)) or (A and (not C)) or (A and (not B));
    Fg <= ((not A) and B) or (A and (not C)) or (A and (not B));

end architecture;
```

Example 6.6
7-Segment Display Decoder - Modeling using Logical Operators

Again, a more compact description of the decoder can be accomplished if the ports are described as vectors and a conditional or select signal assignment is used. Example 6.7 shows how to model the 7-segment decoder in VHDL using conditional and selected signal assignments.

Example: 7-Segment Decoder – VHDL Modeling – Conditional/Select Signal Assignments

The block diagram and truth table for this system are as follows:

ABC	a F(6)	b F(5)	c F(4)	d F(3)	e F(2)	f F(1)	g F(0)
"000"	1	1	1	1	1	1	0
"001"	0	1	1	0	0	0	0
"010"	1	1	0	1	1	0	1
"011"	1	1	1	1	0	0	1
"100"	0	1	1	0	0	1	1
"101"	1	0	1	1	0	1	1
"110"	1	0	1	1	1	1	1
"111"	1	1	1	0	0	0	0

The following is the entity for this design that uses bit_vectors for the inputs and outputs.

```
entity decoder_7seg is
  port (ABC  : in  bit_vector(2 downto 0);
        F    : out bit_vector(6 downto 0));
end entity;
```

The following are two different ways to implement the behavior of the decoder: (1) conditional signal assignments and (2) selected signal assignments.

(1)
```
architecture decoder_7seg_arch of decoder_7seg is
begin
  F <= "1111110" when (ABC = "000") else
       "0110000" when (ABC = "001") else
       "1101101" when (ABC = "010") else
       "1111001" when (ABC = "011") else
       "0110011" when (ABC = "100") else
       "1011011" when (ABC = "101") else
       "1011111" when (ABC = "110") else
       "1110000" when (ABC = "111");
end architecture;
```

(2)
```
architecture decoder_7seg_arch of decoder_7seg is
begin
  with (ABC) select
    F <= "1111110" when "000",
         "0110000" when "001",
         "1101101" when "010",
         "1111001" when "011",
         "0110011" when "100",
         "1011011" when "101",
         "1011111" when "110",
         "1110000" when "111";
end architecture;
```

Example 6.7
7-Segment Display Decoder - Modeling using Conditional and Selected Signal Assignments

CONCEPT CHECK

CC6.1   In a decoder, a logic expression is created for each output. Once all of the output logic expressions are found, how can the decoder logic be further minimized?

A)   By using K-maps to find the output logic expressions.

B)   By buffering the inputs so that they can drive a large number of other gates.

C)   By identifying any logic terms that are used in multiple locations (inversions, product terms, and sum terms) and sharing the interim results among multiple circuits in the decoder.

D)   By ignoring fan-out.

6.2 Encoders

An encoder works in the opposite manner as a decoder. An assertion on a specific input port corresponds to a unique code on the output port.

6.2.1 Example: One-Hot Binary Encoder

A one-hot binary encoder has n outputs and 2^n inputs. The output will be an n-bit, binary code which corresponds to an assertion on one and only one of the inputs. Example 6.8 shows the process of designing a 4-to-2 binary encoder by hand (i.e., using the classical digital design approach).

Example 6.8
4-to-2 Binary Encoder - Logic Synthesis by Hand

In VHDL this can be implemented using logical operators, conditional signal assignments or selected signal assignments. In the conditional and selected signal assignments, if an output is not listed for each and every input possibility, then an output must be specified to cover any remaining inputs conditions. In the conditional signal assignment, the covering value is specified after the final *else* statement. In the selected signal assignment, the covering value is specified using the *when others* clause. Example 6.9 shows how to model the encoder in VHDL using each of the above-mentioned modeling techniques.

Example: 4-to-2 Binary Encoder – VHDL Modeling

The block diagram and truth table for this system are as follows:

encoder_1hot_4to2

ABCD	YZ
"0001"	"00"
"0010"	"01"
"0100"	"10"
"1000"	"11"

The following is the entity for this design that uses bit_vectors for the inputs and outputs.

```
entity encoder_1hot_4to2 is
    port (ABCD : in  bit_vector(3 downto 0);
          YZ   : out bit_vector(1 downto 0));
end entity;
```

The following are three different ways to implement the behavior of the encoder: (1) concurrent signal assignments with logical operators; (2) conditional signal assignment; and (3) selected signal assignments.

(1)
```
architecture encoder_1hot_4to2_arch of encoder_1hot_4to2 is

begin

  YZ(1) <= ABCD(3) or ABCD(2);
  YZ(0) <= ABCD(3) or ABCD(1);

end architecture;
```

(2)
```
architecture encoder_1hot_4to2_arch of encoder_1hot_4to2 is

begin

  YZ <= "00" when (ABCD = "0001") else
        "01" when (ABCD = "0010") else
        "10" when (ABCD = "0100") else
        "11" when (ABCD = "1000") else
        "00";

end architecture;
```

(3)
```
architecture encoder_1hot_4to2_arch of encoder_1hot_4to2 is

begin

  with (ABCD) select
    YZ <= "00" when "0001",
          "01" when "0010",
          "10" when "0100",
          "11" when "1000",
          "00" when others;

end architecture;
```

Example 6.9
4-to-2 Binary Encoder - VHDL Modeling

CONCEPT CHECK

CC6.2   If it is desired to have the outputs of an encoder produce 0's for all input codes not defined in the truth table, can "don't cares" be used when deriving the minimized logic expressions? Why?

  A) No. Don't cares aren't used in encoders.

  B) Yes. Don't cares can always be used in K-maps.

  C) Yes. All that needs to be done is to treat each X as a 0 when forming the most minimal prime implicant.

  D) No. Each cell in the K-map corresponding to an undefined input code needs to contain a 0 so don't cares are not applicable.

6.3 Multiplexers

A multiplexer is a circuit that passes one of its multiple inputs to a single output based on a select input. This can be thought of as a digital switch. The multiplexer has n select lines, 2^n inputs, and one output. Example 6.10 shows the process of designing a 2-to-1 multiplexer by hand (i.e., using the classical digital design approach).

Example 6.10
2-to-1 Multiplexer – Logic Synthesis by Hand

Again, in VHDL a multiplexer can be implemented using different behavioral models. Let's look at the modeling of a 4-to-1 multiplexer in VHDL using logical operators, conditional signal assignments and selected signal assignments. This multiplexer requires two select lines to address each of the four input lines. Each of the product terms in the multiplexer logic expression must include both select lines. The polarity of the select lines is chosen so that when an input is selected, its product term will allow the input to pass to the OR gate. In the VHDL implementation of the multiplexer using conditional and selected signal assignments, since every possible value of *Sel* is listed, it is not necessary to use a final *else* or *when others* clause. Example 6.11 shows the VHDL modeling of a 4-to-1 multiplexer.

Example: 4-to-1 Multiplexer – VHDL Modeling

The symbol and truth table for the 4-to-1 multiplexer are as follows:

Sel	F
"00"	A
"01"	B
"10"	C
"11"	D

The following is the entity for this design that uses type bit_vector for the select input.

```
entity mux_4to1 is
    port (A,B,C,D : in  bit;
          Sel     : in  bit_vector(1 downto 0);
          F       : out bit);
end entity;
```

The following are three different ways to implement the behavior of the mux: (1) concurrent signal assignments with logical operators; (2) conditional signal assignment; and (3) selected signal assignments.

(1)
```
architecture mux_4to1_arch of mux_4to1 is

begin

    F <= (A and not Sel(0) and not Sel(1)) or
         (B and not Sel(0) and     Sel(1)) or
         (C and     Sel(0) and not Sel(1)) or
         (D and     Sel(0) and     Sel(1));

end architecture;
```

(2)
```
architecture mux_4to1_arch of mux_4to1 is

begin

    F <= A when (Sel = "00") else
         B when (Sel = "01") else
         C when (Sel = "10") else
         D when (Sel = "11");

end architecture;
```

(3)
```
architecture mux_4to1_arch of mux_4to1 is

begin

    with (Sel) select
        F <= A when "00",
             B when "01",
             C when "10",
             D when "11";

end architecture;
```

Example 6.11
4-to-1 Multiplexer – VHDL Modeling

CONCEPT CHECK

CC6.3 How are the product terms in a multiplexer based on the identity theorem?

A) Only the select product term will pass its input to the final sum term. Since all of the unselected product terms output 0, the input will be passed through the sum term because anything OR'd with a 0 is itself.

B) The select lines are complemented such that they activate only one OR gate.

C) The select line inputs will produce 1's on the inputs of the selected product term. This allows the input signal to pass through the selected AND gate because anything AND'd with a 1 is itself.

D) The select line inputs will produce 0's on the inputs of the selected sum term. This allows the input signal to pass through the selected OR gate because anything OR'd with a 0 is itself.

6.4 Demultiplexers

A demultiplexer works in a complementary fashion to a multiplexer. A demultiplexer has one input that is routed to one of its multiple outputs. The output that is active is dictated by a select input. A demux has n select lines that chooses to route the input to one of its 2^n outputs. When an output is not selected, it outputs a logic 0. Example 6.12 shows the process of designing a 1-to-2 demultiplexer by hand (i.e., using the classical digital design approach).

Example 6.12
1-to-2 Demultiplexer – Logic Synthesis by Hand

Again, in VHDL a demultiplexer can be implemented using different behavioral models. Example 6.13 shows the modeling of a 1-to-4 demultiplexer in VHDL using logical operators, conditional signal assignments and selected signal assignments. This demultiplexer requires two select lines in order to choose between the four outputs.

Example: 1-to-4 Demultiplexer – VHDL Modeling

The symbol and truth table for the 1-to-4 demultiplexer are as follows:

Sel	W	X	Y	Z
"00"	A	0	0	0
"01"	0	A	0	0
"10"	0	0	A	0
"11"	0	0	0	A

The following is the entity for this design that uses type bit_vector for the select input.

```
entity demux_1to4 is
    port (A      : in  bit;
          Sel    : in  bit_vector(1 downto 0);
          W,X,Y,Z : out bit);
end entity;
```

The following shows the behavior of the demux using: (1) concurrent signal assignments with logical operators; (2) conditional signal assignment; and (3) selected signal assignments.

(1)
```
architecture demux_1to4_arch of demux_1to4 is

 begin

  W <=  A and not Sel(0) and not Sel(1);
  X <=  A and not Sel(0) and     Sel(1);
  Y <=  A and     Sel(0) and not Sel(1);
  Z <=  A and     Sel(0) and     Sel(1);

end architecture;
```

(2)
```
architecture demux_1to4_arch of demux_1to4 is

 begin

  W <= A when (Sel = "00") else '0';
  X <= A when (Sel = "01") else '0';
  Y <= A when (Sel = "10") else '0';
  Z <= A when (Sel = "11") else '0';

end architecture;
```

(3)
```
architecture demux_1to4_arch of demux_1to4 is

 begin

  with (Sel) select
    W <= A when "00",'0' when others;

  with (Sel) select
    X <= A when "01",'0' when others;

  with (Sel) select
    Y <= A when "10",'0' when others;

  with (Sel) select
    Z <= A when "11",'0' when others;

end architecture;
```

Example 6.13
1-to-4 Demultiplexer – VHDL Modeling

CONCEPT CHECK

CC6.4 How many select lines are needed in a 1-to-64 demultiplexer?

A) 1   B) 4   C) 6   D) 64

Summary

❖ The term medium scale integrated circuit (MSI) logic refers to a set of basic combinational logic circuits that implement simple, commonly used functions such as decoders, encoders, multiplexers, and demultiplexers. MSI logic can also include operations such as comparators and simple arithmetic circuits.

❖ While an MSI logic circuit may have multiple outputs, each output requires its own unique logic expression that is based on the system inputs.

❖ A decoder is a system that has a greater number of outputs than inputs. The behavior of each output is based on each unique input code.

❖ An encoder a system that has a greater number of inputs than outputs. A compressed output code is produced based on which input(s) lines are asserted.

❖ A multiplexer is a system that has <u>one output</u> and multiple inputs. At any given time, one and only one input is routed to the output based on the value on a set of *select lines*. For n select lines, a multiplexer can support 2^n inputs.

❖ A demultiplexer is a system that has <u>one input</u> and multiple outputs. The input is routed to one of the outputs depending on the value on a set of select lines. For n select lines, a demultiplexer can support 2^n outputs.

❖ HDLs are particularly useful for describing MSI logic due to their abstract modeling capability. Through the use of Boolean conditions and vector assignments, the behavior of MSI logic can be modeled in a compact and intuitive manner.

Exercise Problems

Section 6.1 – Decoders

6.1.1 Design a 4-to-16 one-hot decoder by hand. The block diagram and truth table for the decoder are given in Figure 6.1. Give the minimized logic expressions for each output (i.e., F_0, F_1, ..., F_{15}) and the full logic diagram for the system.

Figure 6.1

6.1.2 Design a VHDL model for a 4-to-16 one-hot decoder using <u>concurrent signal assignments and logical operators</u>. Use the entity definition given in Figure 6.2.

```
entity decoder_1hot_4to16 is
    port (A  : in  bit_vector (3 downto 0);
          F  : out bit_vector (15 downto 0));
end entity;
```

Figure 6.2

6.1.3 Design a VHDL model for a 4-to-16 one-hot decoder using <u>conditional signal assignments</u>. Use the entity definition given in Figure 6.2.

6.1.4 Design a VHDL model for a 4-to-16 one-hot decoder using <u>selected signal assignments</u>. Use the entity definition given in Figure 6.2.

6.1.5 Design a 4-input, 7-segment HEX character decoder by hand. The system has four inputs called A, B, C and D. The system has 7 outputs called F_a, F_b, F_c, F_d, F_e, F_f, and F_g. These outputs drive the individual LEDs within the display. A logic 1 on an output corresponds to the LED being ON. The display will show the HEX characters 0-9, A, b, c, d, E, and F corresponding to the 4-bit input code on A. A template for creating the truth tables for this system is provided in Figure 6.3. Provide the minimized logic expressions for each of the seven outputs and the overall logic diagram for the decoder.

**7-Segment
Display Decoder**

**7-Segment Display
Layout**

A	B	C	D		F_a	F_b	F_c	F_d	F_e	F_f	F_g
0	0	0	0								
0	0	0	1								
0	0	1	0								
0	0	1	1								
0	1	0	0								
0	1	0	1								
0	1	1	0								
0	1	1	1								
1	0	0	0								
1	0	0	1								
1	0	1	0								
1	0	1	1								
1	1	0	0								
1	1	0	1								
1	1	1	0								
1	1	1	1								

Figure 6.3

6.1.6 Design a VHDL model for a 4-input, 7-segment HEX character decoder using <u>conditional signal assignments</u>. Use the entity definition given in Figure 6.4 for your design. The system has a 4-bit input vector called A and a 7-bit output vector called F. The individual scalars within the output vector (i.e., F(6 downto 0)) correspond to the character display segments a, b, c, d, e, f, and g respectively. A logic 1 on an output corresponds to the LED being ON. The display will show the HEX characters 0-9, A, b, c, d, E, and F corresponding to the 4-bit input code on A. A template for creating the truth table is provided in Figure 6.3. The signals in this table correspond to the entity in this problem as follows: A=A(3), B=A(2), C=A(1), D=A(0), F_a=F(6), F_b=F(5), F_c=F(4), F_d=F(3), F_e=F(2), F_f=F(1), and F_g=F(0).

```
entity decoder_7seg_4in is
  port (A   : in  bit_vector(3 downto 0);
        F   : out bit_vector(6 downto 0));
end entity;
```

Figure 6.4

6.1.7 Design a VHDL model for a 4-input, 7-segment HEX character decoder using <u>selected signal assignments</u>. Use the entity definition given in Figure 6.4 for your design. The system has a 4-bit input vector called A and a 7-bit output vector called F. The individual scalars within the output vector (i.e., F(6 downto 0)) correspond to the character display segments a, b, c, d, e, f, and g respectively. A logic 1 on an output corresponds to the LED being ON. The display will show the HEX characters 0-9, A, b, c, d, E, and F corresponding to the 4-bit input code on A. A template for creating the truth table for this system is provided in Figure 6.3. The signals in this table correspond to the entity in this problem as follows: A=A(3), B=A(2), C=A(1), D=A(0), F_a=F(6), F_b=F(5), F_c=F(4), F_d=F(3), F_e=F(2), F_f=F(1), and F_g=F(0).

Section 6.2 – Encoders

6.2.1 Design an 8-to-3 binary encoder by hand. The block diagram and truth table for the encoder are given in Figure 6.5. Give the logic expressions for each output and the full logic diagram for the system.

8-to-3 One-Hot Encoder

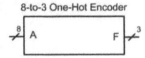

A(7)	A(6)	A(5)	A(4)	A(3)	A(2)	A(1)	A(0)	F(2)	F(1)	F(0)
0	0	0	0	0	0	0	1	0	0	0
0	0	0	0	0	0	1	0	0	0	1
0	0	0	0	0	1	0	0	0	1	0
0	0	0	0	1	0	0	0	0	1	1
0	0	0	1	0	0	0	0	1	0	0
0	0	1	0	0	0	0	0	1	0	1
0	1	0	0	0	0	0	0	1	1	0
1	0	0	0	0	0	0	0	1	1	1

Figure 6.5

6.2.2 Design a VHDL model for an 8-to-3 binary encoder using <u>concurrent signal assignments and logical operators</u>. Use the entity definition given in Figure 6.6 for your design.

```
entity encoder_8to3_binary is
  port (A   : in  bit_vector (7 downto 0);
        F   : out bit_vector (2 downto 0));
end entity;
```

Figure 6.6

6.2.3 Design a VHDL model for an 8-to-3 binary encoder using <u>conditional signal assignments</u>. Use the entity definition given in Figure 6.6 for your design.

6.2.4 Design a VHDL model for an 8-to-3 binary encoder using <u>selected signal assignments</u>. Use the entity definition given in Figure 6.6 for your design.

Section 6.3 – Multiplexers

6.3.1 Design an 8-to-1 multiplexer by hand. The block diagram and truth table for the multiplexer are given in Figure 6.7. Give the minimized logic expressions for the output and the full logic diagram for the system.

8-to-1 Multiplexer

Figure 6.7

6.3.2 Design a VHDL model for an 8-to-1 multiplexer using <u>concurrent signal assignments and logical operators</u>. Use the entity definition given in Figure 6.8 for your design.

```
entity mux_8to1 is
  port (A   : in  bit_vector (7 downto 0);
        Sel : in  bit_vector (2 downto 0);
        F   : out bit);
end entity;
```

Figure 6.8

6.3.3 Design a VHDL model for an 8-to-1 multiplexer using <u>conditional signal assignments</u>. Use the entity definition given in Figure 6.8 for your design.

6.3.4 Design a VHDL model for an 8-to-1 multiplexer using <u>selected signal assignments</u>. Use the entity definition given in Figure 6.8 for your design.

Section 6.4 – Demultiplexers

6.4.1 Design a 1-to-8 demultiplexer by hand. The block diagram and truth table for the demultiplexer are given in Figure 6.9. Give the minimized logic expressions for each output and the full logic diagram for the system.

1-to-8 Demultiplexer

Sel$_2$	Sel$_1$	Sel$_0$	F$_7$	F$_6$	F$_5$	F$_4$	F$_3$	F$_2$	F$_1$	F$_0$
0	0	0	0	0	0	0	0	0	0	A
0	0	1	0	0	0	0	0	0	A	0
0	1	0	0	0	0	0	0	A	0	0
0	1	1	0	0	0	0	A	0	0	0
1	0	0	0	0	0	A	0	0	0	0
1	0	1	0	0	A	0	0	0	0	0
1	1	0	0	A	0	0	0	0	0	0
1	1	1	A	0	0	0	0	0	0	0

Figure 6.9

6.4.2 Design a VHDL model for a 1-to-8 demultiplexer using <u>concurrent signal assignments and logical operators</u>. Use the entity definition given in Figure 6.10 for your design.

```
entity demux_1to8 is
    port (A    : in  bit;
          Sel : in  bit_vector (2 downto 0);
          F    : out bit_vector (7 downto 0));
end entity;
```

Figure 6.10

6.4.3 Design a VHDL model for a 1-to-8 demultiplexer using <u>conditional signal assignments</u>. Use the entity definition given in Figure 6.10 for your design.

6.4.4 Design a VHDL model for a 1-to-8 demultiplexer using <u>selected signal assignments</u>. Use the entity definition given in Figure 6.10 for your design.

Chapter 7: Sequential Logic Design

In this chapter we begin looking at sequential logic design. Sequential logic design differs from combinational logic design in that the outputs of the circuit depend not only on the current values of the inputs but also on the *past* values of the inputs. This is different from the combinational logic design where the output of the circuitry depends only on the current values of the inputs. The ability of a sequential logic circuit to base its outputs on both the current and past inputs allows more sophisticated and intelligent systems to be created. We begin by looking at sequential logic storage devices, which are used to hold the past values of a system. This is followed by an investigation of timing considerations of sequential logic circuits. We then look at some useful circuits that can be created using only sequential logic storage devices. Finally, we look at one of the most important logic circuits in digital systems, the finite state machine.

Learning Outcomes – After completing this chapter, you will be able to:

7.1   Describe the operation of a sequential logic storage device.
7.2   Describe how the state encoding approach selected in a finite state machine correlates to the number of storage devices required in the circuit.
7.3   Design a finite state machine using the classical digital design approach from a state diagram.
7.4   Design a finite state machine using the classical digital design approach from a word description.
7.5   Describe the difference between a Mealy and Moore finite state machine architecture.
7.6   Design a VHDL model of a finite state machine using concurrent behavior modeling techniques for both the next state and output logic and a structural modeling technique for the state memory where the storage device is provided as a black box and instantiated as a component.
7.7   Design a binary ripple counter using only D-Flip-Flops.
7.8   Design a counter that is implemented as a finite state machine using the classical digital design approach.
7.9   Design a VHDL model of a counter using concurrent behavior modeling techniques for the next state and output logic and a structural modeling technique for the state memory where the storage device is provided as a black box and instantiated as a component.
7.10 Analyze the logic diagram of a FSM to find its next state logic and output logic expressions.
7.11 Analyze the logic diagram of a FSM to find its state transition table.
7.12 Analyze the logic diagram of a FSM to find its state diagram.
7.13 Analyze the logic diagram of a FSM to find its maximum clock frequency.

7.1 Sequential Logic Storage Devices

7.1.1 The Cross-Coupled Inverter Pair

The first thing that is needed in sequential logic is a storage device. The fundamental storage device in sequential logic is based on a positive feedback configuration. Consider the circuit in Figure 7.1. This circuit configuration is called the *cross-coupled inverter pair*. In this circuit if the input of U1 starts with a value of 1, it will produce an output of Q=0. This output is fed back to the input of U2, thus producing an output of Qn=1. Qn is fed back to the original input of U1, thus reinforcing the initial condition. This circuit will *hold*, or *store,* a logic 0 without being driven by any other inputs. This circuit operates in a complementary manner when the initial value of U1 is a 0. With this input condition, the circuit will store a logic 1 without being driven by any other inputs.

Figure 7.1
Storage using a Cross-Coupled Inverter Pair

7.1.2 Metastability

The cross-coupled inverter pair in Figure 7.1 exhibits what is called *metastable* behavior due to its positive feedback configuration. Metastability refers to when a system can exist in a state of equilibrium when undisturbed but can be moved to a different, more stable state of equilibrium when sufficiently disturbed. Systems that exhibit *high levels* of metastability have an equilibrium state that is highly unstable, meaning that if disturbed even slightly the system will move rapidly to a more stable point of equilibrium. The cross-coupled inverter pair is a highly metastable system. This system actually contains three equilibrium states. The first is when the input of U1 is exactly between a logic 0 and logic 1 (i.e., $V_{CC}/2$). In this state, the output of U1 is also exactly $V_{CC}/2$. This voltage is fed back to the input of U2, thus producing an output of exactly $V_{CC}/2$ on U2. This in turn is fed back to the original input on U1 reinforcing the initial state. Despite this system being at equilibrium in this condition, this state is highly unstable. With minimal disturbance to any of the nodes within the system, it will move rapidly to one of two more stable states. The two stable states for this system are when Q=0 or when Q=1 (see Figure 7.1). Once the transition begins between the unstable equilibrium state toward one of the two more stable states, the positive feedback in the system continually reinforces the transition until the system reaches its final state. In electrical systems, this initial disturbance is caused by the presence of *noise*, or unwanted voltage in the system. Noise can come from many sources including random thermal motion of charge carriers in the semiconductor materials, electromagnetic energy, or naturally occurring ionizing particles. Noise is present in every electrical system so the cross-coupled inverter pair will never be able to stay in the unstable equilibrium state where all nodes are at $V_{CC}/2$.

The cross-coupled inverter pair has two stable states, thus it is called a *bistable* element. In order to understand the bistable behavior of this circuit, let's look at its behavior when the initial input value on U1 is set directly between a logic 0 and logic 1 (i.e., $V_{CC}/2$) and how a small amount of noise will cause the system to move toward a stable state. Recall that an inverter is designed to have an output that quickly transitions between a logic LOW and HIGH in order to minimize the time spent in the uncertainty region. This is accomplished by designing the inverter to have what is called *gain*. Gain can be thought of as a multiplying factor that is applied to the input of the circuit when producing the output (i.e., $V_{out}=gain \cdot V_{in}$). The gain for an inverter will be negative since the output moves in the opposite direction of the input. The inverter is designed to have a very high gain such that even the smallest change on the input when in the transition region will result in a large change on the output. Consider the behavior of this circuit shown in Figure 7.2. In this example, let's represent the gain of the inverter as $-g$ and see how the system responds when a small positive voltage noise (V_n) is added to the $V_{CC}/2$ input on U1.

Examining Metastability – Moving Toward the State Q=0.

Let's consider how this circuit responds when its initial value at the input to U1 is directly in between a 0 and a 1 (e.g., $V_{CC}/2$).

The input to U1 is $V_{CC}/2$, which creates an output of $V_{CC}/2$.

The output of U1 is fed to the input of U2, again producing an output of $V_{CC}/2$ on U2.

The output of U2 is fed to the input of U1, thus reinforcing the original value of $V_{CC}/2$. We can say that the circuit is in an *equilibrium state*.

Now let's consider how this circuit responds when a small amount of positive noise (V_n) is added to the input of U1 when it is at $V_{CC}/2$. The $V_{CC}/2$ component is not shown for simplicity.

(1) A small amount of noise is added to $V_{CC}/2$ at the input of U1. This pushes it slightly toward a logic 1.

(2) This noise is amplified by the inverter with a negative gain, pushing it slightly toward a logic 0.

(3) The amplified noise is fed to the input of U2.

(4) The noise is amplified again, thus creating an even larger, positive voltage that is fed back to the original input of U1.

(5) When the noise is fed back to the input of U1, it pushes it even more toward a logic 1.

(6) The noise is amplified further, pushing the output even more toward a logic 0.

(7) The amplified noise is fed to the input of U2.

(8) The noise is amplified again, thus creating an even larger, positive voltage that is fed back to the original input of U1.

This process continues until the voltage at the input of U1 reaches V_{CC} and cannot be increased further. Simultaneously, the voltage at the input to U2 is decreased until it reaches GND and cannot be decreased further. At that point, the system is at a stable state and will store Q=0.

The system reaches stability once the input of U1 cannot be increased any further.

In this stable state, the system is holding, or storing a value of Q=0.

Figure 7.2
Examining Metastability Moving Toward the State Q=0

Figure 7.3 shows how the system responds when a small negative voltage noise ($-V_n$) is added to the $V_{CC}/2$ input on U1.

Examining Metastability – Moving Toward the State Q=1.

Now let's consider how this circuit responds when a small amount of negative noise (-V$_n$) is added to the input of U1 when it is at V$_{CC}$/2. The V$_{CC}$/2 component is not shown for simplicity.

(1) A small amount of negative noise is added to V$_{CC}$/2 at the input of U1. This pushes it slightly toward a logic 0.

(2) This noise is amplified by the inverter with a negative gain, thus creating a positive voltage and pushing it slightly toward a logic 1.

(3) The amplified noise is fed to the input of U2.

(4) The noise is amplified again, thus creating an even more negative voltage that is fed back to the original input of U1.

(5) When the noise is fed back to the input of U1, it pushes it even more toward a logic 0.

(6) The noise is amplified further, pushing the output even more toward a logic 1.

(7) The amplified noise is fed to the input of U2.

(8) The noise is amplified again, thus creating an even more negative voltage that is fed back to the original input of U1.

This process continues until the voltage at the input of U1 reaches GND and cannot be decreased further. Simultaneously, the voltage at the input to U2 is increased until it reaches V$_{CC}$ and cannot be increased further. At that point, the system is at a stable state and will store Q=1.

The system reaches stability once the input of U1 cannot be decreased any further.

In this stable state, the system is holding, or storing a value of Q=1.

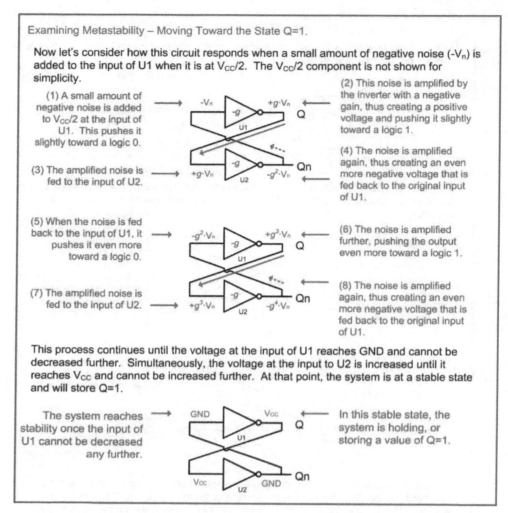

Figure 7.3
Examining Metastability Moving Toward the State Q=1

7.1.3 The SR Latch

While the cross-coupled inverter pair is the fundamental storage concept for sequential logic, there is no mechanism to set the initial value of Q. All that is guaranteed is that the circuit will store a value in one of two stable states (Q=0 or Q=1). The *SR Latch* provides a means to control the initial values in this positive feedback configuration by replacing the inverters with NOR gates. In this circuit, S stands for *set* and indicates when the output is forced to a logic 1 (Q=1), and R stands for *reset* and indicates when the output is forced to a logic 0 (Q=0). When both S=0 and R=0, the SR Latch is put into a *store* mode and it will hold the last value of Q. In all of these input conditions, Qn is the complement of Q. Consider the behavior of the SR Latch during its store state shown in Figure 7.4.

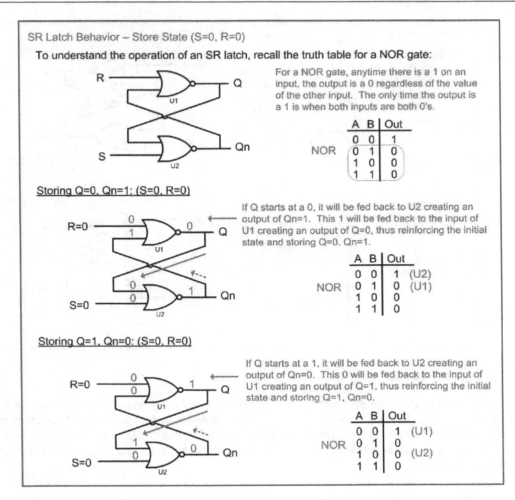

Figure 7.4
SR Latch Behavior - Store State (S=0, R=0)

The SR Latch has two input conditions that will force the outputs to known values. The first condition is called the *set* state. In this state, the inputs are configured as S=1 and R=0. This input condition will force the outputs to Q=1 (e.g, setting Q) and Qn=0. The second input condition is called the *reset* state. In this state the inputs are configured as S=0 and R=1. This input condition will force the outputs to Q=0 (i.e., resetting Q) and Qn=1. Consider the behavior of the SR Latch during its set and reset states shown in Figure 7.5.

Figure 7.5
SR Latch Behavior - Set (S=1, R=0) and Reset (S=0, R=1) States

The final input condition for the SR Latch leads to potential metastability and should be avoided. When S=1 and R=1, the outputs of the SR Latch will both go to logic 0's. The problem with this state is that if the inputs subsequently change to the store state (S=0, R=0), the outputs will go metastable and then settle in one of the two stable states (Q=0 or Q=1). The reason this state is avoided is because the final resting state of the SR Latch is random and unknown. Consider this operation shown in Figure 7.6.

Figure 7.6
SR Latch Behavior – Don't Use State (S=1 and R=1)

Figure 7.7 shows the final truth table for the SR Latch.

SR Latch Truth Table

The following is the final truth table for the SR Latch.

S	R	Q	Qn	
0	0	Last Q	Last Qn	Hold or Store
0	1	0	1	Reset
1	0	1	0	Set
1	1	0	0	Don't Use

Figure 7.7
SR Latch Truth Table

The SR Latch has some drawbacks when it comes to implementation with real circuitry. First, it takes two independent inputs to control the outputs. Second, the state where S=1 and R=1 causes problems when real propagation delays are considered through the gates. Since it is impossible to match the delays exactly between U1 and U2, the SR Latch may occasionally enter this state and experience momentary metastable behavior. In order to address these issues, a number of improvements can be made to this circuit to create two of the most commonly used storage devices in sequential logic, the *D-Latch* and the *D-Flip-Flop*. In order to understand the operation of these storage devices, two incremental modifications are made to the SR Latch. The first is called the *S'R' Latch* and the second is the *SR Latch with enable*. These two circuits are rarely implemented and are only explained to understand how the SR Latch is modified to create a D-Latch and ultimately a D-Flip-Flop.

7.1.4 The S'R' Latch

The S'R' Latch operates in a similar manner as the SR Latch with the exception that the input codes corresponding to the store, set, and reset states are complemented. To accomplish this complementary behavior, the S'R' Latch is implemented with NAND gates configured in a positive feedback configuration. In this configuration, the S'R' Latch will store the last output when S'=1, R'=1. It will set the output (Q=1) when S'=0, R'=1. Finally, it will reset the output (Q=0) when S'=1, R'=0. Consider the behavior of the S'R' Latch during its store state shown in Figure 7.8.

Figure 7.8
S'R' Latch Behavior - Store State (S'=1, R'=1)

Just as with the SR Latch, the S'R' Latch has two input configurations to control the values of the outputs. Consider the behavior of the S'R' Latch during its set and reset states shown in Figure 7.9.

Figure 7.9
S'R' Latch Behavior - Set (S'=0, R'=1) and Reset (S'=1, R'=0) States

And finally, just as with the SR Latch, the S'R' Latch has a state that leads to potential metastability and should be avoided. Consider the operation of the S'R' Latch when the inputs are configured as S'=0 and R'=0 shown in Figure 7.10.

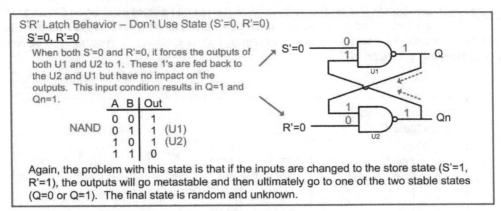

Figure 7.10
S'R' Latch Behavior - Don't Use State (S'=0 and R'=0)

The final truth table for the S'R' Latch is given in Figure 7.11.

Figure 7.11
S'R' Latch Truth Table

7.1.5 SR Latch with Enable

The next modification that is made in order to move toward a D-Latch and ultimately a D-Flip-Flop is to add an *enable* line to the S'R' Latch. The enable is implemented by adding two NAND gates on the input stage of the S'R' Latch. The SR Latch with enable is shown in Figure 7.12. In this topology, the use of NAND gates changes the polarity of the inputs so this circuit once again has a set state where S=1, R=0 and a reset state of S=0, R=1. The enable line is labeled *C*, which stands for *clock*. The rationale for this will be demonstrated upon moving through the explanation of the D-Latch.

Figure 7.12
SR Latch with Enable Schematic

Recall that any time a 0 is present on one of the inputs to a NAND gate, the output will always be a 1 regardless of the value of the other inputs. In the SR Latch with enable configuration, any time C=0, the outputs of U3 and U4 will be 1's and will be fed into the inputs of the cross-coupled NAND gate configuration (U1 and U2). Recall that the cross-coupled configuration of U1 and U2 is an S'R' Latch and will be put into a store state when S'=1 and R'=1. This is the *store state* (C=0). When C=1, it has the effect of inverting the values of the S and R inputs before they reach U1 and U2. This condition allows the *set state* to be entered when S=1, R=0, C=1 and the *reset state* to be entered when S=0, R=1, C=1. Consider this operation in Figure 7.13.

Figure 7.13
SR Latch with Enable Behavior – Store, Set, and Reset

Again, there is a potential metastable state when S=1, R=1 and C=1 that should be avoided. There is also a second store state when S=0, R=0 and C=1 that is not used because storage is to be dictated by the C input.

7.1.6 The D-Latch

The SR Latch with enable can be modified to create a new storage device called a D-Latch. Instead of having two separate input lines to control the outputs of the latch, the R input of the latch is instead driven with an inverted version of the S input. This prevents the S and R inputs from ever being the same value and removes the two "Don't Use" states in the truth table shown in Figure 7.12. The new, single input is renamed D to stand for *data*. This new circuit still has the behavior that it will store the last value of Q and Qn when C=0. When C=1, the output will be Q=1 when D=1 and will be Q=0 when D=0. The behavior of the output when C=1 is called *tracking* the input. The D-Latch schematic, symbol and truth table are given in Figure 7.14.

Figure 7.14
D-Latch Schematic, Symbol and Truth Table

The timing diagram for the D-Latch is shown in Figure 7.15.

Figure 7.15
D-Latch Timing Diagram

7.1.7 The D-Flip-Flop

The final and most widely used storage device in sequential logic is the *D-Flip-Flop*. The D-Flip-Flop is similar in behavior to the D-Latch with the exception that the store mode is triggered by a transition, or edge on the clock signal instead of a level. This allows the D-Flip-Flop to implement higher frequency systems since the outputs are updated in a shorter amount of time. The schematic, symbol and truth table are given in Figure 7.16 for a rising edge triggered D-

Flip-Flop. To indicate that the device is edge sensitive, the input for the clock is designated with a ">". The U3 inverter in this schematic creates the rising edge behavior. If U3 is omitted, this circuit would be a negative edge triggered D-Flip-Flop.

Figure 7.16
D-Flip-Flop (Rising Edge Triggered) Schematic, Symbol, and Truth Table

The D-Flip-Flop schematic shown above is called a *master / slave* configuration because of how the data is passed through the two D-Latches (U1 and U2). Due to the U4 inverter, the two D-Latches will always be in complementary modes. When U1 is in hold mode, U2 will be in track mode and vice versa. When the clock signal transitions HIGH, U1 will store the last value of data. During the time when the clock is HIGH, U2 will enter track mode and pass this value to Q. In this way, the data is latched into the storage device on the rising edge of the clock and is present on Q. This is the *master* operation of the device because U1, or the first D-Latch, is holding the value, and the second D-Latch (the *slave*) is simply passing this value to the output Q. When the clock transitions LOW, U2 will store the output of U1. Since there is a finite delay through U1, the U2 D-Latch is able to store the value before U1 fully enters track mode. U2 will drive Q for the duration of the time that the clock is LOW. This is the *slave* operation of the device because U2, or the second D-Latch, is holding the value. During the time the clock is LOW, U1 is in track mode, which passes the input data to the middle of the D-Flip-Flop preparing for the next rising edge of the clock. The master / slave configuration creates a behavior where the Q output of the D-Flip-Flop is only updated with the value of D on a rising edge of the clock. At all other times, Q holds the last value of D. An example timing diagram for the operation of a rising edge D-Flip-Flop is given in Figure 7.17.

D-Flip-Flop (Rising Edge Triggered) Timing Diagram

① On this rising edge of clock, Q is updated with the value of D (Q=1).

To accomplish this, U1 goes into hold mode when the clock goes HIGH, which stores the input 1. U2 goes into track mode, passing the 1 to the output Q. This configuration keeps Q=1 for the first part of the clock cycle.

② When the clock goes LOW, U2 goes into hold mode, which stores the 1 from U1 and drives Q=1 for the rest of the clock period.

U1 goes into track mode to get ready for the next rising edge of the clock.

Figure 7.17
D-Flip-Flop (Rising Edge Triggered) Timing Diagram

D-Flip-Flops often have additional signals that will set the initial conditions of the outputs that are separate from the clock. A *reset* input is used to force the outputs to Q=0, Qn=1. A *preset* input is used to force the outputs to Q=1, Qn=0. In most modern D-Flip-Flops, these inputs are active LOW, meaning that the line is asserted when the input is a 0. Active LOW inputs are indicated by placing an inversion bubble on the input pin of the symbol. These lines are typically *asynchronous*, meaning that when they are asserted, action is immediately taken to alter the outputs. This is different from a *synchronous* input in which action is only taken on the edge of the clock. Figure 7.18 shows the symbols and truth tables for two D-Flip-Flop variants, one with an active LOW reset and another with both an active LOW reset and active LOW preset.

Figure 7.18
D-Flip-Flop with Asynchronous Reset and Preset

D-Flip-Flops can also be created with an *enable* line. An enable line controls whether or not the output is updated. Enable lines are synchronous, meaning that when they are asserted, the outputs will be updated on the rising edge of the clock. When de-asserted, the outputs are not updated. This behavior in effect ignores the clock input when de-asserted. Figure 7.19 shows the symbol and truth table for a D-Flip-Flop with a synchronous enable.

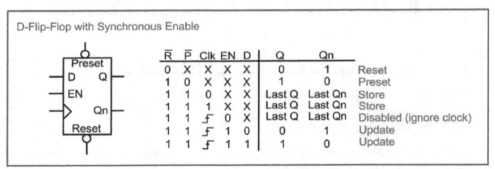

Figure 7.19
D-Flip-Flop with Synchronous Enable

The behavior of the D-Flip-Flop allows us to design systems that are *synchronous* to a clock signal. A clock signal is a periodic square wave that dictates when events occur in a digital system. A synchronous system based on D-Flip-Flops will allow the outputs of its storage devices to be updated upon a rising edge of the clock. This is advantageous because when the Q outputs are storing values they can be used as inputs for combinational logic circuits. Since combinational logic circuits contain a certain amount of propagation delay before the final output is calculated, the D-Flip-Flop can hold the inputs at a steady value while the output is generated. Since the input on a D-Flip-Flop is ignored during all other times, the output of a combinational logic circuit can be fed back as an input to a D-Flip-Flop. This gives a system the ability to generate outputs based on the current values of inputs in addition to past values of the inputs that are being held on the outputs of D-Flip-Flops. This is the definition of sequential logic. An example synchronous, sequential system is shown in Figure 7.20.

Figure 7.20
An Example Synchronous System Based on a D-Flip-Flop

CONCEPT CHECK

CC7.1(a) What will always cause a digital storage device to come out of metastability and settle in one of its two stable states? Why?

   A) The power supply. The power supply provides the necessary current for the device to overcome metastability.

   B) Electrical noise. Noise will always push the storage device toward one state or another. Once the storage device starts moving toward one of its stable states, the positive feedback of the storage device will reinforce the transition until the output eventually comes to rest in a stable state.

   C) A reset. A reset will put the device into a known stable state.

   D) A rising edge of clock. The clock also puts the device into a known stable state.

CC7.1(b) What was the purpose of replacing the inverters in the cross-coupled inverter pair with NOR gates to form the SR Latch?

   A) NOR gates are easier to implement in CMOS.

   B) To provide the additional output Qn.

   C) To provide more drive strength for storing.

   D) To provide inputs to explicitly set the value being stored.

7.2 Sequential Logic Timing Considerations

There are a variety of timing specifications that need to be met in order to successfully design circuits using sequential storage devices. The first specification is called the *setup time* (t_{setup} or t_s). The setup time specifies how long the data input needs to be at a steady state *before* the clock event. The second specification is called the *hold time* (t_{hold} or t_h). The hold time specifies how long the data input needs to be at a steady state *after* the clock event. If these specifications are violated (i.e., the input transitions too close to the clock transition), the storage device will not be able to determine whether the input was a 1 or 0 and will go metastable. The time a storage device will remain metastable is a deterministic value and is specified by the part manufacturer (t_{meta}). In general, metastability should be avoided; however, knowing the maximum duration of metastability for a storage device allows us to design circuits to overcome potential metastable conditions. During the time the device is metastable, the output will have random behavior. It may go to a steady state 1, a steady state 0, or toggle between a 0 and 1 uncontrollably. Once the device comes out of metastability, it will come to rest in one of its two stable states (Q=0 or Q=1). The final resting state is random and unknown. Another specification for sequential storage devices is the delay from the time a clock transition occurs to the point that the data is present on the Q output. This specification is called the *Clock-to-Q* delay and is given the notation t_{CQ}. These specifications are shown in Figure 7.21.

Figure 7.21
Sequential Storage Device Timing Specifications

CC7.2 Which D-flop-flop timing specification requires all of combinational logic circuits in the system to settle on their final output before a triggering clock edge can occur?

A) t_{setup} B) t_{hold} C) t_{CQ} D) t_{meta}

7.3 Common Circuits Based on Sequential Storage Devices

Sequential logic storage devices give us the ability to create sophisticated circuits that can make decisions based on the current and past values of the inputs; however, there are a variety of simple, yet useful circuits that can be created with only these storage devices. This section will introduce a few of these circuits.

7.3.1 Toggle Flop Clock Divider

A *Toggle Flop* is a circuit that contains a D-Flip-Flop configured with its Qn output wired back to its D input. This configuration is also commonly referred to as a *T-Flip-Flop* or *T-Flop*. In this circuit, the only input is the clock signal. Let's examine the behavior of this circuit when its outputs are initialized to Q=0, Qn=1. Since Qn is wired to the D input, a logic 1 is present on the input before the first clock edge. Upon a rising edge of the clock, Q is updated with the value of D. This puts the outputs at Q=1, Qn=0. With these outputs, now a logic 0 is present on the input before the next clock edge. Upon the next rising edge of the clock, Q is updated with the value of D. This time the outputs go to Q=0, Qn=1. This behavior continues indefinitely. The circuit is called a toggle flop because the outputs simply toggle between a 0 and 1 every time there is a rising edge of the clock. This configuration produces outputs that are square waves with exactly half the frequency of the incoming clock. As a result, this circuit is also called a *clock divider*. This circuit can be given its own symbol with a label of "T" indicating it is a toggle flop. The configuration of a Toggle Flop (T-Flop) and timing diagram are shown in Figure 7.22.

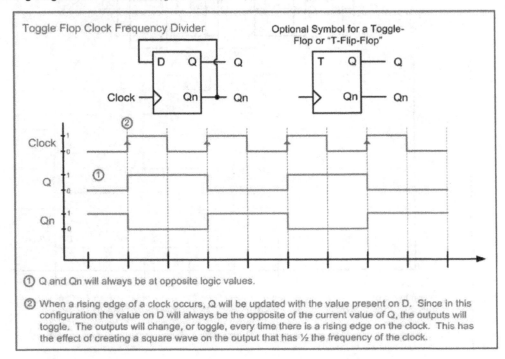

Figure 7.22
Toggle Flop Clock Frequency Divider

7.3.2 Ripple Counter

The toggle flop configuration can be used to create a simple binary counter called a *ripple counter*. In this configuration, the Qn output of a toggle flop is used as the clock for a subsequent toggle flop. Since the output of the first toggle flop is a square wave that is ½ the frequency of the incoming clock, this configuration will produce an output on the second toggle flop that is ¼ the frequency of the incoming clock. This is by nature the behavior of a binary counter. The output of this counter is present on the Q pins of each toggle flop. Toggle flops are added until the desired width of the counter is achieved with each toggle flop representing one bit of the counter. Since each toggle flop produces the clock for the subsequent latch, the clock is said to *ripple* through the circuit, hence the name ripple counter. A 3-bit ripple counter is shown in Figure 7.23.

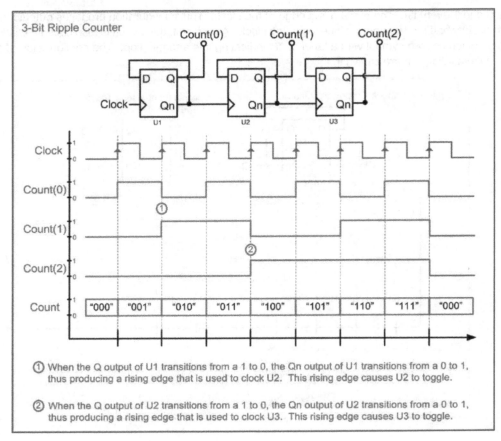

Figure 7.23
3-Bit Ripple Counter

7.3.3 Switch Debouncing

Another useful circuit based on sequential storage devices is a switch debouncer. Mechanical switches have a well-known issue of not producing clean logic transitions on their outputs when pressed. This becomes problematic when using a switch to create an input for a digital device because it will cause unwanted logic level transitions on the output of the gate. In the case of a clock input, this unwanted transition can cause a storage device to unintentionally latch incorrect data.

The primary cause of these unclean logic transitions is due to the physical vibrations of the metal contacts when they collide with each other during a button press or switch actuation. Within a mechanical switch, there is typically one contact that is fixed and another that is designed to move when the button is pressed. The contact that is designed to move can be thought of as a beam that is fixed on one side and free on the other. As the free side of the beam moves toward the fixed contact in order to close the circuit, it will collide and then vibrate just as a tuning fork does when struck. The vibration will eventually diminish and the contact will come to rest, thus making a clean electrical connection; however, during the vibration period the moving contact will *bounce* up and down on the destination contact. This bouncing causes the switch to open and close multiple times before coming to rest in the closed position. This phenomenon is accurately referred to as *switch bounce*. Switch bounce is present in all mechanical switches and gets progressively worse as the switches are used more and more.

Figure 7.24 shows some of the common types of switches found in digital systems. The term *pole* is used to describe the number of separate circuits controlled by the switch. The term *throw* is used to describe the number of separate closed positions the switch can be in.

Figure 7.24
Common Types of Mechanical Switches

Let's look at switch bounce when using a SPST switch to provide an input to a logic gate. A SPST requires a resistor and can be configured to provide either a logic HIGH or LOW when in the open position and the opposite logic level when in the closed position. The example configuration in Figure 7.25 provides a logic LOW when in the open position and a logic HIGH when in the closed position. In the open position, the input to the gate (SW) is pulled to GND to create a logic LOW. In the closed position, the input to the gate is pulled to Vcc to create a logic HIGH. A resistor is necessary to prevent a short circuit between Vcc and GND when the switch is closed. Since the input current specification for a logic gate is very small, the voltage developed across the resistor due to the gate input current is negligible. This means that the resistor can be inserted in the pull-down network without developing a noticeable voltage. When the switch closes, the free-moving contact will bounce off of the destination contact numerous times before settling in the closed position. During the time while the switch is bouncing, the switch will repeatedly toggle between the open (HIGH) and closed (LOW) positions.

Figure 7.25
Switch Bouncing in a Single Pole, Single Throw Switch

A possible solution to eliminate this switch bounce is to instead use a SPDT switch in conjunction with a sequential storage device. Before looking at this solution, we need to examine an additional condition introduced by the SPDT switch. The SPDT switch has what is known as *break-before-make* behavior. The term *break* is used to describe when a switch is open while the term *make* is used to describe when the switch is closed. When a SPDT switch is pressed, the input will be floating during the time when the free-moving contact is transitioning toward the destination contact. During this time, the output of the switch is unknown and can cause unwanted logic transitions if it is being used to drive the input of a logic gate.

Let's look at switch bounce when using a SPDT switch without additional circuitry to handle bouncing. A SPDT has two positions that the free-moving contact can make a connection to (i.e., double throw). When using this switch to drive a logic level into a gate, one position is configured as a logic HIGH and the other a logic LOW. Consider the SPDT switch configuration in Figure 7.26. Position 1 of the SPDT switch is connected to GND, while position 2 is connect to V_{CC}. When unpressed the switch is in position 1. When pressed, the free-moving contact will transition from position 1 to 2. During the transition the free-moving contact is floating. This creates a condition where the input to the gate (SW) is unknown. This floating input will cause unpredictable behavior on the output of the gate. Upon reaching position 2, the free-moving contact will bounce off of the destination contact. This will cause the input of the logic gate to toggle between a logic HIGH and floating repeatedly until the free-moving contact comes to rest in position 2.

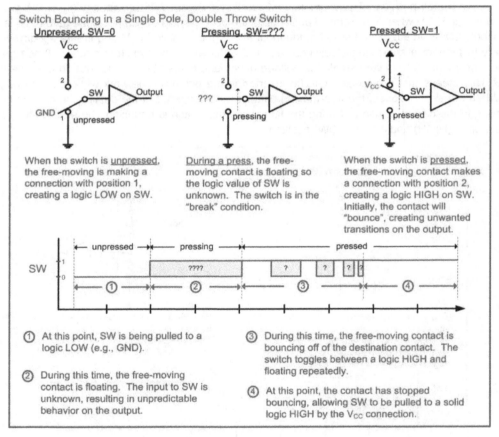

Figure 7.26
Switch Bouncing in a Single Pole, Double Throw Switch

The SPDT switch is ideal for use with an S'R' Latch in order to produce a clean logic transition. This is because during the *break* portion of the transition, an S'R' Latch can be used to hold the last value of the switch. This is unique to the SPDT configuration. The SPST switch in comparison does not have the *break* characteristic, rather it always drives a logic level in both of its possible positions. Consider the debounce circuit for a SPDT switch in Figure 7.27.

This circuit is based on an S'R' Latch with two pull-up resistors. Since the S'R' Latch is created using NAND gates, this circuit is commonly called a *NAND-Debounce* circuit. In the unpressed configuration, the switch drives S'=0 and the R2 pull-up resistor drives R'=1. This creates a logic 0 on the output of the circuit (Qn=0). During a switch press, the free-moving contact is floating, thus it is not driving in a logic level into the S'R' Latch. Instead, both pull-up resistors pull S' and R' to 1's. This puts the latch into its hold mode and the output will remain at a logic 0 (Qn=0). Once the free-moving contact reaches the destination contact, the switch will drive R'=0. Since at this point the R1 pull-up is driving S'=1, the latch outputs a logic 1 (Qn=1). When the free-moving contact bounces off of the destination contact, it will put the latch back into the hold mode; however, this time the last value that will be held is Qn=1. As the switch continues to bounce, the latch will move between the Qn=1 and Qn="Last Qn" states, both of which produce an output of 1. In this way, the SPDT switch in conjunction with the S'R' Latch produces a clean 0 to 1 logic transition despite the break-before-make behavior of the switch and the contact bounce.

Figure 7.27
NAND Debounce Circuit for a SPDT Switch

7.3.4 Shift Registers

A *shift register* is a chain of D-Flip-Flops that each are connected to a common clock. The output of the first D-Flip-Flop is connected to the input of the second D-Flip-flop. The output of the second D-Flip-Flop is connected to the input of the third D-Flip-Flop, and so on. When data is present on the input to the first D-Flip-Flop, it will be latched upon the first rising edge of the clock. On the second rising edge of the clock, the same data will be latched into the second D-Flip-Flop. This continues on each rising edge of the clock until the data has been *shifted* entirely through the chain of D-Flip-Flops. Shift registers are commonly used to convert a serial string of data into a parallel format. If an n-bit, serial sequence of information is clocked into the shift register, after n clocks the data will be held on each of the D-Flip-Flop outputs. At this moment, the n-bits can be read as a parallel value. Consider the shift register configuration shown in Figure 7.28.

① After the first four clock edges, the first sequence of bits are held by the shift register and can be read out as a 4-bit value.

Figure 7.28
4-Bit Shift Register

CONCEPT CHECK

CC7.3   Which D-flip-flop timing specification is most responsible for the ripple delay in a ripple counter?

A) t_{setup} B) t_{hold} C) t_{CQ} D) t_{meta}

7.4 Finite State Machines

Now we turn our attention to one of the most powerful sequential logic circuits, the finite state machine (FSM). A FSM, or *state machine*, is a circuit that contains a pre-defined number of states (i.e., a finite number of states). The machine can exist in one and only one state at a time. The circuit *transitions* between states based on a triggering event, most commonly the edge of a clock, in addition to the values of any inputs of the machine. The number of states and all possible transitions are pre-defined. Through the use of states and a pre-defined sequence of transitions, the circuit is able to make decisions on the next state to transition to based on a history of past states. This allows the circuit to create outputs that are more intelligent compared to a simple combinational logic circuit that has outputs based only on the current values of the inputs.

7.4.1 Describing the Functionality of a FSM

The design of a state machine begins with an abstract word description of the desired circuit behavior. We will use a design example of a push-button motor controller to describe all of the steps involved in creating a finite state machine. Example 7.1 starts the FSM design process by stating the word description of the system.

Example: Push-Button Window Controller - Word Description

Design a system that will allow a user to open and close a window with the push of a button. The window is connected to a motor that has two inputs. The first input to the motor is asserted when the motor needs to spin in a clockwise (CW) direction to open the window, while the second input is asserted when the motor needs to spin in a counterclockwise (CCW) direction to close the window. The signals to the motor do not need to be held for the duration of the window opening/closing. Once the motor observes an assertion on one of its inputs, it will spin until the window is in the correct position and then stop. The inputs are not allowed to be asserted at the same time. The user will press a single button to either open or close the window so the system must keep track of whether the window is in the open or closed position in order to send the correct signals to the motor when the button is pressed.

Example 7.1
Push-Button Window Controller - Word Description

7.4.1.1 State Diagrams

A state diagram is a graphical way to describe the functionality of a finite state machine. A state diagram is a form of a directed graph, in which each state (or vertex) within the system is denoted as a circle and given a descriptive name. The names are written inside of the circles. The transitions between states are denoted using arrows with the input conditions causing the transitions written next to them. Transitions (or edges) can move to different states upon particular input conditions or remain in the same state. For a state machine implemented using sequential logic storage, an evaluation of when to transition states is triggered every time the storage devices update their outputs. For example, if the system was implemented using rising edge triggered D-flip-Flops, then an evaluation would occur on every rising edge of the clock.

There are two different types of output conditions for a state machine. The first is when the output only depends on the current state of the machine. This type of system is called a *Moore Machine*. In this case, the outputs of the system are written inside of the state circles. This indicates the output value that will be generated for each specific state. The second output condition is when the outputs depend on both the current state and the system inputs. This type of system is called a *Mealy Machine*. In this case, the outputs of the system are written next to the state transitions corresponding to the appropriate input values. Outputs in a state diagram are typically written inside of parentheses. Example 7.2 shows the construction of the state diagram for our push-button window controller design.

Example: Push-Button Window Controller - State Diagram

1) <u>Defining the States</u> - For this design, we will define two finite states. The first state is when the window is in the closed position. Let's call this state "w_closed". The second state is when the window is in the open position. Let's call this state "w_open". Each of these two states will be represented in the state diagram as circles. The names of the states are written inside of the circles.

2) <u>Defining the Transitions</u> - We now describe the transitions between states using arrows and labeling the arrows with the input conditions that trigger each transition. For this design, when the machine is in the "w_closed" state, a button press (Press=1) will cause a transition to the "w_open" state. When the button is not pressed, the machine will remain in the "w_closed" state (Press=0). When the machine is in the "w_open" state, a button press (Press=1) will cause a transition to the "w_closed" state, while the button not being pressed (Press=0) will keep the machine in the "w_open" state.

3) <u>Defining the Outputs</u> – We now describe the outputs of the system. For this design, the system will output the appropriate motor control signals upon a button press. This means that the outputs depend on both the current state and the current inputs. This is by definition a *Mealy Machine*. As such, the outputs are listed next to the state transitions. By listing the outputs in this location, both the current state and the input values producing the outputs are indicated. When this machine is in either the w_closed or w_open states and the button is NOT pressed, the outputs Open_CW and Close_CCW are both 0's. When the machine is in w_closed state and the button is pressed, the Open_CW output is asserted to rotate the motor clockwise and open the window. When the machine is in w_open state and the button is pressed, the Close_CCW output is asserted to rotate the motor counterclockwise and close the window. The final state diagram for this system is shown below.

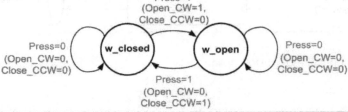

Example 7.2
Push-Button Window Controller - State Diagram

7.4.1.2 State Transition Tables

The state diagram can now be described in a table format that is similar to a truth table. This puts the state machine behavior in a form that makes logic synthesis straightforward. The table contains the same information as in the state diagram. The state that the machine exists in is called the *current state*. For each current state that the machine can reside in, every possible input condition is listed along with the destination state of each transition. The destination state for a transition is called the *next state*. Also listed in the table are the outputs corresponding to each current state and, in the case of a Mealy Machine, the output corresponding to each input condition. Example 7.3 shows the construction of the state transition table for the push-button window controller design. This information is identical to the state diagram given in Example 7.2.

Example: Push-Button Window Controller - State Transition Table

A state transition table contains the same information as the state diagram but in a tabular format. This format is similar to a truth table and makes logic synthesis straight forward. Each state and input condition is listed in the table along with the corresponding next state and outputs.

	(Input)		(Outputs)	
Current State	Press	Next State	Open_CW	Close_CCW
w_closed	0	w_closed	0	0
w_closed	1	w_open	1	0
w_open	0	w_open	0	0
w_open	1	w_closed	0	1

Example 7.3
Push-Button Window Controller - State Transition Table

7.4.2 Logic Synthesis for a FSM

Once the behavior of the state machine has been described, it can be directly synthesized. There are three main components of a state machine: the state memory; the next state logic; and the output logic. Figure 7.29 shows a block diagram of a state machine highlighting these three components. The *next state logic* block is a group of combinational logic that produces the next state signals based on the current state and any system inputs. The *state memory* holds the current state of the system. The current state is updated with next state on every rising edge of the clock, which is indicated with the ">" symbol within the block. This behavior is created using D-Flip-Flops where the current state is held on the Q outputs of the D-Flip-Flops, while the next state is present on the D inputs of the D-Flip-Flops. In this way, every rising edge of the clock will trigger an evaluation of which state to move to next. This decision is based on the current state and the current inputs. The *output logic* block is a group of combinational logic that creates the outputs of the system. This block always uses the current state as an input and, depending on the type of machine (Mealy vs. Moore), uses the system inputs. It is useful to keep this block diagram in mind when synthesizing finite state machines as it will aid in keeping the individual design steps separate and clear.

Figure 7.29
Main Components of a Finite State Machine

7.4.2.1 State Memory

The state memory is the circuitry that will hold the current state of the machine. Upon a rising edge of a clock it will update the current state with the next state. At all other times, the next state input is ignored. This gives time for the next state logic circuitry to compute the results for the next state. This behavior is identical to that of a D-Flip-Flop, thus the state memory is simply one or more D-Flip-Flops. The number of D-Flip-Flops required depends on how the states are *encoded*. *State encoding* is the process of assigning a binary value to the descriptive names of the states from the state diagram and state transition tables. Once the descriptive names have been converted into representative codes using 1's and 0's, the states can be implemented in real circuitry. The assignment of codes is arbitrary and can be selected in order to minimize the circuitry needed in the machine.

There are three main styles of state encoding. The first is straight **binary encoding**. In this approach the state codes are simply a set of binary counts (i.e., 00, 01, 10, 11...). The binary counts are assigned starting at the beginning of the state diagram and incrementally assigned toward the end. This type of encoding has the advantage that it is very efficient in minimizing the number of D-Flip-Flops needed for the state memory. With n D-Flip-Flops, 2^n states can be encoded. When a large number of states is required, the number of D-Flip-Flops can be calculated using the rules of logarithmic math. Example 7.4 shows how to solve for the number of bits needed in the binary state code based on the number of states in the machine.

Solving For the Number of Bits Needed for Binary State Encoding

Problem: You are designing a state machine that has 41 unique states and are going to encode the states in binary. How many D-Flip-Flops do you need?

Solution: Each D-Flip-Flops will hold one bit of the state code. If the state memory has n-bits, it can encode 2^n states using binary encoding. We can use logarithms in order to solve for the n in the exponent.

$$2^n = (\text{\# of states})$$

$$\log(2^n) = \log(\text{\# of states})$$

$$n \cdot \log(2) = \log(\text{\# of states})$$

$$n = \frac{\log(\text{\# of states})}{\log(2)}$$

$$n = \frac{\log(41)}{\log(2)}$$

$$n = 5.36$$

Rounding up to the next whole number means that we need 6 bits, or 6-D-Flip-Flops to encode 41 states in binary.

Check: To check this, let's plug 6 back into the original expression. If we have 6 bits, we can encode 2^6 states, or 64 states. This is enough to encode our 41 states. If we had 1 less bit (e.g., 5), we could only encode up to $2^5 = 32$ states, so we require 6 bits for this state encoding. Note that not all of the possible binary values are used as state codes.

Example 7.4
Solving For the Number of Bits Needed for Binary State Encoding

The second type of state encoding is called **gray code encoding**. A gray code is one in which the value of a code differs by only one bit from any of its neighbors, (i.e., 00, 01, 11, 10...). A gray code is useful for reducing the number of bit transitions on the state codes when the machine has a transition sequence that is linear. Reducing the number of bit transitions can reduce the amount of power consumption and noise generated by the circuit. When the state transitions of a machine are highly non-linear, a gray code encoding approach does not provide any benefit. Gray code is also an efficient coding approach. With n D-Flip-Flops, 2^n states can be encoded just as in binary encoding. Figure 7.30 shows the process of creating n-bit, gray code patterns.

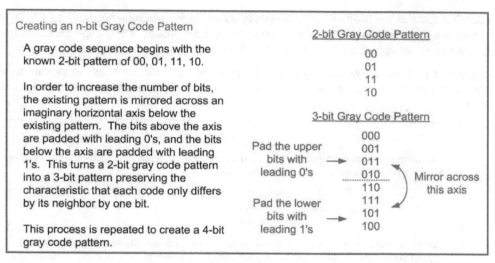

Figure 7.30
Creating an n-bit Gray Code Pattern

The third common technique to encode states is using ***one-hot encoding***. In this approach, a separate D-Flip-Flop is asserted for each state in the machine. For an *n-state* machine, this encoding approach requires *n* D-Flip-Flops. For example, if a machine had 3 states, the one-hot state codes would be "001", "010" and "100". This approach has the advantage that the next state logic circuitry is very simple; further, there is less chance that the different propagation delays through the next state logic will cause an inadvertent state to be entered. This approach is not as efficient as binary and gray code in terms of minimizing the number of D-Flip-Flops because it requires one D-Flip-Flop for each state; however, in modern digital integrated circuits that have abundant D-Flip-Flops, one-hot encoding is commonly used.

Figure 7.31 shows the differences between these three state encoding approaches.

Comparison of Different State Encoding Approaches

A state machine has eight unique states named S0, S1, ... S7. The following is an example of how these states can be encoded using binary, gray code and one-hot.

State Name	Binary	Gray Code	One-Hot
S0	000	000	00000001
S1	001	001	00000010
S2	010	011	00000100
S3	011	010	00001000
S4	100	110	00010000
S5	101	111	00100000
S6	110	101	01000000
S7	111	100	10000000

Figure 7.31
Comparison of Different State Encoding Approaches

Once the codes have been assigned to the state names, each of the bits within the code must be given a unique signal name. The signal names are necessary because the individual bits within the state code are going to be implemented with real circuitry so each signal name will correspond to an actual node in the logic diagram. These individual signal names are called ***state variables***. Unique variable names are needed for both the current state and next state signals. The current state variables are driven by the Q outputs of the D-Flip-Flops holding the state codes. The next state variables are driven by the next state logic circuitry and are connected to the D inputs of the D-Flip-Flops. State variable names are commonly chosen that are descriptive both in terms of their purpose and connection location. For example, current state variables are often given the names Q, Q_cur or Q_current to indicate that they come from the Q outputs of the D-Flip-Flops. Next state variables are given names such as Q*, Q_nxt or Q_next to indicate that they are the *next* value of Q and are connected to the D input of the D-Flip-Flops. Once state codes and state variable names are assigned, the state transition table is updated with the detailed information.

Returning to our push-button window controller example, let's encode our states in straight binary and use the state variable names of Q_cur and Q_nxt. Example 7.5 shows the process of state encoding and the new state transition table.

Example: Push-Button Window Controller - State Encoding

This state machine contains two states, w_closed and w_open. The following are the three possible ways these states could be encoded.

State Name	Binary	Gray Code	One-Hot
w_closed	0	0	01
w_open	1	1	10

Since this machine is so small, there is no difference between the binary and gray code approaches. Both of these techniques will require one D-Flip-Flop to hold the state code. The one-hot approach will require two D-Flip-Flops. Let's choose binary state encoding for this example. Let's use the state variable names Q_cur and Q_nxt.

Once the state codes and state variables are chosen, the state transition table is updated with the new detailed information about the design.

Current State		Input	Next State		Outputs	
	Q_cur	Press		Q_nxt	Open_CW	Close_CCW
w_closed	0	0	w_closed	0	0	0
w_closed	0	1	w_open	1	1	0
w_open	1	0	w_open	1	0	0
w_open	1	1	w_closed	0	0	1

Example 7.5
Push-Button Window Controller - State Encoding

7.4.2.2 Next State Logic

The next step in the state machine design is to synthesize the next state logic. The next state logic will compute the values of the next state variables based on the current state and the system inputs. Recall that a combinational logic function drives one and only one output bit. This means that every bit within the next state code needs to have a dedicated combinational logic circuit. The state transition table contains all of the necessary information to synthesize the next state logic including the exact output values of each next state variable for each and every input combination of state code and system input(s).

In our push-button window controller example, we only need to create one combinational logic circuit because there is only one next state variable (Q_nxt). The inputs to the combinational logic circuit are Q_cur and Press. Notice that the state transition table was created such that the order of the input values are listed in a binary count just as in a formal truth table formation. This makes synthesizing the combinational logic circuit straightforward. Example 7.6 shows the steps to synthesize the next state logic for this the push-button window controller.

Example: Push-Button Window Controller - Next State Logic

We need to synthesize the combinational logic circuit that will create the next state logic for Q_nxt. The behavior of this combinational logic circuit is described in the state transition table. In order to visualize where this information is within the table, let's pull it out and put it into a traditional truth table format.

Current State		Input	Next State		Outputs	
	Q_cur	Press		Q_nxt	Open_CW	Close_CCW
w_closed	0	0	w_closed	0	0	0
w_closed	0	1	w_open	1	1	0
w_open	1	0	w_open	1	0	0
w_open	1	1	w_closed	0	0	1

These columns are the inputs to the next state logic.

This column is the desired output for the next state logic variable Q_nxt.

Q_cur	Press	Q_nxt
0	0	0
0	1	1
1	0	1
1	1	0

$$Q\_nxt = (Q\_cur' \cdot Press) + (Q\_cur \cdot Press')$$

or

$$Q\_nxt = Q\_cur \oplus Press$$

Example 7.6
Push-Button Window Controller - Next State Logic

7.4.2.3 Output Logic

The next step in the state machine design is to synthesize the output logic. The output logic will compute the values of the system outputs based on the current state and, in the case of a Mealy machine, the system inputs. Each of the output signals will require a dedicated combinational logic circuit. Again, the state transition table contains all of the necessary information to synthesize the output logic.

In our push-button window controller example, we need to create one circuit to compute the output "Open_CW" and one circuit to compute the output "Close_CCW". In this example, the inputs to these circuits are the current state (Q_cur) and the system input (Press). Example 7.7 shows the steps to synthesize the output logic for the push-button window controller.

Example: Push-Button Window Controller - Output Logic

We need to synthesize the combinational logic circuits that will create the output logic for the signals "Open_CW" and "Close_CCW". The behavior of this combinational logic circuit is described in the state transition table. Again, in order to visualize where this information is within the table, let's pull it out and put it into traditional truth table formats.

Example 7.7
Push-Button Window Controller - Output Logic

7.4.2.4 The Final Logic Diagram

The final step is the design of the state machine is to create the logic diagram. It is useful to recall the block diagram for a state machine from Figure 7.29. A logic diagram begins by entering the state memory. Recall that the state memory consists of D-Flip-Flops that hold the current state code. One D-Flip-Flop is needed for every current state variable. When entering the D-Flip-Flops, it is useful to label them with the current state variable they will be holding. The next part of the logic diagram is the next state logic. Each of the combinational logic circuits that compute the next state variables should be drawn to the left of D-Flip-Flop holding the corresponding current state variable. The output of each next state logic circuit is connected to the D input of the corresponding D-Flip-Flop. Finally, the output logic is entered with the inputs to the logic coming from the current state and potentially from the system inputs.

Example 7.8 shows the process for creating the final logic diagram for our push-button window controller. Notice that the state memory is implemented with one D-Flip-Flop since there is only 1-bit in the current state code (Q_cur). The next state logic is a combinational logic circuit that computes Q_nxt based on the values of Q_cur and Press. Finally, the output logic consists of two separate combinational logic circuits to compute the system outputs Open_CW and Close_CCW based on Q_cur and Press. In this diagram the Qn output of the D-Flip-Flop could have been used for the inverted versions of Q_cur; however, inversion bubbles were used instead in order to make the diagram more readable.

Example 7.8
Push-Button Window Controller - Logic Diagram

7.4.3 FSM Design Process Overview

The entire finite state machine design process is given in Figure 7.32.

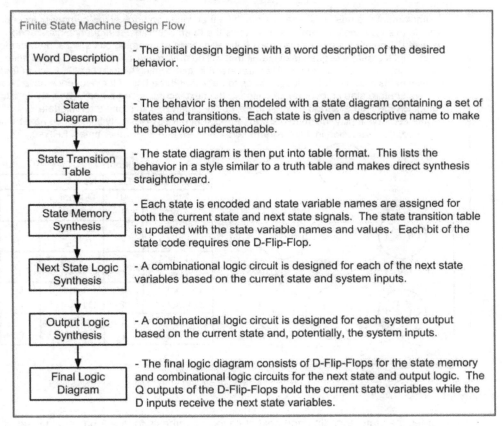

Figure 7.32
Finite State Machine Design Flow

7.4.4 FSM Design Examples

7.4.4.1 Serial Bit Sequence Detector

Let's consider the design of a 3-bit serial sequence detector. Example 7.9 provides the word description, state diagram, and state transition table for this finite state machine.

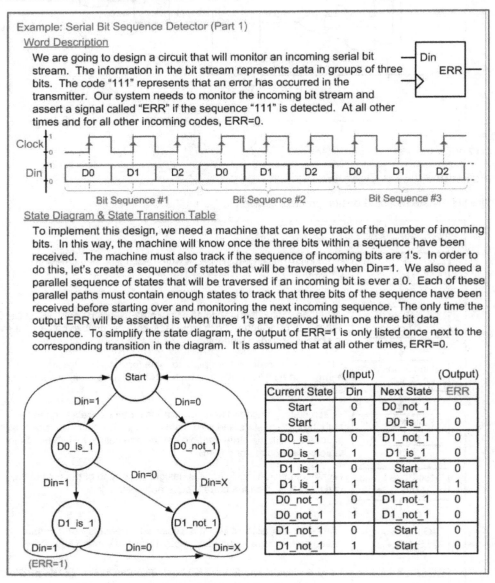

Example: Serial Bit Sequence Detector (Part 1)

Word Description

We are going to design a circuit that will monitor an incoming serial bit stream. The information in the bit stream represents data in groups of three bits. The code "111" represents that an error has occurred in the transmitter. Our system needs to monitor the incoming bit stream and assert a signal called "ERR" if the sequence "111" is detected. At all other times and for all other incoming codes, ERR=0.

State Diagram & State Transition Table

To implement this design, we need a machine that can keep track of the number of incoming bits. In this way, the machine will know once the three bits within a sequence have been received. The machine must also track if the sequence of incoming bits are 1's. In order to do this, let's create a sequence of states that will be traversed when Din=1. We also need a parallel sequence of states that will be traversed if an incoming bit is ever a 0. Each of these parallel paths must contain enough states to track that three bits of the sequence have been received before starting over and monitoring the next incoming sequence. The only time the output ERR will be asserted is when three 1's are received within one three bit data sequence. To simplify the state diagram, the output of ERR=1 is only listed once next to the corresponding transition in the diagram. It is assumed that at all other times, ERR=0.

	(Input)		(Output)
Current State	Din	Next State	ERR
Start	0	D0_not_1	0
Start	1	D0_is_1	0
D0_is_1	0	D1_not_1	0
D0_is_1	1	D1_is_1	0
D1_is_1	0	Start	0
D1_is_1	1	Start	1
D0_not_1	0	D1_not_1	0
D0_not_1	1	D1_not_1	0
D1_not_1	0	Start	0
D1_not_1	1	Start	0

Example 7.9
Serial Bit Sequence Detector (Part 1)

Example 7.10 provides the state encoding and next state logic synthesis for the 3-bit serial bit sequence detector.

Example: Serial Bit Sequence Detector (Part 2)

State Encoding

Let's encode the states in binary in order to minimize the number of D-Flip-Flops. Encoding in Gray Code will not benefit this design since the state transitions are not linear. Since there are 5 unique states, we'll need 3 bits to encode all of the states. At this point, we also need to assign the state variable names. Let's call the three variables for the current state Q2_cur, Q1_cur, and Q0_cur. Let's call the three variables for the next state Q2_nxt, Q1_nxt, and Q0_nxt. After the state codes are assigned, we can update the state transition table.

State	Code
Start	= "000"
D0_is_1	= "001"
D1_is_1	= "010"
D0_not_1	= "011"
D1_not_1	= "100"

Current State				Input	Next State				Output
	Q2_cur	Q1_cur	Q0_cur	Din		Q2_nxt	Q1_nxt	Q0_nxt	ERR
Start	0	0	0	0	D0_not_1	0	1	1	0
Start	0	0	0	1	D0_is_1	0	0	1	0
D0_is_1	0	0	1	0	D1_not_1	1	0	0	0
D0_is_1	0	0	1	1	D1_is_1	0	1	0	0
D1_is_1	0	1	0	0	Start	0	0	0	0
D1_is_1	0	1	0	1	Start	0	0	0	1
D0_not_1	0	1	1	0	D1_not_1	1	0	0	0
D0_not_1	0	1	1	1	D1_not_1	1	0	0	0
D1_not_1	1	0	0	0	Start	0	0	0	0
D1_not_1	1	0	0	1	Start	0	0	0	0

Next State Logic

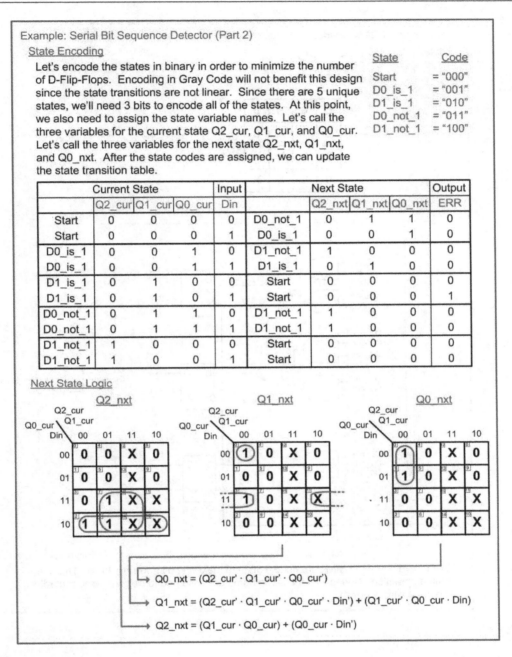

$$Q0\_nxt = (Q2\_cur' \cdot Q1\_cur' \cdot Q0\_cur')$$

$$Q1\_nxt = (Q2\_cur' \cdot Q1\_cur' \cdot Q0\_cur' \cdot Din') + (Q1\_cur' \cdot Q0\_cur \cdot Din)$$

$$Q2\_nxt = (Q1\_cur \cdot Q0\_cur) + (Q0\_cur \cdot Din')$$

Example 7.10
Serial Bit Sequence Detector (Part 2)

Example 7.11 shows the output logic synthesis and final logic diagram for the 3-bit serial bit sequence detector.

Example: Serial Bit Sequence Detector (Part 3)

Output Logic

ERR

$$ERR = Q1\_cur \cdot Q0\_cur' \cdot Din$$

Logic Diagram

"Next State Logic"   "State Memory"   "Output Logic"

Note that many of the wires are not drawn in to make the diagram readable. This is a common practice. Nodes with the same name are assumed to be connected regardless of whether a wire is drawn.

Example 7.11
Serial Bit Sequence Detector (Part 3)

7.4.4.2 Vending Machine Controller

Let's now look at the design of a simple vending machine controller. Example 7.12 provides the word description, state diagram, and state transition table for this finite state machine.

Example: Vending Machine Controller (Part 1)

Word Description

We are going to design a simple vending machine controller. The vending machine will sell bottles of water for 75¢. Customers can enter either a dollar bill or quarters. Once a sufficient amount of money is entered, the vending machine will dispense a bottle of water. If the user entered a dollar it will return one quarter in change. A "Money Receiver" detects when money has been entered. The receiver sends two logic signals to our circuit indicating whether a dollar bill or quarter was received. A "Bottle Dispenser" system holds the water bottles and will release one bottle when its input signal is asserted. A "Coin Return" system holds quarters for change and will release one quarter when its input signal is asserted. The money receiver will reject money if a dollar and quarter are entered simultaneously or if a dollar is entered once the user has started entering quarters.

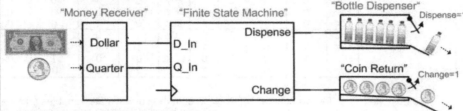

State Diagram and State Transition Table

To implement this state machine, we will need an initial state that the machine will wait in until a customer enters money (Wait). If a dollar is entered, the machine will assert the "Dispense" signal to release a bottle of water and assert the "Change" signal to give one quarter in change. We do not need an additional state for the condition of when a dollar is entered because the machine will simply assert the output signals and return to the Wait state. When the customer pays with quarters, our machine needs to keep track of how many quarters have been received. We'll need two interim states that keep track of how many quarters have been entered (25¢ and 50¢). Once the third quarter has been entered, our machine will assert the "Dispense" signal and return to the Wait state.

	(Inputs)			(Outputs)	
Current State	Q_in	D_in	Next State	Dispense	Change
Wait	0	0	Wait	0	0
Wait	0	1	Wait	1	1
Wait	1	0	25¢	0	0
25¢	0	X	25¢	0	0
25¢	1	X	50¢	0	0
50¢	0	X	50¢	0	0
50¢	1	X	Wait	1	0

State diagrams can be simplified by only drawing transitions when a signal is asserted.

Example 7.12
Vending Machine Controller (Part 1)

Example 7.13 provides the state encoding and next state logic synthesis for the simple vending machine controller.

Example: Vending Machine Controller (Part 2)

State Encoding

Let's encode the states in binary and name the current state variables Q1_cur and Q0_cur and the next state variables Q1_nxt and Q0_nxt. In this table we list out all possible values the current state and the inputs to make the table more complete.

State	Code
Wait	= "00"
25¢	= "01"
50¢	= "10"

	Current State		Input			Next State		Outputs	
	Q1_cur	Q0_cur	Q_in	D_in		Q1_nxt	Q0_nxt	Dispense	Change
Wait	0	0	0	0	Wait	0	0	0	0
Wait	0	0	0	1	Wait	0	0	1	1
Wait	0	0	1	0	25¢	0	1	0	0
Wait	0	0	1	1	Wait	0	0	0	0
25¢	0	1	0	0	25¢	0	1	0	0
25¢	0	1	0	1	25¢	0	1	0	0
25¢	0	1	1	0	50¢	1	0	0	0
25¢	0	1	1	1	25¢	0	1	0	0
50¢	1	0	0	0	50¢	1	0	0	0
50¢	1	0	0	1	50¢	1	0	0	0
50¢	1	0	1	0	Wait	0	0	1	0
50¢	1	0	1	1	50¢	1	0	0	0

Next State Logic

The next state logic for this counter depends on both the current state variables and the system input Up. We can again take advantage of don't cares for the unused state code to minimize the logic.

$$Q0\_nxt = (Q0\_cur \cdot Q\_in') + (Q0\_cur \cdot D\_in) + (Q1\_cur' \cdot Q0\_cur' \cdot Q\_in \cdot D\_in')$$
$$Q1\_nxt = (Q1\_cur \cdot Q\_in') + (Q1\_cur \cdot D\_in) + (Q0\_cur \cdot Q\_in \cdot D\_in')$$

Example 7.13
Vending Machine Controller (Part 2)

Example 7.14 shows the output logic synthesis and final logic diagram for the vending machine controller.

Example 7.14
Vending Machine Controller (Part 3)

CONCEPT CHECK

CC7.4(a) What allows a finite state machine to make more intelligent decisions about the system outputs compared to combinational logic alone?

    A) A finite state machine has knowledge about the past inputs.

    B) The D-flip-flops allow the outputs to be generated more rapidly.

    C) The next state and output logic allows the finite state machine to be more complex and implement larger truth tables.

    D) A synchronous system is always more intelligent.

CC7.4(b) When designing a finite state machine, many of the details of the implementation can be abstracted. At what design step do the details of the implementation start being considered?

    A) The state diagram step.

    B) The state transition table step.

    C) The state memory synthesis step.

    D) The word description.

CC7.4(c) What impact does adding an additional state have on the implementation of the state memory logic in a finite state machine?

    A) It adds an additional D-flip-flop.

    B) It adds a new state code that must be supported.

    C) It adds more combinational logic to the logic diagram.

    D) It reduces the speed that the machine can run at.

CC7.4(d) Which of the following statements about the next state logic is FALSE?

    A) It is always combinational logic.

    B) It always uses the current state as one of its inputs.

    C) Its outputs are connected to the D inputs of the D-flip-flops in the state memory.

    D) It uses the results of the output logic as part of its inputs.

CC7.4(e) Why does the output logic stage of a finite state machine always use the current state as one of its inputs?

    A) If it didn't, it would simply be a separate combinational logic circuit and not be part of the finite state machine.

    B) To make better decisions about what the system outputs should be.

    C) Because the next state logic is located too far away.

    D) Because the current state is produced on every triggering clock edge.

CC7.4(f) What impact does asserting a reset have on a finite state machine?

    A) It will cause the output logic to produce all zeros.

    B) It will cause the next state logic to produce all zeros.

    C) It will set the current state code to all zeros.

    D) It will start the system clock.

7.5 Counters

A *counter* is a special type of finite state machine. A counter will traverse the states within a state diagram in a linear fashion continually circling around all states. This behavior allows a special type of output topology called *state-encoded outputs*. Since each state in the counter represents a unique counter output, the states can be encoded with the associated counter output value. In this way, the current state code of the machine can be used as the output of the entire system.

7.5.1 2-Bit Binary Up Counter

Let's consider the design of a 2-bit binary up counter. Example 7.15 provides the word description, state diagram, state transition table, and state encoding for this counter.

Example 7.15
2-bit Binary Up Counter (Part 1)

Example 7.16 shows the next state and output logic synthesis, the final logic diagram, and resultant representative timing diagram for the 2-bit binary up counter.

Example 7.16
2-bit Binary Up Counter (Part 2)

7.5.2 2-Bit Binary Up/Down Counter

Let's now consider a 2-bit binary up/down counter. In this type of counter, there is an input that dictates whether the counter increments or decrements. This counter can still be implemented as a Moore machine and use state-encoded outputs. Example 7.17 provides the word description, state diagram, state transition table, and state encoding for this counter.

Example: 2-Bit Binary Up/Down Counter (Part 1)

Word Description

We are going to design a 2-bit binary up/down counter. When the
system input "Up" is asserted, the counter will increment by 1 on every
rising edge of the clock. When Up=0, the counter will decrement by 1 on
every rising edge of the clock. The output of the counter is called CNT.

State Diagram & State Transition Table

The state diagram for this counter is below. In this diagram, if the input Up=1, the machine
will traverse the states in order to create an incrementing count. If the input Up=0, the
machine will traverse the states in the opposite order. The outputs of this machine again
only depend on the current state so they are written inside of the state circles. This is a
Moore machine.

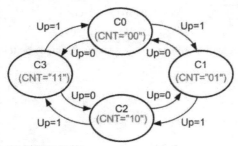

Current State	Up	Next State	CNT
C0	0	C3	"00"
	1	C1	
C1	0	C0	"01"
	1	C2	
C2	0	C1	"10"
	1	C3	
C3	0	C2	"11"
	1	C0	

(Input) ... (Output)

State Encoding

Again, this counter will use "state-encoded outputs". Let's name the current state variables
$Q1\_cur$ and $Q0\_cur$ and the next state variables $Q1\_nxt$ and $Q0\_nxt$. The state code
assignments and updated state transition table are below.

State Code
C0 = "00"
C1 = "01"
C2 = "10"
C3 = "11"

	Current State		Input		Next State		Outputs
	Q1_cur	Q0_cur	Up		Q1_nxt	Q0_nxt	CNT
C0	0	0	0	C3	1	1	"00"
C0	0	0	1	C1	0	1	"00"
C1	0	1	0	C0	0	0	"01"
C1	0	1	1	C2	1	0	"01"
C2	1	0	0	C1	0	1	"10"
C2	1	0	1	C3	1	1	"10"
C3	1	1	0	C2	1	0	"11"
C3	1	1	1	C0	0	0	"11"

Example 7.17
2-bit Binary Up/Down Counter (Part 1)

Example 7.18 shows the next state and output logic synthesis, the final logic diagram, and resultant representative
timing diagram for the 2-bit binary up/down counter.

Example: 2-Bit Binary Up/Down Counter (Part 2)

Next State Logic

The next state logic for this counter depends on both the current state variables and the input Up.

$$Q1\_nxt = Q1\_cur \oplus Q0\_cur \oplus Up$$

$$Q0\_nxt = Q0\_cur'$$

Output Logic

Since we are using state-encoded outputs, the outputs of the system will simply be the current state variables.

$$CNT(1) = Q1\_cur$$
$$CNT(0) = Q0\_cur$$

Logic Diagram

Timing Diagram

Example 7.18
2-bit Binary Up/Down Counter (Part 2)

7.5.3 2-Bit Gray Code Up Counter

A gray code counter is one in which the output only differs by one bit from its prior value. This type of counter can be implemented using state-encoded outputs by simply encoding the states in gray code. Let's consider the design of a 2-bit gray code up counter. Example 7.19 provides the word description, state diagram, state transition table, and state encoding for this counter.

Example: 2-Bit Gray Code Up Counter (Part 1)

Word Description

We are going to design a 2-bit gray code up counter. The counter will output an incrementing gray code pattern on every rising edge of the clock ("00", "01", "11", "10"). When the counter reaches "11", it will start over counting at "00". The output of the counter is called Gray.

State Diagram & State Transition Table

The state diagram for this counter is below. Notice that there are no inputs to the state machine. Also notice that the machine transitions in a linear pattern through the states and continually repeats the sequence of states. The outputs of this machine depend only on the current state, so they are written inside of the state circles. This is a Moore machine.

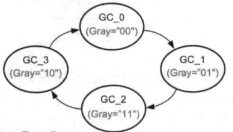

(Output)

Current State	Next State	Gray
GC_0	GC_1	"00"
GC_1	GC_2	"01"
GC_2	GC_3	"11"
GC_3	GC_0	"10"

State Encoding

When implementing this counter, we can use "state-encoded outputs". This means that we choose the state codes so that they match the desired output at each state. This allows the machine to simply use the current state variables for the system outputs. Let's name the current state variables Q1_cur and Q0_cur and the next state variables Q1_nxt and Q0_nxt. The state code assignments and updated state transition table are below.

State	Code
GC_0	= "00"
GC_1	= "01"
GC_2	= "11"
GC_3	= "10"

	Current State			Next State			Outputs
	Q1_cur	Q0_cur			Q1_nxt	Q0_nxt	Gray
GC_0	0	0	GC_1		0	1	"00"
GC_1	0	1	GC_2		1	1	"01"
GC_2	1	1	GC_3		1	0	"11"
GC_3	1	0	GC_0		0	0	"10"

Example 7.19
2-bit Gray Code Up Counter (Part 1)

Example 7.20 shows the next state and output logic synthesis, the final logic diagram, and resultant representative timing diagram for the 2-bit gray code up counter.

Example: 2-Bit Gray Code Up Counter (Part 2)

Next State Logic

The next state logic for this counter only depends on the current state variables since there are no inputs to the system. Care must be taken when synthesizing the next state logic because the order of the current state variable values in the state transition table is not in a binary count order as in prior examples.

$$Q1\_nxt = Q0\_cur$$

$$Q0\_nxt = Q1\_cur'$$

Output Logic

Since we are using state-encoded outputs, the outputs of the system will simply be the current state variables.

$$Gray(1) = Q1\_cur$$

$$Gray(0) = Q0\_cur$$

Logic Diagram

Timing Diagram

Example 7.20
2-bit Gray Code Up Counter (Part 2)

7.5.4 2-Bit Gray Code Up/Down Counter

Let's now consider a 2-bit gray code up/down counter. In this type of counter, there is an input that dictates whether the counter increments or decrements. This counter can still be implemented as a Moore machine and use state-encoded outputs. Example 7.21 provides the word description, state diagram, state transition table, and state encoding for this counter.

Example: 2-Bit Gray Code Up/Down Counter (Part 1)

Word Description

We are going to design a 2-bit gray code up/down counter. When the system input "Up" is asserted, the counter will output an incrementing gray code pattern on every rising edge of the clock ("00", "01", "11", "10"). When the input Up=0, the counter will output a decrementing gray code pattern. The output of the counter is called Gray.

State Diagram & State Transition Table

The state diagram for this counter is below. The outputs of this machine again only depend on the current state, so they are written inside of the state circles. This is a Moore machine.

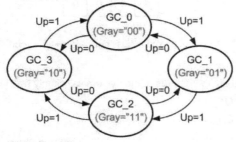

Current State	Up	Next State	Gray
GC_0	0	GC_3	"00"
	1	GC_1	
GC_1	0	GC_0	"01"
	1	GC_2	
GC_2	0	GC_1	"11"
	1	GC_3	
GC_3	0	GC_2	"10"
	1	GC_0	

(Input)   (Output)

State Encoding

Again, this counter will use "state-encoded outputs". Let's name the current state variables $Q1\_cur$ and $Q0\_cur$ and the next state variables $Q1\_nxt$ and $Q0\_nxt$. The state code assignments and updated state transition table are below.

State   Code

GC_0 = "00"
GC_1 = "01"
GC_2 = "11"
GC_3 = "10"

Current State			Input	Next State			Outputs
	Q1_cur	Q0_cur	Up		Q1_nxt	Q0_nxt	Gray
GC_0	0	0	0	GC_3	1	0	"00"
GC_0	0	0	1	GC_1	0	1	"00"
GC_1	0	1	0	GC_0	0	0	"01"
GC_1	0	1	1	GC_2	1	1	"01"
GC_2	1	1	0	GC_1	0	1	"11"
GC_2	1	1	1	GC_3	1	0	"11"
GC_3	1	0	0	GC_2	1	1	"10"
GC_3	1	0	1	GC_0	0	0	"10"

Example 7.21
2-bit Gray Code Up/Down Counter (Part 1)

Example 7.22 shows the next state and output logic synthesis, the final logic diagram, and resultant representative timing diagram for the 2-bit gray code up/down counter.

Example: 2-Bit Gray Code Up/Down Counter (Part 2)

Next State Logic

The next state logic for this counter depends on both the current state variables and the input Up. Again, care must be taken when synthesizing the next state logic due to the non-regular pattern of the current state codes in the state transition table.

$$Q1\_nxt = (Q0\_cur' \cdot Up') + (Q0\_cur \cdot Up) \qquad Q0\_nxt = (Q1\_cur \cdot Up') + (Q1\_cur' \cdot Up)$$

Output Logic

Since we are using state-encoded outputs, the outputs of the system will simply be the current state variables.

$$Gray(1) = Q1\_cur$$
$$Gray(0) = Q0\_cur$$

Logic Diagram

Timing Diagram

Example 7.22
2-bit Gray Code Up/Down Counter (Part 2)

7.5.5 3-Bit One-Hot Up Counter

A one-hot counter creates an output in which one and only one bit is asserted at a time. In an *up counter* configuration, the assertion is made on the least significant bit first, followed by the next higher significant bit, and so on (i.e., 001, 010, 100, 001...). A one-hot counter can be created using state-encoded outputs. For a *n*-bit counter, the machine will require *n* D-Flip-Flops. Let's consider a 3-bit one-hot up counter. Example 7.23 provides the word description, state diagram, state transition table, and state encoding for this counter.

Example: 3-Bit One-Hot Up Counter (Part 1)

Word Description

We are going to design a 3-bit one-hot up counter. The counter will output an incrementing one-hot pattern on every rising edge of the clock ("001", "010", "100"). When the counter reaches "100", it will start over counting at "001". The output of the counter is called Hot.

State Diagram & State Transition Table

The state diagram for this counter is below. Notice that there are no inputs to the state machine. The outputs of this machine depend only on the current state so they are written inside of the state circles. This is a Moore machine.

Current State	Next State	(Output) Hot
Hot_0	Hot_1	"001"
Hot_1	Hot_2	"010"
Hot_2	Hot_0	"100"

State Encoding

When implementing this counter, we can use "state-encoded outputs". Using one-hot state encoding requires three bits to encode the states. This means we'll need three variables for both the current state and next state. Let's name the current state variables Q2_cur, Q1_cur and Q0_cur and the next state variables Q2_nxt, Q1_nxt and Q0_nxt. The state code assignments and updated state transition table are below.

State	Code		Current State				Next State			Outputs
			Q2_cur	Q1_cur	Q0_cur		Q2_nxt	Q1_nxt	Q0_nxt	Hot
Hot_0 = "001"		Hot_0	0	0	1	Hot_1	0	1	0	"001"
Hot_1 = "010"		Hot_1	0	1	0	Hot_2	1	0	0	"010"
Hot_2 = "100"		Hot_2	1	0	0	Hot_0	0	0	1	"100"

Example 7.23
3-bit One-Hot Up Counter (Part 1)

Example 7.24 shows the next state and output logic synthesis, the final logic diagram, and resultant representative timing diagram for the 3-bit one-hot up counter.

Example: 3-Bit One-Hot Up Counter (Part 2)

Next State Logic

The next state logic for this counter only depends on the current state variables since there are no inputs to the system. We can take advantage of don't cares to minimize the logic.

$Q2\_nxt = Q1\_cur$

$Q1\_nxt = Q0\_cur$

$Q0\_nxt = Q2\_cur$

Output Logic

Since we are using state-encoded outputs, the outputs of the system will simply be the current state variables.

$Hot(2) = Q2\_cur$

$Hot(1) = Q1\_cur$

$Hot(0) = Q0\_cur$

Logic Diagram

Timing Diagram

Example 7.24
3-bit One-Hot Up Counter (Part 2)

7.5.6 3-Bit One-Hot Up/Down Counter

Let's now consider a 3-bit one-hot up/down counter. In this type of counter, there is an input that dictates whether the counter increments or decrements. This counter can still be implemented as a Moore machine and use state-encoded outputs. Example 7.25 provides the word description, state diagram, state transition table, and state encoding for this counter.

Example: 3-Bit One-Hot Up/Down Counter (Part 1)

Word Description

We are going to design a 3-bit one-hot up/down counter. When the system input "Up" is asserted, the counter will output an incrementing one-hot pattern on every rising edge of the clock ("001", "010", "100"). When the input Up=0, the counter will output a decrementing one-hot pattern ("100", "010", "001"). The output of the counter is called Hot.

State Diagram & State Transition Table

The state diagram and state transition table for this counter are below.

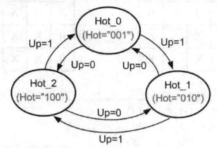

| | (Input) | | (Output) |
Current State	Up	Next State	Hot
Hot_0	0	Hot_2	"001"
Hot_0	1	Hot_1	"001"
Hot_1	0	Hot_0	"010"
Hot_1	1	Hot_2	"010"
Hot_2	0	Hot_1	"100"
Hot_2	1	Hot_0	"100"

State Encoding

Let's use "state-encoded outputs" and name the current state variables Q2_cur, Q1_cur and Q0_cur and the next state variables Q2_nxt, Q1_nxt and Q0_nxt. The state code assignments and updated state transition table are below.

| State | Code | | Current State | | | Input | | Next State | | | Outputs |
			Q2_cur	Q1_cur	Q0_cur	Up		Q2_nxt	Q1_nxt	Q0_nxt	Hot
		Hot_0	0	0	1	0	Hot_2	1	0	0	"001"
Hot_0	= "001"	Hot_0	0	0	1	1	Hot_1	0	1	0	"001"
Hot_1	= "010"	Hot_1	0	1	0	0	Hot_0	0	0	1	"010"
Hot_2	= "100"	Hot_1	0	1	0	1	Hot_2	1	0	0	"010"
		Hot_2	1	0	0	0	Hot_1	0	1	0	"100"
		Hot_2	1	0	0	1	Hot_0	0	0	1	"100"

Example 7.25
3-bit One-Hot Up/Down Counter (Part 1)

Example 7.26 shows the next state and output logic synthesis for the 3-bit one-hot up/down counter.

Example 7.26
3-bit One-Hot Up/Down Counter (Part 2)

Finally, Example 7.27 shows the logic diagram and resultant representative timing diagram for the counter.

Example: 3-Bit One-Hot Up/Down Counter (Part 3)

Logic Diagram

Timing Diagram

Example 7.27
3-bit One-Hot Up/Down Counter (Part 3)

CONCEPT CHECK

CC7.5 What characteristic of a counter makes it a special case of a finite state machine?

A) The state transitions are mostly linear, which reduces the implementation complexity.

B) The outputs are always a gray code.

C) The next state logic circuitry is typically just sum terms.

D) There is never a situation where a counter could be a Mealy machine.

7.6 Finite State Machine's Reset Condition

The one-hot counter designs in Example 7.23 and Example 7.25 where the first FSM examples that had an initial state that was not encoded with all 0's. Notice that all of the other FSM examples had initial states with state codes comprised of all 0's (e.g., w_closed=0, S0="00", C0="00", GC_0="00", etc.). When the initial state is encoded with all 0's, the FSM can be put into this state by asserting the reset line of all of the D-Flip-Flops in the state memory. By asserting the reset line, the Q outputs of all of the D-Flip-Flips are forced to 0's. This sets the initial current state value to whatever state is encoded with all 0's. The initial state of a machine is often referred to as the *reset state*. The circuitry to initialize state machines is often omitted from the logic diagram as it is assumed that the necessary circuitry will exist in order to put the state machine into the reset state. If the reset state is encoded with all 0's, then the reset line can be used alone; however, if the reset state code contains 1's, then both the reset *and* preset lines must be used to put the machine into the reset state upon start up. Let's look at the behavior of the one-hot up counter again. Figure 7.33 shows how using the reset lines of the D-Flip-Flops alone will cause the circuit to operate incorrectly. Instead, a combination of the reset and preset lines must be used to get the one-hot counter into its initial state of Hot_0="001".

Figure 7.33
Finite State Machine Reset State

Resets are most often asynchronous so that they can immediately alter the state of the FSM. If a reset was implemented in a sycnronous manner and there was a clock failure, the system could not be reset since there would be no more subsequent clock edges that would recognize that the reset line was asserted. An asynchronous reset allows the system to be fully restarted even in the event of a clock failure.

CONCEPT CHECK

CC7.6 What is the downside of using D-flip-flops that do not have preset capability in a finite state machine?

A) The finite state machine will run slower.

B) The next state logic will be more complex.

C) The output logic will not be able to support both Mealy and Moore type machine architectures.

D) The finite state machine can never have a start-up state with a state code of all zeros.

7.7 Sequential Logic Analysis

Sequential logic analysis refers to the act of deciphering the operation of a circuit from its final logic diagram. This is similar to combinational logic analysis with the exception that the storage capability of the D-flip-flops must be considered. This analysis is also used to understand the timing of a sequential logic circuit and can be used to predict the maximum clock rate that can be used.

7.7.1 Finding the State Equations and Output Logic Expressions of a FSM

When given the logic diagram for a finite state machine and it is desired to reverse-engineer its behavior, the first step is to determine the next state logic and output logic expressions. This can be accomplished by first labeling the current and next state variables on the inputs and outputs of the D-flip-flops that are implementing the state memory of the FSM. The outputs of the D-flip-flops are labeled with arbitrary current state variable names (e.g., Q1_cur, Q0_cur, etc.) and the inputs are labeled with arbitrary next state variable names (e.g., Q1_nxt, Q0_nxt, etc.). The numbering of the state variables can be assigned to the D-flip-flops arbitrarily as long as the current and next state bit numbering is matched. For example, if a D-flip-flop is labeled to hold bit 0 of the state code, its output should be labeled Q**0**_cur and its input should be labeled Q**0**_nxt.

Once the current state variable nets are labeled in the logic diagram, the expressions for the next state logic can be found by analyzing the combinational logic circuity driving the next state variables (e.g., Q1_nxt, Q0_nxt). The next state logic expressions will be in terms of the current state variables (e.g., Q1_cur, Q0_cur) and any inputs to the FSM.

The output logic expressions can also be found by analyzing the combinational logic driving the outputs of the FSM. Again, these will be in terms of the current state variables and potentially the inputs to the FSM. When analyzing the output logic, the type of machine can be determined. If the output logic only depends on combinational logic that is driven by the current state variables, the FSM is a Moore machine. If the output logic depends on both the current state variables and the FSM inputs, the FSM is a Mealy machine. An example of this analysis approach is given in Example 7.28.

Example 7.28
Determining the Next State Logic and Output Logic Expression of a FSM

7.7.2 Finding the State Transition Table of a FSM

Once the next state logic and output logic expressions are known, the state transition table can be created. It is useful to assign more descriptive names to all possible state codes in the FSM. The number of unique states possible depends on how many D-flip-flops are used in the state memory of the FSM. For example, if the FSM uses two D-flip-flops there are four unique state codes (i.e., 00, 01, 10, 11). We can assign descriptive names such as S0=00, S1=01, S2=10, S3=11.   When first creating the transition table, we assign labels and list each possible state code. If a particular code is not used, it can be removed from the transition table at the end of the analysis. The state code that the machine will start in can be found by analyzing its reset and preset connections. This code is typically listed first in the table. The transition table is then populated with all possible combinations of current states and inputs. The next state codes and output logic values can then be populated by evaluating the next state logic and output logic expressions found earlier. An example of this analysis is shown in Example 7.29.

Example: Determining the State Transition Table of a FSM

Given: The following finite state machine logic diagram.

Find: The state transition table.

Solution: Since there are two D-Flip-Flops in this circuit there can be four unique state codes (00, 01, 10, and 11). We notice that the reset condition for this FSM will initialize this machine to state 00. We will insert this state code in the table as the first state. Also, we can assign four arbitrary state names to these codes. Let's use S0=00, S1=01, S2=10, and S3=11. We can list these state names and current state codes in the table along with every possible value of the input. The last step is to simply evaluate the logic expressions for the next state variables and the output to complete the table.

	Current State		Input		Next State		Outputs
	Q1_cur	Q0_cur	Go		Q1_nxt	Q0_nxt	Done
S0	0	0	0	S0	0	0	0
S0	0	0	1	S1	0	1	0
S1	0	1	0	S2	1	0	0
S1	0	1	1	S2	1	0	0
S2	1	0	0	S3	1	1	0
S2	1	0	1	S3	1	1	0
S3	1	1	0	S0	0	0	1
S3	1	1	1	S0	0	0	1

The current state codes and Go are used as the inputs into the next state logic and output logic expressions.

These values are calculated using the next state logic and output logic expressions. The state names for the next states are added last.

Example 7.29
Determining the State Transition Table of a FSM

7.7.3 Finding the State Diagram of a FSM

Once the state transition table is found, creating the state diagram becomes possible. We start the diagram with the state corresponding to the reset state. We then draw how the FSM transitions between each of its possible states based on the inputs to the machine and list the corresponding outputs. An example of this analysis is shown in Example 7.30.

Example: Determining the State Diagram of a FSM

Given: The following state transition table that has been created from a FSM logic diagram.

Current State			Input		Next State			Outputs
	Q1_cur	Q0_cur	Go			Q1_nxt	Q0_nxt	Done
S0	0	0	0	S0		0	0	0
S0	0	0	1	S1		0	1	0
S1	0	1	0	S2		1	0	0
S1	0	1	1	S2		1	0	0
S2	1	0	0	S3		1	1	0
S2	1	0	1	S3		1	1	0
S3	1	1	0	S0		0	0	1
S3	1	1	1	S0		0	0	1

Find: The state diagram.

Solution: The reset condition for this FSM is S0=00 based on the way that the resets of the D-Flip-Flops were connected in the prior logic diagram. This allows us to begin drawing the state diagram starting in S0. From this state we simply list the next state based on the input Go. We notice that the machine will stay in S0 when Go=0 and will transition to S1 when Go=1. We then notice that the machine transitions from S1-to-S2, from S2-to-S3, and from S3-to-S0 regardless of the input value. We can draw these transitions with the input condition Go=X.

For the output Done, we notice that it only depends on the current state, thus this is a Moore machine. For this type of machine we can write the output value within the state bubbles. The final state diagram is as follows.

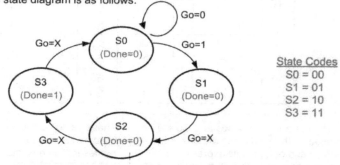

State Codes
S0 = 00
S1 = 01
S2 = 10
S3 = 11

Example 7.30
Determining the State Diagram of a FSM

7.7.4 Determining the Maximum Clock Frequency of a FSM

The maximum clock frequency is often one of the banner specifications for a digital system. The clock frequency of a FSM depends on a variety of timing specifications within the sequential circuit including the setup and hold time of the D-flip-flop, the clock-to-Q delay of the D-flip-flop, the combinational logic delay driving the input of the D-flip-flop, the delay of the interconnect that wires the circuit together, and the desired margin for the circuit. The basic concept of analyzing the timing of FSM is to determine how long we must wait after a rising (assuming a rising edge triggered D-flip-flop) clock edge occurs until the subsequent rising clock edge can occur. The amount of time that must be allowed between rising clock edges depends on how much delay exists in the system. A sufficient amount of time must exist between clock edges to allow the logic computations to settle so that on the next clock edge the D-flip-flops can latch in a new value on their inputs.

Let's examine all of the sources of delay in a FSM. Let's being by assuming that all logic values are at a stable value and we experience a rising clock edge. The value present on the D input of the D-flip-flop is latched into the storage device and will appear on the Q output after one clock-to-Q delay of the device (t_{CQ}). Once the new value is produced on the output of the D-flip-flop, it is then used by a variety of combinational logic circuits to produce the next state codes and the outputs of the FSM. The next state code computation is typically longer than the output computation so let's examine that path. The new value on Q propagates through the combinational logic circuitry and produces the next state code at the D input of the D-flip-flop. The delay to produce this next state code includes wiring delay in addition to gate delay. When analyzing the delay of the combinational logic circuitry (t_{cmb}) and the delay of the interconnect (t_{int}), the worst case path is always considered. Once the new logic value is produced by the next state logic circuitry, it must remain stable for a certain amount of time in order to meet the D-flip-flop's setup specification (t_{setup}). Once this specification is met, the D-flip-flop *could* be clocked with the next clock edge; however, this represents a scenario without any *margin* in the timing. This means that if anything in the system caused the delay to increase even slightly, the D-flip-flop could go metastable. To avoid this situation, margin is included in the delay (t_{margin}). This provides some padding so that the system can reliably operate. A margin of 10% is typical in digital systems. The time that must exist between rising clock edges is then simply the sum of all of these sources of delay ($t_{CQ} + t_{cmb} + t_{int} + t_{setup} + t_{margin}$). Since the time between rising clock edges is defined as the period of the signal (T), this value is also the definition of the period of the fastest clock. Since the frequency of a signal is simply f=1/T, the maximum clock frequency for the FSM is the reciprocal of the sum of the delay.

One specification that is not discussed in the above description is the hold time of the D-flip-flop (t_{hold}). The hold specification is the amount of time that the input to the D-flip-flop must remain constant after the clock edge. In modern storage devices, this time is typically very small and considerably less than the t_{CQ} specification. If the hold specification is less than t_{CQ} it can be ignored because the output of the D-flip-flop will not change until after one t_{CQ} anyway. This means that the hold requirements are inherently met. This is the situation with the majority of modern D-flip-flops. In the rare case that the hold time is greater than t_{CQ}, then it is used in place of t_{CQ} in the summation of delays. Figure 7.34 gives the summary of the maximum clock frequency calculation when analyzing a FSM.

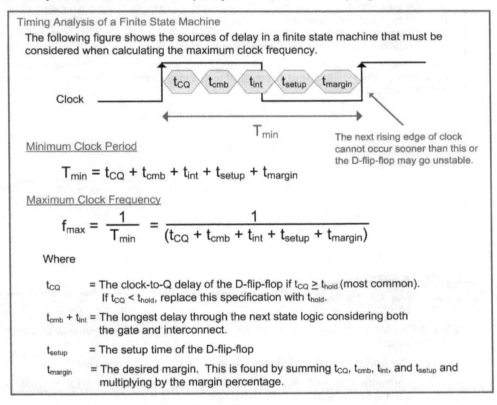

Timing Analysis of a Finite State Machine

The following figure shows the sources of delay in a finite state machine that must be considered when calculating the maximum clock frequency.

Minimum Clock Period

$$T_{min} = t_{CQ} + t_{cmb} + t_{int} + t_{setup} + t_{margin}$$

Maximum Clock Frequency

$$f_{max} = \frac{1}{T_{min}} = \frac{1}{(t_{CQ} + t_{cmb} + t_{int} + t_{setup} + t_{margin})}$$

Where

t_{CQ} = The clock-to-Q delay of the D-flip-flop if $t_{CQ} \geq t_{hold}$ (most common). If $t_{CQ} < t_{hold}$, replace this specification with t_{hold}.

$t_{cmb} + t_{int}$ = The longest delay through the next state logic considering both the gate and interconnect.

t_{setup} = The setup time of the D-flip-flop

t_{margin} = The desired margin. This is found by summing t_{CQ}, t_{cmb}, t_{int}, and t_{setup} and multiplying by the margin percentage.

Figure 7.34
Timing Analysis of a Finite State Machine

Let's take a look at an example of how to use this analysis. Example 7.31 shows this analysis for the FSM analyzed in prior sections but this time considering the delay specifications of each device.

Example: Determining the Maximum Clock Frequency of a FSM

Given: The following finite state machine logic diagram with the associated delays.

t_{setup} = 0.5 ns
t_{hold} = 0.5 ns
t_{CQ} = 1 ns

t_{XOR} = 4 ns
t_{AND} = 1 ns
t_{OR} = 2 ns

t_{int} = 0.5 ns
(for all paths)

Find: The maximum clock frequency this FSM can operate at with a timing margin of 10%.

Solution: First, we need to decide whether to use t_{CQ} or t_{hold} in our delay calculation. In this example, $t_{CQ} > t_{hold}$ so we will use t_{CQ}. When $t_{CQ} \geq t_{hold}$ the hold specification of the D-flip-flop is inherently met.

Next, we need to find the longest combinational logic and interconnect path. Since it is given that all interconnect paths are identical at 0.5ns, we simply need to find the longest gate delay path. There are three paths in this FSM. The first is the next state logic circuit using the XOR gate with 4ns of delay (t_{XOR}). The second is the next state logic expression using the SOP form with a delay of 3ns ($t_{AND} + t_{OR}$ =1ns + 2ns). The third path is through the output logic circuit with a delay of 1ns (t_{AND}). The longest combinational logic path is through the XOR gate so in our calculation we will use t_{cmb}=4ns.

Next, we need to calculate the exact value of the 10% margin required. The margin is found by summing all other real delays in the signal path and multiplying by the margin percentage. For this example:

$$t_{margin} = (t_{CQ} + t_{cmb} + t_{int} + t_{setup}) \cdot (0.1)$$
$$t_{margin} = (1ns + 4ns + 0.5ns + 0.5ns) \cdot (0.1)$$
$$t_{margin} = 0.6ns$$

Now we can plug all of our delays directly into the equation for the maximum clock frequency:

$$f_{max} = \frac{1}{(t_{CQ} + t_{cmb} + t_{int} + t_{setup} + t_{margin})} = \frac{1}{(1ns + 4ns + 0.5ns + 0.5ns + 0.6ns)}$$

$$f_{max} = 151 \text{ MHz}$$

Example 7.31
Determining the Maximum Clock Frequency of a FSM

CONCEPT CHECK

CC7.7 What is the risk of running the clock above its maximum allowable frequency in a finite state machine?

A) The power consumption may drop below the recommended level.

B) The setup and hold specifications of the D-flip-flops may be violated, which may put the machine into an unwanted state.

C) The states may transition too quickly to be usable.

D) The crystal generating the clock may become unstable.

Summary

❖ Sequential logic refers to a circuit that bases its outputs on both the present and past values of the inputs. Past values are held in sequential logic storage device.

❖ All sequential logic storage devices are based on a cross-coupled feedback loop. The positive feedback loop formed in this configuration will hold either a 1 or a 0. This is known as a bistable device.

❖ If the inputs of the feedback loop in a sequential logic storage device are driven to exactly between a 1 and a 0 (i.e., $V_{cc}/2$) and then released, the device will go *metastable*. Metastability refers to the behavior where the device will ultimately be pushed toward one of the two stable states in the system, typically by electrical noise. Once the device begins moving toward one of the stable states, the positive feedback will reinforce the transition until it reaches the stable state. The stable state that the device will move toward is random and unknown.

❖ Cross-coupled inverters are the most basic form of the positive feedback loop configuration. To give the ability to drive the outputs of the storage device to known values, the inverters are replaced with NOR gates to form the SR Latch. A variety of other modifications can be made to the loop configuration to ultimately produce a D-latch and D-flip-flop.

❖ A D-flip-flop will update its Q output with the value on its D input on every triggering edge of a clock. The amount of time that it takes for the Q output to update after a triggering clock edge is called the "t-clock-to-Q" (t_{CQ}) specification.

❖ The setup and hold times of a D-flip-flop describe how long before (t_{setup}) and after (t_{hold}) the triggering clock edge that the data on the D input of the device must be stable. If the D input transitions too close to the triggering clock edge (i.e., violating a setup or hold specification) then the device will go metastable and the ultimate value on Q is unknown.

❖ A synchronous system is one in which all logic transitions occur based on a single timing event. The timing event is typically the triggering edge of a clock.

❖ There are a variety of common circuits that can be accomplished using just sequential storage devices. Examples of these circuits include switch debouncing, toggle-flops, ripple counters, and shift registers.

❖ A finite state machine (FSM) is a system that produces outputs based on the current value of the inputs and a history of past inputs. The history of inputs are recorded as *states* that the machine has been in. As the machine responds to new inputs, it transitions between states. This allows a finite state machine to make more sophisticated decisions about what outputs to produce by knowing its history.

❖ A state diagram is a graphical way to describe the behavior of a FSM. States are represented using circles and transitions are represented using arrows. Outputs are listed either inside of the state circle or next to the transition arrow.

❖ A state transition table contains the same information as a state diagram, but in tabular format. This allows the system to be more easily synthesized because the information is in a form similar to a truth table.

❖ The first step in FSM synthesis is creating the *state memory*. The state memory consists of a set of D-flip-flops that hold the current state of the FSM. Each state in the FSM must be assigned a binary code. The type of encoding is arbitrary; however, there are certain encoding types that are commonly used such as binary, gray code, and one-hot. Once the codes are assigned, state variables need to be defined for each bit position for both the current state and the next state codes. The state variables for the current state represent the Q outputs of the D-flip-flops, which hold the current state code. The state variables for the next state code represent the D inputs of the D-flip-flops. A D-flip-flop is needed for each bit in the state code. On the triggering edge of a clock, the current state will be updated with the next state code.

❖ The second step in FSM synthesis is creating the *next state logic*. The next state logic is combinational logic circuitry that produces the next state codes based on the current state variables and any system inputs. The next state logic drives the D inputs of the D-flip-flops in the state memory.

❖ The third step in FSM synthesis is creating the *output logic*. The output logic is combinational logic circuitry that produces the system outputs based on the current state, and potentially, the system inputs.

❖ The output logic always depends on the current state of a FSM. If the output logic also depends on the system inputs, the machine is a *Mealy* machine. If the output logic does not depend on the system inputs, the machine is a *Moore* machine.

❖ A counter is a special type of finite state machine in which the states are traversed linearly. The linear progression of states allows the next state logic to be simplified. The complexity of the output logic in a counter can also be reduced by encoding the states with the desired counter output for that state. This technique, known as *state-encoded outputs*, allows the system outputs to simply be the current state of the FSM.

❖ The *reset state* of a FSM is the state that the machine will go to when it begins operation. The state code for the reset state must be configured using the reset and/or preset lines of the D-flip-flops.

If only reset lines are used on the D-flip-flops, the reset state must be encoded using only zeros.

❖ Given the logic diagram for a state machine, the logic expression for the next state memory and the output logic can be determined by analyzing the combinational logic driving the D inputs of the state memory (i.e., the next state logic) and the combinational logic driving the system outputs (i.e., the output logic).

❖ Given the logic diagram for a state diagram, the state diagram can be determined by first finding the logic expressions for the next state and output logic. The number of D-flip-flops in the logic diagram can then be used to calculate the possible number of state codes that the machine has. The state codes are then used to calculate the next state logic and output values. From this information a state transition table can be created and in turn, the state diagram.

❖ The maximum frequency of a FSM is found by summing all sources of time delay that must be

accounted for before the next triggering edge of the clock can occur. These sources include t_{CQ}, the worst case combinational logic path, the worst case interconnect delay path, the setup/hold time of the D-flip-flops, and any margin that is to be included. The sum of these timing delays represents the smallest period (T) that the clock can have. This is then converted to frequency.

❖ If the t_{CQ} time is greater than or equal to the hold time, the hold time can be ignored in the maximum frequency calculation. This is because the outputs of the D-flip-flops are inherently *held* while the D-flip-flops are producing the next output value. The time it takes to change the outputs after a triggering clock edge is defined as t_{CQ}. This means as long as $t_{CQ} \geq t_{hold}$, the hold time specification is inherently met since the logic driving the next state codes uses the Q outputs of the D-flip-flops.

Exercise Problems

For some of the following exercise problems you will be asked to design a VHDL model and perform a functional simulation. You will be provided with a test bench for each of these problems. The details of how to create your own VHDL test bench are provided later in Chapter 8. For some of the following exercise problems you will be asked to use D-Flip-Flops as part of a VHDL design. You will be provided with the model of the D-Flip-Flop and can declare it as a component in your design. The VHDL entity for a D-Flip-Flop is given in Figure 7.35. Keep in mind that this D-Flip-Flop has an active LOW reset. This means that when the reset line is pulled to a 0, the outputs will go to Q=0, Qn=1. When the reset line is LOW, the incoming clock is ignored. Once the reset line goes HIGH, the D-Flip-Flop resumes normal behavior. The details of how to create your own model of a D-Flip-Flop are provided later in Chapter 8.

Rising Edge Triggered D-Flip-Flop with Active LOW Reset

```
dflipflop.vhd
entity dflipflop is
    port    (Clock   : in    bit;
             Reset   : in    bit;
             D       : in    bit;
             Q, Qn   : out   bit);
end entity;
```

Figure 7.35

Section 7.1 – Sequential Logic Storage Devices

7.1.1 What does the term *metastability* refer to in a sequential storage device?

7.1.2 What does the term *bistable* refer to in a sequential storage device?

7.1.3 You are given a cross-coupled inverter pair in which all nodes are set to $V_{cc}/2$. Why will this configuration always move to a more stable state?

7.1.4 An SR Latch essentially implements the same cross-coupled feedback loop to store information as in a cross-coupled inverter pair. What is the purpose of using NOR gates instead of inverters in the SR Latch configuration?

7.1.5 Why isn't the input condition S=R=1 used in an SR Latch?

7.1.6 How will the output Q behave in an SR Latch if the inputs continuously switch between S=0, R=1 and S=1, R=1 every 10ns?

7.1.7 How do D-flip-flops enable synchronous systems?

7.1.8 What signal in the D-flip-flop in Figure 7.35 has the highest priority?

7.1.9 For the timing diagram shown in Figure 7.36, draw the outputs Q and Qn for a rising edge triggered D-flip-flop with active LOW.

Figure 7.36

7.1.10 For the timing diagram shown in Figure 7.37, draw the outputs Q and Qn for a rising edge triggered D-flip-flop with active LOW .

Figure 7.37

7.1.11 For the timing diagram shown in Figure 7.38, draw the outputs Q and Qn for a rising edge triggered D-flip-flop with active LOW .

Figure 7.38

Section 7.2 – Sequential Logic Timing Considerations

7.2.1 What timing specification is violated in a D-flip-flop when the data is not held long enough *before* the triggering clock edge occurs?

7.2.2 What timing specification is violated in a D-flip-flop when the data is not held long enough *after* the triggering clock edge occurs?

7.2.3 What is the timing specification for a D-flip-flop that describes how long after the triggering clock edge occurs that the new data will be present on the Q output?

7.2.4 What is the timing specification for a D-flip-flop that describes how long after the device goes metastable that the outputs will settle to known states.

7.2.5 If the Q output of a D-flip-flop is driving the D input of another D-flip-flop from the same logic family, can the hold time be ignored if it is less than the clock-to-Q delay? Provide an explanation as to why or why not.

Section 7.3 – Common Circuits Based on Sequential Storage Devices

7.3.1 In a Toggle Flop (T-flop) configuration, the Qn output of the D-flip-flop is routed back to the D input. This can lead to a hold time violation if the output arrives on the input too quickly. Under what condition(s) is a hold time violate not an issue?

7.3.2 In a Toggle Flop (T-flop) configuration, what timing specifications dictate how quickly the next edge of the incoming clock can occur?

7.3.3 One drawback of a ripple counter is that the delay through the cascade of D-flip-flops can become considerable for large counters. At what point does the delay of a ripple counter prevent it from being useful?

7.3.4 A common use of a ripple counter is in the creation of a 2^n *programmable clock divider*. In a ripple counter, bit(0) has a frequency that is exactly $1/2$ of the incoming clock, bit(1) has a frequency that is exactly $1/4$ of the incoming clock, bit(2) has a frequency that is exactly $1/8$ of the incoming clock, etc. This behavior can be exploited to create a divided down output clock that is divided by multiples of 2^n by selecting a particular bit of the counter. The typical configuration of this programmable clock divider is to route each bit of the counter to an input of a multiplexer. The select lines going to the multiplexer choose which bit of the counter are used as the divided down clock output. This architecture is shown in Figure 7.39. Design a VHDL model to implement the programmable clock divider shown in this figure. Use the entity definition provided in this figure for your design. Use a 4-bit ripple counter to produce four divided versions of the clock (1/2, 1/4, 1/8, and 1/16). Your system will take in two select lines that will choose which version of the clock is to be routed to the output. Instantiate the D-flip-flops model provided to implement the ripple counter. Implement the 4-to-1 multiplexer using conditional signal assignments. The multiplexer does not need to be its own component.

prog_clock_div.vhd

Figure 7.39

7.3.5 What phenomenon causes switch bounce in a SPST switch?

7.3.6 What two phenomena causes switch bounce in a SPDT switch?

Section 7.4 – Finite State Machines

7.4.1 For the state diagram in Figure 7.40, answer the following questions regarding the number of D-Flip-

Flops needed to implement the state memory of the finite state machine.

a) How many D-Flip-Flops will this machine take if the states are encoded in binary?
b) How many D-Flip-Flops will this machine take if the states are encoded in gray code?
c) How many D-Flip-Flops will this machine take if the states are encoded in one-hot?

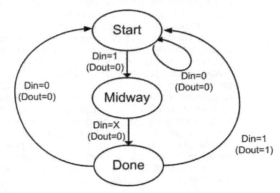

Figure 7.40

7.4.2 For the state diagram in Figure 7.40, is this a Mealy or Moore machine?

7.4.3 Design the finite state machine circuitry by hand to implement the behavior described by the state diagram in Figure 7.40. Name the current state variables Q1_cur and Q0_cur and name the next state variables Q1_nxt and Q0_nxt. Use the following state codes:

Start = "00"
Midway = "01"
Done = "10"

a) What is the next state logic expression for Q1_nxt?
b) What is the next state logic expression for Q0_nxt?
c) What is the output logic expression for Dout?
d) Draw the final logic diagram for this machine.

7.4.4 Design a VHDL model to implement the behavior described by the state diagram in Figure 7.40. Use the entity definition provided in Figure 7.41 for your design. Name the current state variables Q1_cur and Q0_cur and name the next state variables Q1_nxt and Q0_nxt. Instantiate the D-Flip-Flop model provided to implement your state memory. Use concurrent signal assignments with logical operators for the implementation of your next state and output logic.

```
fsm1.vhd

entity fsm1 is
    port    (Clock   : in   bit;
             Reset   : in   bit;
             Din     : in   bit;
             Dout    : out  bit);
end entity;
```

Figure 7.41

7.4.5 Design a VHDL model to implement the behavior described by the state diagram in Figure 7.40. Use the entity definition provided in Figure 7.41 for your design. Name the current state variables Q1_cur and Q0_cur and name the next state variables Q1_nxt and Q0_nxt.

Instantiate the D-Flip-Flop model provided to implement your state memory. Use conditional signal assignments for the implementation of your next state and output logic.

7.4.6 Design a VHDL model to implement the behavior described by the state diagram in Figure 7.40. Use the entity definition provided in Figure 7.41 for your design. Name the current state variables Q1_cur and Q0_cur and name the next state variables Q1_nxt and Q0_nxt. Instantiate the D-Flip-Flop model provided to implement your state memory. Use selected signal assignments for the implementation of your next state and output logic.

7.4.7 For the state diagram in Figure 7.42, answer the following questions regarding the number of D-Flip-Flops needed to implement the state memory of the finite state machine.

a) How many D-Flip-Flops will this machine take if the states are encoded in binary?
b) How many D-Flip-Flops will this machine take if the states are encoded in gray code?
c) How many D-Flip-Flops will this machine take if the states are encoded in one-hot?

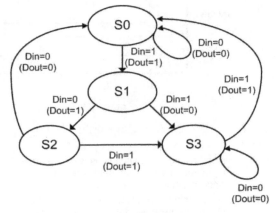

Figure 7.42

7.4.8 For the state diagram in Figure 7.42, is this a Mealy or Moore machine?

7.4.9 Design the finite state machine circuitry by hand to implement the behavior described by the state diagram in Figure 7.42. Name the current state variables Q1_cur and Q0_cur and name the next state variables Q1_nxt and Q0_nxt. Also, use the following state codes:

S0 = "00"
S1 = "01"
S2 = "10"
S3 = "11"

a) What is the next state logic expression for Q1_nxt?
b) What is the next state logic expression for Q0_nxt?
c) What is the output logic expression for Dout?
d) Draw the final logic diagram for this machine.

7.4.10 Design a VHDL model to implement the behavior described by the state diagram in Figure 7.42. Use the entity definition provided in Figure 7.43 for your design. Name the current state variables Q1_cur and Q0_cur and name the next state variables Q1_nxt and Q0_nxt. Instantiate the D-Flip-Flop model provided to implement your state memory. Use <u>concurrent signal assignments with logical operators</u> for the implementation of your next state and output logic.

```
fsm2.vhd

entity fsm2 is
    port  (Clock  : in   bit;
           Reset  : in   bit;
           Din    : in   bit;
           Dout   : out  bit);
end entity;
```

Figure 7.43

7.4.11 Design a VHDL model to implement the behavior described by the state diagram in Figure 7.42. Use the entity definition provided in Figure 7.43 for your design. Name the current state variables Q1_cur and Q0_cur and name the next state variables Q1_nxt and Q0_nxt. Instantiate the D-Flip-Flop model provided to implement your state memory. Use <u>conditional signal assignments</u> for the implementation of your next state and output logic.

7.4.12 Design a VHDL model to implement the behavior described by the state diagram in Figure 7.42. Use the entity definition provided in Figure 7.43 for your design. Name the current state variables Q1_cur and Q0_cur and name the next state variables Q1_nxt and Q0_nxt. Instantiate the D-Flip-Flop model provided to implement your state memory. Use <u>selected signal assignments</u> for the implementation of your next state and output logic.

7.4.13 Design a 4-bit serial bit sequence detector by hand similar to the one described in Example 7.9. The input to your state detector is called DIN and the output is called FOUND. Your detector will assert FOUND anytime there is a 4-bit sequence of "0101". For all other input sequences the output is not asserted.

a) Provide the state diagram for this FSM.
b) Provide the state transition table for this FSM.
c) Encode your states using binary encoding. How many D-Flip-Flops does it take to implement the state memory for this FSM?
d) Synthesize the combinational logic expressions for the next state logic.
e) Synthesize the combinational logic expressions for the output logic.
f) Is this machine a Mealy or Moore machine?
g) Draw the logic diagram for this FSM.

7.4.14 Design a 25 cent vending machine controller by hand similar to the one described in Example 7.12. Your controller will take in nickels and dimes and dispense a product anytime the customer has entered 25 cents. Your FSM has two inputs, Nin and Din. Nin is asserted whenever the customer enters a nickel while Din is asserted anytime the customer enters a dime. Your FSM has two outputs, Dispense and Change. Dispense is asserted anytime the customer has entered at least 25 cents and Change is asserted anytime the customer has entered more than 25 cents and needs a nickel in change.

a) Provide the state diagram for this FSM.
b) Provide the state transition table for this FSM.
c) Encode your states using binary encoding. How many D-Flip-Flops does it take to implement the state memory for this FSM?

d) Synthesize the combinational logic expressions for the next state logic.
e) Synthesize the combinational logic expressions for the output logic.
f) Is this machine a Mealy or Moore machine?
g) Draw the logic diagram for this FSM.

7.4.15 Design a finite state machine by hand that controls a traffic light at the intersection of a busy highway and a seldom used side road. You will be designing the control signals for just the red, yellow, and green lights facing the highway. Under normal conditions, the highway has a green light. The side road has a car detector that indicates when a car pulls up by asserting a signal called CAR. When CAR is asserted, you will change the highway traffic light from green to yellow. Once yellow, you will always go to red. Once in the red position, a built in timer will begin a countdown and provide your controller a signal called TIMEOUT when 15 seconds has passed. Once TIMEOUT is asserted, you will change the highway traffic light back to green. Your system will have three outputs GRN, YLW, and RED that control when the highway facing traffic lights are on (1=ON, 0=OFF).

a) Provide the state diagram for this FSM.
b) Provide the state transition table for this FSM.
c) Encode your states using binary encoding. How many D-Flip-Flops does it take to implement the state memory for this FSM?
d) Synthesize the combinational logic expressions for the next state logic.
e) Synthesize the combinational logic expressions for the output logic.
f) Is this machine a Mealy or Moore machine?
g) Draw the logic diagram for this FSM.

Section 7.5 – Counters

7.5.1 Design a <u>3-bit binary up counter</u> by hand. This state machine will need eight states and require three bits for the state variable codes. Name the current state variables Q2_cur, Q1_cur, and Q0_cur and the next state variables Q2_nxt, Q1_nxt, and Q0_nxt. The output of your counter will be a 3-bit vector called Count.

a) What is the next state logic expression for Q2_nxt?
b) What is the next state logic expression for Q1_nxt?
c) What is the next state logic expression for Q0_nxt?
d) What is the output logic expression for Count(2)?
e) What is the output logic expression for Count(1)?
f) What is the output logic expression for Count(0)?
g) Draw the logic diagram for this counter.

7.5.2 Design a VHDL model for a <u>3-bit binary up counter</u>. Instantiate the D-Flip-Flop model provided to implement your state memory. Use whatever concurrent signal assignment modeling approach you wish to model the next state and output logic. Use the VHDL entity provided in Figure 7.44 for your design.

```
counter_3bit_binary_up.vhd

entity counter_3bit_binary_up is
  port (Clock : in   bit;
        Reset : in   bit;
        Count : out  bit_vector (2 downto 0));
end entity;
```

Figure 7.44

7.5.3 Design a <u>3-bit binary up/down counter</u> by hand. The counter will have an input called "Up" that will dictate the direction of the counter. When Up=1, the counter should increment and when Up=0 it should decrement. This state machine will need eight states and require three bits for the state variable codes. Name the current state variables Q2_cur, Q1_cur, and Q0_cur and the next state variables Q2_nxt, Q1_nxt, and Q0_nxt. The output of your counter will be a 3-bit vector called Count.

a) What is the next state logic expression for Q2_nxt?
b) What is the next state logic expression for Q1_nxt?
c) What is the next state logic expression for Q0_nxt?
d) What is the output logic expression for Count(2)?
e) What is the output logic expression for Count(1)?
f) What is the output logic expression for Count(0)?
g) Draw the logic diagram for this counter.

7.5.4 Design a VHDL model for a <u>3-bit binary up/down counter</u>. Instantiate the D-Flip-Flop model provided to implement your state memory. Use whatever concurrent signal assignment modeling approach you wish to model the next state and output logic. Use the VHDL entity provided in Figure 7.45 for your design.

counter_3bit_binary_up_down.vhd

```
entity counter_3bit_binary_up_down is
  port (Clock : in   bit;
        Reset : in   bit;
        Up    : in   bit;
        Count : out  bit_vector (2 downto 0));
end entity;
```

Figure 7.45

7.5.5 Design a <u>3-bit gray code up counter</u> by hand. This state machine will need eight states and require three bits for the state variable codes. Name the current state variables Q2_cur, Q1_cur, and Q0_cur and the next state variables Q2_nxt, Q1_nxt, and Q0_nxt. The output of your counter will be a 3-bit vector called Count.

a) What is the next state logic expression for Q2_nxt?
b) What is the next state logic expression for Q1_nxt?
c) What is the next state logic expression for Q0_nxt?
d) What is the output logic expression for Count(2)?
e) What is the output logic expression for Count(1)?
f) What is the output logic expression for Count(0)?
g) Draw the logic diagram for this counter.

7.5.6 Design a VHDL model for a <u>3-bit gray code up counter</u>. Instantiate the D-Flip-Flop model provided to implement your state memory. Use whatever concurrent signal assignment modeling approach you wish to model the next state and output logic. Use the VHDL entity provided in Figure 7.46 for your design.

counter_3bit_graycode_up.vhd

```
entity counter_3bit_graycode_up is
  port (Clock : in   bit;
        Reset : in   bit;
        Count : out  bit_vector (2 downto 0));
end entity;
```

Figure 7.46

7.5.7 Design a <u>3-bit gray code up/down counter</u> by hand. The counter will have an input called "Up" that will dictate the direction of the counter. When Up=1, the counter should increment and when Up=0 it should decrement. This state machine will need eight states and require three bits for the state variable codes. Name the current state variables Q2_cur, Q1_cur, and Q0_cur and the next state variables Q2_nxt, Q1_nxt, and Q0_nxt. The output of your counter will be a 3-bit vector called Count.

a) What is the next state logic expression for Q2_nxt?
b) What is the next state logic expression for Q1_nxt?
c) What is the next state logic expression for Q0_nxt?
d) What is the output logic expression for Count(2)?
e) What is the output logic expression for Count(1)?
f) What is the output logic expression for Count(0)?
g) Draw the logic diagram for this counter.

7.5.8 Design a VHDL model for a <u>3-bit gray code up/down counter</u>. Instantiate the D-Flip-Flop model provided to implement your state memory. Use whatever concurrent signal assignment modeling approach you wish to model the next state and output logic. Use the VHDL entity provided in Figure 7.47 for your design.

counter_3bit_graycode_up_down.vhd

```
entity counter_3bit_graycode_up_down is
  port (Clock : in   bit;
        Reset : in   bit;
        Up    : in   bit;
        Count : out  bit_vector (2 downto 0));
end entity;
```

Figure 7.47

Section 7.6 – Finite State Machine's Reset Condition

7.6.1 Are resets typically synchronous or asynchronous?

7.6.2 Why is it necessary to have a reset/preset condition in a finite state machine?

7.6.3 How does the reset/preset condition correspond to the behavior described in the state diagram?

7.6.4 When is it necessary to also use the preset line(s) of a D-flip-flop instead of just the reset line(s) when implementing the state memory of a finite state machine?

7.6.5 If a finite state machine has eight unique states that are encoded in binary and all D-flip-flops used for the state memory use their reset lines, what is the state code that the machine will go to upon reset?

Section 7.7 – Sequential Logic Analysis

7.7.1 For the finite state machine logic diagram in Figure 7.48, give the next state logic expression for Q_nxt.

t_{setup}	= 1 ns
t_{hold}	= 1 ns
t_{CQ}	= 1 ns
t_{XOR}	= 2 ns
t_{int}	= 0
t_{margin}	= 10%

Figure 7.48

7.7.2 For the finite state machine logic diagram in Figure 7.48, give the output logic expression for Tout.

7.7.3 For the finite state machine logic diagram in Figure 7.48, give the state transition table.

7.7.4 For the finite state machine logic diagram in Figure 7.48, give the state diagram.

7.7.5 For the finite state machine logic diagram in Figure 7.48, give the maximum clock frequency.

7.7.6 For the finite state machine logic diagram in Figure 7.49, give the next state logic expression for *Q_nxt*.

t_{setup}	= 1 ns
t_{hold}	= 0.5 ns
t_{CQ}	= 1 ns
t_{AND}	= 1 ns
t_{OR}	= 1 ns
t_{int}	= 1 ns
t_{margin}	= 10%

Figure 7.49

7.7.7 For the finite state machine logic diagram in Figure 7.49, give the output logic expression for *F*.

7.7.8 For the finite state machine logic diagram in Figure 7.49, give the state transition table.

7.7.9 For the finite state machine logic diagram in Figure 7.49, give the state diagram.

7.7.10 For the finite state machine logic diagram in Figure 7.49, give the maximum clock frequency.

7.7.11 For the finite state machine logic diagram in Figure 7.50, give the next state logic expressions for *Q1_nxt* and *Q0_nxt*.

t_{setup}	= 2 ns
t_{hold}	= 1 ns
t_{CQ}	= 2 ns
t_{AND}	= 0.5 ns
t_{OR}	= 0.5 ns
t_{INV}	= 0.5 ns
t_{int}	= 0.5 ns (all paths)
t_{margin}	= 10%

Figure 7.50

7.7.12 For the finite state machine logic diagram in Figure 7.50, give the output logic expression for *Return*.

7.7.13 For the finite state machine logic diagram in Figure 7.50, give the state transition table.

7.7.14 For the finite state machine logic diagram in Figure 7.50, give the state diagram.

7.7.15 For the finite state machine logic diagram in Figure 7.50, give the maximum clock frequency.

Chapter 8: VHDL (Part 2)

In Chapter 5 VHDL was presented as a way to describe the behavior of concurrent systems. The modeling techniques presented were appropriate for combinational logic because these types of circuits have outputs dependent only on the current values of their inputs. This means a model that continuously performs signal assignments provides an accurate model of this circuit behavior. In Chapter 7 sequential logic storage devices were presented that did not continuously update their outputs based on the instantaneous values of their inputs. Instead, sequential storage devices only update their outputs based upon an event, most often the edge of a clock signal. The modeling techniques presented in Chapter 5 are unable to accurately describe this type of behavior. In this chapter we describe the VHDL constructs to model signal assignments that are triggered by an event in order to accurately model sequential logic. We can then use these techniques to describe more complex sequential logic circuits such as finite state machines and register transfer level systems. This chapter will also present how to create test benches and look at commonly used packages that increase the capability and accuracy with which VHDL can model modern systems.

Learning Outcomes – After completing this chapter, you will be able to:

8.1   Design a VHDL model for a combinational logic circuit using a process and an if/then statement.
8.2   Design a VHDL model for a combinational logic circuit using a process and a case statement.
8.3   Design a VHDL test bench to exhaustively stimulate a device under test.
8.4   Design a VHDL test bench to automatically verify the proper operation of a device under test using report and assert statements.
8.5   Design a VHDL test bench that reads in test vectors from an external file.
8.6   Design a VHDL test bench that writes the status of the test to an external file.
8.7   Design a VHDL test bench that writes the status of the test to a computer's STD_OUTPUT.
8.8   Design a VHDL model of a sequential logic circuit using a process and sequential signal assignments.

8.1 The Process

VHDL uses a *process* to model signal assignments that are based on an event. A process is a technique to model behavior of a system, thus a process is placed in the VHDL architecture after the begin statement. The signal assignments within a process have unique characteristics that allow them to accurately model sequential logic. First, the signal assignments do not take place until the process ends or is suspended. Second, the signal assignments will be made only once each time the process is triggered. Finally, the signal assignments will be executed in the order that they appear within the process. This assignment behavior is called a *sequential signal assignment*. Sequential signal assignments allow a process to model register transfer level behavior where a signal can be used as both the operand of an assignment and the destination of a different assignment within the same process. VHDL provides two techniques to trigger a process, the *sensitivity list* and the *wait statement*.

8.1.1 Sensitivity List

A *sensitivity list* is a mechanism to control when a process is triggered (or started). A sensitivity list contains a list of signals that the process is sensitive to. If there is a transition on any of the signals in the list, the process will be triggered and the signal assignments in the process will be made. The following is the syntax for a process that uses a sensitivity list.

```
process_name : process (<signal_name1>, <signal_name2>, ...)

    -- variable declarations

  begin

      sequential_signal_assignment_1
      sequential_signal_assignment_2
                      :
  end process;
```

Let's look at a simple model for a flip flop.

Example:

```
FlipFlop : process (Clock)
    begin
        Q <= D;
end process;
```

In this example, a transition on the signal Clock (LOW to HIGH or HIGH to LOW) will trigger the process. The signal assignment of D to Q will be executed once the process ends. When the signal Clock is not transitioning, the process will not trigger and no assignments will be made to Q, thus modeling the behavior of Q holding its last value. This behavior is close to modeling the behavior of a real D-Flip-Flop, but more constructs are needed to model behavior that is sensitive to only a particular type of transition (i.e., rising or falling edge). These constructs will be covered later.

8.1.2 The Wait Statement

A *wait statement* is a mechanism to suspend (or stop) a process and allow signal assignments to be executed without the need for the process to end. When using a wait statement, a sensitivity list is not used. Without a sensitivity list, the process will immediately trigger. Within the process, the wait statement is used to stop and start the process. There are three ways in which wait statements can be used. The first is an indefinite wait. In the following example, the process does not contain a sensitivity list so it will trigger immediately. The keyword **wait** is used to suspend the process. Once this statement is reached, the signal assignments to Y1 and Y2 will be executed and the process will suspend indefinitely.

Example:

```
Proc_Ex1 : process
    begin
        Y1 <= '0';
        Y2 <= '1';
        wait;
end process;
```

The second technique to use a wait statement to suspend a process is to use it in conjunction with the keyword **for** and a time expression. In the following example, the process will trigger immediately since it does not contain a sensitivity list. Once the process reaches the wait statement, it will suspend and execute the first signal assignment to CLK (CLK <= '0'). After 5ns, the process will start again. Once it reaches the second wait statement, it will suspend and execute the second signal assignment to CLK (CLK <= '1'). After another 5ns, the process will start again and immediately end due to the *end process* statement. After the process ends, it will immediately trigger again due to the lack of a sensitivity list and repeat the behavior just described. This behavior will continue indefinitely. This example creates a square wave called CLK with a period of 10ns.

Example:

```
Proc_Ex2 : process
    begin
        CLK <= '0'; wait for 5 ns;
        CLK <= '1'; wait for 5 ns;
end process;
```

The third technique to use a wait statement to suspend a process is to use it in conjunction with the keyword **until** and a Boolean condition. In the following example, the process will again trigger immediately because there is not a sensitivity list present. The process will then immediately suspend and only resume once a Boolean condition becomes true (i.e., Counter > 15). Once this condition is True, the process will start again. Once it reaches the second wait statement, it will execute the first signal assignment to RollOver (RollOver <= '1'). After 1ns, the process will resume. Once the process ends, it will execute the second signal assignment to RollOver (RollOver <= '0').

Example:

```
Proc_Ex3 : process
    begin
        wait until (Counter > 15);        -- first wait statement
        RollOver <= '1'; wait for 1 ns;   -- second wait statement
        RollOver <= '0';
end process;
```

Wait statements are typically not synthesizable and are most often used for creating stimulus patterns in test benches.

8.1.3 Sequential Signal Assignments

One of the more confusing concepts of a process is how sequential signal assignments behave. The rules of signal assignments within a process are as follows:

- Signals cannot be declared within a process.
- Signal assignments do not take place until the process ends or suspends.
- Signal assignments are executed in the sequence they appear in the process (once the process ends or process suspends).

Let's take a look at an example of how signals behave in a process. Example 8.1 shows the behavior of sequential signal assignments when executed within a process. Intuitively, we would assume that F will be the complement of A; however, due to the way that sequential signal assignments are performed within a process, this not the case. In order to understand this behavior, let's look at the situation where A transitions from a 0 to a 1 with B=0 and F=0 initially. This transition triggers the process since A is listed in the sensitivity list. When the process triggers, A=1 since this is where the input resides after the triggering transition. The first signal assignment (B <= A) will cause B=1, but this assignment occurs only after the process ends. This means that when the second signal assignment is evaluated (F <= not B), it uses the initial value of B from when the process triggered (B=0) since B is not updated to a 1 until the process ends. The second assignment yields F=1. When the process ends, A=1, B=1 and F=1. The behavior of this process will always result in A=B=F. This is counterintuitive because the statement F <= not B leads us to believe that F will always be the complement of A and B; however, this is not the case due to the way that signal assignments are only updated in a process upon suspension or when the process ends.

Example 8.1
Behavior of Sequential Signal Assignments within a Process

Now let's consider how these assignments behave when executed as concurrent signal assignments. Example 8.2 shows the behavior of the same signal assignments as in Example 8.1, but this time outside of a process. In this model, the statements are executed concurrently and produce the expected behavior of F being the complement of A.

Example: Behavior of Concurrent Signal Assignments outside a Process

For the following system:

```
entity Ex is
  port (A : in  bit;
        F : out bit);
end entity;
```

The output F will be the complement of input A when the assignments are executed concurrently.

```
architecture Ex_arch of Ex is

  signal B : bit;

begin

    B <= A;
    F <= not B;

end architecture;
```

Example 8.2
Behavior of Concurrent Signal Assignments outside a Process

While the behavior of the sequential signal assignments initially seems counterintuitive, it is necessary in order to model the behavior of sequential storage devices and will become clear once more VHDL constructs have been introduced.

8.1.4 Variables

There are situations inside of processes in which it is desired for assignments to be made instantaneously instead of when the process suspends. For these situations, VHDL provides the concept of a *variable*. A variable has the following characteristics:

- Variables only exist within a process.
- Variables are defined in a process before the begin statement.
- Once the process ends, variables are removed from the system. This means that assignments to variables cannot be made by systems outside of the process.
- Assignments to variables are made using the ":=" operator.
- Assignments to variables are made instantaneously.

A variable is declared before the begin statement in a process. The syntax for declaring a variable is as follows:

```
variable variable_name : <type> := <initial_value>;
```

Let's reconsider the example in Example 8.1, but this time we'll use a variable in order to accomplish instantaneous signal assignments within the process. Example 8.3 shows this approach to model the behavior where F is the complement of A.

Example 8.3
Variable Assignment Behavior

CONCEPT CHECK

CC8.1 If a model of a combinational logic circuit excludes one of its inputs from the sensitivity list, what is the implied behavior?

A) A storage element because the output will be held at its last value when the unlisted input transitions.

B) An infinite loop.

C) A don't care will be used to form the minimal logic expression.

D) Not applicable because this syntax will not compile.

8.2 Conditional Programming Constructs

One of the more powerful features that processes provide in VHDL is the ability to use conditional programming constructs such as if/then clauses, case statements, and loops. These constructs are only available within a process, but their use is not limited to modeling sequential logic. As we'll see, the characteristics of a process also support modeling of combinational logic circuits, so these conditional constructs are a very useful tool in VHDL. This provides the ability to model both combinational and sequential logic using the more familiar programming language constructs.

8.2.1 If / Then Statements

An *if/then* statement provides a way to make conditional signal assignments based on Boolean conditions. The **if** portion of statement is followed by a Boolean condition that if evaluated TRUE will cause the signal assignment after the **then** statement to be performed. If the Boolean condition is evaluated FALSE, no assignment is made. VHDL provides multiple variants of the if/then statement. An *if/then/else* statement provides a final signal assignment that will be made if the Boolean condition is evaluated false. An *if/then/elsif* statement allows multiple Boolean conditions to be used. The syntax for the various forms of the VHDL if/then statement are as follows:

```
if boolean_condition then sequential_statement
end if;


if boolean_condition then sequential_statement_1
else sequential_statement_2
end if;


if boolean_condition_1 then sequential_statement_1
elsif boolean_condition_2 then sequential_statement_2
   :
   :
elsif boolean_condition_n then sequential_statement_n
end if;


if boolean_condition_1 then sequential_statement_1
elsif boolean_condition_2 then sequential_statement_2
   :
   :
elsif boolean_condition_n then sequential_statement_n
else sequential_statement_n+1
end if;
```

Let's take a look at using an if/then statement to describe the behavior of a combinational logic circuit. Recall that a combinational logic circuit is one in which the output depends on the instantaneous values of the inputs. This behavior can be modeled by placing all of the inputs to the circuit in the sensitivity list of a process. A change on any of the inputs in the sensitivity list will trigger the process and cause the output to be updated. Example 8.4 shows how to model a 3-input combinational logic circuit using if/then statements within a process.

Example: Using If/Then Statements to Model Combinational Logic

Implement the following truth table using an <u>if/then statement</u> within a process.

A	B	C	F
0	0	0	1
0	0	1	0
0	1	0	1
0	1	1	0
1	0	0	0
1	0	1	0
1	1	0	1
1	1	1	0

```
entity SystemX is
    port (A, B, C  :  in  bit;
          F        :  out bit);
end entity;
```

Recall that an if/then statement is only legal within a process. In order to create a process that models combinational logic, we need to list each of the inputs to the circuit in the sensitivity list. This will cause the process to trigger and make an assignment to the output whenever there is a change on any of the inputs.

```
architecture SystemX_arch of SystemX is

begin

  SystemX_Proc : process (A, B, C)
    begin
      if    (A='0' and B='0' and C='0') then F <= '1';
      elsif (A='0' and B='0' and C='1') then F <= '0';
      elsif (A='0' and B='1' and C='0') then F <= '1';
      elsif (A='0' and B='1' and C='1') then F <= '0';
      elsif (A='1' and B='0' and C='0') then F <= '0';
      elsif (A='1' and B='0' and C='1') then F <= '0';
      elsif (A='1' and B='1' and C='0') then F <= '1';
      elsif (A='1' and B='1' and C='1') then F <= '0';
      end if;
  end process;

end architecture;
```

A more compact version of this behavior can be created by taking advantage of the else clause. In this model, only Boolean conditions are listed for outputs corresponding to 1's.

```
architecture SystemX_arch of SystemX is

begin

  SystemX_Proc : process (A, B, C)
    begin
      if    (A='0' and B='0' and C='0') then F <= '1';
      elsif (A='0' and B='1' and C='0') then F <= '1';
      elsif (A='1' and B='1' and C='0') then F <= '1';
      else F <= '0';
      end if;
  end process;

end architecture;
```

Example 8.4
Using If/Then Statements to Model Combinational Logic

8.2.2 Case Statements

A *case* statement is another technique to model signal assignments based on Boolean conditions. As with the if/then statement, a case statement can only be used inside of a process. The statement begins with the keyword **case** followed by the input signal name that assignments will be based off of. The input signal name can be optionally enclosed in parentheses for readability. The keyword **when** is used to specify a particular value (or choice) of the input signal that will result in associated sequential signal assignments. The assignments are listed after the **=>** symbol. The following is the syntax for a case statement.

```
case (input_name) is
   when choice_1 => sequential_statement(s);
   when choice_2 => sequential_statement(s);
                       :
                       :
   when choice_n => sequential_statement(s);
end case;
```

When not all of the possible input conditions (or choices) are specified, a **when others** clause is used to provide signal assignments for all other input conditions. The following is the syntax for a case statement that uses a *when others* clause.

```
case (input_name) is
   when choice_1 => sequential_statement(s);
   when choice_2 => sequential_statement(s);
                       :
                       :
   when others   => sequential_statement(s);
end case;
```

Multiple choices that correspond to the same signal assignments can be pipe-delimited in the case statement. The following is the syntax for a case statement with pipe-delimited choices.

```
case (input_name) is
   when choice_1 | choice_2 => sequential_statement(s);
   when others              => sequential_statement(s);
end case;
```

The input signal for a case statement must be a single signal name. If multiple scalars are to be used as the input expression for a case statement, they should be concatenated either outside of the process resulting in a new signal vector or within the process resulting in a new variable vector. Example 8.5 shows how to model a 3-input combinational logic circuit using case statements within a process.

Example: Using Case Statements to Model Combinational Logic

Implement the following truth table using a <u>case statement</u> within a process.

A	B	C	F
0	0	0	1
0	0	1	0
0	1	0	1
0	1	1	0
1	0	0	0
1	0	1	0
1	1	0	1
1	1	1	0

```
entity SystemX is
   port (A, B, C  :  in  bit;
         F         :  out bit);
end entity;
```

A case statement is only legal within a process. In the following example, the three input scalars (A,B,C) are concatenated into a new variable for use as the input signal to the case statement.

```
architecture SystemX_arch of SystemX is

begin

  SystemX_Proc : process (A, B, C)

    variable ABC : bit_vector (2 downto 0) := "000";

    begin

      ABC := A & B & C;

        case (ABC) is
          when "000" => F <= '1';
          when "001" => F <= '0';
          when "010" => F <= '1';
          when "011" => F <= '0';
          when "100" => F <= '0';
          when "101" => F <= '0';
          when "110" => F <= '1';
          when "111" => F <= '0';
        end case;

  end process;

end architecture;
```

More compact forms of the case statement can be created using the *when others* clause and pipe delimited inputs.

```
case (ABC) is
  when "000"   => F <= '1';
  when "010"   => F <= '1';
  when "110"   => F <= '1';
  when others  => F <= '0';
end case;
```

```
case (ABC) is
  when "000" | "010" | "110"  => F <= '1';
  when others                 => F <= '0';
end case;
```

Example 8.5
Using Case Statements to Model Combinational Logic

If/then statements can be embedded within a case statement and, conversely, case statements can be embedded within an if/then statement.

8.2.3 Infinite Loops

A *loop* within VHDL provides a mechanism to perform repetitive assignments infinitely. This is useful in test benches for creating stimulus such as clocks or other periodic waveforms. A loop can only be used within a process. The keyword **loop** is used to signify the beginning of the loop. Sequential signal assignments are then inserted. The end of the loop is signified with the keywords **end loop**. Within the loop, the *wait for, wait until* and *after* statements are all legal. Signal assignments within a loop will be executed repeatedly forever unless an **exit** or **next** statement is encountered. The *exit* clause provides a Boolean condition that will force the loop to end if the condition is evaluated true. When using the exit statement, an additional signal assignment is typically placed after the loop to provide the desired behavior when the loop is not active. Using flow control statements such as *wait for* and *wait after* provide a means to avoid having the loop immediately executed again after exiting. The *next* clause provides a way to skip the remaining signal assignments and begin the next iteration of the loop. The following is the syntax for an infinite loop in VHDL.

```
loop
    exit when boolean_condition;         -- optional exit statement
    next when boolean_condition;         -- optional next statement
    sequential_statement(s);
end loop;
```

Consider the following example of an infinite loop that generates a clock signal (CLK) with a period of 100ns. In this example, the process does not contain a sensitivity list, so, a wait statement must be used to control the signal assignments. This process in this example will trigger immediately and then enter the infinite loop and never exit.

Example:

```
Clock_Proc1 : process
  begin
    loop
       CLK <= not CLK;
       wait for 50 ns;
    end loop;
end process;
```

Now consider the following loop example that will generate a clock signal with a period of 100ns with an enable (EN) line. This loop will produce a periodic clock signal as long as EN=1. When EN=0, the clock output will remain at CLK=0. An exit condition is placed at the beginning of the loop to check if EN=0. If this condition is true, the loop will exit and the clock signal will be assigned a 0. The process will then wait until EN=1. Once EN=1, the process will end and then immediately trigger again and reenter the loop. When EN=1, the clock signal will be toggled (CLK <= not CLK) and then wait for 50ns. This toggling behavior will repeat as long as EN=1.

Example:

```
Clock_Proc2 : process
  begin
    loop
       exit when EN='0';
       CLK <= not CLK;
       wait for 50 ns;
    end loop;

    CLK <= '0';
    wait until EN='1';

end process;
```

It is important to keep in mind that infinite loops that continuously make signal assignments without the use of sensitivity lists or wait statements will cause logic simulators to hang.

8.2.4 While Loops

A *while loop* provides a looping structure with a Boolean condition that controls its execution. The loop will only execute as long as its condition is evaluated true. The following is the syntax for a VHDL while loop.

```
while boolean_condition loop
    sequential_statement(s);
end loop;
```

Let's implement the previous example of a loop that generates a clock signal (CLK) with a period of 100ns as long as EN=1. The Boolean condition for the while loop is EN=1. When EN=1, the loop will be executed indefinitely. When EN=0, the while loop will be skipped. In this case, an additional signal assignment is necessary to model the desired behavior when the loop is not used (i.e., CLK=0).

Example:

```
Clock_Proc3 : process
   begin
     while (EN='1') loop
       CLK <= not CLK;
        wait for 50 ns;
     end loop;

       CLK <= '0';
       wait until EN='1';

   end process;
```

8.2.5 For Loops

A *for loop* provides the ability to create a loop that will execute a predefined number of times. The range of the loop is specified with integers (*min, max*) at the beginning of the for loop. A *loop variable* is implicitly declared in the loop that will increment (or decrement) from *min* to *max* of the range. The loop variable is of type integer. If it is desired to have the loop variable increment from min to max, the keyword **to** is used when specifying the range of the loop. If it is desired to have the loop variable decrement max to min, the keyword **downto** is used when specifying the range of the loop. The loop variable can be used within the loop as an index for vectors, thus the for loop is useful for automatically accessing and assigning multiple signals within a single loop structure. The following is the syntax for a VHDL for loop in which the loop variable will increment from min to max of the range.

```
for loop_variable in min to max loop
   sequential_statement(s);
end loop;
```

The following is the syntax for a VHDL for loop in which the loop variable will decrement from max to min of the range.

```
for loop_variable in max downto min loop
   sequential_statement(s);
end loop;
```

For loops are useful for test benches in which a range of patterns are to be created. For loops are also synthesizable as long as the complete behavior of the desired system is described by the loop. The following is an example of creating a simple counter using the loop variable. The signal Count_Out in this example is of type integer. This allows the loop variable *i* to be assigned to Count_Out each time through the loop since the loop variable is also of type integer. This counter will count from 0 to 15 and then repeat. The count will increment every 50ns.

Example:

```
Counter_Proc : process
   begin
     for i in 0 to 15 loop
       Count_Out <= i;
        wait for 50 ns;
     end loop;
   end process;
```

CONCEPT CHECK

CC8.2   When using an if/then statement to model a combinational logic circuit, is using the *else* clause the same as using *don't cares* when minimizing a logic expression with a K-map?

A)   Yes. The else clause allows the synthesizer to assign whatever output values are necessary in order to create the most minimal circuit.

B)   No. The else clause explicitly states the output values for all input codes not listed in the if/elsif portion of the if/then construct. This is the same as filling in the truth table with specific values for all input codes covered by the else clause and the synthesizer will create the logic expression accordingly.

8.3 Signal Attributes

There are situations where we want to describe behavior that is based on more than just the current value of a signal. For example, a real D-Flip-Flop will only update its outputs on a particular type of transition (i.e., rising or falling). In order to model this behavior, we need to specify more information about the signal. This is accomplished by using *attributes*. Attributes provide additional information about a signal other than just its present value. An attribute can provide information such as past values, whether an assignment was made to a signal, or when the last time an assignment resulted in a value change. A signal attribute is implemented by placing an apostrophe (') after the signal name and then listing the VHDL attribute keyword. Different attributes will result in different output types. Attributes that yield Boolean output types can be used as inputs to Boolean decision conditions for other VHDL constructs. Other attributes can be used to define the range of new vectors by referencing the size of existing vectors or automatically defining the number of iterations in a loop. Finally, some attributes can be used to create self-checking test benches that monitor the impact of circuit delays on the functionality of a system. The following are a list of the commonly used, pre-defined VHDL signal attributes. The example signal name *A* is used to illustrate how scalar attributes operate. The example signal **B** is used to illustrate how vector attributes operate with type bit_vector (7 downto 0).

Attribute	Information Returned	Type Returned
A'**event**	true when signal A changes, false otherwise	boolean
A'**active**	true when an assignment is made to A, false otherwise	boolean
A'**last_event**	time when signal A last changed	time
A'**last_active**	time when signal A was last assigned to	time
A'**last_value**	the previous value of A	same type as A
B'**length**	size of the vector (e.g., 8)	integer
B'**left**	left bound of the vector (e.g., 7)	integer
B'**right**	right bound of the vector (e.g., 0)	integer
B'**range**	range of the vector "(7 downto 0)"	string

Signal attributes can be used to model edge sensitive behavior. Let's look at the model for a simple D-Flip-Flop. A process is used to model the synchronous behavior of the D-Flip-Flop. The sensitivity list contains only the *Clock* input. The *D* input is not included in the sensitivity list because a change on D should not trigger the process. Attributes and logical operators are not allowed in the sensitivity list of a process. As a result, the process will trigger on every edge of the clock signal. Within the process, an if/then statement is used with the Boolean condition **(Clock'event and Clock='1')** in order to make signal assignments only on a rising edge of the clock. The syntax for this Boolean condition is understood and is synthesizable by all CAD tools. An else clause is not included in the if/then statement. This implies that when there is not a rising edge, no assignments will be made to the outputs and they will simply hold their last value. Example 8.6 shows how to model a simple D-Flip-Flop using attributes.   Note that this example does not model the reset behavior of a real D-Flip-Flop.

Example: Behavioral Modeling of a Rising Edge Triggered D-Flip-Flop Using Attributes

Clk	D	Q	
0	X	Last Q	Store
1	X	Last Q	Store
⌐	0	0	Update
⌐	1	1	Update

```
entity Dflipflop is
    port   (Clock      : in    bit;
            D          : in    bit;
            Q          : out   bit);
end entity;

architecture Dflipflop_arch of Dflipflop is

  begin

     D_FLIP_FLOP  : process (Clock)
        begin
          if (Clock'event and Clock='1') then
             Q <= D;
          end if;
       end process;

end architecture;
```

Example 8.6
Behavioral Modeling of a Rising Edge Triggered D-Flip-Flop Using Attributes

CONCEPT CHECK

CC8.3   If the D input to a D-flip-flop is tied to a 0, which of the following conditions will return true on every triggering edge of the clock?

    A)   Q'event and Q='0'

    B)   Q'active and Q='0'

    C)   Q'last_event='0' and Q='0'

    D)   Q'last_active='0' and Q='0'

8.4 Test Benches

The functional verification of VHDL designs is accomplished through simulation using a *test bench*. A test bench is a VHDL system that instantiates the system to be tested as a component and then generates the inputs patterns and observes the outputs. The system being tested is often called a *device under test (DUT)* or *unit under test (UUT)*. Test benches are only used for simulation so we can use abstract modeling techniques that are unsynthesizable to generate the stimulus patterns. VHDL also contains specific functionality to report on the status of a test and also automatically check that the outputs are correct. Example 8.7 shows how to create a simple test bench to verify the operation of SystemX. The test bench does not have any inputs or outputs, thus there are no ports declared in the entity. SystemX is declared as a component in the test bench and then instantiated (DUT1). Internal signals are declared to connect to the component under test (A_TB, B_TB, C_TB, F_TB). A process is then used to drive the inputs of SystemX. Within the process, wait statements are used to control the execution of the signal assignments, thus the process does not have a sensitivity list. Each possible input code is generated within the process. The output (F_TB) is observed using a simulation tool in either the form of a waveform or a table listing.

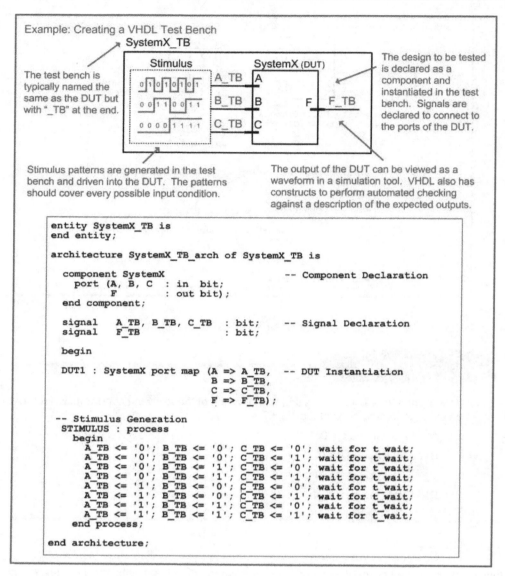

Example: Creating a VHDL Test Bench

The test bench is typically named the same as the DUT but with "_TB" at the end.

The design to be tested is declared as a component and instantiated in the test bench. Signals are declared to connect to the ports of the DUT.

Stimulus patterns are generated in the test bench and driven into the DUT. The patterns should cover every possible input condition.

The output of the DUT can be viewed as a waveform in a simulation tool. VHDL also has constructs to perform automated checking against a description of the expected outputs.

```
entity SystemX_TB is
end entity;

architecture SystemX_TB_arch of SystemX_TB is

  component SystemX                    -- Component Declaration
    port (A, B, C  : in  bit;
          F        : out bit);
  end component;

  signal  A_TB, B_TB, C_TB  : bit;     -- Signal Declaration
  signal  F_TB              : bit;

  begin

  DUT1 : SystemX port map (A => A_TB,  -- DUT Instantiation
                           B => B_TB,
                           C => C_TB,
                           F => F_TB);

  -- Stimulus Generation
  STIMULUS : process
    begin
      A_TB <= '0'; B_TB <= '0'; C_TB <= '0'; wait for t_wait;
      A_TB <= '0'; B_TB <= '0'; C_TB <= '1'; wait for t_wait;
      A_TB <= '0'; B_TB <= '1'; C_TB <= '0'; wait for t_wait;
      A_TB <= '0'; B_TB <= '1'; C_TB <= '1'; wait for t_wait;
      A_TB <= '1'; B_TB <= '0'; C_TB <= '0'; wait for t_wait;
      A_TB <= '1'; B_TB <= '0'; C_TB <= '1'; wait for t_wait;
      A_TB <= '1'; B_TB <= '1'; C_TB <= '0'; wait for t_wait;
      A_TB <= '1'; B_TB <= '1'; C_TB <= '1'; wait for t_wait;
    end process;

end architecture;
```

Example 8.7
Creating a VHDL Test Bench

8.4.1 Report Statement

The keyword **report** can be used within a test bench in order to provide the status of the current test. A report statement will print a string to the transcript window of the simulation tool. The report output also contains an optional severity level. There are four levels of severity (ERROR, WARNING, NOTE and FAILURE). The severity level *FAILURE* will halt a simulation while the levels *ERROR*, *WARNING* and *NOTE* will allow the simulation to continue. If the severity level is omitted, the report is assumed to be a severity level of NOTE. The syntax for using a report statement is as follows:

```
report "string to be printed" severity <level>;
```

Let's look at how we could use the report function within the example test bench to print the current value of the input pattern to the transcript window of the simulator. Example 8.8 shows the new process and resulting transcript output of the simulator when using report statements.

Example: Using Report Statements in a VHDL Test Bench

Report statements are inserted in the process to indicate the current stimulus pattern.

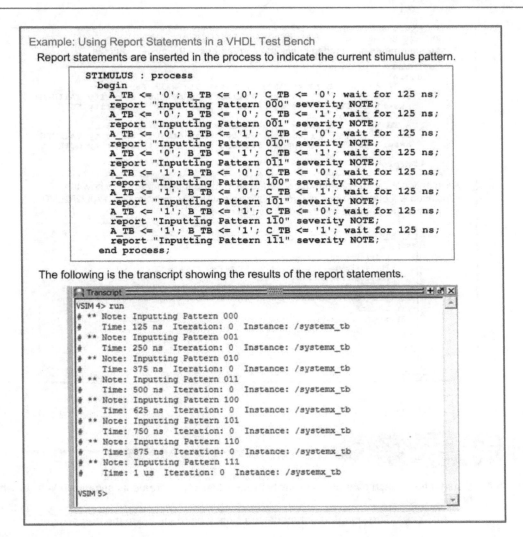

```
STIMULUS : process
  begin
    A_TB <= '0'; B_TB <= '0'; C_TB <= '0'; wait for 125 ns;
    report "Inputting Pattern 000" severity NOTE;
    A_TB <= '0'; B_TB <= '0'; C_TB <= '1'; wait for 125 ns;
    report "Inputting Pattern 001" severity NOTE;
    A_TB <= '0'; B_TB <= '1'; C_TB <= '0'; wait for 125 ns;
    report "Inputting Pattern 010" severity NOTE;
    A_TB <= '0'; B_TB <= '1'; C_TB <= '1'; wait for 125 ns;
    report "Inputting Pattern 011" severity NOTE;
    A_TB <= '1'; B_TB <= '0'; C_TB <= '0'; wait for 125 ns;
    report "Inputting Pattern 100" severity NOTE;
    A_TB <= '1'; B_TB <= '0'; C_TB <= '1'; wait for 125 ns;
    report "Inputting Pattern 101" severity NOTE;
    A_TB <= '1'; B_TB <= '1'; C_TB <= '0'; wait for 125 ns;
    report "Inputting Pattern 110" severity NOTE;
    A_TB <= '1'; B_TB <= '1'; C_TB <= '1'; wait for 125 ns;
    report "Inputting Pattern 111" severity NOTE;
  end process;
```

The following is the transcript showing the results of the report statements.

```
Transcript
VSIM 4> run
# ** Note: Inputting Pattern 000
#    Time: 125 ns  Iteration: 0  Instance: /systemx_tb
# ** Note: Inputting Pattern 001
#    Time: 250 ns  Iteration: 0  Instance: /systemx_tb
# ** Note: Inputting Pattern 010
#    Time: 375 ns  Iteration: 0  Instance: /systemx_tb
# ** Note: Inputting Pattern 011
#    Time: 500 ns  Iteration: 0  Instance: /systemx_tb
# ** Note: Inputting Pattern 100
#    Time: 625 ns  Iteration: 0  Instance: /systemx_tb
# ** Note: Inputting Pattern 101
#    Time: 750 ns  Iteration: 0  Instance: /systemx_tb
# ** Note: Inputting Pattern 110
#    Time: 875 ns  Iteration: 0  Instance: /systemx_tb
# ** Note: Inputting Pattern 111
#    Time: 1 us  Iteration: 0  Instance: /systemx_tb

VSIM 5>
```

Example 8.8
Using Report Statements in a VHDL Test Bench

8.4.2 Assert Statement

The **assert** statement provides a mechanism to check a Boolean condition before using the report statement. This allows report outputs to be selectively printed based on the values of signals in the system under test. This can be used to either print the successful operation or the failure of a system. If the Boolean condition associated with the assert statement is evaluated True, it *will not* execute the subsequent report statement. If the Boolean condition is evaluated False, it will execute the subsequent report statement. The assert statement is always used in conjunction with the report statement. The following is the syntax for the assert statement.

```
assert boolean_condition report "string" severity <level>;
```

Let's look at how we could use the assert function within the example test bench to check whether the output (F_TB) is correct. In the example in Example 8.9, the system passes the first pattern but fails the second.

Example: Using Assert Statements in a VHDL Test Bench
Assert statements are used to check the correctness of the system outputs.

```
STIMULUS : process
  begin
    A_TB <= '0'; B_TB <= '0'; C_TB <= '0'; wait for 125 ns;
    assert (F_TB='1') report "Failed test at 000" severity FAILURE;
    assert (F_TB='0') report "Passed test at 000" severity NOTE;

    A_TB <= '0'; B_TB <= '0'; C_TB <= '1'; wait for 125 ns;
    assert (F_TB='1') report "Failed test at 001" severity FAILURE;
    assert (F_TB='0') report "Passed test at 001" severity NOTE;
                             :
  end process;
```

An intentional failure was introduced at the second input pattern to show how the simulation will end if a report statement is issued with a severity level of FAILURE. The following is the output of the transcript for this case.

```
Transcript                                                        + ⊠ ×
VSIM 6> run
# ** Note: Passed test at 000
#    Time: 125 ns  Iteration: 0  Instance: /systemx_tb
# ** Failure: Failed test at 001
#    Time: 250 ns  Iteration: 0  Process: /systemx_tb/STIMULUS File: C:/
Users/lameres/Desktop/EE261_VHDL/ModelSim/Ch08_VHDL_Part2/Test_Bench_Sys
temX/SystemX_TB.vhd
# Break in Process STIMULUS at C:/Users/lameres/Desktop/EE261_VHDL/Model
Sim/Ch08_VHDL_Part2/Test_Bench_SystemX/SystemX_TB.vhd line 35

VSIM 7>
```

Example 8.9
Using Assert Statements in a VHDL Test Bench

CONCEPT CHECK

CC8.4   Could a test bench ever use sensitivity lists exclusively to create its stimulus? Why or why not?

A) Yes. The signal assignments will simply be made when the process ends.

B) No. Since a sensitivity list triggers when there is a chance on one or more of the signals listed, the processes in the test bench would never trigger because there is no method to make the initial signal transition.

8.5 Packages

One of the drawbacks of the VHDL standard package is that it provides limited functionality in its synthesizable data types. The bit and bit_vector, while synthesizable, lack the ability to accurately model many of the topologies implemented in modern digital systems. Of primary interest are topologies that involve multiple drivers connected to a single wire. The standard package will not permit this type of connection; however, this type of topology is a common way to interface multiple nodes on a shared interconnection. Furthermore, the standard package does not provide many useful features for these types, such as don't cares, arithmetic using the + and − operators, type conversion functions or the ability to read/write external files. To increase the functionality of VHDL, packages are included in the design.

8.5.1 STD_LOGIC_1164

In the late 1980's, the IEEE 1164 standard was released that added functionality to VHDL to allow a multi-valued logic system (i.e., a signal can take on more values than just 0 and 1). This standard also provided a mechanism for multiple drivers to be connected to the same signal. An updated release in 1993 called IEEE 1164-1993 was the most significant update to this standard and contains the majority of functionality used in VHDL today. Nearly all systems described in VHDL include the 1164 standard as a package. This package is included by adding the following syntax at the beginning of the VHDL file.

```
library IEEE;
use IEEE.std_logic_1164.all;
```

This package defines four new data types: **std_ulogic**, **std_ulogic_vector**, **std_logic,** and **std_logic_vector**. The std_ulogic and std_logic are enumerated, scalar types that can provide a multi-valued logic system. The types std_ulogic_vector and std_logic_vector are vector types containing a linear array of scalar types std_ulogic and std_logic respectively. The scalar types can take on nine different values as described below.

Value	Description	Notes
U	uninitialized	default initial value
X	forcing unknown	
0	forcing 0	
1	forcing 1	
Z	high impedance	
W	weak unknown	
L	weak 0 pull-down	
H	weak 1 pull-up	
-	don't care	used for synthesis only

These values can be assigned to signals by enclosing them in single quotes (scalars) or double quotes (vectors).

Example:

```
A <= 'X';       -- assignment to a scalar (std_ulogic or std_logic)
V <= "01ZH";    -- assignment to a 4-bit vector (std_ulogic_vector or
                --                               std_logic_vector)
```

The type std_ulogic is *unresolved*, (note: the "u" standard for "unresolved"). This means that if a signal is being driven by two circuits with type std_ulogic, the VHDL simulator will not be able to *resolve* the conflict and it will result in a compiler error. The std_logic type is *resolved*. This means that if a signal is being driven by two circuits with type std_logic, the VHDL simulator *will* be able to resolve the conflict and will allow the simulation to continue. Figure 8.1 shows an example of a shared signal topology and how conflicts are handled when using various data types.

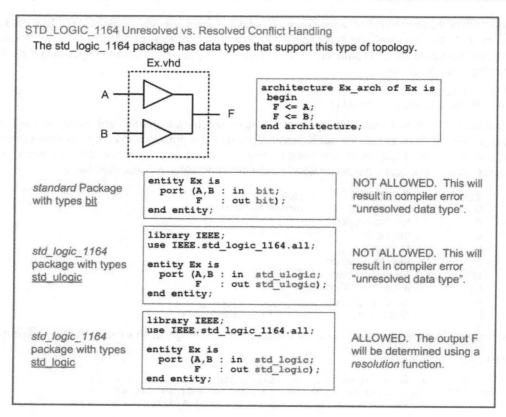

Figure 8.1
STD_LOGIC_1164 Unresolved vs. Resolved Conflict Handling

8.5.1.1 STD_LOGIC Resolution Function

The std_logic_1164 will resolve signal conflict of type std_logic using a **resolution function**. The nine allowed values each have a relative drive strength that allows a resolution to be made in the event of conflict. Whenever there is a conflict, the simulator will consult the resolution function to determine the value of the signal. Figure 8.2 shows the relative drive strengths of the nine possible signal values provided by the std_logic_1164 package and the resolution function table.

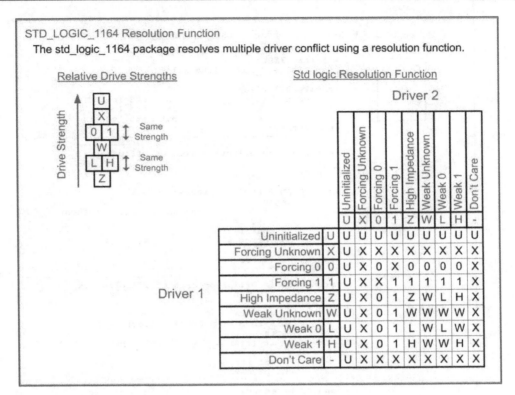

Figure 8.2
STD_LOGIC_1164 Resolution Function

8.5.1.2 STD_LOGIC_1164 Logical Operators

The std_logic_1164 also contains new definitions for all of the logical operators (**and, nand, or, nor, xor, xnor, not)** for types std_ulogic and std_logic. These are required since these data types can take on more logic values than just a 0 or 1, thus the logical operator definitions from the standard package are not sufficient.

8.5.1.3 STD_LOGIC_1164 Edge Detection Functions

The std_logic_1164 also provides functions for the detection of rising or falling transitions on a signal. The functions **rising_edge()** and **falling_edge()** provide a more readable form of this functionality compared to the (Clock'event and Clock='1') approach. Example 8.10 shows the use of the rising_edge() function to model the behavior of a rising edge triggered D-Flip-Flop.

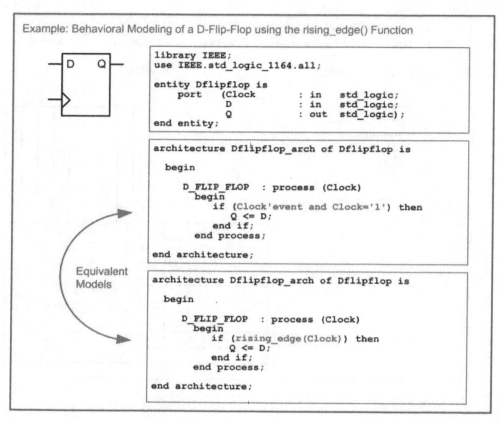

Example 8.10
Behavioral Modeling of a D-Flip-Flop using the rising_edge() Function

8.5.1.4 STD_LOGIC Type Conversion Functions

The std_logic_1164 package also provides functions to convert between data types. Functions exist to convert between bit, std_ulogic and std_logic. Functions also exist to convert between these types' vector forms (bit_vector, std_ulogic_vector and std_logic_vector). The functions are listed below.

Name	Input Type	Return Type
To_bit()	std_ulogic	bit
To_bitvector()	std_ulogic_vector	bit_vector
To_bitvector()	std_logic_vector	bit_vector
To_StdULogic()	bit	std_ulogic
To_StdULogicVector()	bit_vector	std_ulogic_vector
To_StdULogicVector()	std_logic_vector	std_ulogic_vector
To_StdLogicVector()	bit_vector	std_logic_vector
To_StdLogicVector()	std_ulogic_vector	std_logic_vector

When using these functions, the function name and input signal are placed to the right of the assignment operator and the target signal is placed on the left.

Example:

```
A <= To_bit(B);                -- B is type std_ulogic, A is type bit
V <= To_StdLogicVector(C);     -- C is type bit_vector, V is std_logic_vector
```

When identical function names exist that can have different input data types, the VHDL compiler will automatically decide which function to use based on the input argument type. For example, the function "To_bitvector" exists for an input of std_ulogic_vector *and* std_logic_vector. When using this function, the compiler will automatically detect which input type is being used and select the corresponding function variant. No additional syntax is required by the designer in this situation.

8.5.2 NUMERIC_STD

The *numeric_std* package provides numerical computation for types std_logic and std_logic_vector. When performing binary arithmetic, the results of arithmetic operations and comparisons vary greatly depending on whether the binary number is unsigned or signed. As a result, the numeric_std package defines two new data types, **unsigned** and **signed**. An unsigned type is defined to have its MSB in the leftmost position of the vector, and the LSB in the rightmost position of the vector. A signed number uses two's complement representation with the leftmost bit of the vector being the sign bit. When declaring a signal to be one of these types, it is implied that these represent the encoding of an underlying native type of std_logic/std_logic_vector. The use of unsigned/signed types provides the interpretation of how arithmetic, logical and comparison operators will perform. This also implies that the numeric_std package requires the std_logic_1164 to always be included. While the numeric_std package includes an inclusion call of the std_logic_1164 package, it is common to explicitly include both the std_logic_1164 and the numeric_std packages in the main VHDL file. The VHDL compiler will ignore redundant package statements. The syntax for including these packages is as follows:

```
library IEEE;
use IEEE.std_logic_1164.all;    -- defines types std_ulogic and std_logic
use IEEE.numeric_std.all;       -- defines types unsigned and signed
```

8.5.2.1 NUMERIC_STD Arithmetic Functions

The numeric_std package provides support for a variety of arithmetic functions for the types unsigned and signed. These include **+, -, *, /, mod, rem** and **abs** functions. These arithmetic operations behave differently for the unsigned versus signed types, but the VHDL compiler will automatically use the correct operation based on the types of the input arguments.

Most synthesis tools support the addition, subtraction and multiplication operators in this package. This provides a higher level of abstraction when modeling arithmetic circuitry. Recall that the VHDL standard package does not support addition, subtraction and multiplication of types bit/bit_vector using the +, - and * operators. Using the numeric_std package gives the ability to model these arithmetic operations with a synthesizable data type using the more familiar mathematical operators. The division, modulo, remainder and absolute value functions are not synthesizable directly from this package.

Example:

```
F <= A + B;                     -- A, B, F are type unsigned(3 downto 0)
F <= A - B;
```

8.5.2.2 NUMERIC_STD Logical Functions

The numeric_std package provides support for all of the logical operators (**and, nand, or, nor, xor, xnor, not**) for types unsigned and signed. It also provides two new shift functions **shift_left()** and **shift(right)**. These shift functions will fill the vacant position in the vector after the shift with a 0, thus these are *logical shifts*. This package also provides two new rotate functions **rotate_left()** and **rotate_right()**.

8.5.2.3 NUMERIC_STD Comparison Functions

The numeric_std package provides support for all of the comparison functions for types unsigned and signed. These include **>, <, <=, >=, =** and **/=**. These comparisons return type Boolean.

Example: (A="0000", B="1111")

```
if (A < B) then       -- This condition is TRUE if A and B are UNSIGNED
    :

if (A < B) then       -- This condition is FALSE if A and B are SIGNED
```

8.5.2.4 NUMERIC_STD Edge Detection Functions

The numeric_std also provides the functions **rising_edge()** and **falling_edge()** for the detection of rising or falling edge transition detection for types unsigned and signed.

8.5.2.5 NUMERIC_STD Conversion Functions

The numeric_std package contains a variety of useful conversion functions. Of particular usefulness are functions between the type *integer* and to/from *unsigned/signed*. This allows behavioral models for counters, adders and subtractors to be implemented using the more readable type integer. After the functionally has been described, a conversion can be used to turn the result into types unsigned or signed to provide a synthesizable output. When converting an integer to a vector, a *size* argument is included. The size argument is of type integer and provides the number of bits in the vector that the integer will be converted to.

Name	Input Type	Return Type
To_integer()	unsigned	integer
To_integer()	signed	integer
To_unsigned()	integer, \<size>	unsigned (size-1 downto 0)
To_signed()	integer, \<size>	signed (size-1 downto 0)

8.5.2.6 NUMERIC_STD Type Casting

VHDL contains a set of built-in *type casting* operations that are commonly used with the numeric_std package to convert between *std_logic_vector* and *unsigned/signed*. Since the types unsigned/signed are based on the underlying type std_logic_vector, the conversion between types simple and known as casting. The following are the built-in type casting capabilities in VHDL.

Name	Input Type	Return Type
std_logic_vector()	unsigned	std_logic_vector
std_logic_vector()	signed	std_logic_vector
unsigned()	std_logic_vector	unsigned
signed()	std_logic_vector	signed

When using these type casts, they are placed on the right-hand side of the assignment exactly as a conversion function.

Example:

```
A <= std_logic_vector(B); -- B is unsigned, A is std_logic_vector
C <= unsigned(D);         -- D is std_logic_vector, A is unsigned
```

Type casts and conversion functions can be compounded in order to perform multiple conversions in one assignment. This is useful when converting between types that do not have a direct cast or conversion function. Let's look at the example of converting an integer to an 8-bit std_logic_vector where the number being represented is unsigned. The first step is to convert the integer to an unsigned type. This can be accomplished with the *to_unsigned* function defined in the numeric_std package. This can be embedded in a second cast from unsigned to std_logic_vector. In the following example, E is the target of the operation and is of type std_logic vector. F is the argument of assignment and is of type integer. Recall that the to_unsigned conversions requires both the input integer name and the size of the unsigned vector being converted to.

Example:

```
E <= std_logic_vector(to_unsigned(F, 8));
```

8.5.3 NUMERIC_STD_UNSIGNED

When using the numeric_std package, the data types unsigned and signed must be used in order to get access to the numeric operators. While this provides ultimate control over the behavior of the signal operations and comparisons, many designs may only use unsigned types. In order to provide a mechanism to treat all vectors as unsigned while leaving their type as std_logic_vector, the numeric_std_unsigned package was created. When this package is used, it will treat all std_logic_vectors in the design as unsigned. This package requires the std_logic_1164 and numeric_std packages to be previously included. When used, all signals and ports can be declared as std_logic/std_logic_vector and they will be treated as unsigned when performing arithmetic operations and comparisons. The following is an example of how to include this package.

```
library IEEE;
use IEEE.std_logic_1164.all;
use IEEE.numeric_std.all;
use IEEE.numeric_std_unsigned.all;
```

8.5.3.1 NUMERIC_STD_UNSIGNED Conversion Functions

The numeric_std_unsigned package contains a few more type conversions beyond the numeric_std package. These additional conversions are as follows:

Name	Input Type	Return Type
To_Integer	std_logic_vector	integer
To_StdLogicVector	unsigned	std_logic_vector

8.5.4 NUMERIC_BIT

The *numeric_bit* package provides numerical computation for types bit and bit_vector. Since the vast majority of VHDL designs today use types std_logic/std_logic_vector instead of bit/bit_vector, this package is rarely used. This package is included by adding the following syntax at the beginning of the VHDL file in the design.

```
library IEEE;
use IEEE.numeric_bit.all;      -- defines types unsigned and signed
```

The numeric_bit package is nearly identical to numeric_std. It defines data types **unsigned** and **signed**, which provide information on the encoding style of the underlying data types bit and bit_vector. All of the arithmetic, logical and comparison functions defined in numeric_std are supported in numeric_bit (**+, -, *, /, mod, rem, abs, and, nand, or, nor, xor, xnor, not, >, <, <=, >=, =, /=**) for types unsigned and signed. This package also provides the same edge detection (**rising_edge(), falling_edge()**), shift (**shift_left(), shift_right()**) and rotate (**rotate_left(), rotate_right()**) functions for types unsigned and signed.

The primary difference between numeric_bit and numeric_std is that numeric_bit also provides support for the shift/rotate operators from the standard package (**sll**, **srl**, **rol**, **ror**). Also, the conversion functions are defined only for conversions between integer, unsigned, and signed.

Name	Input Type	Return Type
To_integer	unsigned	integer
To_integer	signed	integer
To_unsigned	integer, <size>	unsigned (size-1 downto 0)
To_signed	integer, <size>	signed (size-1 downto 0)

8.5.5 NUMERIC_BIT_UNSIGNED

The numeric_bit_unsigned package provides a way to treat all bit/bit_vectors in a design as unsigned numbers. The syntax for including the numeric_bit_unsigned package is shown below. In this example, all bit/bit_vectors will be treated as unsigned numbers for all arithmetic operations and comparisons.

```
library IEEE;
use IEEE.numeric_bit.all;
use IEEE.numeric_bit_unsigned.all;
```

8.5.5.1 NUMERIC_BIT_UNSIGNED Conversion Functions

The numeric_bit_unsigned package contains a few more type conversions beyond the numeric_bit package. These additional conversions are as follows:

Name	Input Type	Return Type
To_integer	std_logic_vector	integer
To_BitVector	unsigned	bit_vector

8.5.6 MATH_REAL

The *math_real* package provides numerical computation for the type *real*. The type *real* is the VHDL type used to describe a 32-bit floating point number. None of the operators provided in the math_real package are synthesizable. This package is primarily used for test benches. This package is included by adding the following syntax at the beginning of the VHDL file in the design.

```
library IEEE;
use IEEE.math_real.all;
```

The math_real package defines a set of commonly used constants, which are shown below.

Constant Name	Type	Value	Description
MATH_E	real	2.718	value of e
MATH_1_E	real	0.367	value of 1/e
MATH_PI	real	3.141	value of pi
MATH_1_PI	real	0.318	value of 1/pi
MATH_LOG_OF_2	real	0.693	natural log of 2
MATH_LOG_OF_10	real	2.302	natural log of10
MATH_LOG2_OF_E	real	1.442	log base 2 of e
MATH_LOG10_OF_E	real	0.434	log base 10 of e
MATH_SQRT2	real	1.414	sqrt of 2
MATH_SQRT1_2	real	0.707	sqrt of 1/2
MATH_SQRT_PI	real	1.772	sqrt of pi
MATH_DEG_TO_RAD	real	0.017	conversion factor from degree to radian
MATH_RAD_TO_DEG	real	57.295	conversion factor from radian to degree

Only three digits of accuracy are shown in this table; however, the constants defined in the math_real package have full 32-bit accuracy. The math_real package provides a set of commonly used floating point operators for the type real.

Function Name	Return Type	Description
SIGN	real	returns sign of input
CEIL	real	returns smallest integer value
FLOOR	real	returns largest integer value
ROUND	real	rounds input up/down to whole number
FMAX	real	returns largest of two inputs
FMIN	real	returns smallest of two inputs
SQRT	real	returns square root of input
CBRT	real	returns cube root of input
**	real	raise to power of (X**Y)
EXP	real	e^x
LOG	real	log(X)
SIN	real	sin(X)
COS	real	cos(X)
TAN	real	tan(X)
ASIN	real	asin(X)
ACOS	real	acos(X)
ATAN	real	atan(X)
ATAN2	real	atan(X/Y)
SINH	real	sinh(X)
COSH	real	cosh(X)
TANH	real	tanh(X)
ASINH	real	asinh(X)
ACOSH	real	acosh(X)
ATANH	real	atanh(X)

8.5.7 MATH_COMPLEX

The *math_complex* package provides numerical computation for complex numbers. Again, nothing in this package is synthesizable and is typically used only for test benches. This package is included by adding the following syntax at the beginning of the VHDL file in the design.

```
library IEEE;
use IEEE.math_complex.all;
```

This package defines three new data types, **complex**, **complex_vector** and **complex_polar**. The type *complex* is defined with two fields, *real* and *imaginary*. The type *complex_vector* is a linear array of type complex. The type *complex_polar* is defined with two fields, *magnitude* and *angle*. This package provides a set of common operations for use with complex numbers. This package also supports the arithmetic operators **+**, **-**, * and / for the type complex.

Function Name	Return Type	Description
CABS	real	absolute value of complex number
CARG	real (radians)	returns angle of complex number
CMPLX	complex	returns complex number form of input
CONJ	complex or complex_polar	returns complex conjugate
CSQRT	real	returns square root
CEXP	real	returns e^z of complex input
COMPLEX_TO_POLAR	complex_polar	convert complex to complex_polar
POLAR_TO_COMPLEX	complex	convert complex_polar to complex

8.5.8 TEXTIO and STD_LOGIC_TEXTIO

The *textio* package provides the ability to read and write to/from external input/output (I/O). External I/O refers to items such as files or the standard input/output of a computer. This package contains functions that allow the values of signals and variables to be read and written in addition to strings. This allows more sophisticated output messages to be created compared to the *report* statement alone, which can only output strings. The ability to read in values from a file allows sophisticated test patterns to be created outside of VHDL and then read in during simulation for testing a system. It is important to keep in mind that the term "I/O" refers to external files or the transcript window, not the inputs and outputs of a system model. The textio package is not synthesizable and is only used in test benches. The textio package is within the STD library and is included in a VHDL design using the following syntax.

```
library STD;
use STD.textio.all;
```

This package by itself only supports reading and writing types bit, bit_vector, integer, character and string. Since the majority of synthesizable designs use types std_logic and std_logic_vector, an additional package was created that added support for these types. The package is called *std_logic_textio* and is located within the IEEE library. The syntax for including this package is below.

```
library IEEE;
use IEEE.std_logic_textio.all;
```

The textio package defines two new types for interfacing with external I/O. These types are **file** and **line**. The type *file* is used to identify or create a file for reading/writing within the VHDL design. The syntax for declaring a file is as follows:

```
file file_handle : <file_type> open <file_mode> is <"filename">;
```

Declaring a file will automatically open the file and keep it open until the end of the process that is using it. The *file_handle* is a unique identifier for the file that is used in subsequent procedures. The file handle name is user-defined. A file handle eliminates the need to specify the entire file name each time a file access procedure is called. The *file_type* describes the information within the file. There are two supported file types, **TEXT** and **INTF**. A *TEXT* file is one that contains strings of characters. This is the most common type of file used as there are functions that can convert between types string, bit/bit_vector and std_logic/std_logic_vector. This allows all of the information in the file to be stored as characters, which makes the file readable by other programs. An *INTF* file type contains only integer values and the information is stored as a 32-bit, signed binary number. The *file_mode* describes whether the file will be read from or written to. There are two supported modes, **WRITE_MODE** and **READ_MODE**. The *filename* is given within double quotes and is user-defined. It is common to enter an extension on the file so that it can be opened by other programs (e.g., output.txt). Declaring a file always takes place within a process before the process begin statement. The following are examples of how to declare files.

```
file Fout: TEXT open WRITE_MODE is "output_file.txt";
file Fin:  TEXT open READ_MODE  is "input_file.txt";
```

The information within a file is accessed (either read or written) using the concept of a *line*. In the textio package, a file is interpreted as a sequence of lines, each containing either a string of characters or an integer value. The type *line* is used as a temporary buffer when accessing a line within the file. When accessing a file, a variable is created of type *line*. This variable is then used to either hold information that is *read* from a line in the file or to hold the information that is to be *written* to a line in the file. A variable is necessary for this behavior since assignments to/from the file must be made immediately. As such, a line variable is always declared within a process before the process begin statement. The syntax for declaring a variable of type line is as follows:

```
variable <line_variable_name> : line;
```

There are two procedures that allow information to be transferred between a line variable in VHDL and a line in a file. These procedures are **readline()** and **writeline()**. Their syntax is as follows:

```
readline(<file_handle>, <line_variable_name>);
writeline(<file_handle>, <line_variable_name>);
```

The transfer of information between a line variable and a line in a file using these procedures is accomplished on the entire line. There is no mechanism to read or write only a portion of the line in a file. Once a file is opened/created using a file declaration, the lines are accessed in the order they appear in the file. The first procedure called (either readline() or writeline()) will access the first line of the file. The next time a procedure is called, it will access the second line of the file. This will continue until all of the lines have been accessed. The textio package provides a function to indicate when the end of the file has been reached when performing a readline(). This function is called **endfile()** and returns type boolean. This function will return True once the end of the file has been reached. Figure 8.3 shows a graphical representation of how the textio package handles external file access.

Figure 8.3
IEEE.textio Package Interpretation of Files

Two additional procedures are provided to add or retrieve information to/from the line variable within the VHDL test bench. These procedures are **read()** and **write()**. The syntax for these procedures is as follows:

```
read(<line_variable_name>, <destination_variable>);
write(<line_variable_name>, <source_variable>);
```

When using the read() procedure, the information in the line variable is treated as *space-delimited*. This means that each read() procedure will retrieve the information from the line variable until it reaches a white space. This allows multiple read() procedures to be used in order to parse the information into separate *destination_variable* names. The destination_variable must be of the appropriate type and size of the information being read from the file. For example, if the field in the line being read is a 4 character string ("wxyz"), then a destination variable must be defined of type *string(1 to 4)*. If the field being read is a 2-bit std_logic_vector, then a destination variable must be defined of type *std_logic_vector(1 downto 0)*. The read() procedure will ignore the delimiting white space character.

When using the write() procedure, the *source_destination* is assumed to be of type bit, bit_vector, integer, std_logic or std_logic_vector. If it is desired to enter a text string directly, then the function **string** is used with the format *string'<"characters...">*. Multiple write() procedures can be used to insert information into the line variable. Each subsequent write procedure appends the information to the end of the string. This allows different types of information to be interleaved (e.g., text, signal value, text, etc.).

8.5.8.1 Example: Writing to an External File From a Test Bench

Let's look at an example of a test bench that writes information about the tests being conducted to an external file. Example 8.11 shows the model for the system to be tested (SystemX) and an overview of the test bench approach (SystemX_TB).

Example 8.11
Writing to an External File from a Test Bench (Part 1)

Example 8.12 shows the details of the test bench model. In this test bench, a file is declared in order to create "output_file.txt". This file is given the handle *Fout*. A line variable is also declared called *current_line* to act as a temporary buffer to hold information that will be written to the file. The procedure write() is used to add information to the line variable. The first write() procedure is used to create a text message ("Beginning Test..."). Notice that since the information to be written to the line variable is of type string, a conversion function must be used within the write() procedure (e.g,. string'(Beginning Test...")). This message is written as the first line in the file using the writeline() procedure. After an input vector has been applied to the DUT, a new line is constructed containing both descriptive text, the input vector value and the output value from the DUT. This message is repeated for each input code in the test bench.

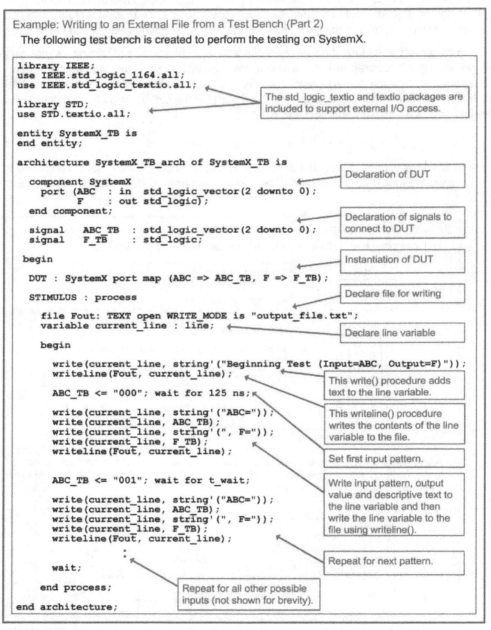

Example 8.12
Writing to an External File from a Test Bench (Part 2)

Example 8.13 shows the resulting file that is created from this test bench.

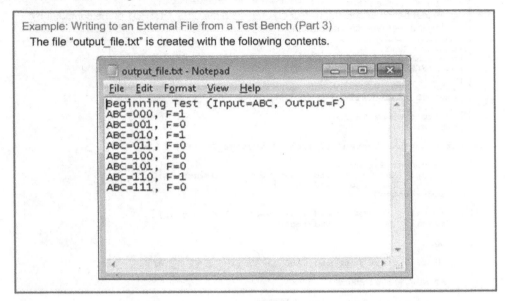

Example: Writing to an External File from a Test Bench (Part 3)
The file "output_file.txt" is created with the following contents.

Example 8.13
Writing to an External File from a Test Bench (Part 3)

8.5.8.2 Example: Writing to STD_OUTPUT From a Test Bench

The textio package also provides the ability to write to the standard output of the computer instead of to an external file. The standard output of the computer is typically routed to the transcript window of the simulator. This is accomplished by using a reserved file handle called **OUTPUT**. When using this file handle, a new file does not need to be declared in the test bench since it is already defined as part of the textio package. The reserved file handle name OUTPUT can be used directly in the writeline() procedure.

Let's look at an example of a test bench that outputs information about the test being conducted to STD_OUT. Example 8.14 shows this test bench approach. The test bench is identical as the one used in Example 8.12 with the exception that the writeline() procedure outputs are directed to the STD_OUTPUT of the computer using the reserved file handle name OUTPUT instead of to an external file.

Example: Writing to STD_OUTPUT from a Test Bench (Part 1)

This test bench directs the writeline() outputs to the STD_OUTPUT of the computer by using the reserved file handle "OUTPUT".

```vhdl
library IEEE;
use IEEE.std_logic_1164.all;
use IEEE.std_logic_textio.all;

library STD;
use STD.textio.all;

entity SystemX_TB is
end entity;

architecture SystemX_TB_arch of SystemX_TB is

  component SystemX
    port (ABC  : in  std_logic_vector(2 downto 0);
          F    : out std_logic);
  end component;

  signal   ABC_TB  : std_logic_vector(2 downto 0);
  signal   F_TB    : std_logic;

begin

  DUT : SystemX port map (ABC => ABC_TB, F => F_TB);

  STIMULUS : process

    variable current_line : line;

    begin

      write(current_line, string'("Beginning Test (Input=ABC, Output=F)"));
      writeline(OUTPUT, current_line);

      ABC_TB <= "000"; wait for 125 ns;

      write(current_line, string'("ABC="));
      write(current_line, ABC_TB);
      write(current_line, string'(", F="));
      write(current_line, F_TB);
      writeline(OUTPUT, current_line);

      ABC_TB <= "001"; wait for t_wait;

      write(current_line, string'("ABC="));
      write(current_line, ABC_TB);
      write(current_line, string'(", F="));
      write(current_line, F_TB);
      writeline(OUTPUT, current_line);

         :

      wait;

    end process;

end architecture;
```

The reserved file handle "OUTPUT" is used to direct the writeline() output to the computer STD_OUTPUT.

Repeat for all other possible inputs (not shown for brevity).

Example 8.14
Writing to STD_OUT from a Test Bench (Part 1)

Example 8.15 shows the output from the test bench. This output is displayed in the transcript window of the simulation tool.

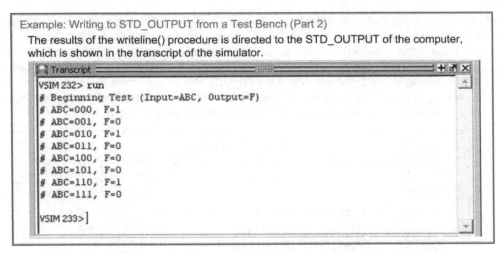

Example 8.15
Writing to STD_OUT from a Test Bench (Part 2)

8.5.8.3 Example: Reading From an External File in a Test Bench

Let's now look at an example of reading test vectors from an external file. Example 8.16 shows the test bench setup. In this example, the SystemX design from the prior example will be tested using vectors provided by an external file (input_file.txt). The test bench will read in each line of the file individually and sequentially. After reading a line, the test bench will drive the DUT with the input vector. In order to verify correct operation, the results will be written to the STD_OUTPUT of the computer.

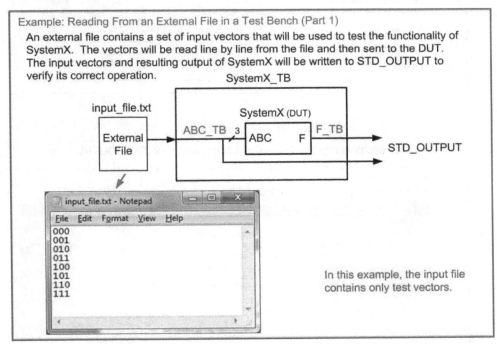

Example 8.16
Reading From an External File in a Test Bench (Part 1)

In order to read the external vectors, a file is declared in READ_MODE. This opens the external file and allows the VHDL test bench to access its lines. A variable is declared to hold the line that is read using the readline() procedure. In this example, the line variable for reading is called "current_read_line". A variable is also declared that will ultimately hold the vector that is extracted from current_read_line. This variable (called current_read_field) is declared to be of type std_logic_vector(2 downto 0) because the vectors in the file are 3-bit values. Once the line is read from the file using the readline() procedure, the vector can be read from the line variable using the read() procedure. Once the value resides in the *current_read_field* variable, it can be assigned to the DUT input signal vector *ABC_TB*. A set of messages are then written to the STD_OUTPUT of the computer using the reserved file handle OUTPUT. The messages contain descriptive text in addition to the values of the input vector and output value of the DUT. Example 8.17 shows the process to implement this behavior in the test bench.

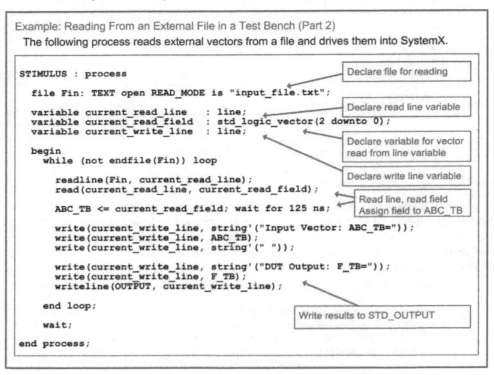

Example: Reading From an External File in a Test Bench (Part 2)

The following process reads external vectors from a file and drives them into SystemX.

```
STIMULUS : process

  file Fin: TEXT open READ_MODE is "input_file.txt";    Declare file for reading

  variable current_read_line    : line;                 Declare read line variable
  variable current_read_field   : std_logic_vector(2 downto 0);  Declare variable for vector
  variable current_write_line   : line;                          read from line variable

  begin                                                 Declare write line variable
    while (not endfile(Fin)) loop

      readline(Fin, current_read_line);                 Declare write line variable
      read(current_read_line, current_read_field);
                                                        Read line, read field
      ABC_TB <= current_read_field; wait for 125 ns;    Assign field to ABC_TB

      write(current_write_line, string'("Input Vector: ABC_TB="));
      write(current_write_line, ABC_TB);
      write(current_write_line, string'(" "));

      write(current_write_line, string'("DUT Output: F_TB="));
      write(current_write_line, F_TB);
      writeline(OUTPUT, current_write_line);

    end loop;
                                                        Write results to STD_OUTPUT
    wait;

end process;
```

Example 8.17
Reading From an External File in a Test Bench (Part 2)

Example 8.18 **shows the results of this test bench, which are written to STD_OUTPUT.**

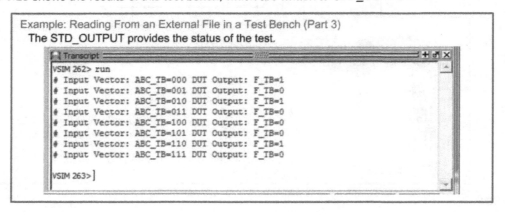

Example: Reading From an External File in a Test Bench (Part 3)

The STD_OUTPUT provides the status of the test.

```
Transcript
VSIM 262> run
# Input Vector: ABC_TB=000 DUT Output: F_TB=1
# Input Vector: ABC_TB=001 DUT Output: F_TB=0
# Input Vector: ABC_TB=010 DUT Output: F_TB=1
# Input Vector: ABC_TB=011 DUT Output: F_TB=0
# Input Vector: ABC_TB=100 DUT Output: F_TB=0
# Input Vector: ABC_TB=101 DUT Output: F_TB=0
# Input Vector: ABC_TB=110 DUT Output: F_TB=1
# Input Vector: ABC_TB=111 DUT Output: F_TB=0

VSIM 263>
```

Example 8.18
Reading From an External File in a Test Bench (Part 3)

8.5.8.4 Example: Reading Space-Delimited Data from an External File in a Test Bench

As mentioned earlier, information in a line variable is treated as white space-delimited by the read() procedure. This allows more information than just a single vector to be read from a file. When a read() procedure is performed on a line variable, it will extract information until it reaches either a white space or the end-of-line character. If a white space is encountered, the read() procedure will end. Let's take a look at an example of how to read information from a file when it contains both strings and vectors. Example 8.19 shows the test bench setup where an external file is to be read that contains both a text heading and test vector on each line. Since the header and the vector are separated with a white space character, two read() procedures need to be used to independently extract these distinct fields from the line variable.

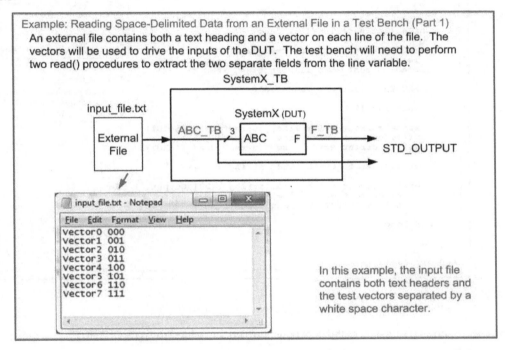

Example 8.19
Reading Space-Delimited Data from an External File in a Test Bench (Part 1)

The test bench will transfer a line from the file into a line variable using the readline() procedure just as in the previous example; however, this time two different variables will need to be defined in order to read the two separate fields in the line. Each variable must be declared to be the proper type and size for the information in the field. For example, the first field in the file is a string of seven characters. As a result, the first variable declared (current_read_field1) will be of type *string(1 to 7)*. Recall that strings are typically indexed incrementally from left to right starting with the index 1. The second field in the file is a 3-bit vector, so the second variable declared (current_read_field2) will be of type std_logic_vector(2 downto 0). Each time a line is retrieved from the file using the readline() procedure, two subsequent read() procedures can be performed to extract the two fields from the line variable. The second field (i.e., the vector) can be used to drive the input of the DUT. In this example, both fields are written to STD_OUTPUT in addition to the output of the DUT to verify proper functionality. Example 8.20 shows the test bench process which models this behavior.

Example: Reading Space-Delimited Data from an External File in a Test Bench (Part 2)

The following process reads external vectors from a file and drives SystemX.

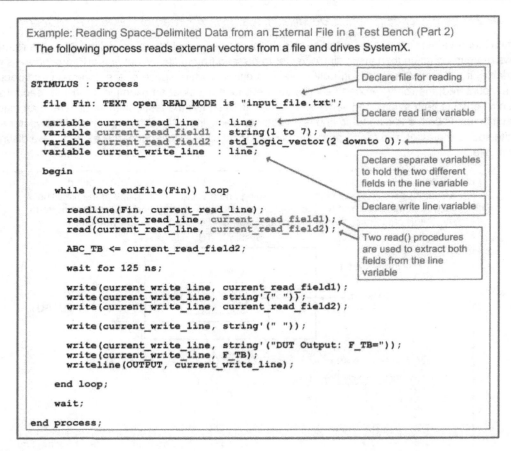

```
STIMULUS : process

  file Fin: TEXT open READ_MODE is "input_file.txt";       → Declare file for reading

  variable current_read_line    : line;                    → Declare read line variable
  variable current_read_field1  : string(1 to 7);     ←
  variable current_read_field2  : std_logic_vector(2 downto 0); ←
  variable current_write_line   : line;                    → Declare separate variables
                                                             to hold the two different
                                                             fields in the line variable
  begin

    while (not endfile(Fin)) loop                          → Declare write line variable

      readline(Fin, current_read_line);
      read(current_read_line, current_read_field1);   ←    Two read() procedures
      read(current_read_line, current_read_field2);   ←    are used to extract both
                                                            fields from the line
      ABC_TB <= current_read_field2;                        variable

      wait for 125 ns;

      write(current_write_line, current_read_field1);
      write(current_write_line, string'(" "));
      write(current_write_line, current_read_field2);

      write(current_write_line, string'(" "));

      write(current_write_line, string'("DUT Output: F_TB="));
      write(current_write_line, F_TB);
      writeline(OUTPUT, current_write_line);

    end loop;

    wait;

end process;
```

Example 8.20
Reading Space-Delimited Data from an External File in a Test Bench (Part 2)

Example 8.21 shows the results of this test bench, which are written to STD_OUTPUT.

Example: Reading Space-Delimited Data from an External File in a Test Bench (Part 3)

The STD_OUTPUT provides the status of the test.

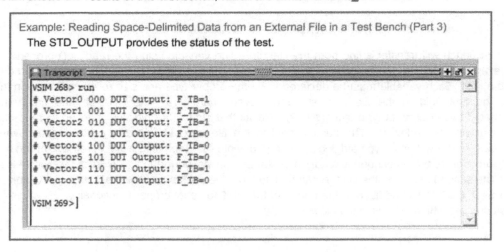

```
Transcript
VSIM 268> run
# Vector0 000 DUT Output: F_TB=1
# Vector1 001 DUT Output: F_TB=0
# Vector2 010 DUT Output: F_TB=1
# Vector3 011 DUT Output: F_TB=0
# Vector4 100 DUT Output: F_TB=0
# Vector5 101 DUT Output: F_TB=0
# Vector6 110 DUT Output: F_TB=1
# Vector7 111 DUT Output: F_TB=0

VSIM 269>
```

Example 8.21
Reading Space-Delimited Data from an External File in a Test Bench (Part 3)

8.5.9 Legacy Packages (STD_LOGIC_ARITH / UNSIGNED / SIGNED)

Prior to the release of the *numeric_std* package by IEEE, Synopsis, Inc. created a set of packages to provide computational operations for types std_logic and std_logic_vector. Since these arithmetic packages were defined very early in the life of VHDL, they were widely adopted. Unfortunately, due to these packages not being standardized through a governing body such as IEEE, vendors began modifying the packages to meet proprietary needs. This led to a variety of incompatibility issues that have plagued these packages. As a result, all new designs requiring computational operations should be based on the IEEE *numeric_std* package. While the IEEE standard is the recommended numerical package for VHDL, the original Synopsis packages are still commonly found in designs and in design examples, so providing an overview of their functionality is necessary.

Synopsis, Inc. created the **std_logic_arith** package to provide computational operations for types std_logic and std_logic_vector. Just as with the *numeric_std* package, this package defines two new types, **unsigned** and **signed**. Arithmetic, comparison and shift operators are provided for these types that include **+, -, *, abs, >, <, <=, >=, =, /=, shl**, and **shr**. This package also provides a set of conversion functions between types unsigned, signed, std_logic_vector and integer. The syntax for these conversions are as follows:

Name	Input Type	Return Type
CONV_INTEGER	unsigned	integer
CONV_INTEGER	signed	integer
CONV_UNSIGNED	integer, \<size>	unsigned
CONV_UNSIGNED	signed	unsigned
CONV_SIGNED	integer, \<size>	signed
CONV_SIGNED	unsigned	signed
CONV_STD_LOGIC_VECTOR	integer, \<size>	std_logic_vector(size-1 downto 0)
CONV_STD_LOGIC_VECTOR	unsigned, \<size>	std_logic_vector(size-1 downto 0)
CONV_STD_LOGIC_VECTOR	signed, \<size>	std_logic_vector(size-1 downto 0)

The Synopsis packages have the ability to treat all std_logic_vectors in a design as either unsigned or signed by including an additional package. The **std_logic_unsigned** package, when included in conjunction with the std_logic_arith package, will treat all std_logic_vectors in the design as unsigned numbers. The syntax for using the Synopsis arithmetic packages on unsigned numbers is as follows. The *std_logic_1164* package is required to define types std_logic/std_logic_vector. The *std_logic_arith* package provides the computational operators for types std_logic/std_logic_vector. Finally, the *std_logic_unsigned* package treats all std_logic/std_logic_vector types as unsigned numbers when performing arithmetic operations.

```
library IEEE;
use IEEE.std_logic_1164.all;
use IEEE.std_logic_arith.all;
use IEEE.std_logic_unsigned.all;
```

The **std_logic_signed** package works in a similar manner with the exception that it treats all std_logic/std_logic_vector types as signed numbers when performing arithmetic operations. The *std_logic_unsigned* and *std_logic_signed* packages are never used together since they will conflict with each other.

The syntax for using the std_logic_signed package is as follows:

```
library IEEE;
use IEEE.std_logic_1164.all;
use IEEE.std_logic_arith.all;
use IEEE.std_logic_signed.all;
```

One of the more confusing aspects of the Synopsis packages is that they are included in the IEEE library. This means that both the *numeric_std* package (IEEE standard) and the *std_logic_arith* package (Synopsis, non-standard) are part of the same library, but one is recommended while the other is not. This is due to the fact that the Synopsis packages were developed first, and putting them into the IEEE library was the most natural location since this library was provided as part of the VHDL standard. When the numeric_std package was standardized by IEEE, it also was naturally inserted into the IEEE library. As a result, today's IEEE library contains both styles of packages.

CONCEPT CHECK

CC8.5(a) Why is standardization important for VHDL packages?

A) So that different CAD/CAE tools are interoperable.

B) To support IEEE.

C) So that synthesis is possible.

D) So that detailed manuals can be created.

CC8.5(b) Why doesn't the VHDL standard package simply include all of the functionality that has been created in all of the packages that were developed later?

A) There was not sufficient funding to keep the VHDL standard package updated.

B) If every package was included, compilation would take an excessive amount of time.

C) Explicitly defining packages helps keep the remind the designer the proper way to create a VHDL model.

D) Because not all designs require all of the functionality in every package. Plus, some packages defined duplicate information. For example, both the numeric_bit and numberic_std have data types called *unsigned*.

Summary

❖ To model sequential logic, an HDL needs to be able to trigger signal assignments based on a triggering event. This is accomplished in VHDL using a *process*.

❖ A *sensitivity* list is a way to control when a VHDL process is triggered. A sensitivity list contains a list of signals. If any of the signals in the sensitivity list transition it will cause the process to trigger. If a sensitivity list is omitted, the process will trigger immediately.

❖ Signal assignments are made when a process suspends. There are two techniques to suspend a process. The first is using the *wait* statement. The second is simply ending the process.

❖ Sensitivity lists and wait statements are never used at the same time. Sensitivity lists are used to model synthesizable logic while wait statements are used for test benches.

❖ When signal assignments are made in a process, they are made in the order they are listed in the process. If assignments are made to the same signal within a process, only the last assignment will take place when the process suspends.

❖ If assignments are needed to occur prior to the process suspending, a *variable* is used. In VHDL, variables only exist within a process. Variables are defined when a process triggers and deleted when the process ends.

❖ Processes also allow more advanced modeling constructs in VHDL. These include *if/then statements*, *case statements*, *infinite loops*, *while loops*, and *for loops*.

❖ *Signal attributes* allow additional information to be observed about a signal other than its value.

❖ A *test bench* is a way to simulate a device under test (DUT) by instantiating it as a component, driving in stimulus, and observing the outputs. Test benches do not have inputs or outputs and are unsynthesizable.

❖ The *report* and *assert* statements provide a way to perform automatic checking of the outputs of a DUT within a test bench.

❖ The IEEE STD_LOGIC_1164 package provides more realistic date types for modeling modern digital systems. This package provides the std_ulogic and std_logic data types. These data types can take on nine different values (U, X, 0, 1, Z, W, L, H, and -). The std_logic data type provides a resolution function that allows multiple outputs to be connected to the same signal. The resolution function will determine the value of the signal based on a predefined priority given in the function.

❖ The IEEE STD_LOGIC_1164 package provides logical operators and edge detection functions for the types std_ulogic and std_logic. It also provides conversion functions to and from the type *bit*.

❖ The IEEE NUMERIC_STD package provides the data types *unsigned* and *signed*. These types use the underlying data type std_logic. These types provide the ability to treat vectors as either unsigned or two's complement codes.

❖ The IEEE NUMERIC_STD package provides arithmetic operations for the types unsigned and signed. This package also provides conversions functions and type casts to and from the types integer and std_logic_vector.

❖ The TEXTIO and STD_LOGIC_TEXTIO packages provide the functionality to read and write to files from within a test benches. This allows more sophisticated vector patterns to be driven into a DUT. This also provides more sophisticated automatic checking of a DUT.

Exercise Problems

Section 8.1 – The Process

8.1.1 When using a sensitivity list in a process, what will cause the process to *trigger*?

8.1.2 When using a sensitivity list in a process, what will cause the process to *suspend*?

8.1.3 When a sensitivity list is <u>not</u> used in a process, when will the process trigger?

8.1.4 Can a sensitivity list and a wait statement be used in the same process at the same time?

8.1.5 Does a wait statement *trigger* or *suspend* a process?

8.1.6 When are signal assignments officially made in a process?

8.1.7 Why are assignments in a process called *sequential signal assignments?*

8.1.8 Can signals be declared in a process?

8.1.9 Are variables declared within a process visible to the rest of the VHDL model (e.g., are they visible outside of the process)?

8.1.10 What happens to a variable when a process ends.

8.1.11 What is the assignment operators for variables?

Section 8.2 – Conditional Programming Constructs

8.2.1 Design a VHDL model to implement the behavior described by the 4-input truth table in Figure 8.4. Use a process and an if/then statement. Use std_logic and std_logic_vector types for your signals. Declare the entity to match the block diagram provided. Hint: Notice that there are far more input codes producing F=0 than producing F=1. Can you use this to your advantage to make your VHDL model simpler?

A	B	C	D	F
0	0	0	0	0
0	0	0	1	1
0	0	1	0	0
0	0	1	1	1
0	1	0	0	0
0	1	0	1	0
0	1	1	0	0
0	1	1	1	0
1	0	0	0	0
1	0	0	1	1
1	0	1	0	0
1	0	1	1	1
1	1	0	0	0
1	1	0	1	0
1	1	1	0	0
1	1	1	1	0

Capital "i"

SystemI.vhd

Note that the input to the VHDL model is declared as a 4-bit vector.

Figure 8.4

8.2.2 Design a VHDL model to implement the behavior described by the 4-input truth table in Figure 8.4. Use a process and a <u>case statement</u>. Use std_logic and std_logic_vector types for your signals. Declare the entity to match the block diagram provided.

8.2.3 Design a VHDL model to implement the behavior described by the 4-input minterm list in Figure 8.5. Use a process and an if/then statement. Use std_logic and std_logic_vector types for your signals. Declare the entity to match the block diagram provided.

$$F = \sum_{A,B,C,D}(4,5,7,12,13,15)$$

SystemJ.vhd

Figure 8.5

8.2.4 Design a VHDL model to implement the behavior described by the 4-input minterm list in Figure 8.5. Use a process and a <u>case statement</u>. Use std_logic and std_logic_vector types for your signals. Declare the entity to match the block diagram provided.

8.2.5 Design a VHDL model to implement the behavior described by the 4-input maxterm list in Figure 8.6. Use a process and an if/then statement. Use std_logic and std_logic_vector types for your signals. Declare the entity to match the block diagram provided.

SystemK.vhd

$$F = \prod_{A,B,C,D}(3,7,11,15)$$

Figure 8.6

8.2.6 Design a VHDL model to implement the behavior described by the 4-input maxterm list in Figure 8.6. Use a process and a <u>case statement</u>. Use std_logic and std_logic_vector types for your signals. Declare the entity to match the block diagram provided.

8.2.7 Design a VHDL model to implement the behavior described by the 4-input truth table in Figure 8.7. Use a process and an if/then statement. Use std_logic and std_logic_vector types for your signals. Declare the entity to match the block diagram provided. Hint: Notice that there are far more input codes producing F=1 than producing F=0. Can you use this to your advantage to make your VHDL model simpler?

A	B	C	D	F
0	0	0	0	1
0	0	0	1	0
0	0	1	0	1
0	0	1	1	1
0	1	0	0	1
0	1	0	1	1
0	1	1	0	1
0	1	1	1	1
1	0	0	0	1
1	0	0	1	0
1	0	1	0	1
1	0	1	1	0
1	1	0	0	1
1	1	0	1	0
1	1	1	0	1
1	1	1	1	1

Figure 8.7

8.2.8 Design a VHDL model to implement the behavior described by the 4-input truth table in Figure 8.7. Use a process and a <u>case statement</u>. Use std_logic and std_logic_vector types for your signals. Declare the entity to match the block diagram provided.

8.2.9 Figure 8.8 shows the topology of a *4-bit shift register* when implemented structurally using D-Flip-Flops. Design a VHDL model to describe this functionality using a <u>single process and sequential signal assignments</u> instead of instantiating D-Flip-Flops. The figure also provides the block diagram for the entity definition. Use std_logic and std_logic_vector types for your signals.

Figure 8.8

8.2.10 Design a VHDL model for a counter using a <u>for loop</u> with an output type of integer. Figure 8.9 shows the block diagram for the entity definition. The counter should increment from 0 to 31 and then start over. Use wait statements within your process to update the counter value every 10 ns. Consider using the loop variable of the for loop to generate your counter value. NOTE: This design is <u>not</u> synthesizable.

counter_integer_up.vhd

Figure 8.9

8.2.11 Design a VHDL model for a counter using a <u>for loop</u> with an output type of std_logic_vector(4 downto 0). Figure 8.10 shows the block diagram for the entity definition. The counter should increment from 00000_2 to 11111_2 and then start over. Use wait statements within your process to update the counter value every 10ns. Consider using the loop variable of the for loop to generate an integer version of your count value, and then use a type conversion function to convert the integer to std_logic_vector. NOTE: This design is <u>not</u> synthesizable.

counter_5bit_binary_up.vhd

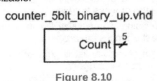

Figure 8.10

Section 8.3 – Signal Attributes

8.3.1 What is the purpose of a signal attribute?

8.3.2 What is the data type returned when using the signal attribute *'event*?

8.3.3 What is the data type returned when using the signal attribute *'last_event*?

8.3.4 What is the data type returned when using the signal attribute *'length*?

Section 8.4 – Test Benches

8.4.1 Design a VHDL <u>test bench</u> to verify the functional operation of the system in Figure 8.4. Your test bench should drive in each input code for the vector ABCD in the order they appear in the truth table (i.e., "0000", "0001", "0010", …). Have your test bench change the input pattern every 10 ns using the *wait for* statement within your stimulus process.

8.4.2 Design a VHDL <u>test bench</u> to verify the functional operation of the system in Figure 8.4 using <u>report and assert statements</u>. Your test bench should drive in each input code for the vector ABCD in the order they appear in the truth table (i.e., "0000", "0001", "0010", …). Have your test bench change the input pattern every 10 ns using the *wait for* statement within your stimulus process. Use the report and assert statements to output a message on the status of each test to the simulation transcript window. For each input vector, create a message that indicates the current input vector being tested, the resulting output of your DUT, and whether the DUT output is correct.

8.4.3 Design a VHDL <u>test bench</u> to verify the functional operation of the system in Figure 8.5. Your test bench should drive in each input code for the vector ABCD in the order they appear in the truth table (i.e., "0000", "0001", "0010", …). Have your test bench change the input pattern every 10 ns using the *wait for* statement within your stimulus process.

8.4.4 Design a VHDL <u>test bench</u> to verify the functional operation of the system in Figure 8.5 using <u>report and assert statements</u>. Your test bench should drive in each input code for the vector ABCD in the order they appear in the truth table (i.e., "0000", "0001", "0010", …). Have your test bench change the input pattern every 10 ns using the *wait for* statement within your stimulus process. Use the report and assert statements to output a message on the status of each test to the simulation transcript window. For each input vector, create a message that indicates the current input vector being tested, the resulting output of your DUT, and whether the DUT output is correct.

8.4.5 Design a VHDL <u>test bench</u> to verify the functional operation of the system in Figure 8.6. Your test bench should drive in each input code for the vector ABCD in the order they appear in the truth table (i.e., "0000", "0001", "0010", ...). Have your test bench change the input pattern every 10 ns using the *wait for* statement within your stimulus process.

8.4.6 Design a VHDL <u>test bench</u> to verify the functional operation of the system in Figure 8.6 using <u>report and assert statements</u>. Your test bench should drive in each input code for the vector ABCD in the order they appear in the truth table (i.e., "0000", "0001", "0010", ...). Have your test bench change the input pattern every 10 ns using the *wait for* statement within your stimulus process. Use the report and assert statements to output a message on the status of each test to the simulation transcript window. For each input vector create a message that indicates the current input vector being tested, the resulting output of your DUT, and whether the DUT output is correct.

8.4.7 Design a VHDL <u>test bench</u> to verify the functional operation of the system in Figure 8.7. Your test bench should drive in each input code for the vector ABCD in the order they appear in the truth table (i.e., "0000", "0001", "0010", ...). Have your test bench change the input pattern every 10 ns using the *wait for* statement within your stimulus process.

8.4.8 Design a VHDL <u>test bench</u> to verify the functional operation of the system in Figure 8.7 using <u>report and assert statements</u>. Your test bench should drive in each input code for the vector ABCD in the order they appear in the truth table (i.e., "0000", "0001", "0010", ...). Have your test bench change the input pattern every 10 ns using the *wait for* statement within your stimulus process. Use the report and assert statements to output a message on the status of each test to the simulation transcript window. For each input vector, create a message that indicates the current input vector being tested, the resulting output of your DUT, and whether the DUT output is correct.

Section 8.5 – Packages

8.5.1 What are all possible values that a signal of type *std_logic* can take on?

8.5.2 What is the difference between the types *std_ulogic* and *std_logic*?

8.5.3 If a signal of type *std_logic* is assigned both a 0 and Z at the same time, what will final signal value be?

8.5.4 If a signal of type *std_logic* is assigned both a 1 and X at the same time, what will final signal value be?

8.5.5 If a signal of type *std_logic* is assigned both a 0 and L at the same time, what will final signal value be?

8.5.6 Are any arithmetic operations provided for the type *std_logic_vector* in the STD_LOGIC_1164 package?

8.5.7 If you declare a signal of type *unsigned* from the NUMBERIC_STD package, what are all the possible values that the signal can take on?

8.5.8 If you declare a signal of type *signed* from the NUMERIC_STD package, what are all the possible values that the signal can take on?

8.5.9 If two signals (A and B) are declared of type *signed* from the NUMERIC_STD package and hold the values A <= "1111" and B <= "0000", which signal has a greater value?

8.5.10 If two signals (A and B) are declared of type *unsigned* from the NUMERIC_STD package and hold the values A <= "1111" and B <= "0000", which signal has a greater value?

8.5.11 If you are using the NUMERIC_STD package, what is the syntax to convert a signal of type *unsigned* into *std_logic*?

8.5.12 If you are using the NUMERIC_STD package, what is the syntax to convert a signal of type *integer* into *std_logic*?

8.5.13 Design a self-checking VHDL <u>test bench that reads in test vectors from an external file</u> to verify the functional operation of the system in Figure 8.7. Create an input text file called "input_vectors.txt" that contains each input code for the vector ABCD in the order they appear in the truth table (i.e., "0000", "0001", "0010", ...) on a separate line. The test bench should read in each line of the file individually and use the corresponding input vector to drive the DUT. Write the output results to an external file called "<u>output_vectors.txt</u>".

8.5.14 Design a self-checking VHDL <u>test bench that reads in test vectors from an external file</u> to verify the functional operation of the system in Figure 8.7. Create an input text file called "input_vectors.txt" that contains each input code for the vector ABCD in the order they appear in the truth table (i.e., "0000", "0001", "0010", ...) on a separate line. The test bench should read in each line of the file individually and use the corresponding input vector to drive the DUT. Write the output results to the <u>STD OUTPUT</u> of the simulator.

Chapter 9: Behavioral Modeling of Sequential Logic

In this chapter, we will look at modeling sequential logic using the more sophisticated behavioral modeling techniques presented in Chapter 8. We will begin by looking at modeling sequential storage devices. Next, we will look at the behavioral modeling of finite state machines. Finally, we will look at register transfer level, or RTL modeling.

Learning Outcomes – After completing this chapter, you will be able to:

9.1   Design a VHDL model of a finite state machine using a three process, behavioral modeling approach from a state diagram.
9.2   Design a VHDL model of a finite state machine with states modeled using a user-enumerated type.
9.3   Design a VHDL model of a finite state machine with states explicitly encoded using subtypes.
9.4   Design a VHDL model of a finite state machine using a three process, behavioral modeling approach from a word description.
9.5   Design a VHDL model of a counter using a single process, behavioral modeling approach.
9.6   Design a VHDL model of a synchronous system using a register transfer level (RTL) modeling approach.

9.1 Modeling Sequential Storage Devices in VHDL

9.1.1 D-Latch

Let's begin with the model of a simple D-Latch. Since the outputs of this sequential storage device are not updated continuously, its behavior is modeled using a process. Since we want to create a synthesizable model, we use a sensitivity list to trigger the process instead of wait statements. In the sensitivity list we need to include the C input since it controls when the D-Latch is in track or store mode. We also need to include the D input in the sensitivity list because during the track mode, the output Q will be continuously assigned the value of D so any change on D needs to trigger the process. The use of an if/then statement is used to model the behavior during track mode (C=1). Since the behavior is not explicitly stated for when C=0, the outputs will hold their last value, which allows us to simply end the if/then statement to complete the model.. Example 9.1 shows the behavioral model for a D-Latch.

Example 9.1
Behavioral Model of a D-Latch in VHDL

9.1.2 D-Flip-Flop

The rising edge behavior of a D-Flip-Flop is modeled using a (Clock'event and Clock='1') boolean condition within a process. The (rising_edge(Clock)) function can also be used for type std_logic. Example 9.2 shows the behavioral model for a rising edge triggered D-Flip-Flop with both Q and Qn outputs.

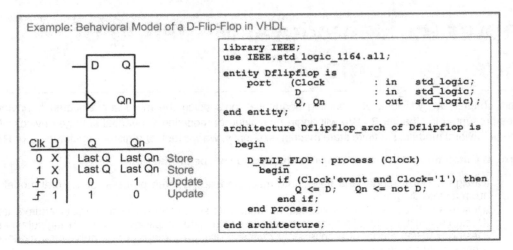

Example: Behavioral Model of a D-Flip-Flop in VHDL

Clk D	Q	Qn	
0 X	Last Q	Last Qn	Store
1 X	Last Q	Last Qn	Store
ꜛ 0	0	1	Update
ꜛ 1	1	0	Update

```
library IEEE;
use IEEE.std_logic_1164.all;

entity Dflipflop is
    port    (Clock          : in     std_logic;
             D              : in     std_logic;
             Q, Qn          : out    std_logic);
end entity;

architecture Dflipflop_arch of Dflipflop is

  begin

    D_FLIP_FLOP : process (Clock)
      begin
          if (Clock'event and Clock='1') then
              Q <= D;    Qn <= not D;
          end if;
    end process;

end architecture;
```

Example 9.2
Behavioral Model of a D-Flip-Flop in VHDL

9.1.3 D-Flip-Flop with Asynchronous Reset

D-Flip-Flops typically have a reset line in order to initialize their outputs to a known state (e.g., Q=0, Qn=1). Resets are asynchronous, meaning that whenever they are asserted, assignments to the outputs takes place immediately. If a reset was *synchronous*, the output assignments would only take place on the next rising edge of the clock. This behavior is undesirable because if there is a system failure, there is no guarantee that a clock edge will ever occur. Thus the reset may never take place. Asynchronous resets are more desirable not only to put the D-Flip-Flops into a known state at startup, but also to recover from a system failure that may have impacted the clock signal. In order to model this asynchronous behavior, the reset signal is placed in the sensitivity list. This allows both the clock and the reset inputs to trigger the process. Within the process, an if/then/elsif statement is used to determine whether the reset has been asserted or a rising edge of the clock has occurred. The if/then/elsif statement first checks whether the reset input has been asserted. If it has, it makes the appropriate assignments to the outputs (Q=0, Qn=1). If the reset has not been asserted, the *elsif* clause checks whether a rising edge of the clock has occurred using the (Clock'event and Clock='1') boolean condition. If it has, the outputs are updated accordingly (Q <= D, Qn <= not D). A final else statement is not included so that assignments to the outputs are not made under any other condition. This models the store behavior of the D-Flip-Flop. Example 9.3 shows the behavioral model for a rising edge triggered D-Flip-Flop with an asynchronous, active LOW reset.

Example: Behavioral Model of a D-Flip-Flop with Asynchronous Reset in VHDL

$\overline{R}$	Clk	D	Q	Qn	
0	X	X	0	1	Reset
1	0	X	Last Q	Last Qn	Store
1	1	X	Last Q	Last Qn	Store
1	⌐	0	0	1	Update
1	⌐	1	1	0	Update

```vhdl
library IEEE;
use IEEE.std_logic_1164.all;

entity Dflipflop is
    port    (Clock          : in   std_logic;
             Reset          : in   std_logic;
             D              : in   std_logic;
             Q, Qn          : out  std_logic);
end entity;

architecture Dflipflop_arch of Dflipflop is

  begin

      D_FLIP_FLOP : process (Clock, Reset)
        begin
           if (Reset = '0') then
                Q <= '0'; Qn <= '1';
           elsif (Clock'event and Clock='1') then
                Q <= D;    Qn <= not D;
           end if;
      end process;

end architecture;
```

Example 9.3
Behavioral Model of a D-Flip-Flop with Asynchronous Reset in VHDL

9.1.4 D-Flip-Flop with Asynchronous Reset and Preset

A D-Flip-Flop with both an asynchronous reset and asynchronous preset is handled in a similar manner as the D-Flip-Flop in the prior section. The preset input is included in the sensitivity list in order to trigger the process whenever a transition occurs on either the clock, reset, or preset inputs. An if/then/elsif statement is used to first check whether a reset has occurred; then whether a preset has occurred; and finally, whether a rising edge of the clock has occurred. Example 9.4 shows the model for a rising edge triggered D-Flip-Flop with asynchronous, active LOW reset and preset.

Example: Behavioral Model of a D-Flip-Flop with Asynchronous Reset and Preset in VHDL

R	P	Clk	D	Q	Qn	
0	X	X	X	0	1	Reset
1	0	X	X	1	0	Preset
1	1	0	X	Last Q	Last Qn	Store
1	1	1	X	Last Q	Last Qn	Store
1	1	↑	0	0	1	Update
1	1	↑	1	1	0	Update

```vhdl
library IEEE;
use IEEE.std_logic_1164.all;

entity Dflipflop is
    port    (Clock              : in    std_logic;
             Reset, Preset       : in    std_logic;
             D                   : in    std_logic;
             Q, Qn               : out   std_logic);
end entity;

architecture Dflipflop_arch of Dflipflop is

  begin

     D_FLIP_FLOP : process (Clock, Reset, Preset)
        begin
           if (Reset = '0') then
               Q <= '0'; Qn <= '1';
           elsif (Preset = '0') then
               Q <= '1'; Qn <= '0';
           elsif (Clock'event and Clock='1') then
               Q <= D;    Qn <= not D;
           end if;
        end process;

end architecture;
```

Example 9.4
Behavioral Model of a D-Flip-Flop with Asynchronous Reset and Preset in VHDL

9.1.5 D-Flip-Flop with Synchronous Enable

An enable input is also a common feature of modern D-Flip-Flops. Enable inputs are synchronous, meaning that when they are asserted, action is only taken on the rising edge of the clock. This means that the enable input is not included in the sensitivity list of the process. Since action is only taken when there is a rising edge of the clock, a nested if/then statement is included beneath the *elsif (Clock'event and Clock='1')* clause. Example 9.5 shows the model for a D-Flip-Flop with a synchronous enable (EN) input. When EN=1, the D-Flip-Flop is enabled and assignments are made to the outputs only on the rising edge of the clock. When EN=0, the D-Flip-Flop is disabled and assignments to the outputs are not made. When disabled, the D-Flip-Flop effectively ignores rising edges on the clock and the outputs remain at their last values.

Example: Behavioral Model of a D-Flip-Flop with Synchronous Enable in VHDL

$\bar{R}$	$\bar{P}$	Clk	EN	D	Q	Qn	
0	X	X	X	X	0	1	Reset
1	0	X	X	X	1	0	Preset
1	1	0	X	X	Last Q	Last Qn	Store
1	1	1	X	X	Last Q	Last Qn	Store
1	1	⌐	0	X	Last Q	Last Qn	Disabled (ignore clock)
1	1	⌐	1	0	0	1	Update
1	1	⌐	1	1	1	0	Update

```vhdl
library IEEE;
use IEEE.std_logic_1164.all;

entity Dflipflop is
    port    (Clock          : in     std_logic;
             Reset, Preset  : in     std_logic;
             D, EN          : in     std_logic;
             Q, Qn          : out    std_logic);
end entity;

architecture Dflipflop_arch of Dflipflop is

  begin

    D_FLIP_FLOP : process (Clock, Reset, Preset)
      begin
        if (Reset = '0') then
            Q <= '0'; Qn <= '1';
        elsif (Preset = '0') then
            Q <= '1'; Qn <= '0';
        elsif (Clock'event and Clock='1') then
            if (EN = '1') then
                Q <= D;    Qn <= not D;
            end if;
        end if;
    end process;

end architecture;
```

A nested if/then statement is used to model the synchronous enable.

Example 9.5
Behavioral Model of a D-Flip-Flop with Synchronous Enable in VHDL

CONCEPT CHECK

CC9.1   Why is the D input not listed in the sensitivity list of a D-flip-flop?

   A)   To simplify the behavioral model.

   B)   To avoid a setup time violation if D transitions too closely to the clock.

   C)   Because a rising edge of clock is needed to make the assignment.

   D)   Because the outputs of the D-flip-flop are not updated when D changes.

9.2 Modeling Finite State Machines in VHDL

Finite state machines can be easily modeled using the behavioral constructs from Chapter 8. The most common modeling practice for FSMs is to create a new *user-defined* type that can take on the descriptive state names from the state diagram. Two signals are then created of this type, *current_state* and *next_state*. Once these signals are created, all of the functional blocks in the state machine can use the descriptive state names in their conditional signal assignments. The synthesizer will automatically assign the state codes based on the most effective use of the target technology (e.g., binary, gray code, one-hot). Within the VHDL state machine model, three processes are used to describe each of the functional blocks, *state memory, next state logic,* and *output logic.* In order to examine how to model a finite state machine using this approach, let's use the push-button window controller example from Chapter 7.

Example 9.6 gives the overview of the design objectives for this example and the state diagram describing the behavior to be modeled in VHDL.

Example 9.6
Push-Button Window Controller in VHDL – Design Description

Let's begin by defining the entity. The system has an input called *Press* and two outputs called *Open_CW* and *Close_CCW*. The system also has clock and reset inputs. We will design the system to update on the rising edge of the clock and have an asynchronous, active LOW, reset. Example 9.7 shows the VHDL entity definition for this example.

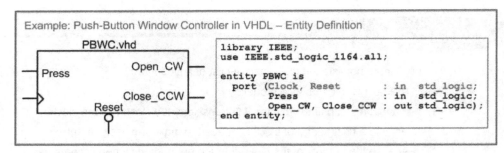

Example 9.7
Push-Button Window Controller in VHDL – Entity Definition

9.2.1 Modeling the States with User-Defined, Enumerated Data Types

Now we begin designing the finite state machine in VHDL using behavioral modeling constructs. The first step is to create a new user-defined, enumerated data type that can take on values that match the descriptive state names we've chosen in the state diagram (i.e., w_closed and w_open). This is accomplished by declaring a new type before the begin statement in the architecture with the keyword *type*. For this example, we will create a new type called *State_Type* and explicitly enumerate the values that it can take on. This type can now be used in future signal declarations. We then create two new signals called *current_state* and *next_state* of type State_Type. These two signals will be used throughout the VHDL model in order to provide a high-level, readable description of the FSM behavior. The following syntax shows how to declare the new type and declare the current_state and next_state signals.

```
type   State_Type is (w_closed, w_open);
signal current_state, next_state : State_Type;
```

9.2.2 The State Memory Process

Now we model the state memory of the FSM using a process. This process models the behavior of the D-Flip-Flops in the FSM that are holding the current state on their Q outputs. Each time there is a rising edge of the clock, the current state is updated with the next state value present on the D inputs of the D-Flip-Flops. This process must also model the reset condition. For this example we will have the state machine go to the *w_closed* state when Reset is asserted. At all other times, the process will simply update current_state with next_state on every rising edge of the clock. The process model is very similar to the model of a D-Flip-Flop. This is as expected since this process will synthesize into one or more D-Flip-Flops to hold the current state. The sensitivity list contains only Clock and Reset and assignments are only made to the signal current_state. The following syntax shows how to model the state memory of this FSM example.

```
STATE_MEMORY : process (Clock, Reset)
  begin
    if (Reset = '0') then
        current_state <= w_closed;
    elsif (Clock'event and Clock='1') then
        current_state <= next_state;
    end if;
end process;
```

9.2.3 The Next State Logic Process

Now we model the next state logic of the FSM using a second process. Recall that the next state logic is combinational logic, thus we need to include all of the input signals that the circuit considers in the next state calculation in the sensitivity list. The current_state signal will always be included in the sensitivity list of the next state logic process in addition to any inputs to the system. For this example the system has one other input called *Press*. This process makes assignments to the next_state signal. It is common to use a case statement to separate out the assignments that occur at each state. At each state within the case statement, an if/then statement is used to model the assignments for different input conditions on Press. The following syntax shows how to model the next state logic of this FSM example. Notice that we include a *when others* clause to ensure that the state machine has a path back to the reset state in the case of an unexpected fault.

```
NEXT_STATE_LOGIC : process (current_state, Press)
    begin
      case (current_state) is
        when w_closed => if (Press = '1') then
                            next_state <= w_open;
                         else
                            next_state <= w_closed;
                         end if;
        when w_open   => if (Press = '1') then
                            next_state <= w_closed;
                         else
                            next_state <= w_open;
                         end if;
        when others   => next_state <= w_closed;
      end case;
    end process;
```

9.2.4 The Output Logic Process

Now we model the output logic of the FSM using a third process. Recall that output logic is combinational logic, thus we need to include all of the input signals that this circuit considers in the output assignments. The current_state will always be included in the sensitivity list. If the FSM is a Mealy machine, then the system inputs will also be included in the sensitivity list. If the machine is a Moore machine, then only the current_state will be present in the sensitivity list. For this example the FSM is a Mealy machine so the input Press needs to be included in the sensitivity list. Note that this process only makes assignments to the outputs of the machine (Open_CW and Close_CCW). The following syntax shows how to model the output logic of this FSM example. Again, we include a *when others* clause to ensure that the state machine has explicit output behavior in the case of a fault.

```
OUTPUT_LOGIC : process (current_state, Press)
  begin
    case (current_state) is
      when w_closed => if (Press = '1') then
                           Open_CW <= '1'; Close_CCW <= '0';
                       else
                           Open_CW <= '0'; Close_CCW <= '0';
                       end if;

      when w_open   => if (Press = '1') then
                           Open_CW <= '0'; Close_CCW <= '1';
                       else
                           Open_CW <= '0'; Close_CCW <= '0';
                       end if;

      when others   => Open_CW <= '0'; Close_CCW <= '0';
    end case;
end process;
```

Putting this all together in the VHDL architecture yields a functional model for the FSM that can be simulated and synthesized. Once again, it is important to keep in mind that since we did not explicitly assign the state codes, the synthesizer will automatically assign the codes based on the most efficient use of the target technology. Example 9.8 shows the entire architecture for this example.

Example: Push-Button Window Controller in VHDL – Architecture

```vhdl
architecture PBWC_arch of PBWC is

  type    State_Type is (w_closed, w_open);          ◄———  Declaration of user
  signal current_state, next_state : State_Type;            defined type for the
                                                            signals current_state
begin                                                       and next_state.
-------------------------------------------------------
  STATE_MEMORY : process (Clock, Reset)
    begin                                              ◄———  The first process is
      if (Reset = '0') then                                 used to model the
        current_state <= w_closed;                          state memory.
      elsif (Clock'event and Clock='1') then
        current_state <= next_state;
      end if;
  end process;
-------------------------------------------------------
  NEXT_STATE_LOGIC : process (current_state, Press)
    begin                                              ◄———  The second
      case (current_state) is                                process is used
        when w_closed => if (Press = '1') then               to model the next
                           next_state <= w_open;              state logic.
                         else
                           next_state <= w_closed;
                         end if;
        when w_open   => if (Press = '1') then
                           next_state <= w_closed;
                         else
                           next_state <= w_open;
                         end if;
        when others   => next_state <= w_closed;
      end case;
  end process;
-------------------------------------------------------
  OUTPUT_LOGIC : process (current_state, Press)◄———    The third process is
    begin                                               used to model the
      case (current_state) is                           output logic.
        when w_closed => if (Press = '1') then
                           Open_CW <= '1'; Close_CCW <= '0';
                         else
                           Open_CW <= '0'; Close_CCW <= '0';
                         end if;
        when w_open   => if (Press = '1') then
                           Open_CW <= '0'; Close_CCW <= '1';
                         else
                           Open_CW <= '0'; Close_CCW <= '0';
                         end if;
        when others   => Open_CW <= '0'; Close_CCW <= '0';
      end case;
  end process;

end architecture;
```

Example 9.8
Push-Button Window Controller in VHDL – Architecture

Example 9.9 shows the simulation waveform for this state machine. This functional simulation was performed using ModelSim-Altera Starter Edition 10.1d.

Example: Push-Button Window Controller in VHDL – Simulation Waveform

The state machine moves to the next state on the rising edge of the clock.

When Press is asserted, the outputs and next_state are updated.

Example 9.9
Push-Button Window Controller in VHDL – Simulation Waveform

9.2.5 Explicitly Defining State Codes with Subtypes

In the prior example, we did not have control over the state variable encoding. While the previous example is the most common way to model FSMs, there are situations where we would like to assign the state variable codes manually. This is accomplished using a *subtype* and constants. A subtype is simply a constrained type, meaning that it defines a subset of values that an existing type can take on. For example, we could create a subtype to constrain the std_logic data type to only allow values of 0 and 1 and *not* the values of U, X, Z, W, L, H, and -. This would not be considered a new type since it is simply a constraint put upon the existing std_logic type. A subtype defines the constraint and has a unique name that can be used to declare other signals. To use this approach for manually encoding the states of a FSM, we first declare a new subtype called *State_Type* that is simply a version of the existing type std_logic. We then create constants to represent the descriptive state names in the state diagram. These constants are given the type State_Type and a specific value. The value given is the state code we wish to assign to the particular state name. Finally, the current_state and next_state signals are declared of type State_Type. In this way, we can use the same VHDL processes as in the previous example that use the descriptive state names from the state diagram. The following is the VHDL syntax for manually assigning the state codes using subtypes. This syntax would replace the State_Type declaration in the previous example. Example 9.10 shows the resulting simulation waveforms.

```
subtype  State_Type is std_logic;
constant w_open   : State_Type := '0';
constant w_closed : State_Type := '1';
signal   current_state, next_state : State_Type;
```

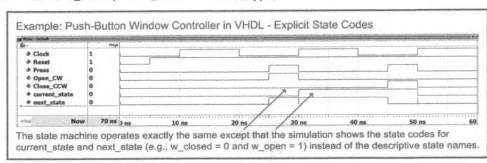

Example: Push-Button Window Controller in VHDL - Explicit State Codes

The state machine operates exactly the same except that the simulation shows the state codes for current_state and next_state (e.g., w_closed = 0 and w_open = 1) instead of the descriptive state names.

Example 9.10
Push-Button Window Controller in VHDL – Explicit State Codes

CONCEPT CHECK

CC9.2   Why is it always a good design approach to model a generic finite state machine using three processes?

    A)   For readability.

    B)   So that it is easy to identify whether the machine is a Mealy or Moore.

    C)   So that the state memory process can be re-used in other FSMs.

    D)   Because each of the three sub-systems of a FSM has unique inputs and outputs that should be handled using a dedicated process.

9.3 FSM Design Examples in VHDL

This section presents a set of example finite state machine designs using the behavioral modeling constructs of VHDL. These example are the same state machines that were presented in Chapter 7.

9.3.1 Serial Bit Sequence Detector in VHDL

Let's look at the design of the serial bit sequence detector finite state machine from Chapter 7 using the behavioral modeling constructs of VHDL. Example 9.11 shows the design description and entity definition for this state machine.

Example 9.11
Serial Bit Sequence Detector in VHDL – Design Description and Entity Definition

Example 9.12 shows the architecture for the serial bit sequence detector. In this example, a user-defined type is created to model the descriptive state names in the state diagram.

Example: Serial Bit Sequence Detector in VHDL – Architecture

```vhdl
architecture Seq_Det_arch of Seq_Det is

  type    State_Type is (Start, D0_is_1, D1_is_1, D0_not_1, D1_not_1);
  signal current_state, next_state : State_Type;

  begin

--------------------------------------------------------------------------
  STATE_MEMORY : process (Clock, Reset)
    begin
      if (Reset = '0') then
        current_state <= Start;
      elsif (Clock'event and Clock='1') then
        current_state <= next_state;
      end if;
  end process;
--------------------------------------------------------------------------
  NEXT_STATE_LOGIC : process (current_state, Din)
    begin
      case (current_state) is
        when Start    => if (Din = '1') then
                              next_state <= D0_is_1;
                         else
                              next_state <= D0_not_1;
                         end if;
        when D0_is_1  => if (Din = '1') then
                              next_state <= D1_is_1;
                         else
                              next_state <= D1_not_1;
                         end if;
        when D1_is_1  => next_state <= Start;
        when D0_not_1 => next_state <= D1_not_1;
        when D1_not_1 => next_state <= Start;
        when others   => next_state <= Start;
      end case;
  end process;
--------------------------------------------------------------------------
  OUTPUT_LOGIC : process (current_state, Din)
    begin
      case (current_state) is
        when D1_is_1  => if (Din = '1') then
                              ERR <= '1';
                         else
                              ERR <= '0';
                         end if;
        when others   => ERR <= '0';
      end case;
  end process;

end architecture;
```

Declaration of user defined type for the signals current_state and next_state.

Note that in this example there are states decisions that don't require if/then statements.

This is a Meally machine so both the current state and the system inputs are present in the sensitivity list.

Example 9.12
Serial Bit Sequence Detector in VHDL – Architecture

Example 9.13 shows the functional simulation waveform for this design.

Example: Serial Bit Sequence Detector in VHDL – Simulation Waveform

The first sequence of 3-bits (1-0-0) does not cause the ERR output to be asserted.

The second sequence of 3-bits (1-1-1) does cause ERR to be asserted.

Example 9.13
Serial Bit Sequence Detector in VHDL – Simulation Waveform

9.3.2 Vending Machine Controller in VHDL

Let's now look at the design of the vending machine controller from Chapter 7 using the behavioral modeling constructs of VHDL. Example 9.14 shows the design description and entity definition.

Example: Vending Machine Controller in VHDL – Design Description and Entity Definition

The vending machine sells bottles of water for 75¢. Customers can enter either a dollar bill or quarters. Once a sufficient amount of money is entered, the vending machine will dispense a bottle of water and, if the user entered a dollar, return one quarter in change.

```
library IEEE;
use IEEE.std_logic_1164.all;

entity Vending is
  port (Clock, Reset      : in  std_logic;
        D_in, Q_in        : in  std_logic;
        Dispense, Change  : out std_logic);
end entity;
```

Example 9.14
Vending Machine Controller in VHDL – Design Description and Entity Definition

Example 9.15 shows the VHDL architecture for the vending machine controller. In this model, the descriptive state names Wait, 25¢, and 50¢ cannot be used directly. This is because Wait is a VHDL keyword and user-defined names cannot begin with a number. Instead, the letter "s" is placed in front of the state names in order to make them legal VHDL names (i.e., sWait, s25, s50).

Example: Vending Machine Controller in VHDL – Architecture

```
architecture Vending_arch of Vending is

  type    State_Type is (sWait, s25, s50);
  signal current_state, next_state : State_Type;

  begin
```

Note that an "s" is added to the beginning of the state names since "Wait" is a VHDL keyword and names cannot start with a number.

```
  ----------------------------------------------------------
  STATE_MEMORY : process (Clock, Reset)
    begin
      if (Reset = '0') then
        current_state <= sWait;
      elsif (Clock'event and Clock='1') then
        current_state <= next_state;
      end if;
  end process;

  ----------------------------------------------------------
  NEXT_STATE_LOGIC : process (current_state, D_in, Q_in)
    begin
      case (current_state) is
        when sWait  => if (Q_in = '1') then
                          next_state <= s25;
                       else
                          next_state <= sWait;
                       end if;
        when s25    => if (Q_in = '1') then
                          next_state <= s50;
                       else
                          next_state <= s25;
                       end if;
        when s50    => if (Q_in = '1') then
                          next_state <= sWait;
                       else
                          next_state <= s50;
                       end if;
        when others => next_state <= sWait;
      end case;
  end process;

  ----------------------------------------------------------
  OUTPUT_LOGIC : process (current_state, D_in, Q_in)
    begin
      case (current_state) is
        when sWait  => if (D_in = '1') then
                          Dispense <= '1'; Change <='1';
                       else
                          Dispense <= '0'; Change <='0';
                       end if;
        when s25    => Dispense <= '0'; Change <='0';
        when s50    => if (Q_in = '1') then
                          Dispense <= '1'; Change <='0';
                       else
                          Dispense <= '0'; Change <='0';
                       end if;
        when others => Dispense <= '0'; Change <='0';
      end case;
  end process;

end architecture;
```

This is a Mealy machine so both the current state and the system inputs are present in the sensitivity list.

Example 9.15
Vending Machine Controller in VHDL – Architecture

Example 9.16 shows the resulting simulation waveform for this design.

Example 9.16
Vending Machine Controller in VHDL – Simulation Waveform

9.3.3 2-Bit, Binary Up/Down Counter in VHDL

Let's now look at how a simple counter can be implemented using the three process behavioral modeling approach in VHDL. Example 9.17 shows the design description and entity definition for the 2-bit, binary up/down counter FSM from Chapter 7.

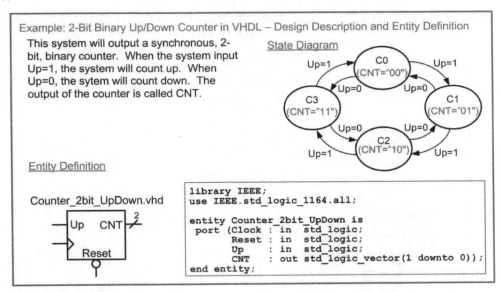

Example 9.17
2-Bit Binary Up/Down Counter in VHDL – Design Description and Entity Definition

Example 9.18 shows the architecture for the 2-bit up/down counter using the three process modeling approach. Since a counter's outputs only depend on the current state, counters are Moore machines. This simplifies the output logic process since it only needs to contain the current state in its sensitivity list.

Example: 2-Bit Binary Up/Down Counter in VHDL – Architecture (Three Process Model)

```vhdl
library IEEE;
use IEEE.std_logic_1164.all;

entity Counter_2bit_UpDown is
 port (Clock, Reset  : in  std_logic;
        Up           : in  std_logic;
        CNT          : out std_logic_vector(1 downto 0));
end entity;

architecture Counter_2bit_UpDown_arch of Counter_2bit_UpDown is

 type    State_Type is (C0, C1, C2, C3);
 signal current_state, next_state : State_Type;

 begin
---------------------------------------------------------------
   STATE_MEMORY : process (Clock, Reset)
     begin
       if (Reset = '0') then
          current_state <= C0;
       elsif (Clock'event and Clock='1') then
          current_state <= next_state;
       end if;
   end process;
---------------------------------------------------------------
   NEXT_STATE_LOGIC : process (current_state, Up)
     begin
       case (current_state) is
         when C0     => if (Up = '1') then
                           next_state <= C1;
                        else
                           next_state <= C3;
                        end if;
         when C1     => if (Up = '1') then
                           next_state <= C2;
                        else
                           next_state <= C0;
                        end if;
         when C2     => if (Up = '1') then
                           next_state <= C3;
                        else
                           next_state <= C1;
                        end if;
         when C3     => if (Up = '1') then
                           next_state <= C0;
                        else
                           next_state <= C2;
                        end if;
         when others => next_state <= C0;
       end case;
   end process;
---------------------------------------------------------------
   OUTPUT_LOGIC : process (current_state)
     begin
       case (current_state) is
         when C0     => CNT <= "00";
         when C1     => CNT <= "01";
         when C2     => CNT <= "10";
         when C3     => CNT <= "11";
         when others => CNT <= "00";
       end case;
   end process;
end architecture;
```

A counter is a Moore machine so the output only depends on the current state.

Example 9.18
2-Bit Binary Up/Down Counter in VHDL – Architecture (Three Process Model)

Example 9.19 shows the resulting simulation waveform for this counter finite state machine.

Example 9.19
2-Bit Binary Up/Down Counter in VHDL – Simulation Waveform

CONCEPT CHECK

CC9.3 The state memory process is nearly identical for all finite state machines with one exception. What is it?

A) The sensitivity list may need to include a preset signal.

B) Sometimes it is modeled using an SR latch storage approach instead of with D-flip-flop behavior.

C) The name of the reset state will be different.

D) The current_state and next_state signals are often swapped.

9.4 Modeling Counters in VHDL

Counters are a special case of finite state machines because they move linearly through their discrete states (either forward or backwards) and typically are implemented with state-encoded outputs. Due to this simplified structure and wide spread use in digital systems, VHDL allows counters to be modeled using a single process and with arithmetic operators (i.e., + and -). This enables a more compact model and allows much wider counters to be implemented.

9.4.1 Counters in VHDL Using the Type UNSIGNED

Let's look at how we can model a 4-bit, binary up counter with an output called *CNT*. First, we want to model this counter using the "+" operator. Recall that the "+" operator is not defined in the std_logic_1164 package. We need to include the numeric_std package in order to add this capability. Within the numeric_std package, the "+" operator is only defined for types signed and unsigned (and not for std_logic_vector) so the output CNT will be declared as type unsigned. Next, we want to implement the counter using a signal assignment in the form *CNT <= CNT + 1*; however, since CNT is an output port, it cannot be used as an argument (right hand side) in an operation. We will need to create an internal signal to implement the counter functionality (i.e., CNT_tmp). Since a signal does not contain directionality, it can be used as both the target and an argument of an operation. Outside of the counter process, a concurrent signal assignment is used to continuously assign CNT_tmp to CNT in order to drive the output of the system. This means that we need to create the internal signal CNT_tmp of type unsigned also to support this assignment. Example 9.20 shows the VHDL model and simulation waveform for this counter. When the counter reaches its maximum value of "1111", it rolls over to "0000" and continues counting because it is defined to only contain 4-bits.

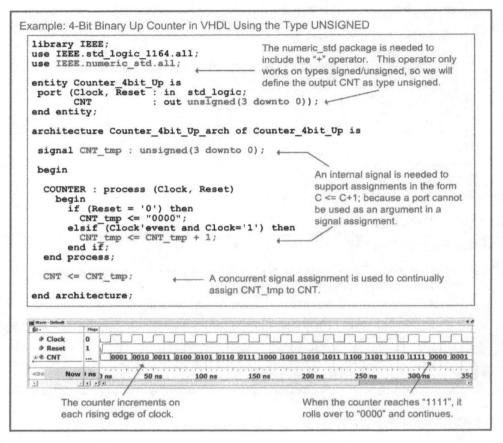

Example: 4-Bit Binary Up Counter in VHDL Using the Type UNSIGNED

```
library IEEE;
use IEEE.std_logic_1164.all;
use IEEE.numeric_std.all;

entity Counter_4bit_Up is
 port (Clock, Reset : in  std_logic;
       CNT          : out unsigned(3 downto 0));
end entity;

architecture Counter_4bit_Up_arch of Counter_4bit_Up is

 signal CNT_tmp : unsigned(3 downto 0);

 begin

   COUNTER : process (Clock, Reset)
     begin
       if (Reset = '0') then
         CNT_tmp <= "0000";
       elsif (Clock'event and Clock='1') then
         CNT_tmp <= CNT_tmp + 1;
       end if;
   end process;

   CNT <= CNT_tmp;

end architecture;
```

The numeric_std package is needed to include the "+" operator. This operator only works on types signed/unsigned, so we will define the output CNT as type unsigned.

An internal signal is needed to support assignments in the form C <= C+1; because a port cannot be used as an argument in a signal assignment.

A concurrent signal assignment is used to continually assign CNT_tmp to CNT.

The counter increments on each rising edge of clock.

When the counter reaches "1111", it rolls over to "0000" and continues.

Example 9.20
4-Bit Binary Up Counter in VHDL Using the Type UNSIGNED

9.4.2 Counters in VHDL Using the Type INTEGER

Another common technique to model counters with a single process is to use the type integer. The numeric_std package supports the "+" operator for type integer. It also contains a conversion between the types integer and unsigned/signed. This means a process can be created to model the counter functionality with integers and then the result can be converted and assigned to the output of the system of type unsigned. One thing that must be considered when using integers is that they are defined as 32-bit, two's complement numbers. This means that if a counter is defined to use integers and the maximum range of the counter is not explicitly controlled, the counter will increment through the entire range of 32-bit values it can take on. There are a variety of ways to explicitly bound the size of an integer counter. The first is to use an if/then clause within the process to check for the upper limit desired in the counter. For example, if we wish to create a 4-bit binary counter, we will check if the integer counter has reached 15 each time through the process. If it has, we will reset it to zero. Synthesizers will recognize that the integer counter is never allowed to exceed 15 (or "1111" for an unsigned counter) and remove the unused bits of the integer type during implementation (i.e., the remaining 28-bits). Example 9.21 shows the VHDL model and simulation waveform for this implementation of the 4-bit counter using integers.

Example: 4-Bit Binary Up Counter in VHDL Using the Type INTEGER

```
library IEEE;
use IEEE.std_logic_1164.all;
use IEEE.numeric_std.all;      ← The numeric_std package contains the "+"
                                 operator for type integer and a conversion
                                 from type integer to type unsigned.
entity Counter_4bit_Up is
 port (Clock, Reset : in  std_logic;
         CNT              : out unsigned(3 downto 0)); ← In this example, the output
end entity;                                              port is defined to be of type
                                                         unsigned.

architecture Counter_4bit_Up_arch of Counter_4bit_Up is

  signal CNT_int : integer;   ← An internal signal of type integer
                                is declared to model the counter
  begin                         functionality.

    COUNTER : process (Clock, Reset)
      begin
        if (Reset = '0') then
          CNT_int <= 0;
        elsif (Clock'event and Clock='1') then

          if (CNT_int = 15) then  ← A nested if/then statement checks
            CNT_int <= 0;           to see if the integer counter has
          else                      reached its maximum value.
            CNT_int <= CNT_int + 1;
          end if;
                                  A concurrent assignment between the
        end if;                   internal counter and the output port is
    end process;                  made that contains the conversion
                                  between type integer and unsigned. The 4
    CNT <= to_unsigned(CNT_int, 4);  ← in this function represents the number of
                                       unsigned bits to convert the integer into.
end architecture;
```

The std_logic_vector is treated as unsigned
and will roll over once it gets to "1111".

Example 9.21
4-Bit Binary Up Counter in VHDL Using the Type INTEGER

9.4.3 Counters in VHDL Using the Type STD_LOGIC_VECTOR

It is often desired to have the ports of a system be defined of type std_logic/std_logic_vector for compatibility with other systems. One technique to accomplish this and also model the counter behavior internally using std_logic_vector is through inclusion of the numeric_std_unsigned package. This package allows the use of std_logic_vector when declaring the ports and signals within the design and treats them as unsigned when performing arithmetic and comparison functions. Example 9.22 shows the VHDL model and simulation waveform for this alternative implementation of the 4-bit counter.

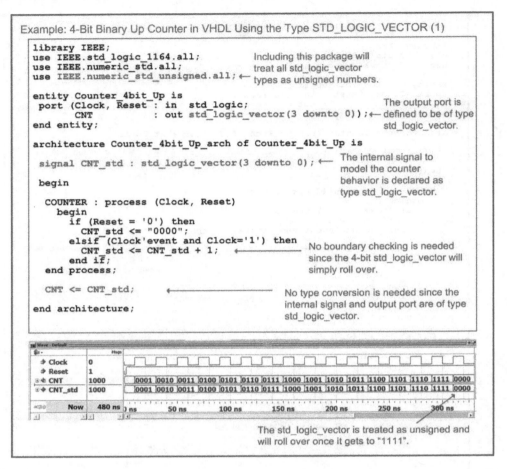

Example 9.22
4-Bit Binary Up Counter in VHDL Using the Type STD_LOGIC_VECTOR (1)

If it is designed to have an output type of std_logic_vector and use an integer in modeling the behavior of the counter, then a double conversion can be used. In the following example, the counter behavior is modeled using an integer type with range checking. A concurrent signal assignment is used at the end of the architecture in order to convert the integer to type std_logic_vector. This is accomplished by first converting the type integer to unsigned and then converting the type unsigned to std_logic_vector. Example 9.23 shows the VHDL model and simulation waveform for this alternative implementation of the 4-bit counter.

Example: 4-Bit Binary Up Counter in VHDL Using the Type STD_LOGIC_VECTOR (2)

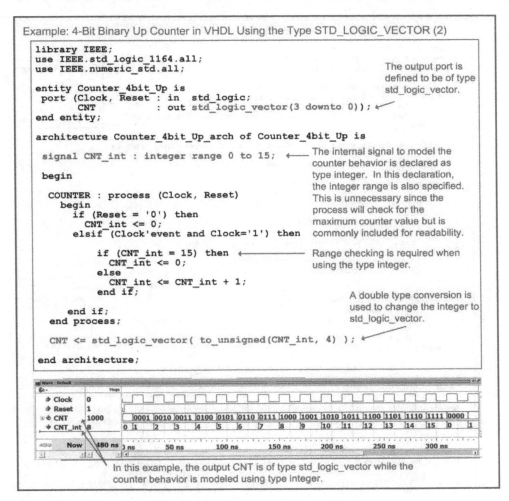

```
library IEEE;
use IEEE.std_logic_1164.all;
use IEEE.numeric_std.all;                    The output port is
                                             defined to be of type
entity Counter_4bit_Up is                    std_logic_vector.
 port (Clock, Reset : in  std_logic;
         CNT            : out std_logic_vector(3 downto 0));  ◄
end entity;

architecture Counter_4bit_Up_arch of Counter_4bit_Up is

  signal CNT_int : integer range 0 to 15;  ◄─── The internal signal to model the
                                             counter behavior is declared as
  begin                                      type integer. In this declaration,
                                             the integer range is also specified.
   COUNTER : process (Clock, Reset)          This is unnecessary since the
     begin                                   process will check for the
        if (Reset = '0') then                maximum counter value but is
          CNT_int <= 0;                      commonly included for readability.
        elsif (Clock'event and Clock='1') then

          if (CNT_int = 15) then  ◄───────── Range checking is required when
            CNT_int <= 0;                    using the type integer.
          else
            CNT_int <= CNT_int + 1;
          end if;                            A double type conversion is
                                             used to change the integer to
      end if;                                std_logic_vector.
    end process;

    CNT <= std_logic_vector( to_unsigned(CNT_int, 4) );  ◄

end architecture;
```

In this example, the output CNT is of type std_logic_vector while the counter behavior is modeled using type integer.

Example 9.23
4-Bit Binary Up Counter in VHDL Using the Type STD_LOGIC_VECTOR (2)

9.4.4 Counters with Enables in VHDL

Including an enable in a counter is a common technique to prevent the counter from running continuously. When the enable is asserted, the counter will increment on the rising edge of the clock as usual. When the enable is de-asserted, the counter will simply hold its last value. Enable lines are synchronous, meaning that they are only evaluated on the rising edge of the clock. As such, they are modeled using a nested if/then statement within the if/then statement checking for a rising edge of the clock. Example 9.24 shows an example model for a 4-bit counter with enable.

Example: 4-Bit Binary Up Counter with Enable in VHDL

```
library IEEE;
use IEEE.std_logic_1164.all;
use IEEE.numeric_std.all;

entity Counter_4bit_wEN is
 port (Clock, Reset : in  std_logic;
       EN           : in  std_logic;
       CNT          : out std_logic_vector(3 downto 0));
end entity;

architecture Counter_4bit_wEN_arch of Counter_4bit_wEN is

 signal CNT_int : integer range 0 to 15;

begin

  COUNTER : process (Clock, Reset)
    begin
      if (Reset = '0') then
        CNT_int <= 0;
      elsif (Clock'event and Clock='1') then

        if (EN='1') then
          if (CNT_int = 15) then
            CNT_int <= 0;
          else
            CNT_int <= CNT_int + 1;
          end if;
        end if;

      end if;
  end process;

  CNT <= std_logic_vector( to_unsigned(CNT_int, 4) );

end architecture;
```

A nested if/then statement is used in order to check if the counter is enabled on each edge of the clock. If EN='1', the counter will increment as usual. If EN='0', the counter will simply hold its last value.

When the counter is NOT enabled, it will hold its last value.

Example 9.24
4-Bit Binary Up Counter with Enable in VHDL

9.4.5 Counters with Loads

A counter with a *load* has the ability to set the counter to a specified value. The specified value is provided on an input port (i.e., CNT_in) with the same width as the counter output (CNT). A synchronous load input signal (i.e., Load) is used to indicate when the counter should set its value to the value present on CNT_in. Example 9.25 shows an example model for a 4-bit counter with load capability.

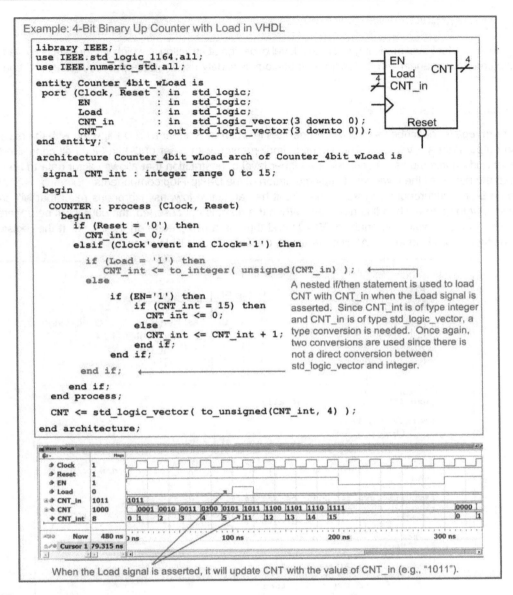

Example: 4-Bit Binary Up Counter with Load in VHDL

```vhdl
library IEEE;
use IEEE.std_logic_1164.all;
use IEEE.numeric_std.all;

entity Counter_4bit_wLoad is
 port (Clock, Reset : in  std_logic;
       EN           : in  std_logic;
       Load         : in  std_logic;
       CNT_in       : in  std_logic_vector(3 downto 0);
       CNT          : out std_logic_vector(3 downto 0));
end entity;

architecture Counter_4bit_wLoad_arch of Counter_4bit_wLoad is

 signal CNT_int : integer range 0 to 15;

 begin

  COUNTER : process (Clock, Reset)
    begin
      if (Reset = '0') then
        CNT_int <= 0;
      elsif (Clock'event and Clock='1') then

        if (Load = '1') then
          CNT_int <= to_integer( unsigned(CNT_in) );
        else

          if (EN='1') then
            if (CNT_int = 15) then
              CNT_int <= 0;
            else
              CNT_int <= CNT_int + 1;
            end if;
          end if;

        end if;

      end if;
    end process;

    CNT <= std_logic_vector( to_unsigned(CNT_int, 4) );

end architecture;
```

A nested if/then statement is used to load CNT with CNT_in when the Load signal is asserted. Since CNT_int is of type integer and CNT_in is of type std_logic_vector, a type conversion is needed. Once again, two conversions are used since there is not a direct conversion between std_logic_vector and integer.

When the Load signal is asserted, it will update CNT with the value of CNT_in (e.g., "1011").

Example 9.25
4-Bit Binary Up Counter with Load in VHDL

CONCEPT CHECK

CC9.4   If a counter is modeled using only one process in VHDL, is it still a finite state machine? Why or why not?

A) Yes. It is just a special case of a FSM that can easily be modeled using one process. Synthesizers will recognize the single process model as a FSM.

B) No. Using only one process will synthesize into combinational logic. Without the ability to store a state, it is not a finite state machines.

9.5 RTL Modeling

Register Transfer Level modeling refers to a level of design abstraction in which vector data is moved and operated on in a synchronous manner. This design methodology is widely used in data path modeling and computer system design.

9.5.1 Modeling Registers in VHDL

The term *register* describes a circuit that operates in a similar manner as a D-Flip-Flop with the exception that the input and output data are vectors. This circuit is implemented with a set of D-Flip-Flops all connected to the same clock, reset and enable inputs. A register is a higher level of abstraction that allows vector data to be stored without getting into the details of the lower level implementation of the D-Flip-Flop components. Example 9.26 shows an RTL model of an 8-bit, synchronous register. This circuit has an active low, asynchronous reset that will cause the 8-bit output *Reg_Out* to go to 0 when it is asserted. When the reset is not asserted, the output will be updated with the 8-bit input *Reg_In* if the system is enabled (EN=1) and there is a rising edge on the clock. If the register is disabled (EN=0), the input clock is ignored. At all other times, the output holds its last value.

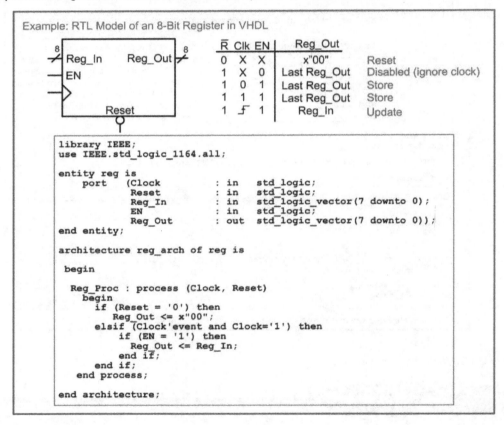

Example 9.26
RTL Model of an 8-Bit Register in VHDL

9.5.2 Shift Registers in VHDL

A shift register is a circuit which consists of multiple registers connected in series. Data is shifted from one register to another on the rising edge of the clock. This type of circuit is often used in serial-to-parallel data converters. Example 9.27 shows an RTL model for a 4-stage, 8-bit shift register. In the simulation waveform, the data is shown in hexadecimal format.

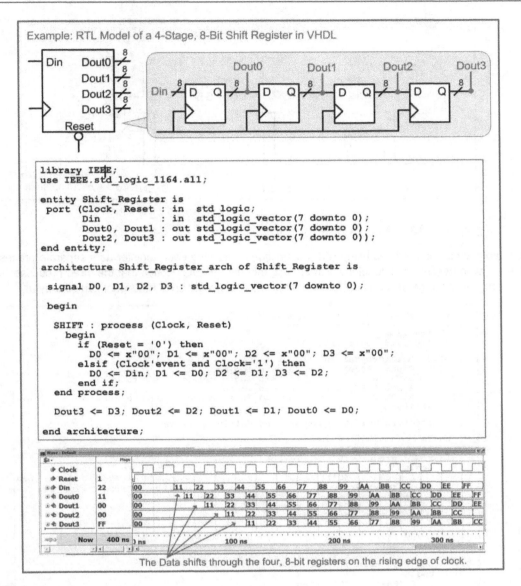

Example 9.27
RTL Model of a 4-Stage, 8-Bit Shift Register in VHDL

9.5.3 Registers as Agents on a Data Bus

One of the powerful topologies that registers can easily model is a multi-drop bus. In this topology, multiple registers are connected to a data bus as receivers or agents. Each agent has an enable line that controls when it latches information from the data bus into its storage elements. This topology is synchronous, meaning that each agent and the driver of the data bus is connected to the same clock signal. Each agent has a dedicated, synchronous enable line that is provided by a system controller elsewhere in the design. Example 9.28 shows this multi-drop bus topology. In this example system, three registers (A, B, and C) are connected to a data bus as receivers. Each register is connected to the same clock and reset signals. Each register has its own dedicated enable line (A_EN, B_EN, and C_EN).

Example 9.28
Registers as Agents on a Data Bus - System Topology

This topology can be modeled using RTL abstraction by treating each register as a separate process. Example 9.29 shows how to describe this topology with an RTL model in VHDL. Notice that the three processes modeling the A, B, and C registers are nearly identical to each other with the exception of the signal names they use.

```
Example: Registers as Agents on a Data Bus – RTL Model in VHDL

library IEEE;
use IEEE.std_logic_1164.all;

entity MultiDropBus is
  port (Clock, Reset      : in  std_logic;
        Data_Bus          : in  std_logic_vector(7 downto 0);
        A_EN, B_EN, C_EN  : in  std_logic;
        A, B, C           : out std_logic_vector(7 downto 0));
end entity;

architecture MultiDropBus_arch of MultiDropBus is

  begin
  --------------------------------------------------         Each register is modeled as a separate
    A_REG : process (Clock, Reset)          <-------         process. The register has a
      begin                                                  synchronous enable that controls when
        if (Reset = '0') then                                it acquires data off of the data bus.
          A <= x"00";
        elsif (Clock'event and Clock='1') then
            if (A_EN = '1') then
              A <= Data_Bus;
            end if;
        end if;
    end process;
  --------------------------------------------------
    B_REG : process (Clock, Reset)
      begin
        if (Reset = '0') then
          B <= x"00";
        elsif (Clock'event and Clock='1') then
            if (B_EN = '1') then
              B <= Data_Bus;                                 All registers are attached
            end if;                                          to the data bus as
        end if;                                              receivers.
    end process;
  --------------------------------------------------
    C_REG : process (Clock, Reset)
      begin
        if (Reset = '0') then
          C <= x"00";
        elsif (Clock'event and Clock='1') then
            if (C_EN = '1') then
              C <= Data_Bus;
            end if;
        end if;
    end process;

end architecture;
```

Example 9.29
Registers as Agents on a Data Bus - RTL Model in VHDL

Example 9.30 shows the resulting simulation waveform for this system. Each register is updated with the value on the data bus whenever its dedicated enable line is asserted.

Example: Registers as Agents on a Data Bus – Simulation Waveform

When a register's synchronous enable is asserted, it will latch the value of data_bus on the next rising edge of clock.

Example 9.30
Registers as Agents on a Data Bus - Simulation Waveform

CONCEPT CHECK

CC9.5 Does RTL modeling synthesize as combinational logic, sequential logic, or both? Why?

A) Combinational logic. Since only one process is used for each register, it will be synthesized using basic gates.

B) Sequential logic. Since the sensitivity list contains clock and reset, it will synthesize into only D-flip-flops.

C) Both. The model has a sensitivity list containing clock and reset and uses an if/then statement indicative of a D-flip-flop. This will synthesize a D-flip-flop to hold the value for each bit in the register. In addition, the ability to manipulate the inputs into the register (using either logical operators, arithmetic operators, or choosing different signals to latch) will synthesize into combinational logic in front of the D input to each D-flip-flop.

Summary

❖ A synchronous system is modeled with a process and a sensitivity list. The clock and reset signals are always listed by themselves in the sensitivity list. Within the process is an if/then statement. The first clause of the if/then statement handles the asynchronous reset condition while the second *elsif* clause handles the synchronous signal assignments.

❖ Edge sensitivity is modeled within a process using either the (*clock'event and clock="1"*) syntax or an edge detection function provided by the STD_LOGIC_1164 package (i.e., *rising_edge()*).

❖ Most D-flip-flops and registers contain a synchronous *enable* line. This is modeled using a nested if/then statement within the main process if/then statement. The nested if/then goes beneath the clause for the synchronous signal assignments.

❖ Generic finite state machines are modeled using three separate processes that describe the behavior of the next state logic, the state memory, and the output logic. Separate processes are used because each of the three functions in a FSM are dependent on different input signals.

❖ In VHDL, descriptive state names can be created for a FSM with a user-defined, enumerated data type. The new type is first declared and each of the descriptive state names are provided that the new data type can take on. Two signals are then created called *current_state* and *next_state* using the new data type. These two signals can then be assigned the descriptive state names of the FSM directly. This approach allows the synthesizer to assign the state codes arbitrarily. A sub-type can be used if it is desired to explicitly define the state codes.

❖ Counters are a special type of finite state machine that can be modeled using a single process. Only the clock and reset signals are listed in the sensitivity list of the counter process.

❖ Registers are modeled in VHDL in a similar manner to a D-flip-flop with a synchronous enable. The only difference is that the inputs and outputs are n-bit vectors.

Exercise Problems

Section 9.1 – Modeling Sequential Storage Devices in VHDL

9.1.1   How does a VHDL model for a D-flip-flop handle treating reset as the highest priority input?

9.1.2   For a VHDL model of a D-flip-flop with a synchronous enable (EN), why isn't EN listed in the sensitivity list?

9.1.3   For a VHDL model of a D-flip-flop with a synchronous enable (EN), what is the impact of listing EN in the sensitivity list?

9.1.4   For a VHDL model of a D-flip-flop with a synchronous enable (EN), why is the behavior of the enable modeled using a nested if/then statement under the clock edge clause rather than an additional elsif clause in the primary if/then statement?

Section 9.2 – Modeling Finite State Machines in VHDL

9.2.1   What is the advantage of using *user-defined, enumerated data types* for the states when modeling a finite state machine?

9.2.2   What is the advantage of using *subtypes* for the states when modeling a finite state machine?

9.2.3   When using the three process behavioral modeling approach for finite state machines, does the next state logic process model combinational or sequential logic?

9.2.4   When using the three process behavioral modeling approach for finite state machines, does the state memory process model combinational or sequential logic?

9.2.5   When using the three process behavioral modeling approach for finite state machines, does the output logic process model combinational or sequential logic?

9.2.6   When using the three process behavioral modeling approach for finite state machines, what inputs are listed in the sensitivity list of the next state logic process?

9.2.7   When using the three process behavioral modeling approach for finite state machines, what inputs are listed in the sensitivity list of the state memory process?

9.2.8   When using the three process behavioral modeling approach for finite state machines, what inputs are listed in the sensitivity list of the output logic process?

9.2.9   When using the three process behavioral modeling approach for finite state machines, how can the signals listed in the sensitivity list of the output logic process immediately tell whether the FSM is a Meally or a Moore machine?

9.2.10   Why is it not a good design approach to combine the next state logic and output logic behavior into a single process?

Section 9.3 – FSM Design Examples in VHDL

9.3.1   Design a VHDL behavioral model to implement the finite state machine described by the state diagram in Figure 9.1. Use the entity definition provided in this figure for your design. Use the three-process approach to modeling FSMs described in this chapter for your design. Model the states in this machine with a user-defined enumerated type.

fsm1_behavioral.vhd

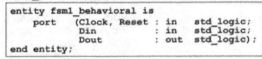

Figure 9.1

9.3.2   Design a VHDL behavioral model to implement the finite state machine described by the state diagram in Figure 9.1. Use the entity definition provided in this figure for your design. Use the three-process approach to modeling FSMs described in this chapter for your design. Explicitly assign binary state codes using VHDL subtypes. Use the following state codes: Start="00", Midway="01", Done="10".

9.3.3   Design a VHDL behavioral model to implement the finite state machine described by the state diagram in Figure 9.2. Use the entity definition provided in this figure for your design. Use the three-process approach to modeling FSMs described in this chapter for your design. Model the states in this machine with a user-defined enumerated type.

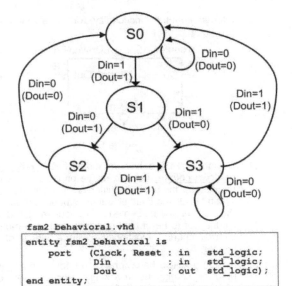

fsm2_behavioral.vhd

```
entity fsm2_behavioral is
    port    (Clock, Reset : in    std_logic;
             Din          : in    std_logic;
             Dout         : out   std_logic);
end entity;
```

Figure 9.2

9.3.4 Design a VHDL behavioral model to implement the finite state machine described by the state diagram in Figure 9.2. Use the entity definition provided in this figure for your design. Use the three-process approach to modeling FSMs described in this chapter for your design. Assign one-hot state codes using VHDL subtypes. Use the following state codes: S0="0001", S1="0010", S2="0100", S3="1000".

9.3.5 Design a VHDL behavioral model for a 4-bit serial bit sequence detector similar to Example 9.11. Use the entity definition provided in Figure 9.3. Use the three-process approach to modeling FSMs described in this chapter for your design. The input to your sequence detector is called *DIN* and the output is called *FOUND*. Your detector will assert FOUND anytime there is a 4-bit sequence of "0101". For all other input sequences the output is not asserted. Model the states in your machine with a user-defined enumerated type.

Seq_Det_behavioral.vhd

```
entity Seq_Det_behavioral is
    port (Clock, Reset : in    std_logic;
          DIN          : in    std_logic;
          FOUND        : out   std_logic);
end entity;
```

Figure 9.3

9.3.6 Design a VHDL behavioral model for a 25 cent vending machine controller similar to Example 9.14. Use the entity definition provided in Figure 9.4. Use the three-process approach to modeling FSMs described in this chapter for your design. Your controller will take in nickels and dimes and dispense a product anytime the customer has entered 25 cents. Your FSM has two inputs, *Nin* and *Din*. Nin is asserted whenever the customer enters a nickel while Din is asserted anytime the customer enters a dime. Your FSM has two outputs, *Dispense* and *Change*. Dispense is asserted anytime the customer has entered at least 25 cents and Change is asserted anytime the customer has entered more than 25 cents and needs a nickel in change.

Model the states in this machine with a user-defined enumerated type.

Vending_behavioral.vhd

```
entity Vending_behavioral is
    port (Clock, Reset     : in    std_logic;
          Nin, Din         : in    std_logic;
          Dispense, Change : out std_logic);
end entity;
```

Figure 9.4

9.3.7 Design a VHDL behavioral model for a finite state machine for a traffic light controller. Use the entity definition provided in Figure 9.5. This is the same problem description as in exercise 7.16. This time, you will implement the functionality using the behavioral modeling techniques presented in this chapter. Your FSM will control a traffic light at the intersection of a busy highway and a seldom used side road. You will be designing the control signals for just the red, yellow, and green lights facing the highway. Under normal conditions, the highway has a green light. The side road has car detector that indicates when car pulls up by asserting a signal called *CAR*. When CAR is asserted, you will change the highway traffic light from green to yellow, and then from yellow to red. Once in the red position, a built in timer will begin a countdown and provide your controller a signal called *TIMEOUT* when 15 seconds has passed. Once TIMEOUT is asserted, you will change the highway traffic light back to green. Your system will have three outputs *GRN*, *YLW*, and *RED*, which control when the highway facing traffic lights are on (1=ON, 0=OFF). Model the states in this machine with a user-defined enumerated type.

tlc_behavioral.vhd

```
entity tlc_behavioral is
    port (Clock, Reset   : in    std_logic;
          CAR, TIMEOUT   : in    std_logic;
          GRN, YLW, RED  : out std_logic);
end entity;
```

Figure 9.5

Section 9.4 – Modeling Counters in VHDL

9.4.1 Design a VHDL behavioral model for a 16-bit, binary up counter using a single process. The block diagram for the entity definition is shown in Figure 9.6. In your model, declare Count_Out to be of type unsigned and implement the internal counter functionality with a signal of type unsigned.

Counter_16bit_Up.vhd

Figure 9.6

9.4.2 Design a VHDL behavioral model for a 16-bit, binary up counter using a single process. The block diagram for the entity definition is shown in Figure 9.6. In your model, declare Count_Out to be of type unsigned and implement the internal counter functionality with a signal of type integer.

9.4.3 Design a VHDL behavioral model for a 16-bit, binary up counter using a single process. The block diagram for the entity definition is shown in Figure 9.6. In your model, declare Count_Out to be of type std logic vector and implement the internal counter functionality with a signal of type integer.

9.4.4 Design a VHDL behavioral model for a 16-bit, binary up counter with enable using a single process. The block diagram for the entity definition is shown in Figure 9.7. In your model, declare Count_Out to be of type unsigned and implement the internal counter functionality with a signal of type unsigned.

Counter_16bit_wEN.vhd

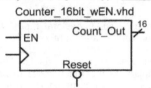

Figure 9.7

9.4.5 Design a VHDL behavioral model for a 16-bit, binary up counter with enable using a single process. The block diagram for the entity definition is shown in Figure 9.7. In your model, declare Count_Out to be of type unsigned and implement the internal counter functionality with a signal of type integer.

9.4.6 Design a VHDL behavioral model for a 16-bit, binary up counter with enable using a single process. The block diagram for the entity definition is shown in Figure 9.7. In your model, declare Count_Out to be of type std logic vector and implement the internal counter functionality with a signal of type integer.

9.4.7 Design a VHDL behavioral model for a 16-bit, binary up counter with enable and load using a single process. The block diagram for the entity definition is shown in Figure 9.8. In your model, declare Count_Out to be of type unsigned and implement the internal counter functionality with a signal of type unsigned.

Counter_16bit_wLoad.vhd

Figure 9.8

9.4.8 Design a VHDL behavioral model for a 16-bit, binary up counter with enable and load using a single process. The block diagram for the entity definition is shown in Figure 9.8. In your model, declare Count_Out to be of type unsigned and implement the internal counter functionality with a signal of type integer.

9.4.9 Design a VHDL behavioral model for a 16-bit, binary up counter with enable and load using a single process. The block diagram for the entity definition is shown in Figure 9.8. In your model, declare Count_Out to be of type std logic vector and implement the internal counter functionality with a signal of type integer.

9.4.10 Design a VHDL behavioral model for a 16-bit, binary up/down counter using a single process. The block diagram for the entity definition is shown in Figure 9.9. When Up=1, the counter will increment. When Up=0, the counter will decrement. In your model, declare Count_Out to be of type unsigned and implement the

internal counter functionality with a signal of type unsigned.

Counter_16bit_UpDown.vhd

Figure 9.9

9.4.11 Design a VHDL behavioral model for a 16-bit, binary up/down counter using a single process. The block diagram for the entity definition is shown in Figure 9.9. When Up=1, the counter will increment. When Up=0, the counter will decrement. In your model, declare Count_Out to be of type unsigned and implement the internal counter functionality with a signal of type integer.

9.4.12 Design a VHDL behavioral model for a 16-bit, binary up/down counter using a single process. The block diagram for the entity definition is shown in Figure 9.9. When Up=1, the counter will increment. When Up=0, the counter will decrement. In your model, declare Count_Out to be of type std logic vector and implement the internal counter functionality with a signal of type integer.

Section 9.5 – RTL Modeling

9.5.1 In *register transfer level* modeling, how does the width of the register relate to the number of D-flip-flops that will be synthesized?

9.5.2 In *register transfer level* modeling, how is the synchronous data movement managed if all registers are using the same clock?

9.5.3 Design a VHDL RTL model of a 32-bit, synchronous register. The block diagram for the entity definition is shown in Figure 9.10. The register has a synchronous enable. The register should be modeled using a single process.

RegisterX_32bit_RTL.vhd

Figure 9.10

9.5.4 Design a VHDL RTL model of an 8-stage, 16-bit shift register. The block diagram for the entity definition is shown in Figure 9.11. Each stage of the shift register will be provided as an output of the system (A, B, C, D, E, F, G, and H). Use std_logic or std_logic_vector for all ports.

Shift_Register_16bit_x8.vhd

Figure 9.11

9.5.5 Design a VHDL RTL model of the multi-drop bus topology in Figure 9.12. Each of the 16 bit registers (RegA, RegB, RegC, and RegD) will latch the contents of the 16-bit data bus if their enable line is asserted. Each register should be modeled using an individual process.

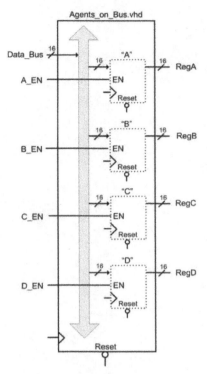

Figure 9.12

Chapter 10: Memory

This chapter introduces the basic concepts, terminology, and roles of memory in digital systems. The material presented here will not delve into the details of the device physics or low-level theory of operation. Instead, the intent of this chapter is to give a general overview of memory technology and its use in computer systems in addition to how to model memory in VHDL.

> Learning Outcomes – After completing this chapter, you will be able to:
>
> 10.1   Describe the functional operation of the most common types of semiconductor memory.
> 10.2   Solve for the final voltage in a DRAM storage cell based on the principles of charge sharing.
> 10.3   Design a VHDL model for an asynchronous read only memory (ROM) system.
> 10.4   Design a VHDL model for a synchronous read only memory (ROM) system.
> 10.5   Design a VHDL model for an asynchronous read/write (R/W) system.
> 10.6   Design a VHDL model for a synchronous read/write (R/W) system.

10.1 Memory Architecture & Terminology

The term *memory* is used to describe a system with the ability to store digital information. The term *semiconductor memory* refers to systems that are implemented using integrated circuit technology. These types of systems store the digital information using transistors, fuses, and/or capacitors on a single semiconductor substrate. Memory can also be implemented using technology other than semiconductors. Disk drives store information by altering the polarity of magnetic fields on a circular substrate. The two magnetic polarities (north and south) are used to represent different logic values (i.e., 0 or 1). Optical disks use lasers to burn pits into reflective substrates. The binary information is represented by light either being reflected (no pit) or not reflected (pit present). Semiconductor memory does not have any moving parts, so it is called *solid state memory* and can hold more information per unit area than disk memory. Regardless of the technology used to store the binary data, all memory has common attributes and terminology that are discussed in this chapter.

10.1.1 Memory Map Model

The information stored in memory is called the **data**. When information is placed into memory, it is called a **write**. When information is retrieved from memory, it is called a **read**. In order to access data in memory, an **address** is used. While data can be accessed as individual bits, in order to reduce the number of address locations needed, data is typically grouped into *N-bit words*. If a memory system has N=8, this means that 8-bits of data are stored at each address. The number of address locations is described using the variable *M*. The overall size of the memory is typically stated by saying "MxN". For example, if we had a 16x8 memory system, that means that there are 16 address locations, each capable of storing a byte of data. This memory would have a **capacity** of 16x8=128 bits. Since the address is implemented as a binary code, the number of lines in the address bus (n) will dictate the number of address locations that the memory system will have ($M=2^n$). Figure 10.1 shows a graphical depiction of how data resides in memory. This type of graphic is called a *memory map model*.

Figure 10.1
Memory Map Model

10.1.2 Volatile vs. Non-Volatile Memory

Memory is classified into two categories depending on whether it can store information when power is removed or not. The term **non-volatile** is used to describe memory that *holds* information when the power is removed, while the

321

term **volatile** is used to describe memory that loses its information when power is removed. Historically, volatile memory is able to run at faster speeds compared to non-volatile memory, so it is used as the primary storage mechanism while a digital system is running. Non-volatile memory is necessary in order to hold critical operation information for a digital system such as start-up instructions, operations systems, and applications.

10.1.3 Read Only vs. Read/Write Memory

Memory can also be classified into two categories with respect to how data is accessed. **Read Only Memory (ROM)** is a device that cannot be written to during normal operation. This type of memory is useful for holding critical system information or programs that should not be altered while the system is running. **Read/Write** memory refers to memory that can be read and written to during normal operation and is used to hold temporary data and variables.

10.1.4 Random Access vs. Sequential Access

Random Access Memory (RAM) describes memory in which any location in the system can be accessed at any time. The opposite of this is **sequential access** memory, in which not all address locations are immediately available. An example of a sequential access memory system is a tape drive. In order to access the desired address in this system, the tape spool must be spun until the address is in a position that can be observed. Most semiconductor memory in modern systems is random access. The terms RAM and ROM have been adopted, somewhat inaccurately, to also describe groups of memory with particular behavior. While the term ROM technically describes a system that cannot be written to, it has taken on the additional association of being the term to describe non-volatile memory. While the term RAM technically describes how data is accessed, it has taken on the additional association of being the term to describe volatile memory. When describing modern memory systems, the terms RAM and ROM are used most commonly to describe the characteristics of the memory being used; however, modern memory systems can be both read/write and non-volatile, and the majority of memory is random access.

CONCEPT CHECK

CC10.1   An 8-bit wide memory has 8 address lines. What is its capacity in bits?

A) 64   B) 256   C) 1024   D) 2048

10.2 Non-Volatile Memory Technology

10.2.1 ROM Architecture

This section describes some of the most common non-volatile memory technologies used to store digital information. An address decoder is used to access individual data words within the memory system. The address decoder asserts one and only one *word line* (WL) for each unique binary address that is present on its input. This operation is identical to a binary-to-one-hot decoder. For an n-bit address, the decoder can access 2^n, or M words in memory. The word lines historically run horizontally across the memory array, thus they are often called *row lines* and the word line decoder is often called the *row decoder*. *Bit lines* (BL) run perpendicular to the word lines in order to provide individual bit storage access at the intersection of the bit and word lines. These lines typically run vertically through the memory array, thus they are often called *column lines*. The output of the memory system (i.e., Data_Out) is obtained by providing an address and then reading the word from buffered versions of the bit lines. When a system provides individual bit access to a row, or access to multiple data words sharing a row line, a column decoder is used to route the appropriate bit line(s) to the data out port.

In a traditional ROM array, each bit line contains a pull-up network to V_{CC}. This provides the ability to store a logic 1 at all locations within the array. If a logic 0 is desired at a particular location, an NMOS pull-down transistor is inserted. The gate of the NMOS is connected to the appropriate word line and the drain of the NMOS is connected to the bit line. When reading, the word line is asserted and turns on the NMOS transistor. This pulls the bit line to GND and produces a logic 0 on the output. When the NMOS transistor is excluded, the bit line remains at a logic 1 due to the pull-up network. Figure 10.2 shows the basic architecture of a ROM.

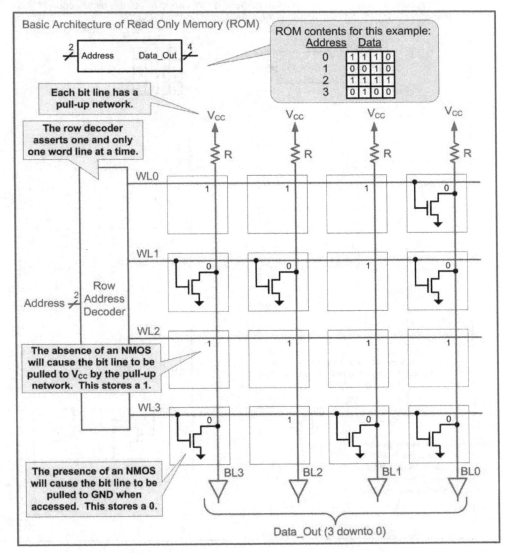

Figure 10.2
Basic Architecture of Read Only Memory (ROM)

Figure 10.3 shows the operation of a ROM when information is being read.

Figure 10.3
ROM Operation During a Read

Memory can be designed to be either asynchronous or synchronous. **Asynchronous memory** updates its data outputs immediately upon receiving an address. **Synchronous memory** only updates its data outputs on the rising edge of a clock. The term *latency* is used to describe the delay between when a signal is sent to the memory (either the address in an asynchronous system or the clock in a synchronous system) and when the data is available. Figure 10.4 shows a comparison of the timing diagrams between asynchronous and synchronous ROM systems during a read cycle.

Figure 10.4
Asynchronous vs. Synchronous ROM Operation During a Read Cycle

10.2.2 Mask Read Only Memory (MROM)

A Mask Read Only Memory (MROM) is a non-volatile device that is programmed during fabrication. The term *mask* refers to a transparent plate that contains patterns to create the features of the devices on an integrated circuit using a process called photolithography. An MROM is fabricated with all of the features necessary for the memory device with the exception of the final connections between the NMOS transistors and the word and bit lines. This allows the majority of the device to be created prior to knowing what the final information to be stored is. Once the desired information to be stored is provided by the customer, the fabrication process is completed by adding connections between certain NMOS transistors and the word/bit lines in order to create logic 0's. Figure 10.5 shows an overview of the MROM programming process.

Figure 10.5
MROM Overview

10.2.3 Programmable Read Only Memory (PROM)

A Programmable Read Only Memory (PROM) is created in a similar manner as an MROM except that the programming is accomplished post-fabrication through the use of fuses or anti-fuses. A **fuse** is an electrical connection that is normally conductive. When a certain amount of current is passed through the fuse it will melt, or *blow*, and create an open circuit. The amount of current necessary to open the fuse is much larger than the current the fuse would conduct during normal operation. An **anti-fuse** operates in the opposite manner as a fuse. An anti-fuse is normally an open circuit. When a certain amount of current is forced into the anti-fuse, the insulating material breaks down and creates a conduction path. This turns the anti-fuse from an open circuit into a wire. Again, the amount of current necessary to close the anti-fuse is much larger than the current the anti-fuse would experience during normal operation. A PROM uses fuses or anti-fuses in order to connect/disconnect the NMOS transistors in the ROM array to the word/bit lines. A PROM programmer is used to *burn* the fuses or anti-fuses. A PROM can only be programmed once in this manner, thus it is a read only memory and non-volatile. A PROM has the advantage that programming can take place quickly as opposed to an MROM that must programmed through device fabrication. Figure 10.6 shows an example PROM device based on fuses.

Figure 10.6
PROM Overview

10.2.4 Erasable Programmable Read Only Memory (EPROM)

As an improvement to the one-time programming characteristic of PROMs, an electrically programmable ROM (EPROM) was created. An EPROM is based on a **floating-gate transistor**. In a floating-gate transistor, an additional metal-oxide structure is added to the gate of an NMOS. This has the effect of increasing the threshold voltage. The geometry of the second metal-oxide is designed such that the threshold voltage is high enough that normal CMOS logic levels are not able to turn the transistor on (i.e., $V_{T1} \geq V_{CC}$). This threshold can be changed by applying a large electric field across the two metal structures in the gate. This causes charge to tunnel into the secondary oxide, ultimately changing it into a conductor. This phenomenon is called Fowler–Nordheim tunneling. The new threshold voltage is low enough that normal CMOS logic levels are not able to turn the transistors off (i.e., $V_{T2} \leq GND$). This process is how the device is *programmed*. This process is accomplished using a dedicated programmer, thus the EPROM must be removed from its system to program. Figure 10.7 shows an overview of a floating-gate transistor and how it is programmed.

Figure 10.7
Floating-Gate Transistor - Programming

In order to change the floating-gate transistor back into its normal state, the device is exposed to a strong ultra-violet (UV) light source. When the UV light strikes the trapped charge in the secondary oxide, it transfers enough energy to the charge particles that they can move back into the metal plates in the gate. This, in effect, *erases* the device and restores it back to a state with a high threshold voltage. EPROMs contain a transparent window on the top of their package that allows the UV light to strike the devices. The EPROM must be removed from its system to perform the erase procedure. When the UV light erase procedure is performed, every device in the memory array is erased. EPROMs are a significant improvement over PROMs because they can be programmed multiple times; however, the programming and erase procedures are manually intensive and require an external programmer and external eraser. Figure 10.8 shows the erase procedure for a floating-gate transistor using UV light.

Figure 10.8
Floating-Gate Transistor - Erasing with UV Light

An EPROM array is created in the exact same manner as in a PROM array with the exception that additional programming circuitry is placed on the IC and a transparent window is included on the package to facilitate erasing. An EPROM is non-volatile and read only since the programming procedure takes place outside of its destination system.

10.2.5 Electrically Erasable Programmable Read Only Memory (EEPROM)

In order to address the inconvenient programming and erasing procedures associated with EPROMs, the electrically erasable programmable ROM (EEPROM) was created. In this type of circuit, the floating-gate transistor is erased by applying a large electric field across the secondary oxide. This electric field provides the energy to move the trapped charge from the secondary oxide back into the metal plates of the gate. The advantage of this approach is that the circuitry to provide the large electric field can be generated using circuitry on the same substrate as the memory array, thus eliminating the need for an external UV light eraser. In addition, since the circuitry exists to generate large on-chip voltages, the device can also be programmed without the need for an external programmer. This allows an EEPROM to be programmed and erased while it resides in its target environment. Figure 10.9 shows the procedure for erasing a floating-gate transistor using an electric field.

Figure 10.9
Floating-Gate Transistor - Erasing with Electricity

Early EEPROMs were very slow and had a limited number of program/erase cycles, thus they were classified into the category of non-volatile, read only memory. Modern floating-gate transistors are now capable of access times on scale with other volatile memory systems, thus they have evolved into one of the few non-volatile, read/write memory technologies used in computer systems today.

10.2.6 FLASH Memory

One of the early drawbacks of EEPROM was that the circuitry that provided the capability to program and erase individual bits also added to the size of each individual storage element. FLASH EEPROM was a technology that attempted to improve the density of floating-gate memory by programming and erasing in large groups of data, known as *blocks*. This allowed the individual storage cells to shrink and provided higher density memory parts. This new architecture was called *NAND FLASH* and provided faster write and erase times coupled with higher density storage elements. The limitation of NAND FLASH was that reading and writing could only be accomplished in a block-by-block basis. This characteristic precluded the use of NAND FLASH for run-time variables and data storage, but was well suited for streaming applications such as audio/video and program loading. As NAND FLASH technology advanced, the block size began to shrink and software adapted to accommodate the block-by-block data access. This expanded the applications that NAND FLASH could be deployed in. Today, NAND FLASH memory is used in nearly all portable devices (e.g., smart phones, tablets, etc.) and its use in solid state hard drives is on pace to replace hard disk drives and optical disks as the primary non-volatile storage medium in modern computers.

In order to provide individual word access, NOR FLASH was introduced. In NOR FLASH, circuitry is added to provide individual access to data words. This architecture provided faster read times than NAND FLASH, but the additional circuitry causes the write and erase times to be slower and the individual storage cell size to be larger. Due to NAND FLASH having faster write times and higher density, it is seeing broader scale adoption compared to NOR FLASH despite only being able to access information in blocks. NOR FLASH is considered random access memory while NAND FLASH is typically not; however, as the block size of NAND FLASH is continually reduced, its use for variable storage is becoming more attractive. All FLASH memory is non-volatile and read/write.

CONCEPT CHECK

CC10.2   Which of the following is suitable for implementation in a read only memory?

A)   Variables that a computer program needs to continuously update.

B)   Information captured by a digital camera.

C)   A computer program on a spacecraft.

D)   Incoming digitized sound from a microphone.

10.3 Volatile Memory Technology

This section describes some common volatile memory technologies used to store digital information.

10.3.1 Static Random Access Memory (SRAM)

Static Random Access Memory (SRAM) is a semiconductor technology that stores information using a cross-coupled inverter feedback loop. Figure 10.10 shows the schematic for the basic SRAM storage cell. In this configuration, two access transistors (M1 and M2) are used to read and write from the storage cell. The cell has two complementary ports called Bit Line (BL) and Bit Line' (BLn). Due to the inverting functionality of the feedback loop, these two ports will always be the complement of each other. This behavior is advantageous because the two lines can be compared to each other to determine the data value. This allows the voltage levels used in the cell to be lowered while still being able to detect the stored data value. Word Lines are used to control the access transistors. This storage element takes six CMOS transistors to implement and is often called a 6T configuration. The advantage of this memory cell is that it has very fast performance compared to other subsystems because of its underlying technology being simple CMOS transistors. SRAM cells are commonly implemented on the same IC substrate as the rest of the system, thus allowing a fully integrated system to be realized. SRAM cells are used for cache memory in computer systems.

Figure 10.10
SRAM Storage Element (6T)

To build an SRAM memory system, cells are arranged in an array pattern. Figure 10.11 shows a 4x4 SRAM array topology. In this configuration, word lines are shared horizontally across the array in order to provide addressing capability. An address decoder is used to convert the binary encoded address into the appropriate word line assertions. N storage cells are attached to the word line to provide the desired data word width. Bit lines are shared vertically across the array in order to provide data access (either read or write). A data line controller handles whether data is read from or written to the cells based on an external write enable (WE) signal. When WE is asserted (WE=1), data will be written to the cells. When WE is de-asserted (WE=0), data will be read from the cells. The data line controller also handles determining the correct logic value read from the cells by comparing BL to BLn. As more cells are added to the bit lines, the signal magnitude being driven by the storage cells diminishes due to the additional loading of the other cells. This is where having complementary data signals (BL and BLn) is advantageous because this effectively doubles the magnitude of the storage cell outputs. The comparison of BL to BLn is handled using a *differential amplifier* that produces a full logic level output even when the incoming signals are very small.

SRAM is volatile memory because when the power is removed, the cross-coupled inverters are not able to drive the feedback loop and the data is lost. SRAM is also read/write memory because the storage cells can be easily read from or written to during normal operation.

Figure 10.11
4x4 SRAM Array Topology

Let's look at the operation of the SRAM array when writing the 4-bit word "0111" to address "01". Figure 10.12 shows a graphical depiction of this operation. In this write cycle, the row address decoder observes the address input "01" and asserts WL1. Asserting this word line enables all of the access transistors (i.e., M1 and M2 in Figure 10.10) of the storage cells in this row. The line drivers are designed to have a stronger drive strength than the inverters in the storage cells so that they can override their values during a write. The information "0111" is present on the Data_In bus and the write enable control line is asserted (WE=1) to indicate a write. The data line controller passes the information to be stored to the line drivers, which in turn converts each input into complementary signals and drives the bit lines. This overrides the information in each storage cell connected to WL1. The address decoder then de-asserts WL1 and the information is stored.

Figure 10.12
SRAM Operation During a Write Cycle – Storing "0111" to Address "01"

Now let's look at the operation of the SRAM array when reading a 4-bit word from address "10". Let's assume that this row was storing the value "1010". Figure 10.13 shows a graphical depiction of this operation. In this read cycle, the row address decoder asserts WL2, which allows the SRAM cells to drive their respective bit lines. Note that each cell drives a complementary version of its stored value. The input control line is de-asserted (WE=0), which indicates that the sense amps will read the BL and BLn lines in order to determine the full logic value stored in each cell. This logic value is then routed to the Data_Out port of the array. In an SRAM array, reading from the cell does not impact the contents of the cell. Once the read is complete, WL2 is de-asserted and the read cycle is complete.

SRAM Operation During a Read Cycle – Reading "1010" from Address "10"

The address decoder asserts WL2. This provides access to all cells on this row.

The sense amps determine whether the storage cell is holding a 0 or 1 by comparing BL to BLn.

Figure 10.13
SRAM Operation During a Read Cycle – Reading "0101" from Address "10"

10.3.2 Dynamic Random Access Memory (DRAM)

Dynamic Random Access Memory (DRAM) is a semiconductor technology that stores information using a capacitor. A capacitor is a fundamental electrical device that stores charge. Figure 10.14 shows the schematic for the basic DRAM storage cell. The capacitor is accessed through a transistor (M1). Since this storage element takes one transistor and one capacitor, it is often referred to as a 1T1C configuration. Just as in SRAM memory, word lines are used to access the storage elements. The term *digit line* is used to describe the vertical connection to the storage cells. DRAM has an advantage over SRAM in that the storage element requires less area to implement. This allows DRAM memory to have much higher density compared to SRAM.

Figure 10.14
DRAM Storage Element (1T 1C)

There are a variety of considerations that must be accounted for when using DRAM. First, the charge in the capacitor will slowly dissipate over time due to the capacitors being non-ideal. If left unchecked, eventually the data held in the capacitor will be lost. In order to overcome this issue, DRAM has a dedicated circuit to *refresh* the contents of the storage cell. A refresh cycle involves periodically reading the value stored on the capacitor and then writing the same value back again at full signal strength. This behavior also means that that DRAM is volatile because when the power is removed and the refresh cycle cannot be performed, the stored data is lost. DRAM is also considered read/write memory because the storage cells can be easily read from or written to during normal operation.

Another consideration when using DRAM is that the voltage of the word line must be larger than V_{cc} in order to turn on the access transistor. In order to turn on an NMOS transistor, the gate terminal must be larger than the source terminal by at least a threshold voltage (V_T). In traditional CMOS circuit design, the source terminal is typically connected to ground (0v). This means the transistor can be easily turned on by driving the gate with a logic 1 (i.e., V_{cc}) since this creates a V_{GS} voltage much larger than V_T. This is not always the case in DRAM. In DRAM, the source terminal is not connected to ground, but rather to the storage capacitor. In the worst-case situation, the capacitor could be storing a logic 1 (i.e., V_{cc}). This means that in order for the word line to be able to turn on the access transistor, it must be equal to or larger than ($V_{cc}+V_T$). This is an issue because the highest voltage that the DRAM device has access to is V_{cc}. In DRAM, a *charge pump* is used to create a voltage larger than $V_{cc}+V_T$ that is driven on the word lines. Once this voltage is used, the charge is lost so the line must be pumped up again before its next use. The process of "pumping up" takes time that must be considered when calculating the maximum speed of DRAM. Figure 10.15 shows a graphical depiction of this consideration.

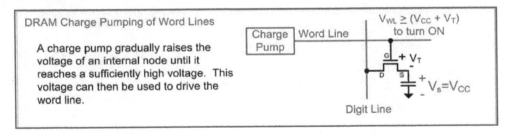

Figure 10.15
DRAM Charge Pumping of Word Lines

Another consideration when using DRAM is how the charge in the capacitor develops into an actual voltage on the digital line when the access transistor is closed. Consider the simple 4x4 array of DRAM cells shown in Figure 10.16. In this topology, the DRAM cells are accessed using the same approach as in the SRAM array from Figure 10.11.

Figure 10.16
Simple 4x4 DRAM Array Topology

One of the limitations of this simple configuration is that the charge stored in the capacitors cannot develop a full voltage level across the digit line when the access transistor is closed. This is because the digit line itself has capacitance that impacts how much voltage will be developed. In practice, the capacitance of the digit line (C_{DL}) is much larger than the capacitance of the storage cell (C_S) due to having significantly more area and being connected to numerous other storage cells. This becomes an issue because when the storage capacitor is connected to the digit line, the resulting voltage on the digit line (V_{DL}) is much less than the original voltage on the storage cell (V_S). This behavior is known as *charge sharing* because when the access transistor is closed, the charge on both capacitors is distributed across both devices and results in a final voltage that depends on the initial charge in the system and the values of the two capacitors. Example 10.1 shows an example of how to calculate the final digit line voltage when the storage cell is connected.

Example: Calculating the Final Digit Line Voltage in a DRAM Based on Charge Sharing

To illustrate how charge sharing limits the voltage that is developed on the digit line, let's consider a simple example where the cell is storing a logic 1 (V_S=+3.3v) and the digit line is initially set to V_{DL}=1.65v. The capacitance of the storage cell is C_S=10 pF while the capacitance of the digit line is C_{DL}=150 pF. We want to solve for the voltage on the digit line after the access transistor is closed.

The principle that guides this problem is "charge conservation". This means that the total amount of charge in the system can neither be created nor destroyed. The amount of charge in the system is dictated by the initial voltage across the capacitors. Since the definition of capacitance is "Charge per Volt", or C=Q/V, we can solve for the total amount of charge in the system prior to the access transistor being closed.

Q_{init} → $\underline{\text{Q in the storage cell}}$ + $\underline{\text{Q on the digital line}}$

$C_S = Q_S / V_S$ $C_{DL} = Q_{DL} / V_{DL}$

10 pF = Q_S / 3.3 v   150 pF = Q_{DL} / 1.65 v

Q_S = 33 pC Q_{DL} = 247.5 pC

$Q_{init} = Q_s + Q_{DL}$ = 33 pC + 247.5 pC = $\underline{\text{280.5 pC}}$

Once the access transistor closes, the two voltages (V_S and V_{DL}) are connected together and are forced to the same voltage (V_S=V_{DL}=V_{final}). Also after the access transistor closes, the final capacitance of the system is the sum of the two capacitors (C_{final}=C_S+C_{DL}=160 pF) since capacitors in parallel are additive. Using charge conservation, the initial charge in the system is equivalent to the final charge in the system (Q_{final}=Q_{init}=280.5 pC). From these values we can calculate the final voltage in the system after the access transistor closes,

$C_{final} = Q_{final} / V_{final}$

160 pF = 280.5 pC / V_{final}

V_{final}=1.75 v

This means that when storage cell is connected to the digit line, it only moves the voltage by 0.1v (1.76v-1.65v), or 100mv. This is a problem because this voltage difference is not sufficient to be detected using a standard logic gate.

Example 10.1
Calculating the Final Digit Line Voltage in a DRAM Based on Charge Sharing

The issue with the charge sharing behavior of a DRAM cell is that the final voltage on the word line is not large enough to be detected by a standard logic gate or latch. In order to overcome this issue, modern DRAM arrays use complementary storage cells and sense amplifiers. The complementary cells store the original data and its complement. Two digit lines (DL and DLn) are used to read the contents of the storage cells. DL and DLn are initially pre-charged to exactly V_{CC}/2. When the access transistors are closed, the storage cells will share their charge with the digit lines and move them slightly away from V_{CC}/2 in different directions. This allows twice the voltage difference to be developed during a read. A sense amplifier is then used to boost this small voltage difference into a full logic level that can be read by a standard logic gate or latch. Figure 10.17 shows the modern DRAM array topology based on complementary storage cells.

Figure 10.17
Modern DRAM Array Topology Based on Complementary Storage Cells

The sense amplifier is designed to boost small voltage deviations from $V_{CC}/2$ on DL and DLn to full logic levels. The sense amplifier sits in-between DL and DLn and has two complementary networks, the N-sense amplifier and the P-sense amplifier. The N-sense amplifier is used to pull a signal that is below $V_{CC}/2$ (either DL or DLn) down to GND. A control signal (N-Latch or NLATn) is used to turn on this network. The P-sense amplifier is used to pull a signal that is above $V_{CC}/2$ (either DL or DLn) up to V_{CC}. A control signal (Active Pull-Up or ACT) is used to turn on this network. The two networks are activated in a sequence with the N-sense network activating first. Figure 10.18 shows an overview of the operation of a DRAM sense amplifier.

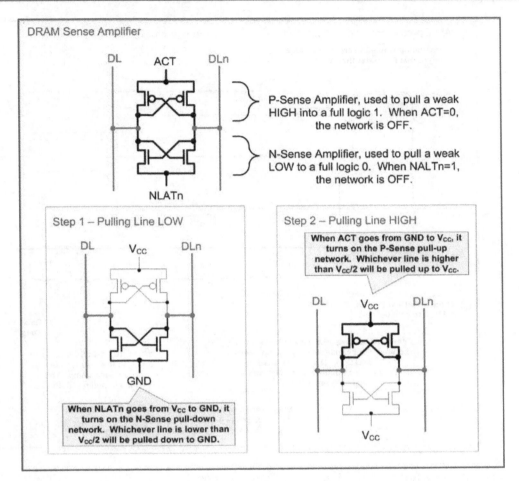

Figure 10.18
DRAM Sense Amplifier

Let's now put everything together and look at the operation of a DRAM system during a read operation. Figure 10.19 shows a simplified timing diagram of a DRAM read cycle. This diagram shows the critical signals and their values when reading a logic 1. Notice that there is a sequence of steps that must be accomplished before the information in the storage cells can be retrieved.

DRAM Operation During a Read Cycle – Reading a 1 from a Storage Cell

A charge pump is used to create a voltage on WL that is greater than $V_{CC}+V_T$.

Control Lines
WL
NALTn
ACT

Digit Lines
V_{CC}
$V_{CC}/2$
0v

DL
DLn

The DL pre-charge drivers set the initial levels of DL and DLn to exactly $V_{CC}/2$.

When WL asserts, the access transistors connect the complementary storage cells to DL and DLn. The charge sharing results in a slight increase in DL and a slight decrease in DLn.

When NALTn switches to GND, it turns on the N-sense network in the sense amp. This results in pulling DLn to GND

When ACT switches to V_{CC}, it turns on the P-sense network in the sense amp. This results in pulling DL to V_{CC}.

Read Data

Figure 10.19
DRAM Operation During a Read Cycle – Reading a 1 from a Storage Cell

A DRAM write operation is accomplished by opening the access transistors to the complementary storage cells using WL, disabling the pre-charge drivers and then writing full logic level signals to the storage cells using the Data_In line driver.

CONCEPT CHECK

CC10.3 Which of the following is suitable for implementation in a read/write memory?

A) A look up table containing the values of sine.

B) Information captured by a digital camera.

C) The boot up code for a computer.

D) A computer program on a spacecraft.

10.4 Modeling Memory with VHDL

10.4.1 Read-Only Memory in VHDL

Modeling of memory in VHDL is accomplished using the *array* data type. Recall the syntax for declaring a new array type below:

```
type name is array (<range>) of <element_type>;
```

To create the ROM memory array, a new type is declared (e.g., ROM_type) that is an array. The *range* represents the addressing of the memory array and is provided as an integer. The *element_type* of the array specifies the data type to be stored at each address and represents the data in the memory array. The type of the element should be std_logic_vector with a width of N. To define a 4x4 array of memory, we would use the following syntax.

Example:

```
type ROM_type is array (0 to 3) of std_logic_vector(3 downto 0);
```

Notice that the address is provided as an integer (0 to 3). This will require two address bits. Also notice that this defines 4-bit data words. Next, we define a new constant of type ROM_type. When defining a constant, we provide the contents at each address.

Example:

```
constant ROM : ROM_type := (0 => "1110",
                            1 => "0010",
                            2 => "1111",
                            3 => "0100");
```

At this point, the ROM array is declared and initialized. In order to model the read behavior, a concurrent signal assignment is used. The assignment will be made to the output data_out based on the incoming address. The assignment to data_out will be the contents of the constant ROM at a particular address. Since the index of a VHDL array needs to be provided as an integer (e.g., 0,1,2,3) and the address of the memory system is provided as a std_logic_vector, a type conversion is required. Since there is not a direct conversion from type std_logic_vector to integer, two conversions are required. The first step is to convert the address from std_logic_vector to unsigned using the *unsigned* type conversion. This conversion exists within the numeric_std package. The second step is to convert the address from unsigned to integer using the *to_integer* conversion. The final assignment is as follows:

Example:

```
data_out <= ROM(to_integer(unsigned(address)));
```

Example 10.2 shows the entire VHDL model for this memory system and the simulation waveform. In the simulation, each possible address is provided (i.e., "00", "01", "10", and "11"). For each address, the corresponding information appears on the data_out port. Since this is an asynchronous memory system, the data appears immediately upon receiving a new address.

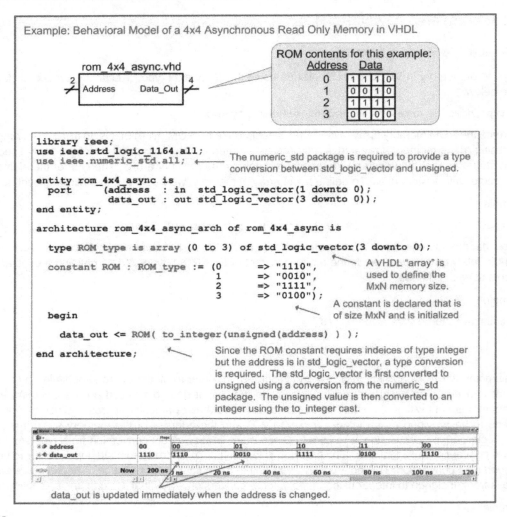

Example: Behavioral Model of a 4x4 Asynchronous Read Only Memory in VHDL

Example 10.2
Behavioral Model of a 4x4 Asynchronous Read Only Memory in VHDL

Latency can be modeled in memory systems by using delayed signal assignments. In the above example, if the memory system had a latency of 5 ns, this could be modeled using the following approach:

Example:

```
data_out <= ROM(to_integer(unsigned(address))) after 5 ns;
```

A synchronous ROM can be created in a similar manner. In this approach, a clock edge is used to trigger when the data_out port is updated. A sensitivity list is used that contains only the signal clock to trigger the assignment. A rising edge condition is then used in an if/then statement to make the assignment only on a rising edge. Example 10.3 shows the VHDL model and simulation waveform for this system. Notice that prior to the first clock edge, the simulator does not know what to assign to data_out so it lists the value as *uninitialized*.

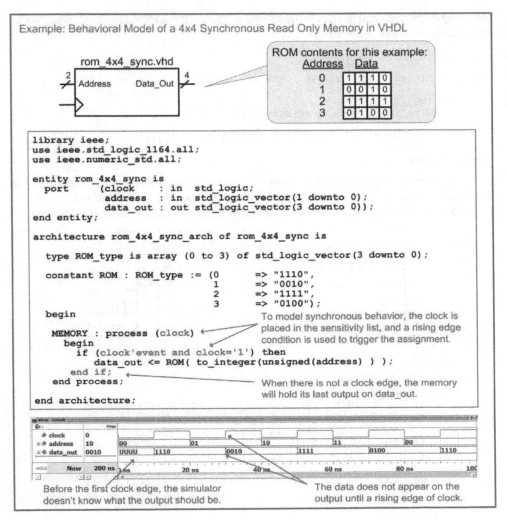

Example 10.3
Behavioral Model of a 4x4 Synchronous Read Only Memory in VHDL

10.4.2 Read/Write Memory in VHDL

In a read/write memory model, a new type is created using a VHDL *array* (e.g., RW_type) that defines the size of the storage system. To create the memory, a new signal is declared with the array type.

Example:

```
type RW_type is array (0 to 3) std_logic_vector(3 downto 0);
signal RW : RW_type;
```

Note that a signal is used in a read/write system as opposed to a constant as in the read only memory system. This is because a read/write system is uninitialized until it is written to. A process is then used to model the behavior of the memory system. Since this is an asynchronous system, all inputs are listed in the sensitivity list (i.e., address, WE, and data_in). The process first checks whether the write enable line is asserted (WE=1), which indicates a write cycle is being performed. If it is, then it makes an assignment to the RW signal at the location provided by the address input with the data provided by the data_in input. Since the RW array is indexed using integers, type conversions are required to convert the address from std_logic_vector to integer. When WE is not asserted (WE=0), a read cycle is being performed. In this case, the process makes an assignment to data_out with the contents stored at the provided address. This assignment also requires type conversions to change the address from std_logic_vector to integer. The following syntax implements this behavior.

Example:

```
MEMORY: process (address, WE, data_in)
  begin
    if (WE = '1') then
      RW(to_integer(unsigned(address))) <= data_in;
    else
      data_out <= RW(to_integer(unsigned(address)));
    end if;
end process;
```

A read/write memory does not contain information until its storage locations are written to. As a result, if the memory is read from before it has been written to, the simulation will return *uninitialized*. Example 10.4 shows the entire VHDL model for an asynchronous read/write memory and the simulation waveform showing read/write cycles.

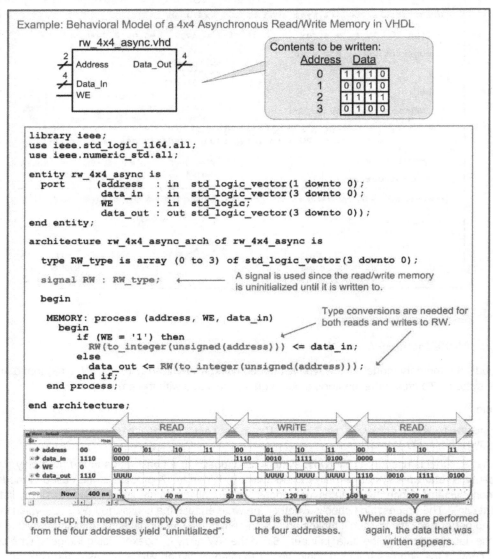

Example: Behavioral Model of a 4x4 Asynchronous Read/Write Memory in VHDL

Example 10.4
Behavioral Model of a 4x4 Asynchronous Read/Write Memory in VHDL

A synchronous read/write memory is made in a similar manner with the exception that a clock is used to trigger the signal assignments in the sensitivity list. The WE signal acts as a synchronous control signal indicating whether assignments are read from or written to the RW array. Example 10.5 shows the entire VHDL model for a synchronous read/write memory and the simulation waveform showing both read and write cycles.

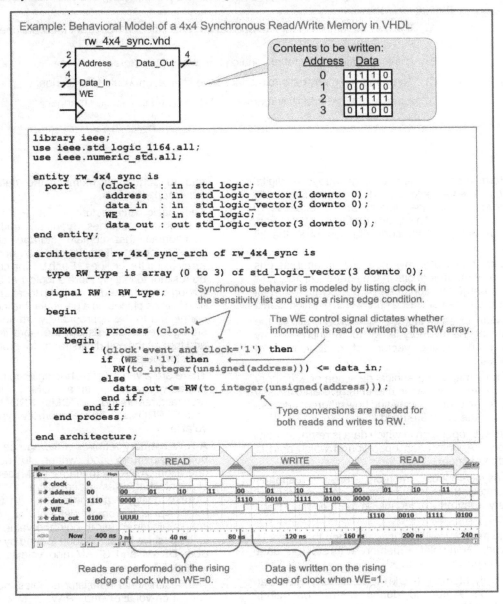

Example 10.5
Behavioral Model of a 4x4 Synchronous Read/Write Memory in VHDL

CONCEPT CHECK

CC10.4 Explain the advantage of modeling memory in VHDL without going into the details of the storage cell operation.

A) It allows the details of the storage cell to be abstracted from the functional operation of the memory system.

B) It is too difficult to model the analog behavior of the storage cell.

C) There are too many cells to model so the simulation would take too long.

D) It lets both ROM and R/W memory to be modeled in a similar manner.

Summary

❖ The term memory refers to large arrays of digital storage. The technology used in memory is typically optimized for storage density at the expense of control capability. This is different from a D-flip-flop, which is optimized for complete control at the bit level.

❖ A memory device always contains an address bus input. The number of bits in the address dictate how many storage locations can be accessed. An n-bit address bus can access 2^n (or M) storage locations.

❖ The width of each storage location (N) allows the density of the memory array to be increased by reading and writing vectors of data instead of individual bits.

❖ A memory map is a graphical depiction of a memory array. A memory map is useful to give an overview of the capacity of the array and how different address ranges of the array are used.

❖ A read is an operation in which data is retrieved from memory. A write is an operation in which data is stored to memory.

❖ An asynchronous memory array responds immediately to its control inputs. A synchronous memory array only responds on the triggering edge of clock.

❖ Volatile memory will lose its data when the power is removed. Non-volatile memory will retain its data when the power is removed.

❖ Read Only Memory (ROM) is a memory type that cannot be written to during normal operation. Read/Write (R/W) memory is a memory type that can be written to during normal operation. Both ROM and R/W memory can be read from during normal operation.

❖ Random Access Memory (RAM) is a memory type in which any location in memory can be accessed at any time. In Sequential Access Memory the data can only be retrieved in a linear sequence. This means that in sequential memory the data cannot be accessed arbitrarily.

❖ The basic architecture of a ROM consists of intersecting bit lines (vertical) and word lines (horizontal) that contain storage cells at their crossing points. The data is read out of the ROM array using the bit lines. Each bit line contains a pull-up resistor to initially store a logic 1 at each location. If a logic 0 is desired at a certain location, a pull-down transistor is placed on a particular bit line with its gate connected to the appropriate word line. When the storage cell is addressed, the word line will assert and turn on the pull-down transistor producing a logic 0 on the output.

❖ There are a variety of technologies to implement the pull-down transistor in a ROM. Different ROM architectures include MROMs, PROMs, EPROMs, and EEPROMs. These memory types are non-volatile.

❖ A R/W memory requires a storage cell that can be both read from and written to during normal operation. A DRAM (dynamic RAM) cell is a storage element that uses a capacitor to hold charge corresponding to a logic value. An SRAM (static RAM) cell is a storage element that uses a cross-coupled inverter pair to hold the value being stored in the positive feedback loop formed by the inverters. Both DRAM and SRAM and volatile and random access.

❖ The floating-gate transistor enables memory that is both non-volatile and R/W. Modern memory systems based on floating-gate transistor technology allow writing to take place using the existing system power supply levels. This type of R/W memory is called FLASH. In FLASH memory, the information is read out in blocks, thus it is not technically random access.

❖ Memory can be modeled in VHDL using the array data type.

Exercise Problems

Section 10.1 – Memory Architecture and Terminology

10.1.1 For a 512k x 32 memory system, how many unique address locations are there? Give the exact number.

10.1.2 For a 512k x 32 memory system, what is the data width at each address location?

10.1.3 For a 512k x 32 memory system, what is the *capacity* in <u>bits</u>?

10.1.4 For a 512k x 32-bit memory system, what is the *capacity* in <u>bytes</u>?

10.1.5 For a 512k x 32 memory system, how wide does the incoming address bus needed to be in order to access every unique address location?

10.1.6 Name the <u>type of memory</u> with the following characteristic: *when power is removed, the data is lost.*

10.1.7 Name the <u>type of memory</u> with the following characteristic: *when power is removed, the memory still holds its information.*

10.1.8 Name the <u>type of memory</u> with the following characteristic: *it can only be read from during normal operation.*

10.1.9 Name the <u>type of memory</u> with the following characteristic: *during normal operation, it can be read and written to.*

10.1.10 Name the <u>type of memory</u> with the following characteristic: *data can be accessed from any address location at any time.*

10.1.11 Name the <u>type of memory</u> with the following characteristic: data can only be accessed in consecutive order, thus not every location of memory is available instantaneously.

Section 10.2 – Non-Volatile Memory Technology

10.2.1 Name the <u>type of memory</u> with the following characteristic: this memory is non-volatile, read/write, and only provides data access in blocks.

10.2.2 Name the <u>type of memory</u> with the following characteristic: this memory uses a floating gate transistor, can be erased with electricity, and provides individual bit access.

10.2.3 Name the <u>type of memory</u> with the following characteristic: this memory is non-volatile, read/write, and provides word-level data access.

10.2.4 Name the <u>type of memory</u> with the following characteristic: this memory uses a floating-gate transistor that is erased with UV light.

10.2.5 Name the <u>type of memory</u> with the following characteristic: *this memory is programmed by blowing fuses or anti-fuses.*

10.2.6 Name the <u>type of memory</u> with the following characteristic: this memory is partially fabricated prior to knowing the information to be stored.

Section 10.3 – Volatile Memory Technology

10.3.1 How many transistors does it take to implement an SRAM cell?

10.3.2 Why doesn't an SRAM cell require a refresh cycle?

10.3.3 Design a VHDL model for the SRAM system shown in Figure 10.20. Your storage cell should be designed such that its contents can be overwritten by the line driver. Consider using a resolved data type for this behavior that models drive strength (e.g., in std_logic, a 1 has a higher drive strength than an H). You will need to create a system for the differential line driver with enable. This driver will need to contain a high impedance state when disabled. Both your line driver (Din) and receiver (Dout) are differential. These systems can be modeled using simple if/then statements. Create a test bench for your system that will write a 0 to the cell, then read it back to verify the 0 was stored and then repeat the write/read cycles for a 1.

Figure 10.20

10.3.4 Why is a DRAM cell referred to as a 1T 1C configuration?

10.3.5 Why is a charge pump necessary on the word lines of a DRAM array?

10.3.6 Why does a DRAM cell require a refresh cycle?

10.3.7 For the DRAM storage cell shown in Figure 10.21, solve for the final voltage on the digit line after the access transistor (M1) closes if initially $V_s = V_{cc}$ (**i.e., the cell is storing a 1**). In this system, $C_s = 5pF$, $C_{DL} = 10pF$, and $V_{cc} = +3.4v$. Prior to the access transistor closing, the digit line is pre-charged to $V_{cc}/2$.

Figure 10.21

10.3.8 For the DRAM storage cell shown in Figure 10.21, solve for the final voltage on the digit line after the access transistor (M1) closes if initially V_S=GND (**i.e., the cell is storing a 0**). In this system, C_S = 5pF, C_{DL}=10pF, and V_{CC}=+3.4v. Prior to the access transistor closing, the digit line is pre-charged to V_{CC}/2.

Section 10.4 – Modeling Memory with VHDL

10.4.1 Design a VHDL model for the <u>16x8, asynchronous, read only memory</u> system shown in Figure 10.22. The system should contain the information provided in the memory map. Create a test bench to simulate your model by reading from each of the 16 unique addresses and observing Data_Out to verify it contains the information in the memory map.

Address	Data
0	x"00"
1	x"11"
2	x"22"
3	x"33"
4	x"44"
5	x"55"
6	x"66"
7	x"77"
8	x"88"
9	x"99"
10	x"AA"
11	x"BB"
12	x"CC"
13	x"DD"
14	x"EE"
15	x"FF"

rom_16x8_async.vhd

Figure 10.22

10.4.2 Design a VHDL model for the <u>16x8, synchronous, read only memory</u> system shown in Figure 10.23. The system should contain the information provided in the memory map. Create a test bench to simulate your model by reading from each of the 16 unique addresses and observing Data_Out to verify it contains the information in the memory map.

Address	Data
0	x"FF"
1	x"EE"
2	x"DD"
3	x"CC"
4	x"BB"
5	x"AA"
6	x"99"
7	x"88"
8	x"77"
9	x"66"
10	x"55"
11	x"44"
12	x"33"
13	x"22"
14	x"11"
15	x"00"

rom_16x8_sync.vhd

Figure 10.23

10.4.3 Design a VHDL model for the <u>16x8, asynchronous, read/write memory</u> system shown in Figure 10.24. Create a test bench to simulate your model. Your test bench should first read from all of the address locations to verify they are uninitialized. Next, your test bench should write unique information to each of the address locations. Finally, your test bench should read from each address location to verify that the information that was written was stored and can be successfully retrieved.

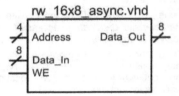

rw_16x8_async.vhd

Figure 10.24

10.4.4 Design a VHDL model for the <u>16x8, synchronous, read/write memory</u> system shown in Figure 10.25. Create a test bench to simulate your model. Your test bench should first read from all of the address locations to verify they are uninitialized. Next, your test bench should write unique information to each of the address locations. Finally, your test bench should read from each address location to verify that the information that was written was stored and can be successfully retrieved.

rw_16x8_sync.vhd

Figure 10.25

Chapter 11: Programmable Logic

This chapter provides an overview of programmable logic devices (PLDs). The term PLD is used as a generic description for any circuit that can be programmed to implement digital logic. The technology and architectures of PLDs have advanced over time. This chapter gives a historical perspective of how the first programmable devices evolved into the programmable technologies that are prevalent today.

Learning Outcomes – After completing this chapter, you will be able to:

11.1   Describe the functional operation of the most common types of programmable logic devices.
11.2   Implement a sum of products logic expression in a programmable array logic (PAL) device.
11.3   Design a look up table (LUT) using a cascade of 2-input multiplexers.

11.1 Programmable Arrays

11.1.1 Programmable Logic Array (PLA)

One of the first commercial PLDs developed using modern integrated circuit technology was the **programmable logic array (PLA)**. In 1970, Texas Instrument introduced the PLA with an architecture that supported the implementation of arbitrary, sum of products logic expressions. The PLA was fabricated with a dense array of AND gates, called an *AND plane*, and a dense array of OR gates, called an *OR plane*. Inputs to the PLA each had an inverter in order to provide the original variable and its complement. Arbitrary SOP logic expressions could be implemented by creating connections between the inputs, the AND plane, and the OR plane. The original PLAs were fabricated with all of the necessary features except the final connections to implement the SOP functions. When a customer provided the desired SOP expression, the connections were added as the final step of fabrication. This configuration technique was similar to an MROM approach. Figure 11.1 shows the basic architecture of a PLA.

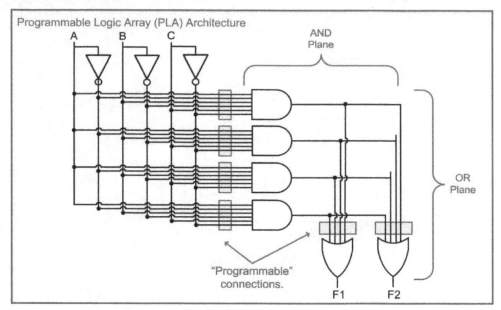

Figure 11.1
Programmable Logic Array (PLA) Architecture

A more compact schematic for the PLA is drawn by representing all of the inputs into the AND and OR gates with a single wire. Connections are indicated by inserting X's at the intersections of wires. Figure 11.2 shows this simplified PLA schematic implementing two different SOP logic expressions.

Figure 11.2
Simplified PLA Schematic

11.1.2 Programmable Array Logic (PAL)

One of the drawbacks of the original PLA was that the programmability of the OR plane caused significant propagation delays through the combinational logic circuits. In order to improve on the performance of PLAs, the **programmable array logic (PAL)** was introduced in 1978 by the company *Monolithic Memories, Inc.* The PAL contained a programmable AND-plane and a *fixed-OR* plane. The fixed-OR plane improved the performance of this programmable architecture. While not having a programmable OR-plane reduced the flexibility of the device, most SOP expressions could be manipulated to work with a PAL. Another contribution of the PAL was that the AND-plane could be programmed using fuses. Initially, all connections were present in the AND-plane. An external programmer was used to blow fuses in order to disconnect the inputs from the AND gates. While the fuse approach provided one-time-only programming, the ability to configure the logic post-fabrication was a significant advancement over the PLA, which had to be programmed at the manufacturer. Figure 11.3 shows the architecture of a PAL.

Figure 11.3
Programmable Array Logic (PAL) Architecture

11.1.3 Generic Array Logic (GAL)

As the popularity of the PAL grew, additional functionality was implemented to support more sophisticated designs. One of the most significant improvements was the addition of an *output logic macrocell (OLMC)*. An OLMC provided a D-Flip-Flop and a selectable mux so that the output of the SOP circuit from the PAL could be used either as the system output or the input to a D-Flip-Flop. This enabled the implementation of sequential logic and finite state machines. The OLMC also could be used to route the I/O pin back into the PAL to increase the number of inputs possible in the SOP expressions. Finally, the OLMC provided a multiplexer to allow feedback from either the PAL output or the output of the D-Flip-Flop. This architecture was named a **generic array logic (GAL)** to distinguish its features from a standard PAL. Figure 11.4 shows the architecture of a GAL consisting of a PAL and an OLMC.

Figure 11.4
Generic Array Logic (GAL) Architecture

11.1.4 Hard Array Logic (HAL)

For mature designs, PALs and GALs could be implemented as a **hard array logic (HAL)** device. A HAL was a version of a PAL or GAL that had the AND plane connections implemented during fabrication instead of through blowing fuses. This architecture was more efficient for high volume applications as it eliminated the programming step post-fabrication and the device did not need to contain the additional programming circuitry.

In 1983, *Altera Inc.,* was founded as a programmable logic device company. In 1984, Altera released its first version of a PAL with a unique feature that it could be programmed and erased multiple times using a programmer and an UV light source similar to an EEPROM.

11.1.5 Complex Programmable Logic Devices (CPLD)

As the demand for larger programmable devices grew, the PAL's architecture was not able to scale efficiently due to a number of reasons: first, as the size of combinational logic circuits increased, the PAL encountered fan-in issues in its AND plane; secondly, for each input that was added to the PAL, the amount of circuitry needed on the chip grew geometrically due to requiring a connection to each AND gate in addition to the area associated with the additional OLMC. This led to a new PLD architecture in which the on-chip interconnect was partitioned across multiple PALs on a single chip. This partitioning meant that not all inputs to the device could be used by each PAL so the design complexity increased; however, the additional programmable resources outweighed this drawback and this architecture was broadly adopted. This new architecture was called a **complex programmable logic device (CPLD)**. The term *simple* **programmable logic device (SPLD)** was created to describe all of the previous PLD architectures (i.e., PLA, PAL, GAL, and HAL). Figure 11.5 shows the architecture of the CPLD.

Figure 11.5
Complex PLD (CPLD) Architecture

CONCEPT CHECK

CC11.1   What is the only source of delay mismatch from the inputs to the outputs in a programmable array?

   A)   The AND gates will have different delays due to having different numbers of inputs.

   B)   The OR gates will have different delays due to having different numbers of inputs.

   C)   An inputs may or may not go through an inverter before reaching the AND gates.

   D)   None. All paths through the programmable array have identical delay.

11.2 Field Programmable Gate Arrays (FPGAs)

To address the need for even more programmable resources, a new architecture was developed by *Xilinx Inc.* in 1985. This new architecture was called a **field programmable gate array (FPGA)**. An FPGA consists of an array of programmable logic blocks (or logic elements) and a network of programmable interconnect that can be used to connect any logic element to any other logic element. Each logic block contained circuitry to implement arbitrary combinational logic circuits in addition to a D-Flip-Flop and a multiplexer for signal steering. This architecture effectively implemented an OLMC within each block, thus providing ultimate flexibility and providing significantly more resources for sequential logic. Today, FPGAs are the most commonly used programmable logic device with Altera Inc. and Xilinx Inc. being the two largest manufacturers. Figure 11.6 shows the generic architecture of an FPGA.

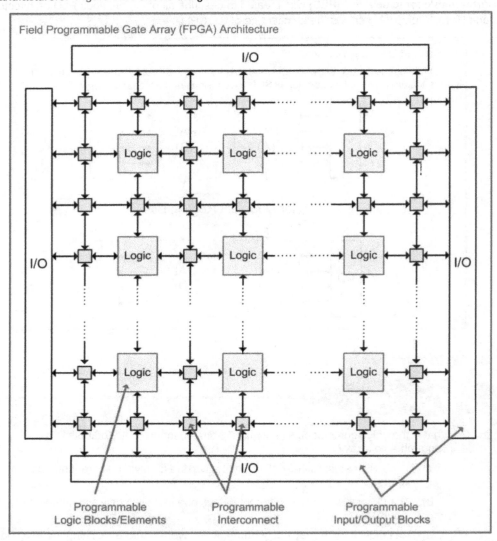

Figure 11.6
Field Programmable Gate Array (FPGA) Architecture

11.2.1 Configurable Logic Block (or Logic Element)

The primary reconfigurable structure in the FPGA is the **configurable logic block (CLB)** or **Logic Element (LE)**. Xilinx Inc. uses the term CLB while Altera uses LE. Combinational logic is implemented using a circuit called a **Look-Up Table (LUT)**, which can implement any arbitrary truth table. The details of a LUT are given in the next section. The CLB/LE also contains a D-Flip-Flop for sequential logic. A signal steering multiplexer is used to select whether the output of the CLB/LE comes from the LUT or from the D-Flip-Flop. The LUT can be used to drive a combinational logic expression into the D input of the D-Flip-Flop, thus creating a highly efficient topology for finite state machines. A global routing network is used to provide common signals to the CLB/LE such as clock, reset and enable. This global routing network can provide these common signals to the entire FPGA or local groups of CLB/LEs. Figure 11.7 shows the topology of a simple CLB/LE.

Figure 11.7
Simple FPGA Configurable Logic Block (or Logic Element)

   CLB/LEs have evolved to include numerous other features such as carry in / carry out signals so that arithmetic operations can be cascaded between multiple blocks in addition to signal feedback and D-flip-Flop initialization.

11.2.2 Look-Up Tables (LUTs)

   A look-up table is the primary circuit used to implement combinational logic in FPGAs. This topology has also been adopted in modern CPLDs. In a LUT, the desired outputs of a truth table are loaded into a local configuration SRAM memory. The SRAM memory provides these values to the inputs of a multiplexer. The inputs to the combinational logic circuit are then used as the select lines to the multiplexer. For an arbitrary input to the combinational logic circuit, the multiplexer selects the appropriate value held in the SRAM and routes it to the output of the circuit. In this way, the multiplexer *looks up* the appropriate output value based on the input code. This architecture has the advantage that any logic function can be created without creating a custom logic circuit. Also, the delay through the LUT is identical regardless of what logic function is being implemented. Figure 11.8 shows a 2-input combinational logic circuit implemented with a 4-input multiplexer.

Figure 11.8
2-Input LUT Implemented with a 4-Input Multiplexer

Fan-in limitations can be encountered quickly in LUTs as the number of inputs of the combinational logic circuit being implemented grows. Recall that multiplexers are implemented with an SOP topology in which each product term in the first level of logic has a number of inputs equal to the number of select lines plus one. Also recall that the sum term in the second level of logic in the SOP topology has a number of inputs equal to the total number of inputs to the multiplexer. In the example circuit shown in Figure 11.8, each product term in the multiplexer will have three inputs and the sum term will have four inputs. As an illustration of how quickly fan-in limitations are encountered, consider the implication of increasing the number of inputs in Figure 11.8 from two to three. In this new configuration, the number of inputs in the product terms will increase from three to four and the number of inputs in the sum term will increase to from four to eight. Eight inputs is often beyond the fan-in specifications of modern devices, meaning that even a 3-input combinational logic circuit will encounter fan-in issues when implemented using a LUT topology.

To address this issue, multiplexer functionality in LUTs is typically implemented as a series of smaller, cascaded multiplexers. Each of the smaller multiplexers progressively select which row of the truth table to route to the output of the LUT. This eliminates fan-in issues at the expense of adding additional levels of logic to the circuit. While cascading multiplexers increases the overall circuit delay, this approach achieves a highly consistent delay because regardless of the truth table output value, the number of levels of logic through the multiplexers is always the same. Figure 11.9 shows how the 2-input truth table from Figure 11.8 can be implemented using a 2-level cascade of 2-input multiplexers.

Figure 11.9
2-Input LUT Implemented with a 2-Level Cascade of 2-Input Multiplexers

If more inputs are needed in the LUT, additional MUX levels are added. Figure 11.10 shows the architecture for a 3-input LUT implemented with a 3-level cascade of 2-input multiplexers.

Figure 11.10
3-Input LUT Implemented with a 3-Level Cascade of 2-Input Multiplexers

Modern FPGAs can have LUTs with up to 6 inputs. If even more inputs are needed in a combinational logic expression, then multiple CLB/LEs are used that form even larger LUTs.

11.2.3 Programmable Interconnect Points (PIPs)

The configurable routing network on an FPGA is accomplished using programmable switches. A simple model for these switches is to use an NMOS transistor. A configuration SRAM bit stores whether the switch is opened or closed. On the FPGA, interconnect is routed vertically and horizontally between the CLB/LEs with switching points placed throughout the FPGA to facilitate any arbitrary routing configuration. Figure 11.11 shows how the routing can be configured into a full cross-point configuration using programmable switches.

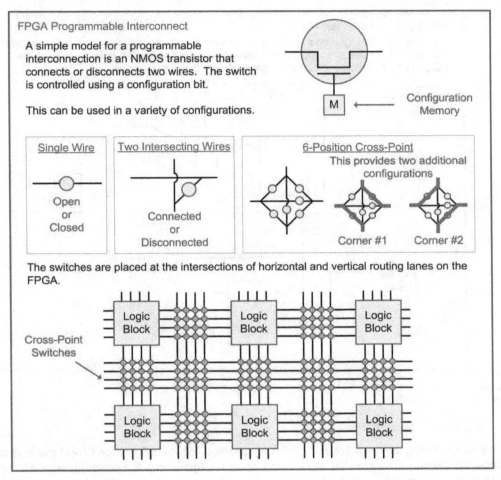

Figure 11.11
FPGA Programmable Interconnect

11.2.4 Input / Output Block (IOBs)

FPGAs also contain **Input / Output Blocks (IOB)** that provide programmable functionality for interfacing to external circuitry. The IOBs contain both driver and receiver circuitry so that they can be programmed to be either inputs or outputs. D-Flip-Flops are included in both the input and output circuitry to support synchronous logic. Figure 11.12 shows the architecture of an FPGA IOB.

Figure 11.12
FPGA Input / Output Block (IOB)

11.2.5 Configuration Memory

All of the programming information for an FPGA is contained within configuration SRAM that is distributed across the IC. Since this memory is volatile, the FPGA will lose its configuration when power is removed. Upon power-up, the FPGA must be programmed with its configuration data. This data is typically held in a non-volatile memory such as FLASH. The "FP" in FPGA refers to the ability to program the device in the *field*, or post-fabrication. The "GA" in FPGA refers to the array topology of the programmable logic blocks or elements.

> **CONCEPT CHECK**
>
> CC11.2   What is the primary difference between an FPGA and a CPLD?
>
> A)   The ability to create arbitrary SOP logic expressions.
>
> B)   The abundance of configurable routing.
>
> C)   The inclusion of D-flip-flops.
>
> D)   The inclusion of programmable I/O pins.

Summary

❖   A *programmable logic device* (PLD) is a generic term for a circuit that can be configured to implement arbitrary logic functions.

❖   There are a variety of PLD architectures that have been used to implement combinational logic. These include the PLA and PAL. These devices contain an AND-plane and an OR-plane. The AND-plane is configured to implement the product terms of a SOP expression. The OR-plane is configured to implement the sum term of a SOP expression.

❖ A GAL increases the complexity of logic arrays by adding sequential logic storage and programmable I/O capability.

❖ A CPLD significantly increases the density of PLDs by connecting an array of PALs together and surrounding the logic with I/O drivers.

❖ FPGAs contain an array of programmable logic elements that each contain programmable combinational logic capability in addition to sequential logic storage. FPGAs also contain a programmable interconnect network that provides the highest level of flexibility in programmable logic.

❖ A look-up-table (LUT) is a simple method to create a programmable combinational logic circuit. A LUT is simply a multiplexer with the inputs to the circuit connected to the select lines of the MUX. The desired outputs of the truth table are connected to the MUX inputs. As different input codes arrive on the select lines of the MUX, they *select* the corresponding logic value to be routed to the system output.

Exercise Problems

Section 11.1 - Programmable Arrays

11.1.1   Name the <u>type of programmable logic</u> described by the characteristic: *this device adds an output logic macrocell to a traditional PAL.*

11.1.2   Name the <u>type of programmable logic</u> described by the characteristic: this device combines multiple PALs on a single chip with a partitioned interconnect system.

11.1.3   Name the <u>type of programmable logic</u> described by the characteristic: *this device has a programmable AND-plane and programmable OR-plane.*

11.1.4   Name the <u>type of programmable logic</u> described by the characteristic: *this device has a programmable AND-plane and fixed OR-plane.*

11.1.5   Name the <u>type of programmable logic</u> described by the characteristic: *this device is a PAL or GAL that is programmed during manufacturing.*

11.1.6   For the following unconfigured PAL schematic in Figure 11.13, draw in the connection points (i.e., the X's) to implement the two SOP logic expressions shown on the outputs.

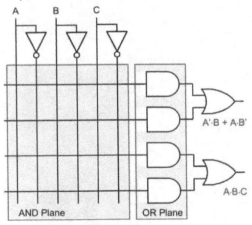

Figure 11.13

Section 11.2 – Field Programmable Gate Arrays (FPGAs)

11.2.1   What <u>type of programmable logic device</u> is described by the following characteristic: this part of an FPGA is used to interface between the internal logic and external circuitry.

11.2.2   What <u>type of programmable logic device</u> is described by the following characteristic: this device consists of programmable logic blocks, programmable interconnect, and programmable input/output blocks.

11.2.3   What <u>type of programmable logic device</u> is described by the following characteristic: *this part of an FPGA is used to configure the on-chip routing.*

11.2.4   What <u>type of programmable logic device</u> is described by the following characteristic: *this part of an FPGA is the primary programmable element.*

11.2.5   What <u>type of programmable logic device</u> is described by the following characteristic: *this part of an FPGA is used to implement combinational logic.*

11.2.6   Draw the logic diagram of a 4-Input Look-Up Table (LUT) to implement the truth table provided in Figure 11.14. Implement the LUT with only 2-input multiplexers. Be sure to label the exact location of the inputs (A, B, C, and D), the desired value for each row of the truth table, and the output (F) in the diagram.

A	B	C	D	F
0	0	0	0	0
0	0	0	1	1
0	0	1	0	0
0	0	1	1	1
0	1	0	0	0
0	1	0	1	0
0	1	1	0	0
0	1	1	1	0
1	0	0	0	0
1	0	0	1	1
1	0	1	0	0
1	0	1	1	1
1	1	0	0	0
1	1	0	1	0
1	1	1	0	0
1	1	1	1	0

4-Input LUT
A
B
C   F
D

Figure 11.14

Chapter 12: Arithmetic Circuits

This chapter presents the design and timing considerations of circuits to perform basic arithmetic operations including addition, subtraction, multiplication, and division. A discussion is also presented on how to model arithmetic circuits in VHDL.

Learning Outcomes – After completing this chapter, you will be able to:

12.1 Describe the architecture of a ripple carry adder.
12.2 Analyze the timing of a ripple carry adder.
12.3 Design a VHDL model for a ripple carry adder using a structural design approach.
12.4 Describe the architecture of a carry look ahead adder.
12.5 Analyze the timing of a carry look ahead adder.
12.6 Design a VHDL model for a carry look ahead adder.
12.7 Describe the architecture of a programmable adder/subtractor circuit.
12.8 Design a VHDL model for a programmable adder/subtractor circuit.
12.9 Describe the architecture of an unsigned combinational multiplier.
12.10 Design a VHDL model for an unsigned combinational multiplier.
12.11 Describe the architecture of a signed combinational multiplier.
12.12 Design a VHDL model for a signed combinational multiplier.
12.13 Describe the architecture of an unsigned combinational divider.
12.14 Design a VHDL model for an unsigned combinational divider.

12.1 Addition

Binary addition is performed in a similar manner to performing decimal addition by hand. The addition begins in the least significant position of the number ($p=0$). The addition produces the sum for this position. In the event that this positional sum cannot be represented by a single symbol, then the higher order symbol is *carried* to the subsequent position ($p=1$). The addition in the next higher position must include the number that was carried in from the lower positional sum. This process continues until all of the symbols in the number have been operated on. The final positional sum can also produce a carry, which needs to be accounted for in a separate system.

Designing a binary adder involves creating a combinational logic circuit to perform the positional additions. Since a combinational logic circuit can only produce a scalar output, circuitry is needed to produce the sum and the carry at each position. The binary adder size is pre-determined and fixed prior to implementing the logic (i.e., an n-bit adder). Both inputs to the adder must adhere to the fixed size, regardless of their value. Smaller numbers simply contain leading zero's in their higher order positions. For an n-bit adder, the largest sum that can be produced will require n+1 bits. To illustrate this, consider a 4-bit adder. The largest numbers that the adder will operate on are $1111_2 + 1111_2$ (or $15_{10} + 15_{10}$). The result of this addition is 11110_2 (or 30_{10}). Notice that the largest sum produced fits within 5 bits, or n+1. When constructing an adder circuit, the sum is always recorded using n-bits with a separate carry out bit. In our 4-bit example, the sum would be expressed as "1110" with a carry out. The carry out bit can be used in multiple word additions, used as part of the number when being decoded for a display, or simply discarded as in the case when using two's complement numbers.

12.1.1 Half Adders

When creating an adder, it is desirable to design incremental sub-systems that can be re-used. This reduces design effort and minimizes troubleshooting complexity. The most basic component in the adder is called a *half adder*. This circuit computes the sum and carry out on two input arguments. The reason it is called a half adder instead of a full adder is because it does not accommodate a *carry in* during the computation, thus is does not provide all of the necessary functionality required for the positional adder. Example 12.1 shows the design of a half adder. Notice that two combinational logic circuits are required in order to produce the sum (the XOR gate) and the carry out (the AND gate). These two gates are in parallel to each other, thus the delay through the half adder is due to only one level of logic.

Example 12.1
Design of a Half Adder

12.1.2 Full Adders

A full adder is a circuit that still produces a sum and carry out, but considers three inputs in the computations (A, B, and C_{in}). Example 12.2 shows the design of a full adder.

Example 12.2
Design of a Full Adder

As mentioned before, it is desirable to re-use design components as we construct more complex systems. One such design re-use approach is to create a full adder using two half adders. This is straightforward for the sum output since the logic is simply two cascaded XOR gates (Sum=A⊕B⊕Cin). The carry out is not as straightforward. Notice that the expression for Cout derived in Example 12.2 contains the term (A+B). If this term could be manipulated to use an XOR gate instead, it would allow the full adder to take advantage of existing circuitry in the system. Figure 12.1 shows a derivation of an equivalency that allows (A+B) to be replaced with (A⊕B) in the Cout logic expression.

A Useful Logic Equivalency that can be Exploited in Arithmetic Circuits
The logic expression for the carry out of a full adder was given as: $C_{out} = A \cdot B + (A + B) \cdot C_{in}$.
It turns out that the exact same output is produced by the expression $A \cdot B + (A \oplus B) \cdot C_{in}$.
Let's examine how this is possible by breaking down the expressions into their individual
parts and solving at each step.

FA Inputs			Desired Output	$C_{out} = A \cdot B + (A + B) \cdot C_{in}$			$C_{out} = A \cdot B + (A \oplus B) \cdot C_{in}$		
C_{in}	A	B	C_{out}	$A \cdot B$	$(A+B) \cdot C_{in}$	$A \cdot B + (A + B) \cdot C_{in}$	$A \cdot B$	$(A \oplus B) \cdot C_{in}$	$A \cdot B + (A \oplus B) \cdot C_{in}$
0	0	0	0	0	0	0	0	0	0
0	0	1	0	0	0	0	0	0	0
0	1	0	0	0	0	0	0	0	0
0	1	1	1	1	0	1	1	0	1
1	0	0	0	0	0	0	0	0	0
1	0	1	1	0	1	1	0	1	1
1	1	0	1	0	1	1	0	1	1
1	1	1	1	1	1	1	1	0	1

$C_{out} = A \cdot B + (A + B) \cdot C_{in} = A \cdot B + (A \oplus B) \cdot C_{in}$

Equivalent !

Figure 12.1
A Useful Logic Equivalency that can be Exploited in Arithmetic Circuits

The ability to implement the carry out logic using the expression $C_{out} = A \cdot B + (A \oplus B) \cdot C_{in}$ allows us to implement a full adder with two half adders and the addition of a single OR gate. Example 12.3 shows this approach. In this new configuration, the sum is produced in two levels of logic while the carry out is produced in three levels of logic.

Example – Design of a Full Adder Out of Two Half Adders
It is often desirable to create a full adder out of two half adders in order to re-use existing design components. The "Sum" of the full adder can be created by using two cascaded XOR gates provided by the half adders.

The expression for the "Carry Out" of the full adder is:
$$C_{out} = A \cdot B + (A + B) \cdot C_{in}$$
or
$$C_{out} = A \cdot B + (A \oplus B) \cdot C_{in}$$

Notice that the carry out of Half Adder 1 produces the $A \cdot B$ term in this expression. Also notice that the carry out of Half Adder 2 produces the $(A \oplus B) \cdot C_{in}$ term. The only remaining logic needed to create the carry out of the full adder is an OR gate. The final logic diagram for the full adder is as follows:

Example 12.3
Design of a Full Adder Out of Half Adders

12.1.3 Ripple Carry Adder (RCA)

The full adder can now be used in the creation of multi-bit adders. The simplest architecture exploiting the full adder is called a *ripple carry adder* (RCA). In this approach, full adders are used to create the sum and carry out of each bit position. The carry out of each full adder is used as the carry in for the next higher position. Since each subsequent full adder needs to wait for the carry to be produced by the preceding stage, the carry is said to *ripple* through the circuit, thus giving this approach its name. Example 12.4 shows how to design a 4-bit ripple carry adder using a chain of full adders. Notice that the carry in for the full adder in position 0 is tied to a logic 0. The 0 input has no impact on the result of the sum but enables a full adder to be used in the 0th position.

Example: Design of a 4-Bit Ripple Carry Adder (RCA)

Full adders can be cascaded together to form a multi-bit adder. The symbols are typically drawn in the following fashion to mirror a positional number system.

The sum of position 1 cannot complete until it receives the carry in (C_1) from the sum in position 0. The position 2 sum cannot complete until it receives the carry in (C_2) from the sum in position 1, etc. In this way, the carry "ripples" through the circuit from right to left. This configuration is known as a Ripple Carry Adder (RCA).

Example 12.4
Design of a 4-Bit Ripple Carry Adder (RCA)

While the ripple carry adder provides a simple architecture based on design re-use, its delay can become considerable when scaling to larger inputs sizes (e.g., n=32 or n=64). A simple analysis of the timing can be stated such that if the time for a full adder to complete its positional sum is t_{FA}, then the time for an n-bit ripple carry adder to complete its computation is $t_{RCA} = n \cdot t_{FA}$.

If we examine the RCA in more detail, we can break down the delay in terms of the levels of logic necessary for the computation. Example 12.5 shows the timing analysis of the 4-bit RCA. This analysis determines the number of logic levels in the adder. The actual gate delays can then be plugged in to find the final delay. The inputs to the adder are A, B and C_{in} and are always assumed to update at the same time. The first full adder requires two levels of logic to produce its sum and three levels to produce its carry out. Since the timing of a circuit is always stated as its worst case delay, we say that the first full adder takes three levels of logic. When the carry (C_1) ripples to the next full adder (FA1), it must propagate through two additional levels of logic in order to produce C_2. Notice that the first half adder in FA1 only depends on A_1 and B_1, thus it is able to perform this computation immediately. This half adder can be considered as first level logic. More importantly, it means that when the carry in arrives (C_1), only two additional levels of logic are needed, not three. The levels of logic for the RCA can be expressed as $3 + 2 \cdot (n-1)$. If each level of logic has a delay of t_{gate}, then a more accurate expression for the RCA delay is $t_{RCA} = (3 + 2 \cdot (n-1)) \cdot t_{gate}$.

Example 12.5
Timing Analysis of a 4-Bit Ripple Carry Adder

12.1.4 Carry Look Ahead Adder (CLA)

In order to address the potentially significant delay of a ripple carry adder, a *carry look ahead* (CLA) adder was created. In this approach, additional circuitry is included that produces the intermediate carry in signals immediately instead of waiting for them to be created by the preceding full adder stage. This allows the adder to complete in a fixed amount of time instead of one that scales with the number of bits in the adder. Example 12.6 shows an overview of the design approach for a CLA.

Example 12.6
Design of a 4-Bit Carry Look Ahead Adder (CLA) – Overview

For the CLA architecture to be effective, the look ahead circuitry needs to be dependent only on the system inputs A, B, and C_{in} (i.e., C_0). A secondary characteristic of the CLA is that it should exploit as much design re-use as possible. In order to examine the design re-use aspects of a multi-bit adder, the concepts of carry **generation** (g) and **propagation** (p) are used. A full adder is said to *generate* a carry if its inputs A and B result in $C_{out}=1$ when $C_{in}=0$. A full adder is said to *propagate* a carry if its inputs A and B result in $C_{out}=1$ when $C_{in}=1$. These simple statements can be used to derive logic expressions for each stage of the adder that can take advantage of existing logic terms from prior stages. Example 12.7 shows the derivation of these terms and how algebraic substitutions can be exploited to create look ahead circuitry for each full adder that is only dependent on the system inputs. In these derivations, the variable *i* is used to represent position since *p* is used to represent the propagate term.

Example: Design of a 4-Bit Carry Look Ahead Adder (CLA) – Algebraic Formation

The look ahead circuitry considers whether the prior adder stages create a carry by considering two conditions: 1) whether a stage will **generate** (*g*) a carry; and 2) whether the stage will **propagate** (*p*) a carry. Let's look at the truth table for a full adder.

C_{in}	A	B	C_{out}
0	0	0	0
0	0	1	0
0	1	0	0
0	1	1	1
1	0	0	0
1	0	1	1
1	1	0	1
1	1	1	1

For the input codes where $C_{in}=0$, the full adder "generates" a new carry when A=1 and B=1. This behavior can be described with the expression: $g = A \cdot B$

For the input codes where $C_{in}=1$, the full adder "propagates" the incoming carry when either A=1 or B=1. This behavior can be described with the expression: $p = A+B$

The entire expression for the carry out can be written as:

$$C_{out} = g + p \cdot C_{in}$$
$$C_{out} = A \cdot B + (A+B) \cdot C_{in}$$

Let's see how this can be used to our advantage in a multiple bit adder. Recall that for any arbitrary adder position, the generate, propagate, and carry out terms are:

$g_i = A_i \cdot B_i$
$p_i = A_i + B_i$
$C_{i+1} = g_i + p_i \cdot C_i$

Note: We'll use the subscript "i" to denote position since we're using "p" for *propagate*.

We can now write expressions for the subsequent carry terms as:

$C_1 = g_0 + p_0 \cdot C_0$

The C_1 expression only depends on the inputs A, B, and C_0.

$C_2 = g_1 + p_1 \cdot C_1$
$C_2 = g_1 + p_1 \cdot (g_0 + p_0 \cdot C_0)$
$C_2 = g_1 + p_1 \cdot g_0 + p_1 \cdot p_0 \cdot C_0$

For C_2, we can plug in the expression for C_1 to create an expression that only depends on A, B, and C_0...

$C_3 = g_2 + p_2 \cdot C_2$
$C_3 = g_2 + p_2 \cdot (g_1 + p_1 \cdot g_0 + p_0 \cdot p_1 \cdot C_0)$
$C_3 = g_2 + p_2 \cdot g_1 + p_2 \cdot p_1 \cdot g_0 + p_2 \cdot p_1 \cdot p_0 \cdot C_0$

and again for C_3...

$C_4 = g_3 + p_3 \cdot C_3$
$C_4 = g_3 + p_3 \cdot (g_2 + p_2 \cdot g_1 + p_2 \cdot p_1 \cdot g_0 + p_2 \cdot p_1 \cdot p_0 \cdot C_0)$
$C_4 = g_3 + p_3 \cdot g_2 + p_3 \cdot p_2 \cdot g_1 + p_3 \cdot p_2 \cdot p_1 \cdot g_0 + p_3 \cdot p_2 \cdot p_1 \cdot p_0 \cdot C_0$

and again for C_4...

All of these expressions only depend on the inputs A, B, and C_0. Also notice that each expression is in a 2-level sum of products form.

Example 12.7
Design of a 4-Bit Carry Look Ahead Adder (CLA) – Algebraic Formation

Example 12.8 shows a timing analysis of the 4-bit carry look ahead adder. Notice that the full adders are modified to add the logic for the generate and propagate bits in addition to removing the unnecessary gates associated with creating the carry out.

Example 12.8
Timing Analysis of a 4-Bit Carry Look Ahead Adder

The 4-bit CLA can produce the sum in four levels of logic as long as fan-in specifications are met. As the CLA width increases, the look ahead circuitry will become fan-in limited and additional stages will be required to address the fan-in. Regardless, the CLA has considerably less delay than a RCA as the width of the adder is increased.

12.1.5 Adders in VHDL

12.1.5.1 Structural Model of a Ripple Carry Adder in VHDL

A structural model of a ripple carry adder is useful to visualize the propagation delay of the circuit in addition to the impact of the carry rippling through the chain. Example 12.9 shows the structural model for a full adder in VHDL consisting of two half adders. The full adder is created by instantiating two versions of the half adder as components. In this example, all gates are modeled with a delay of 1ns.

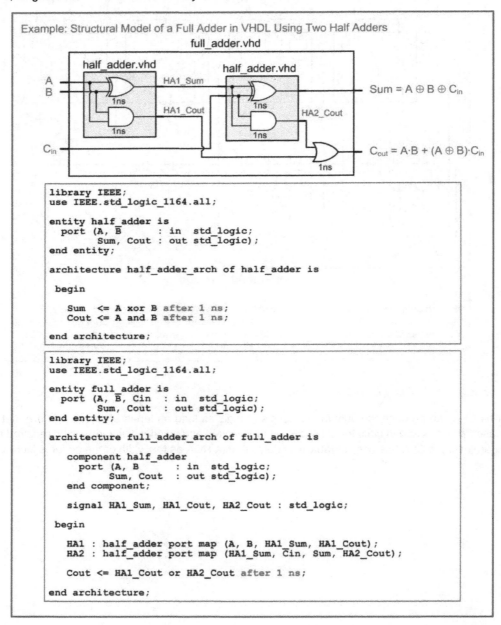

```
Example: Structural Model of a Full Adder in VHDL Using Two Half Adders
                          full_adder.vhd
```

```
library IEEE;
use IEEE.std_logic_1164.all;

entity half_adder is
  port (A, B        : in  std_logic;
        Sum, Cout : out std_logic);
end entity;

architecture half_adder_arch of half_adder is

 begin

   Sum  <= A xor B after 1 ns;
   Cout <= A and B after 1 ns;

end architecture;
```

```
library IEEE;
use IEEE.std_logic_1164.all;

entity full_adder is
  port (A, B, Cin  : in  std_logic;
        Sum, Cout  : out std_logic);
end entity;

architecture full_adder_arch of full_adder is

   component half_adder
     port (A, B        : in  std_logic;
           Sum, Cout  : out std_logic);
   end component;

   signal HA1_Sum, HA1_Cout, HA2_Cout : std_logic;

 begin

   HA1 : half_adder port map (A, B, HA1_Sum, HA1_Cout);
   HA2 : half_adder port map (HA1_Sum, Cin, Sum, HA2_Cout);

   Cout <= HA1_Cout or HA2_Cout after 1 ns;

end architecture;
```

Example 12.9
Structural Model of a Full Adder in VHDL Using Two Half Adders

Example 12.10 shows the structural model of a 4-bit ripple carry adder in VHDL. The RCA is created by instantiating four full adders. Notice that a logic 0 can be directly inserted into the port map of the first full adder to model the behavior of $C_0=0$.

```
Example: Structural Model of a 4-Bit Ripple Carry Adder in VHDL

library IEEE;
use IEEE.std_logic_1164.all;

entity rca_4bit is
  port (A, B  : in  std_logic_vector(3 downto 0);
        Sum   : out std_logic_vector(3 downto 0);
        Cout  : out std_logic);
end entity;

architecture rca_4bit_arch of rca_4bit is

   component full_adder
     port (A, B, Cin  : in  std_logic;
           Sum, Cout  : out std_logic);
   end component;

   signal C1, C2, C3 : std_logic;

 begin

   A0 : full_adder port map (A(0), B(0), '0', Sum(0), C1);
   A1 : full_adder port map (A(1), B(1), C1,  Sum(1), C2);
   A2 : full_adder port map (A(2), B(2), C2,  Sum(2), C3);
   A3 : full_adder port map (A(3), B(3), C3,  Sum(3), Cout);

end architecture;
```

Example 12.10
Structural Model of a 4-bit Ripple Carry Adder in VHDL

When creating arithmetic circuitry, testing under all input conditions is necessary to verify functionality. Testing under each and every input condition can require a large number of input conditions. To test an n-bit adder under each and every numeric input condition will take $(2^n)^2$ test vectors. For our simple 4-bit adder example, this equates to 256 input patterns. The large number of input patterns precludes the use of manual signal assignments in the test bench to stimulate the circuit. One approach to generating the input test patterns is to use nested for loops. Example 12.11 shows a test bench that uses two nested for loops to generate the 256 unique input conditions for the 4-bit ripple carry adder. Note that the loop variables i and j are automatically created when the loops are declared. Since the loop variables are defined as integers, type conversions are required prior to driving the values into the RCA. The simulation waveform illustrates how the ripple carry adder has a noticeable delay before the output sum is produced. During the time the carry is rippling through the adder chain, glitches can appear on each of the sum bits in addition to the carry out signal. The values in this waveform are displayed as unsigned decimal symbols to make the results easier to interpret.

Example: VHDL Test Bench for a 4-Bit Ripple Carry Adder Using Nested For Loops

Nested for loops can be used in order to generate an exhaustive set of test vectors to stimulate the adder.

```
library IEEE;
use IEEE.std_logic_1164.all;
use IEEE.numeric_std.all;

entity rca_4bit_TB is
end entity;

architecture rca_4bit_TB_arch of rca_4bit_TB is

    component rca_4bit
      port (A, B  : in  std_logic_vector(3 downto 0);
            Sum   : out std_logic_vector(3 downto 0);
            Cout  : out std_logic);
    end component;

    signal A_TB, B_TB, Sum_TB  : std_logic_vector(3 downto 0);
    signal Cout_TB             : std_logic;

  begin

    DUT : rca_4bit port map (A_TB, B_TB, Sum_TB, Cout_TB);

    STIM : process
      begin

        for i in 0 to 15 loop
          for j in 0 to 15 loop
            A_TB <= std_logic_vector(to_unsigned(i,4));
            B_TB <= std_logic_vector(to_unsigned(j,4));
            wait for 30 ns;
          end loop;
        end loop;

    end process;

end architecture;
```

The simulation waveform for the ripple carry adder is as follows. The numbers are shown in unsigned decimal format for readability.

Glitches due to ripple delay.

2+12=14, so the adder operates correctly. Notice the effect of the ripple through the circuit. In addition to the correct output being delayed, there are glitches on both the Sum and C_{out} ports.

Example 12.11
VHDL Test Bench for a 4-Bit Ripple Carry Adder Using Nested For Loops

12.1.5.2 Structural Model of a Carry Look Ahead Adder in VHDL

A carry look ahead adder can also be modeled using a combination of concurrent signal assignments with logical operators and modified full adder components. Example 12.12 shows a structural model for a 4-bit CLA in VHDL. In this example, the gate delay is modeled using a constant (tgate) of 1ns. The delay due to multiple levels of logic is entered manually to simplify the model. The two cascaded XOR gates in the modified full adder are modeled using a single signal assignment with 2*tgate of delay.

Example: Structural Model of a 4-Bit Carry Look Ahead Adder in VHDL

```
library IEEE;
use IEEE.std_logic_1164.all;

entity mod_full_adder is
  port (A, B, Cin : in std_logic;
        Sum, p, g : out std_logic);
end entity;

architecture mod_full_adder_arch of mod_full_adder is

   constant tgate : time := 1 ns;

 begin

   Sum   <= (A xor B xor Cin) after 2*tgate;
   p     <= (A or B)          after 1*tgate;
   g     <= (A and B)         after 1*tgate;

end architecture;
```

```
library IEEE;
use IEEE.std_logic_1164.all;

entity cla_4bit is
  port (A, B : in std_logic_vector(3 downto 0);
        Sum  : out std_logic_vector(3 downto 0);
        Cout : out std_logic);
end entity;

architecture cla_4bit_arch of cla_4bit is

   constant tgate : time := 1 ns;

   component mod_full_adder
     port (A, B, Cin  : in  std_logic;
           Sum, p, g : out std_logic);
   end component;

   signal C0, C1, C2, C3 : std_logic;
   signal p, g           : std_logic_vector(3 downto 0);

 begin

   C0   <= '0';
   C1   <= g(0) or (p(0) and C0) after 2*tgate;
   C2   <= g(1) or (p(1) and C1) after 2*tgate;
   C3   <= g(2) or (p(2) and C2) after 2*tgate;
   Cout <= g(3) or (p(3) and C3) after 2*tgate;

   A0 : mod_full_adder port map (A(0), B(0), C0, Sum(0), p(0), g(0));
   A1 : mod_full_adder port map (A(1), B(1), C1, Sum(1), p(1), g(1));
   A2 : mod_full_adder port map (A(2), B(2), C2, Sum(2), p(2), g(2));
   A3 : mod_full_adder port map (A(3), B(3), C3, Sum(3), p(3), g(3));

end architecture;
```

Example 12.12
Structural Model of a 4-Bit Carry Look Ahead Adder in VHDL

Example 12.13 shows the simulation waveform for the 4-bit carry look ahead adder. The outputs still have intermediate transitions while the combinational logic is computing the results; however, the overall delay of the adder is bound to $\leq 4*t_{gate}$.

Example 12.13
4-Bit Carry Look Ahead Adder - Simulation Waveform

12.1.5.3 Behavior Model of an Adder Using UNSIGNED Data Types

VHDL also supports adder models at a higher level of abstraction using the "+" operator. While this operator is supported for the type integer in the std_logic_1164 package, modeling adders using integers can be onerous due to the multiple levels of casting, range checking, and manual handling of carry out. A simpler approach to modeling adder behavior is to use the types unsigned/signed and the "+" operator provided in the numeric_std package. Temporary signals or variables of these types are required to model the adder behavior with the "+" sign. Also, type casting is still required when assigning the values back to the output ports. One advantage of this approach is that range checking is eliminated because rollover is automatically handled with these types.

Example 12.14 shows the behavioral model for a 4-bit adder in VHDL. In this model, a 5-bit unsigned vector is created (Sum_uns). The two inputs, A and B, are concatenated with a leading zero in order to facilitate assigning the sum to this 5-bit vector. The advantage of this approach is that the carry out of the adder is automatically included in the sum as the highest position bit. Since A and B are of type std_logic_vector, they must be converted to unsigned before the addition with the "+" operator can take place. The concatenation, type conversion and addition can all take place in a single assignment.

Example:

```
Sum_uns <= unsigned(('0' & A)) + unsigned(('0' & B));
```

The 5-bit vector Sum_uns now contains the 4-bit sum and carry out. The final step is to assign the separate components of this vector to the output ports of the system. The 4-bit sum portion requires a type conversion back to std_logic_vector before it can be assigned to the output port *Sum*. Since the *Cout* port is a scalar, an unsigned signal can be assigned to it directly without the need for a conversion.

Example:

```
Sum <= std_logic_vector(Sum_uns(3 downto 0));
Cout <= Sum_uns(4);
```

Example: Behavioral Model of a 4-Bit Adder in VHDL

```vhdl
library IEEE;
use IEEE.std_logic_1164.all;
use IEEE.numeric_std.all;

entity adder_4bit is
    port (A, B  : in  std_logic_vector(3 downto 0);
          Sum   : out std_logic_vector(3 downto 0);
          Cout  : out std_logic);
end entity;

architecture adder_4bit_arch of adder_4bit is

    signal Sum_uns : unsigned(4 downto 0);

begin

    Sum_uns <= unsigned(('0' & A)) + unsigned(('0' & B));

    Sum  <= std_logic_vector(Sum_uns(3 downto 0));
    Cout <= Sum_uns(4);

end architecture;
```

A 5-bit unsigned signal is defined to hold the sum and carry.

Adding leading 0's to the inputs enables an assignment to "Sum_uns".

Converting the inputs to unsigned allows the "+" operator to be used.

Finally, the 5-bit vector is broken into its individual Sum and Cout parts.

Since no delay was included in the behavioral model, the outputs are produced instantaneously.

Example 12.14
Behavioral Model of a 4-bit Adder in VHDL

CONCEPT CHECK

CC12.1   Does a binary adder behave differently when its operating on unsigned vs. two's complement numbers? Why or why not?

   A) Yes. The adder needs to keep track of the sign bit, thus extra circuitry is needed.

   B) No. The binary addition is identical. It is up to the designer to handle how the two's complement codes are interpreted and whether two's complement overflow occurred using a separate system.

12.2 Subtraction

Binary subtraction can be accomplished by building a dedicated circuit using a similar design approach as just described for adders. A more effective approach is to take advantage of two's complement representation in order to re-use existing adder circuitry. Recall that taking the two's complement of a number will produce an equivalent magnitude number, but with the opposite sign (i.e., positive to negative or negative to positive). This means that all that is required to create a subtractor from an adder is to first take the two's complement of the subtrahend input. Since the steps to take the two's complement of a number involve complementing each of the bits in the number and then adding 1, the logic required is relatively simple. Example 12.15 shows a 4-bit subtractor using full adders. The subtrahend B is inverted prior to entering the full adders. Also, the carry in bit C_0 is set to 1. This handles the "adding 1" step of the two's complement. All of the carries in the circuit are now treated as *borrows* and the sum is now treated as the *difference*.

Example: Design of a 4-Bit Subtractor Using Full Adders

A subtractor can be made from an adder by taking advantage of two's complement representation. When we wish to perform a subtraction we simply take the two's complement of the subtrahend (e.g., complement all bits and add 1) and then add the two numbers.

Example 12.15
Design of a 4-Bit Subtractor Using Full Adders

    A programmable adder/subtractor can be created with the use of a programmable inverter and a control signal. The control signal will selectively invert B and also change the C_0 bit between a 0 (for adding) and a 1 (for subtracting). Example 12.16 shows how an XOR gate can be used to create a programmable inverter for use in a programmable adder/subtractor circuit.

Example: Creating a Programmable Inverter Using an XOR Gate

An XOR gate can be used as a programmable inverter. Notice that when input A=0, the output F is equal to B. Also notice that when input A=1, the output is the inversion of B. This means we can selectively pass or invert the input B using A as the control signal.

When A=0, F=B. This is simply a buffer.
When A=1, F=B'. This is an inverter.

A	B	F
0	0	0
0	1	1
1	0	1
1	1	0

Example 12.16
Creating a Programmable Inverter Using an XOR Gate

    We can now define a control signal called (ADDn/SUB) that will control whether the circuit performs addition or subtraction. Example 12.17 shows the architecture of a 4-bit programmable adder/subtractor. It should be noted that this programmability adds another level of logic to the circuit, thus increasing its delay. The programmable architecture in Example 12.17 is shown for a ripple carry adder; however, this approach works equally well for a carry look ahead adder architecture.

Example: Design of a 4-Bit Programmable Adder/Subtractor

The control signal "ADDn/SUB" is used to select whether the circuit performs addition (ADDn/SUB=0) or subtraction (ADDn/SUB=1). When in subtraction mode, the XOR gates invert the subtrahend B and add 1 to the first adder stage. These steps take the two's complement of B and allow an add operation to conduct subtraction.

Example 12.17
Design of a 4-Bit Programmable Adder/Subtractor

When using two's complement representation in arithmetic, care must be taken to monitor for two's complement overflow. Recall that when using two's complement representation, the number of bits of the numbers is fixed (e.g., 4-bits) and if a carry/borrow out is generated, it is ignored. This means that the Cout bit does not indicate whether two's complement overflow occurred. Instead, we must construct additional circuitry to monitor the arithmetic operations for overflow. Recall from Chapter 2 that two's complement overflow occurs in any of these situations:

- The sum of like signs results in an answer with opposite sign
  (i.e., Positive + Positive = Negative or Negative + Negative = Positive).
- The subtraction of a positive number from a negative number results in a positive number
  (i.e., Negative – Positive = Positive).
- The subtraction of a negative number from a positive number results in a negative number
  (i.e., Positive – Negative = Negative).

The construction of circuitry for these conditions is straightforward since the sign bit of all numbers involved in the operation indicates whether the number is positive or negative. The sign bits of the input arguments and the output are fed into combinational logic circuitry that will assert for any of the above conditions. These signals are then logically combined to create two's complement overflow signal.

CONCEPT CHECK

CC12.2   What modifications can be made to the programmable adder/subtractor architecture so that it can be used to take the 2's complement of a number?

   A)   Remove the input A.

   B)   Add an additional control signals that will ignore A and just perform a complement on B and then add 1.

   C)   Add an additional 1 to the original number using an OR gate on Cin.

   D)   Set A to 0, put the number to be manipulated on B, and put the system into subtraction mode. The system will then complement the bits on B and then add 1, thus performing two's complement negation.

12.3 Multiplication

12.3.1 Unsigned Multiplication

Binary multiplication is performed in a similar manner to performing decimal multiplication by hand. Recall the process for long multiplication. First, the two numbers are placed vertically over one another with their least significant digits aligned. The upper number is called the *multiplicand* and the lower number is called the *multiplier*. Next, we multiply each individual digit within multiplier with the entire multiplicand, starting with the least position. The result of this interim multiplication is called the *partial product*. The partial product is recorded with its least significant digit aligned with the corresponding position of the multiplier digit. Finally, all partial products are summed to create the final product of the multiplication. This process is often called the *shift and add* approach. Example 12.18 shows the process for performing long multiplication on decimal numbers highlighting the individual steps.

Example 12.18
Performing Long Multiplication on Decimal Numbers

Binary multiplication follows this same process. Example 12.19 shows the process for performing long multiplication on binary numbers. Note that the inputs represent the largest unsigned numbers possible using 4-bits, thus producing the largest possible product. The largest product will require 8-bits to be represented. This means that for any multiplication of n-bit inputs, the product will require 2·n bits for the result.

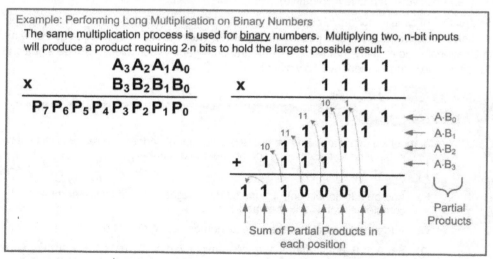

Example 12.19
Performing Long Multiplication on Binary Numbers

The first step in designing a binary multiplier is to create circuitry that can compute the product on individual bits. Example 12.20 shows the design of a single-bit multiplier.

Example 12.20
Design of a Single-Bit Multiplier

We can create all of the partial products in one level of logic by placing an AND gate between each bit pairing in the two input numbers. This will require n^2 AND gates. The next step involves creating adders that can perform the sum of the columns of bits within the partial products. This step is not as straightforward. Notice that in our 4-bit example in Example 12.19 that the number of input bits in the column addition can reach up to 6 (in positions 3). It would be desirable to re-use the full adders previously created; however, the existing full adders could only accommodate 3 inputs (A, B, C_{in}). We can take advantage of the associative property of addition to form the final sum incrementally. Example 12.21 shows the architecture of this multiplier. This approach implements a shift and add process to compute the product and is known as a *combinational multiplier* because it is implemented using only combinational logic. Note that this multiplier only handles unsigned numbers.

Example 12.21
Design of a 4-Bit Unsigned Multiplier

This multiplier can have a significant delay, which is caused by the cascaded full adders. Example 12.22 shows the timing analysis of the combinational multiplier highlighting the worst case path through the circuit.

Example 12.22
Timing Analysis of a 4-Bit Unsigned Multiplier

12.3.2 A Simple Circuit to Multiply by Powers of Two

In digital systems, a common operation is to multiply numbers by powers of two. For unsigned numbers, multiplying by two can be accomplished by performing a logical shift left. In this operation, all bits are moved to the next higher position (i.e., left) by one position and filling the 0th position with a zero. This has the effect of doubling the value of the number. This can be repeated to achieve higher powers of two. This process works as long as the resulting product fits within the number of bits available. Example 12.23 shows this procedure.

Example 12.23
Multiplying an Unsigned Binary Numbers by Two Using a Logical Shift Left

12.3.3 Signed Multiplication

When performing multiplication on signed numbers, it is desirable to re-use the unsigned multiplier in Example 12.21. Let's examine if this is possible. Recall in decimal multiplication that the inputs are multiplied together independent of their sign. The sign of the product is handled separately following these rules:

- A <u>positive</u> number times a <u>positive</u> number produces a <u>positive</u> number.
- A <u>negative</u> number times a <u>negative</u> number produces a <u>positive</u> number.
- A <u>positive</u> number times a <u>negative</u> number produces a <u>negative</u> number.

This process does not work properly in binary due to the way that negative numbers are represented with two's complement. Example 12.24 illustrates how an unsigned multiplier incorrectly handles signed numbers.

Example 12.24
Illustrating How an Unsigned Multiplier Incorrectly Handles Signed Numbers

Instead of building a dedicated multiplier for signed numbers, we can add functionality to the unsigned multiplier previously presented to handle negative numbers. The process involves first identifying any negative numbers. If a negative number is present, the two's complement is taken on it to produce its equivalent magnitude, positive representation. The multiplication is then performed on the positive values. The final step is to apply the correct sign to the product. If the product should be negative due to one of the inputs being negative, the sign is applied by taking the two's complement on the final result. This creates a number that is now in $2 \cdot n$ two's complement format. Example 12.25 shows an illustration of the process to correctly handle signed numbers using an unsigned multiplier.

Example: Process to Correctly Handle Signed Numbers Using an Unsigned Multiplier

The process for handling negative numbers in binary multiplication involves taking the two's complement of any negative numbers to get their positive magnitude equivalents. The unsigned multiplier is then used to create a positive product. If the signs of the inputs should produce a negative product, then the last step is to take the two's complement of the product. Let's do an example of this process on $(-7_{10}) \times (+7_{10}) = (-49_{10})$.

Step 1 – Take the two's complement of any negative inputs.

We notice this number is negative (-7_{10}) so we take its two's complement.

$$\begin{array}{r} 1\ 0\ 0\ 1 \\ \times\ 0\ 1\ 1\ 1 \\ \hline \end{array} \longrightarrow \begin{array}{r} 0\ 1\ 1\ 1 \leftarrow +7_{10} \\ \times\ 0\ 1\ 1\ 1 \\ \hline \end{array}$$

Step 2 – Perform the multiplication.

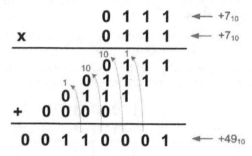

$$\begin{array}{r} 0\ 1\ 1\ 1 \leftarrow +7_{10} \\ \times\quad 0\ 1\ 1\ 1 \leftarrow +7_{10} \\ \hline \end{array}$$

$$0\ 0\ 1\ 1\ 0\ 0\ 0\ 1 \leftarrow +49_{10}$$

Step 3 – Apply the sign to the product (if applicable).

Since we had a (neg)x(pos), the product should be a negative, so we need to apply the sign by taking the two's complement.

$$0\ 0\ 1\ 1\ 0\ 0\ 0\ 1 \leftarrow +49_{10}$$

↓ Two's complement

$$1\ 1\ 0\ 0\ 1\ 1\ 1\ 1 \leftarrow -49_{10}$$

CORRECT!

Notice the result is now in 8-bit two's complement representation.

Example 12.25
Process to Correctly Handle Signed Numbers Using an Unsigned Multiplier

CONCEPT CHECK

CC12.3   Will the AND gates used to compute the partial products in a binary multiplier ever experience an issue with fan-in as the size of the multiplier increases?

   A)   Yes. When the number of bits of the multiplier arguments exceed the fan-in specification of the AND gates used for the partial products, a fan-in issue has occurred.

   B)   No. The number of inputs of the AND gates performing the partial products will always be two, regardless of the size of the input arguments to the multiplier.

12.4 Division

12.4.1 Unsigned Division

There are a variety of methods to perform division, each with trade-offs between area, delay, and accuracy. To understand the general approach to building a divider circuit, let's focus on how a simple iterative divider can be built. Basic division yields a *quotient* and a *remainder*. The process begins by checking whether the *divisor* goes into the highest position digit in the *dividend*. The number of times this dividend digit can be divided is recorded as the highest position value of the quotient. Note that when performing division by hand we typically skip over the condition when the result of these initial operations are zero, but when breaking down the process into steps that can be built with logic circuits, each step needs to be highlighted. The first quotient digit is then multiplied with the divisor and recorded below the original dividend. The next lower position digit of the dividend is brought down and joined with the product from the prior multiplication. This forms a new number to be divided by the divisor to create the next quotient value. This process is repeated until each of the quotient digits have been created. Any value that remains after the last subtraction is recorded as the remainder. Example 12.26 shows the long division process on decimal numbers highlight each incremental step.

Example 12.26
Performing Long Division on Decimal Numbers

Long division in binary follows this same process. Example 12.27 shows the long division process on two 4-bit, unsigned numbers. This division results in a 4-bit quotient and a 4-bit remainder.

Example: Performing Long Division on Binary Numbers

Let's highlight the steps when performing binary division. In the following example, two 4-bit numbers are divided. The dividend is 1111_2 (15_{10}) and the divisor is 0111_2 (7_{10}). The division will yield a 4-bit quotient of 0010_2 (2_{10}) and a 4-bit remainder of 0001_2 (1_{10}).

- The highest digit of the dividend (1, or "0001") is divided to create Q_3.
- Q_3 is then multiplied with the divisor and recorded.
- A subtraction is performed and the next bit of the dividend is brought down to form the next number to be divided ("11", or "0011") to create Q_2.
- This process is repeated to form the next number to be dividend ("111", or "0111") to create Q_1.
- This process is repeated to form the next number to be dividend ("0001") to create Q_0.
- After Q_0 has been created, anything left from the final subtraction is recorded as the "remainder".

Example 12.27
Performing Long Multiplication on Binary Numbers

When building a divider circuit using combinational logic, we can accomplish the computation using a series of iterative subtractors. Performing division is equivalent to subtracting the divisor from the interim dividend. If the subtraction is positive, then the divisor went into the dividend and the quotient is a 1. If the subtraction yields a negative number, then the divisor <u>did not</u> go into the interim dividend and the quotient is 0. We can use the borrow out of a subtraction chain to provide the quotient. This has the advantage that the difference has already been calculated for the next subtraction. A multiplexer is used to select whether the difference is used in the next subtraction (Q=0), or if the interim divisor is simply brought down (Q=1). This inherently provides the functionality of the multiplication step in long division. Example 12.28 shows the architecture of a 4-bit, unsigned divider based on the iterative subtraction approach. Notice that when the borrow out of the 4-bit subtractor chain is a 0, it indicates that the subtraction yielded a positive number. This means that the divisor went into the interim dividend once. In this case, the quotient for this position is a 1. An inverter is required to produce the correct polarity of the quotient. The borrow out is also fed into the multiplexer stage as the select line to pass the difference to the next stage of subtractors. If the borrow out of the 4-bit subtractor chain is a 1, it indicates that the subtraction yielded a negative number. In this case, the quotient is a 0. This also means that the difference calculated is garbage and should not be used. The multiplexer stage instead selects the interim dividend as the input to the next stage of subtractors.

Example: Design of a 4-Bit Unsigned Divider Using a Series of Iterative Subtractors

The following architecture shows a combinational divider that uses a series of iterative subtractions to determine the quotient and remainder.

$$B_3B_2B_1B_0 \overline{)\,\begin{array}{c} Q_3Q_2Q_1Q_0\ ,\ R_3R_2R_1R_0 \\ A_3A_2A_1A_0 \end{array}}$$

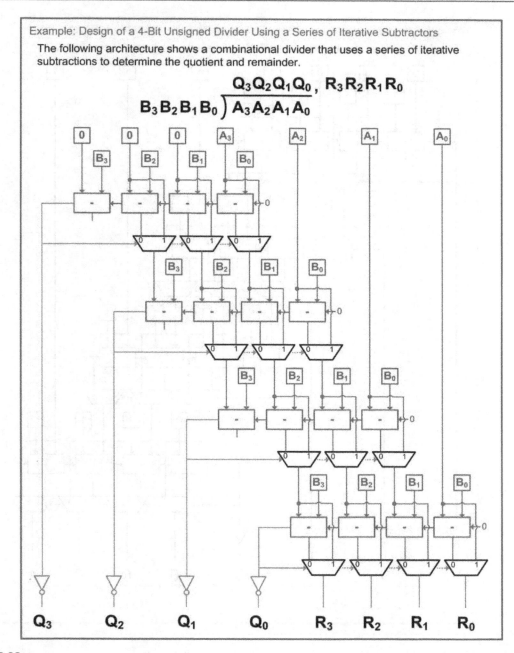

Example 12.28
Design of a 4-Bit Unsigned Divider Using a Series of Iterative Subtractors

To illustrate how this architecture works, Example 12.29 walks through each step in the process where 1111_2 (15_{10}) is divided by 0111_2 (7_{10}). In this example, the calculations propagate through the logic stages from top to bottom in the diagram.

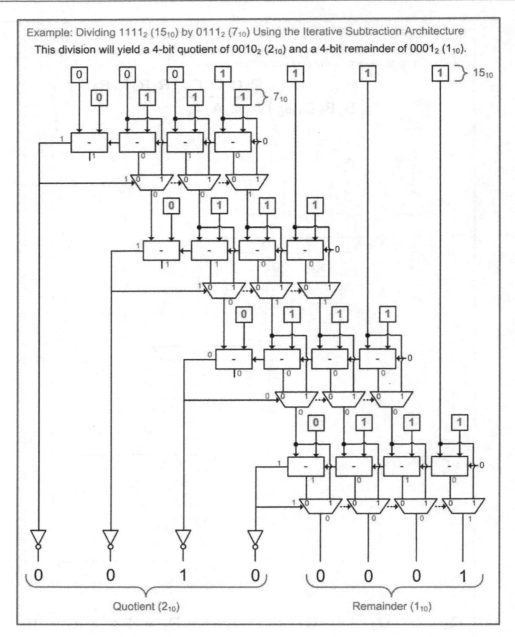

Example: Dividing 1111_2 (15_{10}) by 0111_2 (7_{10}) Using the Iterative Subtraction Architecture

This division will yield a 4-bit quotient of 0010_2 (2_{10}) and a 4-bit remainder of 0001_2 (1_{10}).

Quotient (2_{10}) Remainder (1_{10})

Example 12.29
Dividing 1111_2 (15_{10}) by 0111_2 (7_{10}) Using the Iterative Subtraction Architecture

12.4.2 A Simple Circuit to Divide by Powers of Two

For unsigned numbers, dividing by two can be accomplished by performing a logical shift right. In this operation, all bits are moved to the next lower position (i.e., right) by one position and then filling the highest position with a zero. This has the effect of halving the value of the number. This can be repeated to achieve higher powers of two. This process works until no more ones exist in the number and the result is simply all zero's. Example 12.30 shows this process.

Example 12.30
Dividing an Unsigned Binary Numbers by Two Using a Logical Shift Right

12.4.3 Signed Division

When performing division on signed numbers, a similar strategy as in signed multiplication is used. The process involves first identifying any negative numbers. If a negative number is present, the two's complement is taken on it to produce its equivalent magnitude, positive representation. The division is then performed on the positive values. The final step is to apply the correct sign to the divisor and quotient. This is accomplished by taking the two's complement if a negative number is required. The rules governing the polarities of the quotient and remainders are:

- The quotient will be negative if the input signs are difference (i.e., pos/neg or neg/pos).
- The remainder has the same sign as the dividend.

CONCEPT CHECK

CC12.4 Could a shift register help reduce the complexity of a combinational divider circuit? How?

A) Yes. Instead of having redundant circuits holding the different shifted versions of the divisor, a shift register could be used to hold and shift the divisor after each subtraction.

B) No. A state machine would then be needed to control the divisor shifting, which would make the system even more complex.

Summary

❖ Binary arithmetic is accomplished using combinational logic circuitry. These circuits tend to be the largest circuits in a system and have the longest delay. Arithmetic circuits are often broken up into interim calculations in order to reduce the overall delay of the computation.

❖ A *ripple carry adder* performs addition by reusing lower level components that each perform a small part of the computation. A full adder is made from two half adders and a ripple carry adder is made from a chain of full adders. This approach simplifies the design of the adder but leads to long delay times since the carry from each sum must ripple to the next higher position's addition before it can complete.

❖ A *carry look ahead adder* attempts to eliminate the linear dependence of delay on the number of bits

that exists in a ripple carry adder. The carry look ahead adder contains dedicated circuitry that calculates the carry bits for each position of the addition. This leads to a more constant delay as the width of the adder increases.

❖ A binary multiplier can be created in a similar manner to the way multiplication is accomplished by hand using the *shift and add* approach. The partial products of the multiplication can be performed using 2-input AND gates. The sum of the partial products can have more inputs than the typical ripple carry adder can accommodate. To handle this, the additions are performed two bits at a time using a series of adders.

❖ Division can be accomplished using an iterative subtractor architecture.

Exercise Problems

Section 12.1 - Addition

12.1.1 Give the total delay of the full adder shown in Figure 12.2 if all gates have a delay of 1ns.

Figure 12.2

12.1.2 Give the total delay of the full adder shown in Figure 12.2 if the XOR gates have delays of 5ns while the AND and OR gates have delays of 1ns.

12.1.3 Give the total delay of the 4-bit ripple carry adder shown in Figure 12.3 if all gates have a delay of 2ns.

Figure 12.3

12.1.4 Give the total delay of the 4-bit ripple carry adder shown in Figure 12.3 if the XOR gates have delays of 10ns while the AND and OR gates have delays of 2ns.

12.1.5 Design a VHDL model for an 8-bit Ripple Carry Adder (RCA) using a structural design approach. This involves creating a half adder (half_adder.vhd), full adder (full_adder.vhd), and then finally a top level adder (rca.vhd) by instantiating eight full adder components. Model the ripple delay by inserting 1ns of gate delay for the XOR, AND, and OR operators using a delayed signal assignment. The general topology and entity definition for the design are shown in Figure 12.4. Create a test bench to exhaustively verify this design under all input conditions. The test bench should drive in different values every 30ns in order to give sufficient time for the signals to ripple through the adder.

Figure 12.4

12.1.6 Give the total delay of the 4-bit carry look ahead adder shown in Figure 12.5 if all gates have a delay of 2ns.

Figure 12.5

12.1.7 Give the total delay of the 4-bit carry look ahead adder shown in Figure 12.5 if the XOR gates have delays of 10ns while the AND and OR gates have delays of 2ns.

12.1.8 Design a VHDL model for an 8-bit Carry Look Ahead Adder (cla.vhd). The model should instantiate eight modified full adders (mod_full_adder.vhd). The carry look ahead logic should be implemented using concurrent signal assignments with logical operators. Model each level of gate delay as 1ns using delayed signal assignments. The general topology and entity definition for the design are shown in Figure 12.6. Create a test bench to exhaustively verify this design under all input conditions. The test bench should drive in different values every 30ns in order to give sufficient time for the signals to propagate through the adder.

Figure 12.6

Section 12.2 - Subtraction

12.2.1 How is the programmable adder/subtractor architecture shown in Figure 12.7 analogous to 2's complement arithmetic?

Figure 12.7

12.2.2 Will the programmable adder/subtractor architecture shown in Figure 12.7 work for negative numbers encoded using signed magnitude or 1's complement?

12.2.3 When calculating the delay of the programmable adder/subtractor architecture shown in Figure 12.7 does the delay of the XOR gate that acts as the programmable inverter need to be considered?

12.2.4 Design a VHDL model for an 8-bit, programmable adder/subtractor. The design will have an input called "ADDn_SUB" that will control whether the system behaves as an adder (0) or as a subtractor (1). The design should operate on two's complement signed numbers. The result of the operation(s) will appear on the port called "Sum_Diff". The model should assert the output "Cout" when an addition creates a carry or when a subtraction creates a borrow. The circuit will also assert the output Vout when either operation results in two's complement overflow. The entity definition and block diagram for the system is shown in Figure 12.8. Create a test bench to exhaustively verify this design under all input conditions.

```
entity add_n_sub_8bit is
    port (A, B     : in  std_logic_vector(7 downto 0);
          ADDn_SUB : in  std_logic;
          Sum_Diff : out std_logic_vector(7 downto 0);
          Cout_Bout : out std_logic;
          Vout     : out std_logic);
end entity;
```

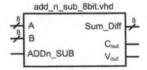

add_n_sub_8bit.vhd

Figure 12.8

Section 12.3 - Multiplication

12.3.1 Give the total delay of the 4-bit unsigned multiplier shown in Figure 12.9 if all gates have a delay of 1ns. The addition is performed using a ripple carry adder.

Figure 12.9

12.3.2 For the 4-bit unsigned multiplier shown in Figure 12.9, how many levels of logic does it take to compute all of the partial products?

12.3.3 For the 4-bit unsigned multiplier shown in Figure 12.9, how many AND gates are needed to compute the partial products?

12.3.4 For the 4-bit unsigned multiplier shown in Figure 12.9, how many total AND gates are used if the additions are implemented using full adders made of half adders?

12.3.5 Based on the architecture of a unsigned multiplier in Figure 12.9, how many AND gates are needed to compute the partial products if the inputs are increased to 8-bits?

12.3.6 For an 8-bit multiplier, how many bits are needed to represent the product?

12.3.7 For an 8-bit *unsigned* multiplier, what is the <u>largest</u> value that the product can ever take on? Give your answer in decimal.

12.3.8 For an 8-bit *signed* multiplier, what is the <u>largest</u> value that the product can ever take on? Give your answer in decimal.

12.3.9 For an 8-bit *signed* multiplier, what is the <u>smallest</u> value that the product can ever take on? Give your answer in decimal.

12.3.10 What is the maximum number of times that a 4-bit multiplicand can be multiplied by two using the *logical shift left* approach before the product is too large to be represented by an 8-bit-product? Hint: The maximum number of times this operation can be performed corresponds to when the multiplicand starts at its lowest possible non-zero value (i.e., 1).

12.3.11 Design a VHDL model for an <u>8-bit unsigned multiplier</u> using the architecture shown in Figure 12.9. Use a structural design approach that consists of full adders in a ripple carry configuration to accomplish the sum of partial products. Model each product term with a logical AND operator. Each logical operation in the design should contain 1ns of delay in order to visualize the delay through the multiplier. Create a test bench to exhaustively verify this design under all input conditions. The entity definition for this multiplier is given in Figure 12.9.

```
entity mul_unsigned_8bit is
  port (A, B : in  std_logic_vector(7 downto 0);
        P     : out std_logic_vector(15 downto 0));
end entity;
```

Figure 12.10

12.3.12 Design a VHDL model for an 8-bit signed multiplier. The multiplier should use the unsigned architecture shown in Figure 12.9 that feeds a second system (or process) that determines the correct sign of the output based on the signs of the inputs. If necessary, the second system will apply a sign to the product by performing two's complement negation. Create a test bench to exhaustively verify the design under all input conditions. The entity definition for this multiplier is given in Figure 12.11.

```
entity mul_signed_8bit is
  port (A, B : in  std_logic_vector(7 downto 0);
        P     : out std_logic_vector(15 downto 0));
end entity;
```

Figure 12.11

Section 12.4 - Division

12.4.1 For a 4-bit divider, how many bits are needed for the quotient?

12.4.2 For a 4-bit divider, how many bits are needed for the remainder?

12.4.3 Explain the basic concept of the iterative-subtractor approach to division.

12.4.4 For the 4-bit divider shown in Example 12.28, estimate the total delay assuming all gates have a delay of 1ns.

12.4.5 Design a VHDL model for an 8-bit unsigned divider using the architecture from Example 12.28. Use full adders configured in subtraction mode to perform the iterative subtractions. Each logical operation in the design should contain 1ns of delay in order to visualize the delay through the multiplier. Create a test bench to exhaustively verify your design under all input conditions.

Chapter 13: Computer System Design

One of the most common digital systems in use today is the computer. A computer accomplishes tasks through an architecture that uses both *hardware* and *software*. The hardware in a computer consists of many of the elements that we have covered so far. These include registers, arithmetic and logic circuits, finite state machines, and memory. What makes a computer so useful is that the hardware is designed to accomplish a predetermined set of **instructions**. These instructions are relatively simple, such as moving data between memory and a register or performing arithmetic on two numbers. The instructions are comprised of binary codes that are stored in a memory device and represent the sequence of operations that the hardware will perform to accomplish a task. This sequence of instructions is called a computer **program**. What makes this architecture so useful is that the preexisting hardware can be *programmed* to perform an almost unlimited number of tasks by simply defining the sequence of instructions to be executed. The process of designing the sequence of instructions, or program, is called *software development* or *software engineering*.

The idea of a general purpose computing machine dates back to the 19th century. The first computing machines were implemented with mechanical systems and were typically analog in nature. As technology advanced, computer hardware evolved from electromechanical switches to vacuum tubes and ultimately to integrated circuits. These newer technologies enabled switching circuits and provided the capability to build binary computers. Today's computers are built exclusively with semiconductor materials and integrated circuit technology. The term *microcomputer* is used to describe a computer that has its processing hardware implemented with integrated circuitry. Nearly all modern computers are binary. Binary computers are designed to operate on a fixed set of bits. For example, an 8-bit computer would perform operations on 8-bits at a time. This means it moves data between registers and memory and performs arithmetic and logic operations in groups of 8-bits.

This chapter will cover the basics of a simple computer system and present the design of an 8-bit system to illustrate the details of instruction execution.

Learning Outcomes – After completing this chapter, you will be able to:

13.1   Describe the role of the main hardware components in a computer system.
13.2   Describe the role of the main software elements in a computer system.
13.3   Describe the three main classes of instructions in a computer system.
13.4   Describe the architecture of a stored program computer.
13.5   Design a VHDL model of a stored program computer.

13.1 Computer Hardware

Computer hardware refers to all of the physical components within the system. This hardware includes all circuit components in a computer such as the memory devices, registers, and finite state machines. Figure 13.1 shows a block diagram of the basic hardware components in a computer.

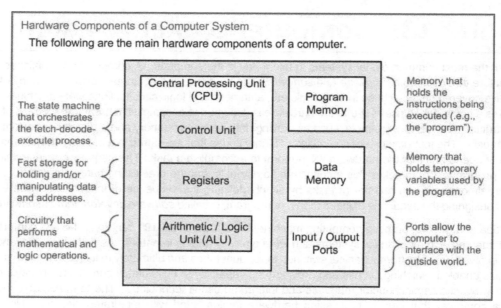

Figure 13.1
Hardware Components of a Computer System

13.1.1 Program Memory

The instructions that are executed by a computer are held in *program memory*. Program memory is treated as read only memory during execution in order to prevent the instructions from being overwritten by the computer. Some computer systems will implement the program memory on a true ROM device (MROM or PROM), while others will use a EEPROM that can be read from during normal operation but can only be written to using a dedicated write procedure. Programs are typically held in non-volatile memory so that the computer system does not lose its program when power is removed. Modern computers will often copy a program from non-volatile memory (e.g., a hard disk drive) to volatile memory after startup in order to speed up instruction execution. In this case, care must be taken that the program does not overwrite itself.

13.1.2 Data Memory

Computers also require *data memory*, which can be written to and read from during normal operation. This memory is used to hold temporary variables that are created by the software program. This memory expands the capability of the computer system by allowing large amounts of information to be created and stored by the program. Additionally, computations can be performed that are larger than the width of the computer system by holding interim portions of the calculation (e.g., performing a 128-bit addition on a 32-bit computer). Data memory is implemented with R/W memory, most often SRAM or DRAM.

13.1.3 Input / Output Ports

The term *port* is used to describe the mechanism to get information from the output world into or out of the computer. Ports can be input, output, or bidirectional. I/O ports can be designed to pass information in a serial or parallel format.

13.1.4 Central Processing Unit

The *central processing unit* (CPU) is considered the *brains* of the computer. The CPU handles reading instructions from memory, decoding them to understand which instruction is being performed, and executing the necessary steps to complete the instruction. The CPU also contains a set of registers that are used for general purpose data storage, operational information, and system status. Finally, the CPU contains circuitry to perform arithmetic and logic operations on data.

13.1.4.1 Control Unit

The *control unit* is a finite state machine that controls the operation of the computer. This FSM has states that perform fetching the instruction (i.e., reading it from program memory), decoding the instruction, and executing the appropriate steps to accomplish the instruction. This process is known as *fetch, decode, and execute* and is repeated each time an instruction is performed by the CPU. As the control unit state machine traverses through its states, it asserts control signals that move and manipulate data in order to achieve the desired functionality of the instruction.

13.1.4.2 Data Path - Registers

The CPU groups its registers and ALU into a subsystem called the *data path*. The data path refers to the fast storage and data manipulations within the CPU. All of these operations are initiated and managed by the control unit state machine. The CPU contains a variety of registers that are necessary to execute instructions and hold status information about the system. Basic computers have the following registers in their CPU:

- **Instruction Register (IR)** – The instruction register holds the current binary code of the instruction being executed. This code is read from program memory as the first part of instruction execution. The IR is used by the control unit to decide which states in its FSM to traverse in order to execute the instruction.

- **Memory Address Register (MAR)** – The memory address register is used to hold the current address being used to access memory. The MAR can be loaded with addresses in order to fetch instructions from program memory or with addresses to access data memory and/or I/O ports.

- **Program Counter (PC)** – The program counter holds the address of the current instruction being executed in program memory. The program counter will increment sequentially through the program memory reading instructions until a dedicated instruction is used to set it to a new location.

- **General Purpose Registers** – These registers are available for temporary storage by the program. Instructions exist to move information from memory into these registers and to move information from these registers into memory. Instructions also exist to perform arithmetic and logic operations on the information held in these registers.

- **Condition Code Register (CCR)** – The condition code register holds status flags that provide information about the arithmetic and logic operations performed in the CPU. The most common flags are *negative* (N), zero (Z), two's complement overflow (V), and carry (C). This register can also contain flags that indicate the status of the computer, such as if an interrupt has occurred or if the computer has been put into a low-power mode.

13.1.4.3 Data Path - Arithmetic Logic Unit (ALU)

The *arithmetic logic unit* is the system that performs all mathematical (i.e., addition, subtraction, multiplication, and division) and logic operations (i.e., and, or, not, shifts, etc.). This system operates on data being held in CPU registers. The ALU has a unique symbol associated with it to distinguish it from other functional units in the CPU.

Figure 13.2 shows the typical organization of a CPU. The registers and ALU are grouped into the data path. In this example, the computer system has two general purpose registers called A and B. This CPU organization will be used throughout this chapter to illustrate the detailed execution of instructions.

Typical CPU Organization

A CPU is functionally organized into a control unit and a data path. The control unit contains the FSM to orchestrate the fetch-decode-execute process. The registers and ALU are grouped into a unit called the data path. The control unit sends control signals to the data path to move and manipulate data. The control unit uses status signals from the data path to decide which states to traverse in its FSM.

Figure 13.2
Typical CPU Organization

13.1.5 A Memory Mapped System

A common way to simplify moving data in or out of the CPU is to assign a unique address to all hardware components in the memory system. Each input/output port and each location in both program and data memory are assigned a unique address. This allows the CPU to access everything in the memory system with a dedicated address. This reduces the number of lines that must pass into the CPU. A *bus system* facilitates transferring information within the computer system. An address bus is driven by the CPU to identify which location in the memory system is being accessed. A data bus is used to transfer information to/from the CPU and the memory system. Finally, a control bus is used to provide other required information about the transactions such as *read* or *write* lines. Figure 13.3 shows the computer hardware in a memory mapped architecture.

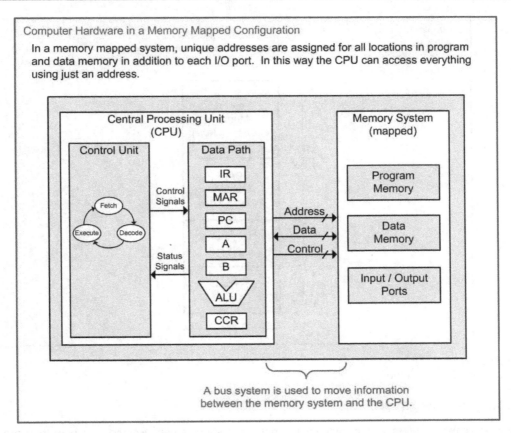

Figure 13.3
Computer Hardware in a Memory Mapped Configuration

To help visualize how the memory addresses are assigned, a *memory map* is used. This is a graphical depiction of the memory system. In the memory map, the ranges of addresses are provided for each of the main subsections of memory. This gives the programmer a quick overview of the available resources in the computer system. Example 13.1 shows a representative memory map for a computer system with an address bus with a width of 8-bits. This address bus can provide 256 unique locations. For this example, the memory system is also 8-bits wide, thus the entire memory system is 256x8 in size. In this example 128 bytes are allocated for program memory; 96 bytes are allocated for data memory; 16 bytes are allocated for output ports; and 16 bytes are allocated for input ports.

CONCEPT CHECK

CC13.1   Is the hardware of a computer programmed in a similar way to a programmable logic device?

A) Yes. The control unit is reconfigured to produce the correct logic for each unique instruction just like a logic element in an FPGA is reconfigured to produce the desired logic expression.

B) No. The instruction code from program memory simply tells the state machine in the control unit which path to traverse in order to accomplish the desired task.

Example 13.1
Memory Map for a 256x8 Memory System

13.2 Computer Software

Computer software refers to the instructions that the computer can execute and how they are designed to accomplish various tasks. The specific group of instructions that a computer can execute is known as its **instruction set**. The instruction set of a computer needs to be defined first before the computer hardware can be implemented. Some computer systems have a very small number of instructions in order to reduce the physical size of the circuitry needed in the CPU. This allows the CPU to execute the instructions very quickly, but requires a large number of operations to accomplish a given task. This architectural approach is called a **reduced instruction set computer** (RISC). The alternative to this approach is to make an instruction set with a large number of dedicated instructions that can accomplish a given task in fewer CPU operations. The drawback of this approach is that the physical size of the CPU must be larger in order to accommodate the various instructions. This architectural approach is called a **complex instruction set computer** (CISC).

13.2.1 Opcodes and Operands

A computer instruction consists of two fields, an *opcode* and an *operand*. The opcode is a unique binary code given to each instruction in the set. The CPU decodes the opcode in order to know which instruction is being executed and then takes the appropriate steps to complete the instruction. Each opcode is assigned a **mnemonic**, which is a descriptive name for the opcode that can be used when discussing the instruction functionally. An operand is additional information for the instruction that may be required. An instruction may have any number of operands including zero. Figure 13.4 shows an example of how the instruction opcodes and operands are placed into program memory.

Anatomy of a Computer Instruction

An instruction consists of a unique opcode and potentially one or more operands.

Opcode, Operand

Each instruction in the set is given a unique code.

An operand (optional) provides additional information needed for the instruction.

The following is an example of how instructions may reside in program memory. Each opcode is decoded to know which instruction is to be executed. The opcode additionally tells the CPU whether or not there are operands required in the instruction.

The program counter contains the address of where to read the instruction from. Each time a part of an instruction is read, it is incremented to point to the next location in memory.

Figure 13.4
Anatomy of a Computer Instruction

13.2.2 Addressing Modes

An *addressing mode* describes the way in which the operand of an instruction is used. While modern computer systems may contain numerous addressing modes with varying complexities, we will focus on just a subset of basic addressing modes. These modes are immediate, direct, inherent, and indexed.

13.2.2.1 Immediate Addressing (IMM)

Immediate addressing is when the operand of an instruction *is* the information to be used by the instruction. For example, if an instruction existed to put a constant into a register within the CPU using immediate addressing, the operand would *be* the constant. When the CPU reads the operand, it simply inserts the contents into the CPU register and the instruction is complete.

13.2.2.2 Direct Addressing (DIR)

Direct addressing is when the operand of an instruction contains the *address* of where the information to be used is located. For example, if an instruction existed to put a constant into a register within the CPU using direct addressing, the operand would contain the address of *where* the constant was located in memory. When the CPU reads the operand, it puts this value out on the address bus and performs an additional read to retrieve the contents located at that address. The value read is then put into the CPU register and the instruction is complete.

13.2.2.3 Inherent Addressing (INH)

Inherent addressing refers to an instruction that does not require an operand because the opcode itself contains all of the necessary information for the instruction to complete. This type of addressing is used on instructions that perform manipulations on data held in CPU registers without the need to access the memory system. For example, if an instruction existed to increment the contents of a register (A), then once the opcode is read by the CPU, it knows everything it needs to know in order to accomplish the task. The CPU simply asserts a series of control signals in order to increment the contents of A and then the instruction is complete. Notice that no operand is needed for this task. Instead, the location of the register to be manipulated (i.e., A) is inherent within the opcode.

13.2.2.4 Indexed Addressing (IND)

Indexed addressing refers to instructions that will access information at an address in memory to complete the instruction, but the address to be accessed is held in another CPU register. In this type of addressing, the operand of the instruction is used as an *offset* that can be applied to the address located in the CPU register. For example, let's say an instruction existed to put a constant into a register (A) within the CPU using indexed addressing. Let's also say that the instruction was designed to use the contents of another register (B) as part of the address of where the constant was located. When the CPU reads the opcode, it understands what the instruction is and that B holds part of the address to be accessed. It also knows that the operand is applied to B to form the actual address to be accessed. When the CPU reads the operand, it adds the value to the contents of B and then puts this new value out on the address bus and performs an additional read. The value read is then put into the CPU register A and the instruction is complete.

13.2.3 Classes of Instructions

There are three general classes of instructions: 1) loads and stores; 2) data manipulations; and 3) branches. To illustrate how these instructions are executed, examples will be given based on the computer architecture shown in Figure 13.3.

13.2.3.1 Loads and Stores

This class of instructions accomplishes moving information between the CPU and memory. A **load** is an instruction that moves information from memory *into* a CPU register. When a load instruction uses immediate addressing, the operand of the instruction *is* the data to be loaded into the CPU register. As an example, let's look at an instruction to load the general purpose register A using immediate addressing. Let's say that the opcode of the instruction is x"86", has a mnemonic LDA_IMM, and is inserted into program memory starting at x"00". Example 13.2 shows the steps involved in executing the LDA_IMM instruction.

Example: Execution of an Instruction to "Load Register A Using Immediate Addressing"

A load instruction using immediate addressing will put the value of the operand into a CPU register. Let's create a program that will load register A in the CPU with the value x"AA". The program is as follows:

Using Mnemonics		Using Hex Values
LDA_IMM x"AA"	or	x"86" x"AA"

When the opcode and operand are put into program memory at x"00", they look like this:

When the CPU begins executing the program, it will perform the following steps:

Step 1 – Fetch the opcode

The program counter begins at x"00", meaning that this address is the location of the first instruction opcode. The PC address is put on the address bus using the MAR and a read is performed. The information read from memory (e.g., the opcode) is placed into the instruction register. The PC is then incremented to point to the next address in program memory. After this step, the IR holds x"86" and the PC holds x"01".

Step 2 – Decode the instruction

The CPU decodes x"86" and understands that it is a "load A with immediate addressing". It also knows from the opcode that the instruction has an operand that exists at the next address location.

Step 3 – Execute the instruction

The CPU now needs to read the operand. It places the PC address (x"01") on the address bus using the MAR and a read is performed. The information read from memory (e.g., the operand) is placed into register A. After this step, A=x"AA". Also in this step, the PC is incremented to point to the next location in memory (x"02"), which holds the opcode of the next instruction to be executed.

Example 13.2
Execution of an Instruction to "Load Register A Using Immediate Addressing"

Now let's look at a load instruction using direct addressing. In direct addressing, the operand of the instruction is the *address* of where the data to be loaded resides. As an example, let's look at an instruction to load the general purpose register A. Let's say that the opcode of the instruction is x"87", has a mnemonic LDA_DIR, and is inserted into program memory starting at x"08". The value to be loaded into A resides at address x"80", which has already been initialized with x"AA" before this instruction. Example 13.3 shows the steps involved in executing the LDA_DIR instruction.

Example: Execution of an Instruction to "Load Register A Using Direct Addressing"

A load instruction using direct addressing will put the value located at the address provided by the operand into a CPU register. Let's create a program that will load register A in the CPU with the contents located at address x"80", which has already been initialized to x"AA". The program is as follows:

Using Mnemonics		Using Hex Values
LDA_DIR x"80"	or	x"87" x"80"

When the opcode and operand are put into program memory at x"08", they look like this:

When the CPU begins executing the program, it will perform the following steps:

Step 1 – Fetch the opcode

The program counter begins at x"08", meaning that this address is the location of the instruction opcode. The PC address is put on the address bus using the MAR and a read is performed. The information read from memory (e.g., the opcode) is placed into the instruction register. The PC is then incremented to point to the next address in program memory. After this step, the IR holds x"87" and the PC holds x"09".

Step 2 – Decode the instruction

The CPU decodes x"87" and understands that it is a "load A with direct addressing". It also knows from the opcode that the instruction has an operand that exists at the next address location.

Step 3 – Execute the instruction

The CPU now needs to read the operand. It places the PC address (x"09") on the address bus using the MAR and a read is performed. The information read from memory (e.g., the operand) is the address that contains the value to be put into A. The operand is immediately put on the address bus using the MAR and another read is performed. The value read from address x"80" is placed into register A. After this step, A=x"AA". Also in this step, the PC is incremented to point to the next location in memory (x"0A"), which holds the opcode of the next instruction to be executed.

Example 13.3
Execution of an Instruction to "Load Register A Using Direct Addressing"

A **store** is an instruction that moves information from a CPU register *into* memory. The operand of a store instruction indicates the address of where the contents of the CPU register will be written. As an example, let's look at an instruction to store the general purpose register A into memory address x"E0". Let's say that the opcode of the instruction is x"96", has a mnemonic STA_DIR, and is inserted into program memory starting at x"04". The initial value of A is x"CC" before the instruction is executed. Example 13.4 shows the steps involved in executing the STA_DIR instruction.

Example: Execution of an Instruction to "Store Register A Using Direct Addressing"

A store instruction using direct addressing will put the value held in a CPU register into memory at the address provided by the operand. Let's create a program that will store register A in the CPU to address location x"E0". We can assume A holds x"CC" prior to this instruction. The program is as follows:

Using Mnemonics   Using Hex Values
STA_DIR   x"E0"   or   x"96"   x"E0"

When the opcode and operand are put into program memory at x"04", they look like this:

When the CPU begins executing the program, it will perform the following steps:

Step 1 – Fetch the opcode

The program counter begins at x"04", meaning that this address is the location of the instruction opcode. The PC address is put on the address bus using the MAR and a read is performed. The information read from memory (e.g., the opcode) is placed into the instruction register. The PC is then incremented to point to the next address in program memory. After this step, the IR holds x"96" and the PC holds x"05".

Step 2 – Decode the instruction

The CPU decodes x"96" and understands that it is a "store A with direct addressing". It also knows from the opcode that the instruction has an operand that exists at the next address location.

Step 3 – Execute the instruction

The CPU now needs to read the operand. It places the PC address (x"05") on the address bus using the MAR and a read is performed. The information read from memory (e.g., the operand) is the address of where A will be written. The operand is immediately put on the address bus using the MAR, A is put on the data bus, and a write is performed. After this step, location x"E0" in memory contains x"CC". Also in this step, the PC is incremented to point to the next location in memory (x"06"), which holds the opcode of the next instruction to be executed. The write did not effect register A so it still contains x"CC" after the instruction completes.

Example 13.4
Execution of an Instruction to "Store Register A Using Direct Addressing"

13.2.3.2 Data Manipulations

This class of instructions refers to ALU operations. These operations take action on data that resides in the CPU registers. These instructions include arithmetic, logic operators, shifts and rotates, and tests and compares. Data manipulation instructions typically use inherent addressing because the operations are conducted on the contents of CPU registers and don't require additional memory access. As an example, let's look at an instruction to perform addition on registers A and B. The sum will be placed back in A. Let's say that the opcode of the instruction is x"42", has a mnemonic ADD_AB, and is inserted into program memory starting at x"04". Example 13.5 shows the steps involved in executing the ADD_AB instruction.

Example: Execution of an Instruction to "Add Registers A and B"

This instruction adds A and B and puts the sum back into A (A = A+B). This instruction does not require an operand because the inputs and output of the operation reside completely within the CPU. This type of instruction uses inherent addressing, meaning that the location of the information impacted is inherent in the opcode. Let's create a program to perform this addition. The program is as follows:

Using Mnemonics		Using Hex Values
ADD_AB	or	x"42"

When the opcode is put into program memory at x"04", it looks like this:

When the CPU begins executing the program, it will perform the following steps:

Step 1 – Fetch the opcode

The program counter begins at x"04", meaning that this address is the location of the instruction opcode. The PC address is put on the address bus using the MAR and a read is performed. The information read from memory (e.g., the opcode) is placed into the instruction register. The PC is then incremented to point to the next address in program memory. After this step, the PC holds x"05" and the IR holds x"42".

Step 2 – Decode the instruction

The CPU decodes x"42" and understands that it is an "Add A and B". It also knows that there is no operand associated with this instruction.

Step 3 – Execute the instruction

The CPU asserts the necessary control signals to route A and B to the ALU, performs the addition, and places the sum back into A. The CCR is also updated to provide additional status information about the operation.

Example 13.5
Execution of an Instruction to "Add Registers A and B"

13.2.3.3 Branches

In the previous examples the program counter was always incremented to point to the address of the next instruction in program memory. This behavior only supports a linear execution of instructions. To provide the ability to specifically set the value of the program counter, instructions called *branches* are used. There are two types of branches: **unconditional** and **conditional**. In an unconditional branch, the program counter is always loaded with the value provided in the operand. As an example, let's look at an instruction to *branch always* to a specific address. This allows the program to perform loops. Let's say that the opcode of the instruction is x"20", has a mnemonic BRA, and is inserted into program memory starting at x"06". Example 13.6 shows the steps involved in executing the BRA instruction.

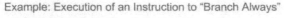

Example: Execution of an Instruction to "Branch Always"

A branch always instruction will set the program counter to the value provided by the operand. Let's create a program that will set the program counter to x"00". The program is as follows:

<u>Using Mnemonics</u>   <u>Using Hex Values</u>
   BRA x"00"   or   x"20" x"00"

When the opcode and operand are put into program memory at x"06", they look like this:

When the CPU begins executing the program, it will perform the following steps:

Step 1 – Fetch the opcode

   The program counter begins at x"06", meaning that this address is the location of the instruction opcode. The PC address is put on the address bus using the MAR and a read is performed. The information read from memory (e.g., the opcode) is placed into the instruction register. The PC is then incremented to point to the next address in program memory. After this step, the PC holds x"07" and the IR holds x"20".

Step 2 – Decode the instruction

   The CPU decodes x"20" and understands that it is a "branch always". It also knows from the opcode that the instruction has an operand that exists at the next address location.

Step 3 – Execute the instruction

   The CPU now needs to read the operand. It places the PC address (x"07") on the address bus using the MAR and a read is performed. The information read from memory (e.g., the operand) is the address to load into the PC. The operand is latched into the PC and the instruction is complete. After this instruction, the PC=x"00" and the program will begin executing instructions at that address.

Example 13.6
Execution of an Instruction to "Branch Always"

In a conditional branch, the program counter is only updated if a particular condition is true. The conditions come from the status flags in the condition code register (NZVC). This allows a program to selectively execute instructions based on the result of a prior operation. Let's look at an example instruction that will branch only if the Z flag is asserted. This instruction is called a *branch if equal to zero*. Let's say that the opcode of the instruction is x"23", has a mnemonic BEQ, and is inserted into program memory starting at x"05". Example 13.7 shows the steps involved in executing the BEQ instruction.

Example: Execution of an Instruction to "Branch if Equal to Zero"

This instruction will update the program counter with the address in the operand if the zero flag (Z) in the condition code register is asserted (Z=1). If Z=0, the program counter will simply increment to the next location in program memory. Let's look at how this program is executed. The instruction resides in program memory at addresses x"05" and x"06".

<u>Using Mnemonics</u>   <u>Using Hex Values</u>
BEQ   x"00"   or   x"23"   x"00"

When the opcode and operand are put into program memory at x"02", they look like this:

When the CPU begins executing the program, it will perform the following steps:

Step 1 – Fetch the opcode

The program counter begins at x"05", meaning that this address is the location of the instruction opcode. The PC address is put on the address bus using the MAR and a read is performed. The information read from memory (e.g., the opcode) is placed into the instruction register. The PC is then incremented to point to the next address in program memory. After this step, the PC holds x"06" and the IR holds x"23".

Step 2 – Decode the instruction

The CPU decodes x"23" and understands that it is a "branch if equal to zero". It also knows from the opcode that the instruction has an operand that exists at the next address location. The FSM now looks at the Z flag and decides which path in the FSM to take in order to execute the instruction properly.

Step 3 – Execute the instruction

<u>Z=1</u> – The branch will be taken by loading the PC with the operand. It places the PC address (x"06") on the address bus using the MAR and a read is performed. The information read from memory (e.g., the operand) is then loaded into the PC. If this action is taken, the PC=x"00".

<u>Z=0</u> – The branch will not be taken. Instead, the PC is simply incremented to point to the next location in memory, bypassing the operand. If this action is taken, the PC=x"07".

Example 13.7
Execution of an Instruction to "Branch if Equal to Zero"

Conditional branches allow computer programs to make *decisions* about which instructions to execute based on the results of previous instructions. This gives computers the ability to react to input signals or take action based on the results of arithmetic or logic operations. Computer instruction sets typically contain conditional branches based on the NZVC flags in the condition code registers. The following instructions are based on the values of the NZVC flags.

- BMI – Branch if minus (N=1)
- BPL – Branch if plus (N=0)
- BEQ – Branch if equal to Zero (Z=1)
- BNE – Branch if not equal to Zero (Z=0)
- BVS – Branch if two's complement overflow occurred, or V is set (V=1)
- BVC – Branch if two's complement overflow did not occur, or V is clear (V=0)
- BCS – Branch if a carry occurred, or C is set (C=1)
- BCC – Branch if a carry did not occur, or C is clear (C=0)

Combinations of these flags can be used to create more conditional branches.

- BHI – Branch if higher (C=1 and Z=0)
- BLS – Branch if lower or the same (C=0 and Z=1)
- BGE – Branch if greater than or equal ((N=0 and V=0) or (N=1 and V=1)), only valid for signed numbers
- BLT – Branch if less than ((N=1 and V=0) or (N=0 and V=1)), only valid for signed numbers
- BGT – Branch if greater than ((N=0 and V=0 and Z=0) or (N=1 and V=1 and Z=0)), only valid for signed numbers
- BLE – Branch if less than or equal ((N=1 and V=0) or (N=0 and V=1) or (Z=1)), only valid for signed numbers

CONCEPT CHECK

CC13.2 Software development consists of choosing which instructions, and in what order, will be executed to accomplish a certain task. The group of instructions is called the *program* and is inserted into program memory. Which of the following might a software developer care about?

A) Minimizing the number of instructions that need to be executed to accomplish the task in order to increase the computation rate

B) Minimizing the number of registers used in the CPU to save power.

C) Minimizing the overall size of the program to reduce the amount of program memory needed.

D) Both A and C.

6406

13.3 Computer Implementation – An 8-Bit Computer Example

13.3.1 Top Level Block Diagram

Let's now look at the detailed implementation and instruction execution of a computer system. In order to illustrate the detailed operation, we will use a simple 8-bit computer system design. Example 13.8 shows the block diagram for the 8-bit computer system. This block diagram also contains the VHDL file and entity names, which will be used when the behavioral model is implemented.

Example 13.8
Top Level Block Diagram for the 8-Bit Computer System

We will use the memory map shown in Example 13.1 for our example computer system. This mapping provides 128 bytes of program memory, 96 bytes of data memory, 16x output ports, and 16x input ports. To simplify the operation of this example computer, the address bus is limited to 8-bits. This only provides 256 locations of memory access, but allows an entire address to be loaded into the CPU as a single operand of an instruction.

13.3.2 Instruction Set Design

Example 13.9 shows a basic instruction set for our example computer system. This set provides a variety of loads and stores, data manipulations, and branch instructions that will allow the computer to be programmed to perform more complex tasks through software development. These instructions are sufficient to provide a baseline of functionality in order to get the computer system operational. Additional instructions can be added as desired to increase the complexity of the system.

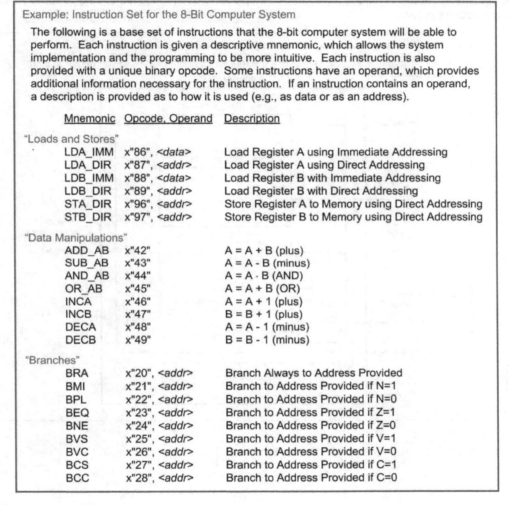

Example: Instruction Set for the 8-Bit Computer System

The following is a base set of instructions that the 8-bit computer system will be able to perform. Each instruction is given a descriptive mnemonic, which allows the system implementation and the programming to be more intuitive. Each instruction is also provided with a unique binary opcode. Some instructions have an operand, which provides additional information necessary for the instruction. If an instruction contains an operand, a description is provided as to how it is used (e.g., as data or as an address).

Mnemonic	Opcode, Operand	Description
"Loads and Stores"		
LDA_IMM	x"86", *<data>*	Load Register A using Immediate Addressing
LDA_DIR	x"87", *<addr>*	Load Register A using Direct Addressing
LDB_IMM	x"88", *<data>*	Load Register B with Immediate Addressing
LDB_DIR	x"89", *<addr>*	Load Register B with Direct Addressing
STA_DIR	x"96", *<addr>*	Store Register A to Memory using Direct Addressing
STB_DIR	x"97", *<addr>*	Store Register B to Memory using Direct Addressing
"Data Manipulations"		
ADD_AB	x"42"	A = A + B (plus)
SUB_AB	x"43"	A = A - B (minus)
AND_AB	x"44"	A = A · B (AND)
OR_AB	x"45"	A = A + B (OR)
INCA	x"46"	A = A + 1 (plus)
INCB	x"47"	B = B + 1 (plus)
DECA	x"48"	A = A - 1 (minus)
DECB	x"49"	B = B - 1 (minus)
"Branches"		
BRA	x"20", *<addr>*	Branch Always to Address Provided
BMI	x"21", *<addr>*	Branch to Address Provided if N=1
BPL	x"22", *<addr>*	Branch to Address Provided if N=0
BEQ	x"23", *<addr>*	Branch to Address Provided if Z=1
BNE	x"24", *<addr>*	Branch to Address Provided if Z=0
BVS	x"25", *<addr>*	Branch to Address Provided if V=1
BVC	x"26", *<addr>*	Branch to Address Provided if V=0
BCS	x"27", *<addr>*	Branch to Address Provided if C=1
BCC	x"28", *<addr>*	Branch to Address Provided if C=0

Example 13.9
Instruction Set for the 8-Bit Computer System

13.3.3 Memory System Implementation

Let's now look at the memory system details. The memory system contains program memory, data memory, and input/output ports. Example 13.10 shows the block diagram of the memory system. The program and data memory will be implemented using lower level components (rom_128x8_sync.vhd and rw_96x8_sync.vhd), while the input and output ports can be modeled using a combination of RTL processes and combinational logic. The program and data memory components contain dedicated circuitry to handle their addressing ranges. Each output port also contains dedicated circuitry to handle its unique address. A multiplexer is used to handle the signal routing back to the CPU based on the address provided.

Example 13.10
Memory System Block Diagram for the 8-Bit Computer System

13.3.3.1 Program Memory Implementation in VHDL

The program memory can be implemented in VHDL using the modeling techniques presented in Chapter 12. To make the VHDL more readable, the instruction mnemonics can be declared as constants. This allows the mnemonic to be used when populating the program memory array. The following VHDL shows how the mnemonics for our basic instruction set can be defined as constants.

```
constant LDA_IMM  : std_logic_vector (7 downto 0) := x"86";
constant LDA_DIR  : std_logic_vector (7 downto 0) := x"87";
constant LDB_IMM  : std_logic_vector (7 downto 0) := x"88";
constant LDB_DIR  : std_logic_vector (7 downto 0) := x"89";
constant STA_DIR  : std_logic_vector (7 downto 0) := x"96";
constant STB_DIR  : std_logic_vector (7 downto 0) := x"97";
constant ADD_AB   : std_logic_vector (7 downto 0) := x"42";
constant SUB_AB   : std_logic_vector (7 downto 0) := x"43";
constant AND_AB   : std_logic_vector (7 downto 0) := x"44";
constant OR_AB    : std_logic_vector (7 downto 0) := x"45";
constant INCA     : std_logic_vector (7 downto 0) := x"46";
constant INCB     : std_logic_vector (7 downto 0) := x"47";
constant DECA     : std_logic_vector (7 downto 0) := x"48";
constant DECB     : std_logic_vector (7 downto 0) := x"49";
constant BRA      : std_logic_vector (7 downto 0) := x"20";
constant BMI      : std_logic_vector (7 downto 0) := x"21";
constant BPL      : std_logic_vector (7 downto 0) := x"22";
constant BEQ      : std_logic_vector (7 downto 0) := x"23";
constant BNE      : std_logic_vector (7 downto 0) := x"24";
constant BVS      : std_logic_vector (7 downto 0) := x"25";
constant BVC      : std_logic_vector (7 downto 0) := x"26";
constant BCS      : std_logic_vector (7 downto 0) := x"27";
constant BCC      : std_logic_vector (7 downto 0) := x"28";
```

Now the program memory can be declared as an array type with initial values to define the program. The following VHDL shows how to declare the program memory and an example program to perform a load, store, and a branch always. This program will continually write x"AA" to port_out_00.

```
type rom_type is array (0 to 127) of std_logic_vector(7 downto 0);

constant ROM : rom_type := (0        => LDA_IMM,
                            1        => x"AA",
                            2        => STA_DIR,
                            3        => x"E0",
                            4        => BRA,
                            5        => x"00",
                            others => x"00");
```

The address mapping for the program memory is handled in two ways. First, notice that the array type defined above uses indices from 0 to 127. This provides the appropriate addresses for each location in the memory. The second step is to create an internal enable line that will only allow assignments from ROM to data_out when a valid address is entered. Consider the following VHDL to create an internal enable (EN) that will only be asserted when the address falls within the valid program memory range of 0 to 127.

```
enable : process (address)
  begin
    if ((to_integer(unsigned(address)) >= 0) and
        (to_integer(unsigned(address)) <= 127)) then
      EN <= '1';
    else
      EN <= '0';
    end if;
end process;
```

If this enable signal is not created, the simulation and synthesis will fail because data_out assignments will be attempted for addresses outside of the defined range of the ROM array. This enable line can now be used in the behavioral model for the ROM process as follows:

```
memory : process (clock)
  begin
    if (clock'event and clock='1') then
      if (EN='1') then
          data_out <= ROM(to_integer(unsigned(address)));
      end if;
    end if;
end process;
```

13.3.3.2 Data Memory Implementation in VHDL

The data memory is created using a similar strategy as the program memory. An array signal is declared with an address range corresponding to the memory map for the computer system (i.e., 128 to 223). An internal enable is again created that will prevent data_out assignments for addresses outside of this valid range. The following is the VHDL to declare the R/W memory array:

```
type rw_type is array (128 to 223) of std_logic_vector(7 downto 0);
signal RW : rw_type;
```

The following is the VHDL to model the local enable and signal assignments for the R/W memory:

```
enable : process (address)
  begin
    if ( (to_integer(unsigned(address)) >= 128) and
         (to_integer(unsigned(address)) <= 223)) then
      EN <= '1';
    else
      EN <= '0';
    end if;
end process;

memory : process (clock)
    begin
      if (clock'event and clock='1') then
          if (EN='1' and write='1') then
            RW(to_integer(unsigned(address))) <= data_in;
          elsif (EN='1' and write='0') then
            data_out <= RW(to_integer(unsigned(address)));
          end if;
      end if;
end process;
```

13.3.3.3 Implementation of Output Ports in VHDL

Each output port in the computer system is assigned a unique address. Each output port also contains storage capability. This allows the CPU to update an output port by writing to its specific address. Once the CPU is done storing to the output port address and moves to the next instruction in the program, the output port holds its information until it is written to again. This behavior can be modeled using an RTL process that uses the address bus and the write signal to create a synchronous enable condition. Each port is modeled with its own process. The following VHDL shows how the output ports at x"E0" and x"E1" are modeled using address specific processes.

```
-- port_out_00 description : ADDRESS x"E0"
 U3 : process (clock, reset)
   begin
     if (reset = '0') then
       port_out_00 <= x"00";
     elsif (clock'event and clock='1') then
       if (address = x"E0" and write = '1') then
         port_out_00 <= data_in;
       end if;
     end if;
   end process;

-- port_out_01 description : ADDRESS x"E1"
 U4 : process (clock, reset)
   begin
     if (reset = '0') then
       port_out_01 <= x"00";
     elsif (clock'event and clock='1') then
       if (address = x"E1" and write = '1') then
         port_out_01 <= data_in;
       end if;
     end if;
   end process;

                    :
    "the rest of the output port models go here…"
                  :
```

13.3.3.4 Implementation of Input Ports in VHDL

The input ports do not contain storage, but do require a mechanism to selectively route their information to the data_out port of the memory system. This is accomplished using the multiplexer shown in Example 13.10. The only functionality that is required for the input ports is connecting their ports to the multiplexer.

13.3.3.5 Memory data_out Bus Implementation in VHDL

Now that all of the memory functionality has been designed, the final step is to implement the multiplexer that handles routing the appropriate information to the CPU on the data_out bus based on the incoming address. The following VHDL provides a model for this behavior. Recall that a multiplexer is combinational logic, so if the behavior is to be modeled using a process, all inputs must be listed in the sensitivity list. These inputs include the outputs from the program and data memory in addition to all of the input ports. The sensitivity list must also include the address bus as it acts as the select input to the multiplexer. Within the process, an if/then statement is used to determine which subsystem drives data_out. Program memory will drive data_out when the incoming address is in the range of 0 to 127 (x"00" to x"7F"). Data memory will drive data_out when the address is in the range of 128 to 223 (x"80" to x"DF"). An input port will drive data_out when the address is in the range of 240 to 255 (x"F0" to x"FF"). Each input port has a unique address so the specific addresses are listed as *elsif* clauses.

```vhdl
    MUX1 : process (address, rom_data_out, rw_data_out,
                    port_in_00, port_in_01, port_in_02, port_in_03,
                    port_in_04, port_in_05, port_in_06, port_in_07,
                    port_in_08, port_in_09, port_in_10, port_in_11,
                    port_in_12, port_in_13, port_in_14, port_in_15)

      begin
        if    ( (to_integer(unsigned(address)) >= 0) and
                (to_integer(unsigned(address)) <= 127)) then
              data_out <= rom_data_out;

        elsif ( (to_integer(unsigned(address)) >= 128) and
                (to_integer(unsigned(address)) <= 223)) then
              data_out <= rw_data_out;

        elsif (address = x"F0") then data_out <= port_in_00;
        elsif (address = x"F1") then data_out <= port_in_01;
        elsif (address = x"F2") then data_out <= port_in_02;
        elsif (address = x"F3") then data_out <= port_in_03;
        elsif (address = x"F4") then data_out <= port_in_04;
        elsif (address = x"F5") then data_out <= port_in_05;
        elsif (address = x"F6") then data_out <= port_in_06;
        elsif (address = x"F7") then data_out <= port_in_07;
        elsif (address = x"F8") then data_out <= port_in_08;
        elsif (address = x"F9") then data_out <= port_in_09;
        elsif (address = x"FA") then data_out <= port_in_10;
        elsif (address = x"FB") then data_out <= port_in_11;
        elsif (address = x"FC") then data_out <= port_in_12;
        elsif (address = x"FD") then data_out <= port_in_13;
        elsif (address = x"FE") then data_out <= port_in_14;
        elsif (address = x"FF") then data_out <= port_in_15;

        else  data_out <= x"00";

        end if;

    end process;
```

13.3.4 CPU Implementation

Let's now look at the central processing unit details. The CPU contains two components, the control unit (control_unit.vhd) and the data path (data_path.vhd). The data path contains all of the registers and the ALU. The ALU is implemented as a sub-component within the data path (alu.vhd). The data path also contains a bus system in order to facilitate data movement between the registers and memory. The bus system is implemented with two multiplxers that are controlled by the control unit. The control unit contains the finite state machine that generates all control signals for the data path as it performs the fetch-decode-execute steps of each instruction. Example 13.11 shows the block diagram of the CPU in our 8-bit microcomputer example.

Example 13.11
CPU Block Diagram for the 8-Bit Computer System

13.3.4.1 Data Path Implementation in VHDL

Let's first look at the data path bus system that handles internal signal routing. The system consists of two 8-bit busses (Bus1 and Bus2) and two multiplexers. Bus1 is used as the destination of the PC, A, and B register outputs, while Bus2 is used as the input to the IR, MAR, PC, A, and B registers. Bus1 is connected directly to the *to_memory* port of the CPU to allow registers to write data to the memory system. Bus2 can be driven by the *from_memory* port of the CPU to allow the memory system to provide data for the CPU registers. The two multiplexers handle all signal routing and have their select lines (Bus1_Sel and Bus2_Sel) driven by the control unit. The following VHDL shows how the multiplexers are implemented. Again, a multiplexer is combinational logic so all inputs must be listed in the sensitivity list of its process. Two concurrent signal assignments are also required to connect the MAR to the address port and to connect Bus1 to the to_memory port.

```vhdl
MUX_BUS1 : process (Bus1_Sel, PC, A, B)
  begin
    case (Bus1_Sel) is
      when "00"   => Bus1 <= PC;
      when "01"   => Bus1 <= A;
      when "10"   => Bus1 <= B;
      when others => Bus1 <= x"00";
    end case;
end process;

MUX_BUS2 : process (Bus2_Sel, ALU_Result, Bus1, from_memory)
  begin
    case (Bus2_Sel) is
      when "00"   => Bus2 <= ALU_Result;
      when "01"   => Bus2 <= Bus1;
      when "10"   => Bus2 <= from_memory;
      when others => Bus2 <= x"00";
    end case;
end process;

address   <= MAR;
to_memory <= Bus1;
```

Next, let's look at implementing the registers in the data path. Each register is implemented using a dedicated process that is sensitive to clock and reset. This models the behavior of synchronous latches, or registers. Each register has a synchronous enable line that dictates when the register is updated. The register output is only updated when the enable line is asserted and a rising edge of the clock is detected. The following VHDL shows how to model the instruction register (IR). Notice that the signal IR is only updated if IR_Load is asserted and there is a rising edge of the clock. In this case, IR is loaded with the value that resides on Bus2.

```vhdl
INSTRUCTION_REGISTER : process (Clock, Reset)
  begin
    if (Reset = '0') then
      IR <= x"00";
    elsif (Clock'event and Clock = '1') then
      if (IR_Load = '1') then
        IR <= Bus2;
      end if;
    end if;
end process;
```

A nearly identical process is used to model the memory address register. A unique signal is declared called *MAR* in order to make the VHDL more readable. MAR is always assigned to address in this system.

```vhdl
MEMORY_ADDRESS_REGISTER : process (Clock, Reset)
  begin
    if (Reset = '0') then
      MAR <= x"00";
    elsif (Clock'event and Clock = '1') then
      if (MAR_Load = '1') then
        MAR <= Bus2;
      end if;
    end if;
  end process;
```

Now let's look at the program counter process. This register contains additional functionality beyond simply latching in the value of Bus2. The program counter also has an increment feature. In order to use the "+" operator, we can declare a temporary unsigned vector called PC_uns. The PC process can model the appropriate behavior using PC_uns and then type cast it back to the original PC signal.

```
PROGRAM_COUNTER : process (Clock, Reset)
  begin
   if (Reset = '0') then
     PC_uns <= x"00";
   elsif (Clock'event and Clock = '1') then
      if (PC_Load = '1') then
        PC_uns <= unsigned(Bus2);
      elsif (PC_Inc = '1') then
        PC_uns <= PC_uns + 1;
      end if;
   end if;
  end process;

  PC <= std_logic_vector(PC_uns);
```

The two general purpose registers A and B are modeled using individual processes as follows:

```
A_REGISTER : process (Clock, Reset)
  begin
   if (Reset = '0') then
     A <= x"00";
   elsif (Clock'event and Clock = '1') then
      if (A_Load = '1') then
        A <= Bus2;
      end if;
   end if;
  end process;

  B_REGISTER : process (Clock, Reset)
  begin
   if (Reset = '0') then
     B <= x"00";
   elsif (Clock'event and Clock = '1') then
      if (B_Load = '1') then
        B <= Bus2;
      end if;
   end if;
  end process;
```

The condition code register latches in the status flags from the ALU (NZVC) when the CCR_Load line is asserted. This behavior is modeled using a similar approach as follows:

```
CONDITION_CODE_REGISTER : process (Clock, Reset)
  begin
   if (Reset = '0') then
     CCR_Result <= x"0";
   elsif (Clock'event and Clock = '1') then
      if (CCR_Load = '1') then
        CCR_Result <= NZVC;
      end if;
   end if;
  end process;
```

13.3.4.2 ALU Implementation in VHDL

The ALU is a set of combinational logic circuitry that performs arithmetic and logic operations. The output of the ALU operation is called *Result*. The ALU also outputs 4 status flags as a 4-bit bus called *NZVC*. The ALU behavior can be modeled using if/then/elsif statements that decide which operation to perform based on the input control signal *ALU_Sel*. The following VHDL shows an example of how to implement the ALU addition functionality. In order to be able to use numerical operators (i.e., +, -, etc.), the numeric_std package is included. Variables can be used within the process to facilitate using the numerical operators. Recall that variables are updated instantaneously so an assignment can be made to the variable and its result is available immediately. Note that in the following VHDL, each operation also updates the NZVC flags. Each of these flags is updated individually. The N flag can be simply driven with position 7 of the ALU result since this bit is the sign bit for signed numbers. The Z flag can be driven using an if/then condition that checks whether the result was x"00". The V flag is updated based on the type of the operation. For the addition operation, the V flag will be asserted if a POS+POS=NEG or a NEG+NEG=POS. These conditions can be checked by looking at the sign bits of the inputs and the sign bit of the result. Finally, the C flag can be directly driven with position 8 of the Sum_uns variable.

```vhdl
ALU_PROCESS : process (A, B, ALU_Sel)

    variable Sum_uns : unsigned(8 downto 0);

    begin
      if (ALU_Sel = "000") then - ADDITION

          --- Sum Calculation -----------------------------------
            Sum_uns := unsigned('0' & A) + unsigned('0' & B);
            Result  <= std_logic_vector(Sum_uns(7 downto 0));

            --- Negative Flag (N) -------------------------------
            NZVC(3) <= Sum_uns(7);

            --- Zero Flag (Z) -----------------------------------
            if (Sum_uns(7 downto 0) = x"00") then
               NZVC(2) <= '1';
            else
               NZVC(2) <= '0';
            end if;

            --- Overflow Flag (V) -------------------------------
            if ((A(7)='0' and B(7)='0' and Sum_uns(7)='1') or
                (A(7)='1' and B(7)='1' and Sum_uns(7)='0')) then
               NZVC(1) <= '1';
            else
               NZVC(1) <= '0';
            end if;

          --- Carry Flag (C) ------------------------------------
            NZVC(0) <= Sum_uns(8);

        elsif (ALU_Sel = …
                              :         "other ALU functionality goes here"

        end if;

    end process;
```

13.3.4.3 Control Unit Implementation in VHDL

Let's now look at how to implement the control unit state machine. We'll first look at the formation of the VHDL to model the FSM and then turn to the detailed state transitions in order to accomplish a variety of the most common instructions. The control unit sends signals to the data path in order to move data in and out of registers and into the ALU to perform data manipulations. The finite state machine is implemented with the behavioral modeling techniques presented in Chapter 9. The model contains three processes in order to implement the state memory, next state logic, and output logic of the FSM. User-defined types are created for each of the states defined in the state diagram of the FSM. The states associated with fetching (S_FETCH_0, S_FETCH_1, S_FETCH_2) and decoding the opcode (S_DECODE_3) are performed each time an instruction is executed. A unique path is then added after the decode state to perform the steps associated with executing each individual instruction. The FSM can be created one instruction at a time by adding additional state paths after the decode state. The following VHDL code shows how the user-defined state names are created for six basic instructions (LDA_IMM, LDA_DIR, STA_DIR, ADD_AB, BRA and BEQ).

```
type state_type is
               (S_FETCH_0, S_FETCH_1, S_FETCH_2,
                S_DECODE_3,
                S_LDA_IMM_4, S_LDA_IMM_5, S_LDA_IMM_6,
                S_LDA_DIR_4, S_LDA_DIR_5, S_LDA_DIR_6, S_LDA_DIR_7,
                S_STA_DIR_4, S_STA_DIR_5, S_STA_DIR_6, S_STA_DIR_7, S_STA_DIR_8,
                S_ADD_AB_4,
                S_BRA_4, S_BRA_5, S_BRA_6,
                S_BEQ_4, S_BEQ_5, S_BEQ_6, S_BEQ_7);

signal current_state, next_state : state_type;
```

Within the architecture of the control unit model, the state memory is implemented as a separate process that will update the current state with the next state on each rising edge of the clock. The reset state will be the first fetch state in the FSM (i.e., S_FETCH_0). The following VHDL shows how the state memory in the control unit can be modeled.

```
STATE_MEMORY : process (Clock, Reset)
  begin
      if (Reset = '0') then
        current_state <= S_FETCH_0;
      elsif (clock'event and clock = '1') then
        current_state <= next_state;
      end if;
end process;
```

The next state logic is also implemented as a separate process. The next state logic depends on the current state, instruction register (IR), and the condition code register (CCR_Result). The following VHDL gives a portion of the next state logic process showing how the state transitions can be modeled.

```
NEXT_STATE_LOGIC : process (current_state, IR, CCR_Result)
  begin
      if (current_state = S_FETCH_0) then
        next_state <= S_FETCH_1;
      elsif (current_state = S_FETCH_1) then
        next_state <= S_FETCH_2;
      elsif (current_state = S_FETCH_2) then
        next_state <= S_DECODE_3;
      elsif (current_state = S_DECODE_3) then
                                                  -- select execution path
          if (IR = LDA_IMM) then                  -- Load A Immediate
              next_state <= S_LDA_IMM_4;
          elsif (IR = LDA_DIR) then               -- Load A Direct
            next_state <= S_LDA_DIR_4;
          elsif (IR = STA_DIR) then               -- Store A Direct
            next_state <= S_STA_DIR_4;
          elsif (IR = ADD_AB) then                -- Add A and B
            next_state <= S_ADD_AB_4;
          elsif (IR = BRA) then                   -- Branch Always
            next_state <= S_BRA_4;
          elsif (IR=BEQ and CCR_Result(2)='1') then  -- BEQ and Z=1
```

```
                        next_state <= S_BEQ_4;
                  elsif (IR=BEQ and CCR_Result(2)='0') then -- BEQ and Z=0
                    next_state <= S_BEQ_7;
                  else
                    next_state <= S_FETCH_0;
                  end if;

           elsif…
                                    :
                 "paths for each instruction go here…"
                                    :
               end if;

      end process;
```

Finally, the output logic is modeled as a third, separate process. It is useful to explicitly state the outputs of the control unit for each state in the machine to allow easy debugging and avoid synthesizing latches. Our example computer system has Moore type outputs so the process only depends on the current state. The following VHDL shows a portion of the output logic process.

```
        OUTPUT_LOGIC : process (current_state)
          begin
            case(current_state) is
              when S_FETCH_0 =>    -- Put PC onto MAR to read Opcode
                  IR_Load   <= '0';
                  MAR_Load  <= '1';
                  PC_Load   <= '0';
                  PC_Inc    <= '0';
                  A_Load    <= '0';
                  B_Load    <= '0';
                  ALU_Sel   <= "000";
                  CCR_Load  <= '0';
                  Bus1_Sel  <= "00"; -- "00"=PC,  "01"=A,    "10"=B
                  Bus2_Sel  <= "01"; -- "00"=ALU_Result, "01"=Bus1, "10"=from_memory
                  write     <= '0';

               when S_FETCH_1 =>    -- Increment PC
                  IR_Load   <= '0';
                  MAR_Load  <= '0';
                  PC_Load   <= '0';
                  PC_Inc    <= '1';
                  A_Load    <= '0';
                  B_Load    <= '0';
                  ALU_Sel   <= "000";
                  CCR_Load  <= '0';
                  Bus1_Sel  <= "00"; -- "00"=PC,  "01"=A,    "10"=B
                  Bus2_Sel  <= "00"; -- "00"=ALU, "01"=Bus1, "10"=from_memory
                  write     <= '0';
                                    :
               "output assignments for all other states go here…"
                                    :
            end case;
          end process;
```

13.3.4.3.1 Detailed Execution of LDA_IMM

Now let's look at the details of the state transitions and output signals in the control unit FSM when executing a few of the most common instructions. Let's begin with the instruction to load register A using immediate addressing (LDA_IMM). Example 13.12 shows the state diagram for this instruction. The first three states (S_FETCH_0, S_FETCH_1, S_FETCH_2) handle fetching the opcode. The purpose of these states is to read the opcode from the address being held by the program counter and put it into the instruction register. Multiple states are needed to handle putting PC into MAR to provide the address of the opcode, waiting for the memory system to provide the opcode, latching the opcode into IR, and incrementing PC to the next location in program memory. Another state is used to decode the opcode (S_DECODE_3) in order to decide which path to take in the state diagram based on the instruction being executed. After the decode state, a series of three more states are needed (S_LDA_IMM_4, S_LDA_IMM_5, S_LDA_IMM_6) to execute the instruction. The purpose of these states is to read the operand from the address being held by the program counter and put it into A. Multiple states are needed to handle putting PC into MAR to provide the address of the operand, waiting for the memory system to provide the operand, latching the operand into A, and incrementing PC to the next location in program memory. When the instruction completes, the value of the operand resides in A and PC is pointing to the next location in program memory, which is the opcode of the next instruction to be executed.

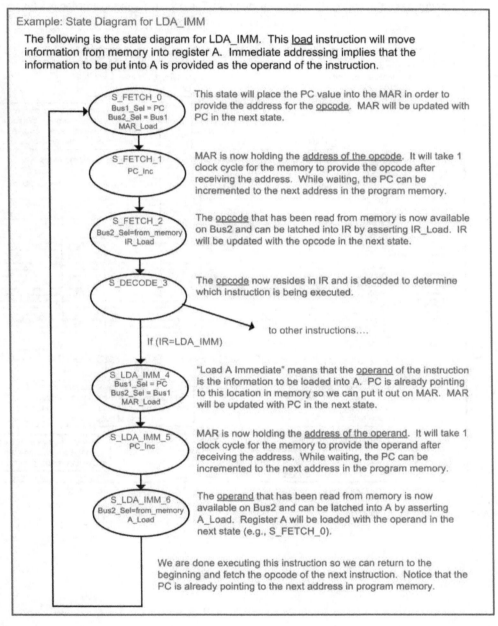

Example: State Diagram for LDA_IMM

The following is the state diagram for LDA_IMM. This load instruction will move information from memory into register A. Immediate addressing implies that the information to be put into A is provided as the operand of the instruction.

S_FETCH_0
Bus1_Sel = PC
Bus2_Sel = Bus1
MAR_Load

This state will place the PC value into the MAR in order to provide the address for the opcode. MAR will be updated with PC in the next state.

S_FETCH_1
PC_Inc

MAR is now holding the address of the opcode. It will take 1 clock cycle for the memory to provide the opcode after receiving the address. While waiting, the PC can be incremented to the next address in the program memory.

S_FETCH_2
Bus2_Sel=from_memory
IR_Load

The opcode that has been read from memory is now available on Bus2 and can be latched into IR by asserting IR_Load. IR will be updated with the opcode in the next state.

S_DECODE_3

The opcode now resides in IR and is decoded to determine which instruction is being executed.

to other instructions....

If (IR=LDA_IMM)

S_LDA_IMM_4
Bus1_Sel = PC
Bus2_Sel = Bus1
MAR_Load

"Load A Immediate" means that the operand of the instruction is the information to be loaded into A. PC is already pointing to this location in memory so we can put it out on MAR. MAR will be updated with PC in the next state.

S_LDA_IMM_5
PC_Inc

MAR is now holding the address of the operand. It will take 1 clock cycle for the memory to provide the operand after receiving the address. While waiting, the PC can be incremented to the next address in the program memory.

S_LDA_IMM_6
Bus2_Sel=from_memory
A_Load

The operand that has been read from memory is now available on Bus2 and can be latched into A by asserting A_Load. Register A will be loaded with the operand in the next state (e.g., S_FETCH_0).

We are done executing this instruction so we can return to the beginning and fetch the opcode of the next instruction. Notice that the PC is already pointing to the next address in program memory.

Example 13.12
State Diagram for LDA_IMM

Example 13.13 shows the simulation waveform for executing LDA_IMM. In this example, register A is loaded with the operand of the instruction, which holds the value x"AA".

Example: Simulation Waveform for LDA_IMM

Let's look at the timing diagram when executing the following load instruction located at addresses x"00" and x"01" in program memory. The opcode for this instruction is x"86".

LDA_IMM   x"AA"

S_FETCH_0 puts PC into MAR to provide the address of the opcode. MAR is updated on the next clock edge.

S_LDA_IMM_4 puts PC into MAR to provide the address of the operand. MAR is updated on the next clock edge.

In S_FETCH_2, the opcode is available from memory. We route it to Bus2 and assert IR_Load. IR will be updated on the next clock edge.

In S_LDA_IMM_6, the operand is available from memory. We route it to Bus2 and assert A_Load. A will be updated on the next clock edge.

In S_FETCH_1, the PC is incremented while waiting for the memory to produce the opcode. PC takes on its new value on the next edge of clock.

In S_LDA_IMM_5, the PC is incremented while waiting for the memory to produce the operand. PC takes on its new value on the next edge of clock.

S_DECODE_3 decodes the opcode and knows that this is a "load A with immediate addressing" and that the operand is the data to be loaded into A.

Register A has been loaded with the operand and the instruction is now complete.

Example 13.13
Simulation Waveform for LDA_IMM

13.3.4.3.2 Detailed Execution of LDA_DIR

Now let's look at the details of the instruction to load register A using direct addressing (LDA_DIR). Example 13.14 shows the state diagram for this instruction. The first four states to fetch and decode the opcode are the same states as in the previous instruction and are performed each time a new instruction is executed. Once the opcode is decoded, the state machine traverses five new states to execute the instruction (S_LDA_DIR_4, S_LDA_DIR_5, S_LDA_DIR_6, S_LDA_DIR_7, S_LDA_DIR_8). The purpose of these states is to read the operand and then use it as the address of where to read the contents to put into A.

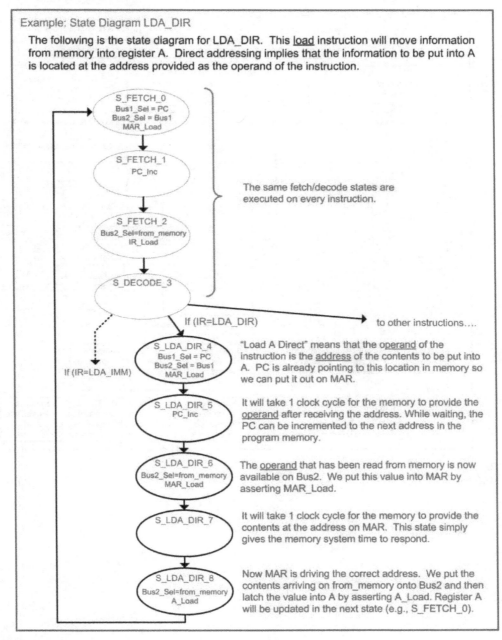

Example: State Diagram LDA_DIR

The following is the state diagram for LDA_DIR. This load instruction will move information from memory into register A. Direct addressing implies that the information to be put into A is located at the address provided as the operand of the instruction.

S_FETCH_0
Bus1_Sel = PC
Bus2_Sel = Bus1
MAR_Load

S_FETCH_1
PC_Inc

S_FETCH_2
Bus2_Sel=from_memory
IR_Load

The same fetch/decode states are executed on every instruction.

S_DECODE_3

If (IR=LDA_DIR)   to other instructions....

If (IR=LDA_IMM)

S_LDA_DIR_4
Bus1_Sel = PC
Bus2_Sel = Bus1
MAR_Load

"Load A Direct" means that the operand of the instruction is the address of the contents to be put into A. PC is already pointing to this location in memory so we can put it out on MAR.

S_LDA_DIR_5
PC_Inc

It will take 1 clock cycle for the memory to provide the operand after receiving the address. While waiting, the PC can be incremented to the next address in the program memory.

S_LDA_DIR_6
Bus2_Sel=from_memory
MAR_Load

The operand that has been read from memory is now available on Bus2. We put this value into MAR by asserting MAR_Load.

S_LDA_DIR_7

It will take 1 clock cycle for the memory to provide the contents at the address on MAR. This state simply gives the memory system time to respond.

S_LDA_DIR_8
Bus2_Sel=from_memory
A_Load

Now MAR is driving the correct address. We put the contents arriving on from_memory onto Bus2 and then latch the value into A by asserting A_Load. Register A will be updated in the next state (e.g., S_FETCH_0).

Example 13.14
State Diagram for LDA_DIR

Example 13.15 shows the simulation waveform for executing LDA_DIR. In this example, register A is loaded with the contents located at address x"80", which has already been initialized to x"AA".

Example: Simulation Waveform for LDA_DIR

Let's look at the timing diagram when executing the following load instruction located at addresses x"08" and x"09" in program memory. The opcode for this instruction is x"87". The address x"80" is in data memory, which in this example is already holding x"AA" prior to this instruction.

LDA_DIR   x"80"

In S_FETCH_2, the opcode is available from memory. We route it to Bus2 and assert IR_Load. IR will be updated on the next clock edge.

In S_LDA_DIR_6, the operand is available from memory. We route it to Bus2 and assert MAR_Load to put it on the address bus.

S_FETCH_0 puts PC into MAR to provide the address of the opcode. MAR is updated on the next clock edge.

S_LDA_DIR_4 puts PC into MAR to provide the address of the operand. MAR is updated on the next clock edge.

S_LDA_DIR_7 waits for the memory system to respond.

In S_FETCH_1, the PC is incremented while waiting for the memory to produce the opcode. PC takes on its new value on the next edge of clock.

In S_LDA_DIR_5, the PC is incremented while waiting for the memory to produce the operand. PC takes on its new value on the next edge of clock.

S_DECODE_3 decodes the opcode and knows that this is a "load A with direct addressing" and that the operand is the address of the contents to be loaded into A.

In S_LDA_DIR_8, the contents of memory are available. We route it to Bus 2 and assert A_Load. A will be updated on the next clock edge.

Example 13.15
Simulation Waveform for LDA_DIR

13.3.4.3.3   Detailed Execution of STA_DIR

Now let's look at the details of the instruction to store register A to memory using direct addressing (STA_DIR). Example 13.16 shows the state diagram for this instruction. The first four states are again the same as prior instructions in order to fetch and decode the opcode. Once the opcode is decoded, the state machine traverses four new states to execute the instruction (S_STA_DIR_4, S_STA_DIR_5, S_STA_DIR_6, S_STA_DIR_7). The purpose of these states is to read the operand and then use it as the address of where to write the contents of A to.

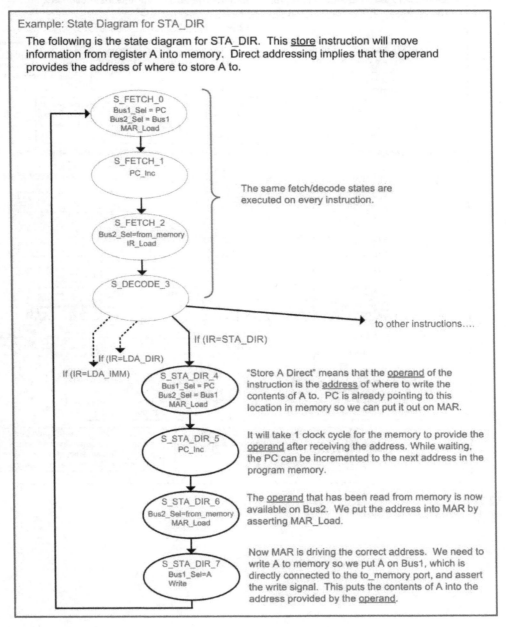

Example: State Diagram for STA_DIR

The following is the state diagram for STA_DIR. This store instruction will move information from register A into memory. Direct addressing implies that the operand provides the address of where to store A to.

Example 13.16
State Diagram for STA_DIR

Example 13.17 shows the simulation waveform for executing STA_DIR. In this example, register A already contains the value x"CC" and will be stored to address x"E0". The address x"E0" is an output port (port_out_00) in our example computer system.

Example 13.17
Simulation Waveform for STA_DIR

13.3.4.3.4 Detailed Execution of ADD_AB

Now let's look at the details of the instruction to add A to B and store the sum back in A (ADD_AB). Example 13.18 shows the state diagram for this instruction. The first four states are again the same as prior instructions in order to fetch and decode the opcode. Once the opcode is decoded, the state machine only requires one more state to complete the operation (S_ADD_AB_4). The ALU is combinational logic so it will begin to compute the sum immediately as soon as the inputs are updated. The inputs to the ALU are Bus1 and register B. Since B is directly connected to the ALU, all that is required to start the addition is to put A onto Bus1. The output of the ALU is put on Bus2 so that it can be latched into A on the next clock edge. The ALU also outputs the status flags NZVC, which are directly connected to the condition code register. A_Load and CCR_Load are asserted in this state. A and CCR_Result will be updated in the next state (i.e., S_FETCH_0).

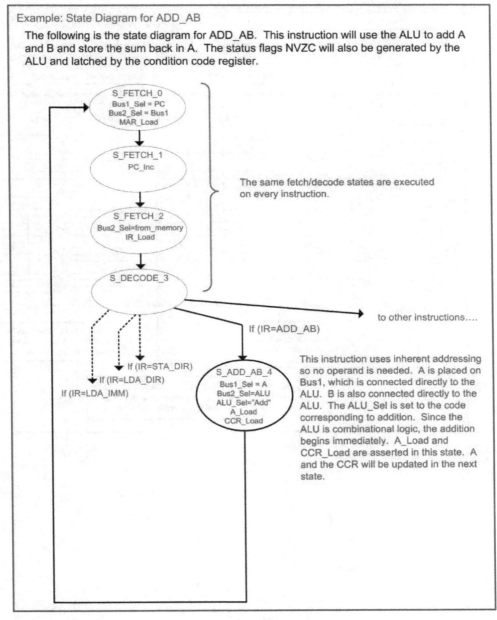

Example 13.18
State Diagram for ADD_AB

Example 13.19 shows the simulation waveform for executing ADD_AB. In this example, two load immediate instructions were used to initialize the general purpose registers to A=x"FF" and B=x"01" prior to the addition. The addition of these values will result in a sum of x"00" and assert the carry (C) and zero (Z) flags in the condition code register.

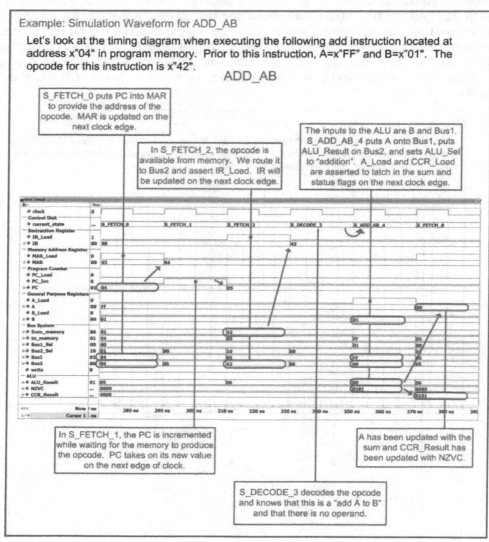

Example: Simulation Waveform for ADD_AB

Let's look at the timing diagram when executing the following add instruction located at address x"04" in program memory. Prior to this instruction, A=x"FF" and B=x"01". The opcode for this instruction is x"42".

ADD_AB

S_FETCH_0 puts PC into MAR to provide the address of the opcode. MAR is updated on the next clock edge.

In S_FETCH_2, the opcode is available from memory. We route it to Bus2 and assert IR_Load. IR will be updated on the next clock edge.

The inputs to the ALU are B and Bus1. S_ADD_AB_4 puts A onto Bus1, puts ALU_Result on Bus2, and sets ALU_Sel to "addition". A_Load and CCR_Load are asserted to latch in the sum and status flags on the next clock edge.

In S_FETCH_1, the PC is incremented while waiting for the memory to produce the opcode. PC takes on its new value on the next edge of clock.

A has been updated with the sum and CCR_Result has been updated with NZVC.

S_DECODE_3 decodes the opcode and knows that this is a "add A to B" and that there is no operand.

Example 13.19
Simulation Waveform for ADD_AB

13.3.4.3.5   Detailed Execution of BRA

Now let's look at the details of the instruction to branch always (BRA). Example 13.20 shows the state diagram for this instruction. The first four states are again the same as prior instructions in order to fetch and decode the opcode. Once the opcode is decoded, the state machine traverses four new states to execute the instruction (S_BRA_4, S_BRA_5, S_BRA_6). The purpose of these states is to read the operand and put its value into PC to set the new location in program memory to execute instructions.

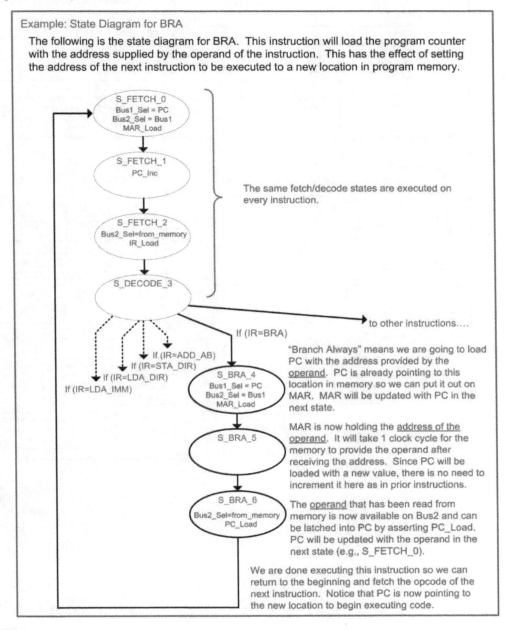

Example: State Diagram for BRA

The following is the state diagram for BRA. This instruction will load the program counter with the address supplied by the operand of the instruction. This has the effect of setting the address of the next instruction to be executed to a new location in program memory.

S_FETCH_0
Bus1_Sel = PC
Bus2_Sel = Bus1
MAR_Load

S_FETCH_1
PC_Inc

S_FETCH_2
Bus2_Sel=from_memory
IR_Load

S_DECODE_3

The same fetch/decode states are executed on every instruction.

If (IR=BRA)

to other instructions....

If (IR=ADD_AB)
If (IR=STA_DIR)
If (IR=LDA_DIR)
If (IR=LDA_IMM)

S_BRA_4
Bus1_Sel = PC
Bus2_Sel = Bus1
MAR_Load

"Branch Always" means we are going to load PC with the address provided by the operand. PC is already pointing to this location in memory so we can put it out on MAR. MAR will be updated with PC in the next state.

S_BRA_5

MAR is now holding the address of the operand. It will take 1 clock cycle for the memory to provide the operand after receiving the address. Since PC will be loaded with a new value, there is no need to increment it here as in prior instructions.

S_BRA_6
Bus2_Sel=from_memory
PC_Load

The operand that has been read from memory is now available on Bus2 and can be latched into PC by asserting PC_Load. PC will be updated with the operand in the next state (e.g., S_FETCH_0).

We are done executing this instruction so we can return to the beginning and fetch the opcode of the next instruction. Notice that PC is now pointing to the new location to begin executing code.

Example 13.20
State Diagram for BRA

Example 13.21 shows the simulation waveform for executing BRA. In this example, PC is set back to address x"00".

Example 13.21
Simulation Waveform for BRA

13.3.4.3.6 Detailed Execution of BEQ

Now let's look at the branch if equal to zero (BEQ) instruction. Example 13.22 shows the state diagram for this instruction. Notice that in this conditional branch, the path that is taken through the FSM depends on both IR and CCR. In the case that Z=1, the branch is taken, meaning that the operand is loaded into PC. In the case that Z=0, the branch is not taken, meaning that PC is simply incremented to bypass the operand and point to the beginning of the next instruction in program memory.

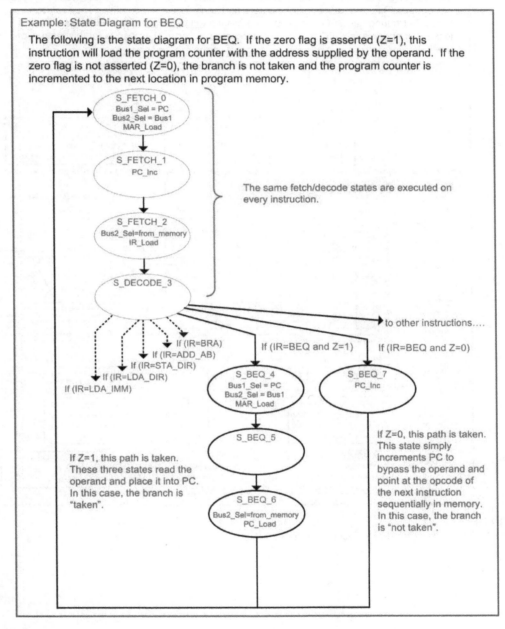

Example: State Diagram for BEQ

The following is the state diagram for BEQ. If the zero flag is asserted (Z=1), this instruction will load the program counter with the address supplied by the operand. If the zero flag is not asserted (Z=0), the branch is not taken and the program counter is incremented to the next location in program memory.

S_FETCH_0
Bus1_Sel = PC
Bus2_Sel = Bus1
MAR_Load

S_FETCH_1
PC_Inc

The same fetch/decode states are executed on every instruction.

S_FETCH_2
Bus2_Sel=from_memory
IR_Load

S_DECODE_3

to other instructions....

If (IR=BRA)
If (IR=ADD_AB)
If (IR=STA_DIR)
If (IR=LDA_DIR)
If (IR=LDA_IMM)

If (IR=BEQ and Z=1)   If (IR=BEQ and Z=0)

S_BEQ_4
Bus1_Sel = PC
Bus2_Sel = Bus1
MAR_Load

S_BEQ_7
PC_Inc

If Z=1, this path is taken. These three states read the operand and place it into PC. In this case, the branch is "taken".

S_BEQ_5

If Z=0, this path is taken. This state simply increments PC to bypass the operand and point at the opcode of the next instruction sequentially in memory. In this case, the branch is "not taken".

S_BEQ_6
Bus2_Sel=from_memory
PC_Load

Example 13.22
State Diagram for BEQ

Example 13.23 shows the simulation waveform for executing BEQ when the branch *is taken*. Prior to this instruction, an addition was performed on x"FF" and x"01". This resulted in a sum of x"00", which asserted the Z and C flags in the condition code register. Since Z=1 when BEQ is executed, the branch is taken.

Example: Simulation Waveform for BEQ When Taking the Branch (Z=1)

Let's look at the timing diagram when executing a branch if equal to zero instruction when the branch is taken. Prior to this instruction, the addition x"FF"+x"01"=x"00" was performed. This prior addition set the zero and carry flag in the condition code register. Since Z=1 during this BEQ instruction, the branch will be taken. The BEQ instruction is located at addresses x"05" and x"06" in program memory. The opcode for this instruction is x"23".

Example 13.23
Simulation Waveform for BEQ When Taking the Branch (Z=1)

Example 13.24 shows the simulation waveform for executing BEQ when the branch *is not taken*. Prior to this instruction, an addition was performed on x"FE" and x"01". This resulted in a sum of x"FF", which did not assert the Z flag. Since Z=0 when BEQ is executed, the branch is not taken. When not taking the branch, PC must be incremented again in order to bypass the operand and point to the next location in program memory.

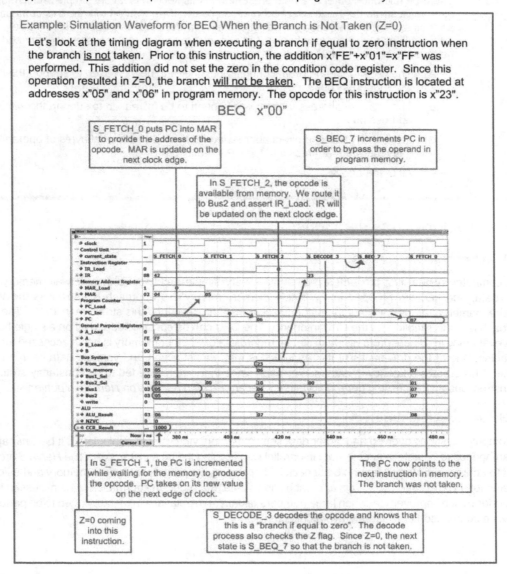

Example: Simulation Waveform for BEQ When the Branch is Not Taken (Z=0)

Let's look at the timing diagram when executing a branch if equal to zero instruction when the branch is not taken. Prior to this instruction, the addition x"FE"+x"01"=x"FF" was performed. This addition did not set the zero in the condition code register. Since this operation resulted in Z=0, the branch will not be taken. The BEQ instruction is located at addresses x"05" and x"06" in program memory. The opcode for this instruction is x"23".

BEQ x"00"

S_FETCH_0 puts PC into MAR to provide the address of the opcode. MAR is updated on the next clock edge.

S_BEQ_7 increments PC in order to bypass the operand in program memory.

In S_FETCH_2, the opcode is available from memory. We route it to Bus2 and assert IR_Load. IR will be updated on the next clock edge.

In S_FETCH_1, the PC is incremented while waiting for the memory to produce the opcode. PC takes on its new value on the next edge of clock.

The PC now points to the next instruction in memory. The branch was not taken.

Z=0 coming into this instruction.

S_DECODE_3 decodes the opcode and knows that this is a "branch if equal to zero". The decode process also checks the Z flag. Since Z=0, the next state is S_BEQ_7 so that the branch is not taken.

Example 13.24
Simulation Waveform for BEQ When the Branch is Not Taken (Z=0)

CC13.3 The 8-bit microcomputer example presented in this section is a very simple architecture used to illustrate the basic concepts of a computer. If we wanted to keep this computer an 8-bit system but increase the depth of the memory, it would require adding more address lines to the address bus. What changes to the computer system would need to be made to accommodate the wider address bus?

    A) The width of the program counter would need to be increased to support the wider address bus.

    B) The memory address register would need to be increased to support the wider address bus.

    C) Instructions that use direct addressing would need additional bytes of operand to pass the wider address into the CPU 8-bits at a time.

    D) All of the above.

13.4 Architecture Considerations

13.4.1 Von Neumann Architecture

The computer system just presented represents a very simple architecture in which all memory devices (i.e., program, data, and I/O) are grouped into a single memory map. This approach is known as the *Von Neumann architecture*, named after the 19th century mathematician that first described this structure in 1945. The advantage of this approach is in the simplicity of the CPU interface. The CPU can be constructed based on a single bus system that executes everything in a linear progression of states, regardless of whether memory is being accessed for an instruction or a variable. One of the drawbacks of this approach is that an instruction and variable data cannot be read at the same time. This creates a latency in data manipulation since the system needed to be constantly switching between reading instructions and accessing data. This latency became known as the *Von Neumann bottleneck.*

13.4.2 Harvard Architecture

As computer systems evolved and larger data sets in memory were being manipulated, it became apparent that it was advantageous to be able to access data in parallel with reading the next instruction. The *Harvard* architecture was proposed to address the Von Neumann bottleneck by separating the program and data memory and using two distinct bus systems for the CPU interface. This approach allows data and program information to be accessed in parallel and leads to performance improvement when large numbers of data manipulations in memory need to be performed. Figure 13.5 shows a comparison between the two architectures.

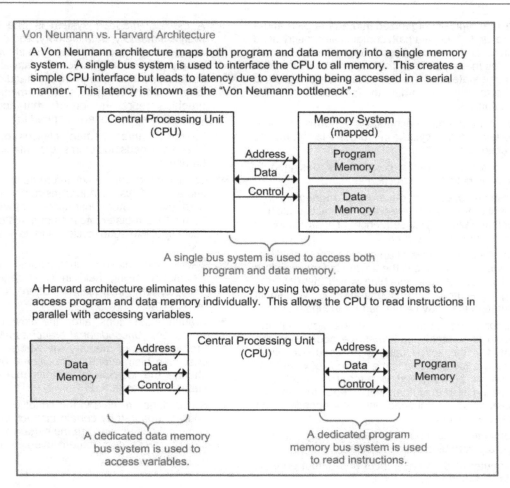

Figure 13.5
Von Neumann vs. Harvard Architecture

CONCEPT CHECK

CC13.4 Does a computer with a Harvard architecture require two control unit state machines?

A) Yes. It has two bus systems that need to be managed separately so two finite state machines are required.

B) No. A single state machine is still used to fetch, decode, and execute the instruction. The only difference is that if data is required for the execute stage, it can be retrieved from data memory at the same time the state machine fetches the opcode of the next instruction from program memory.

Summary

❖ A computer is a collection of hardware components that are constructed to perform a specific set of instructions to process and store data. The main hardware components of a computer are the central processing unit (CPU), program memory, data memory, and input/output ports.

❖ The CPU consists of registers for fast storage, an arithmetic logic unit (ALU) for data manipulation, and a control state machine that directs all activity to execute an instruction.

❖ A CPU is typically organized into a *data path* and a *control unit*. The data path contains all circuitry used to store and process information. The data path includes the registers and the ALU. The control unit is a large state machine that sends control signals to the data path in order to facilitate instruction execution.

❖ The control unit continuously performs a *fetch-decode-execute* cycle in order to complete instructions.

❖ The instructions that a computer is designed to execute is called its *instruction set*.

❖ Instructions are inserted into *program memory* in a sequence that when executed will accomplish a particular task. This sequence of instructions is called a computer *program*.

❖ An instruction consists of an *opcode* and a potential *operand*. The opcode is the unique binary code that tells the control state machine which instruction is being executed. An operand is additional information that may be needed for the instruction.

❖ An *addressing mode* refers to the way that the operand is treated. In *immediate* addressing the operand is the actual data to be used. In *direct* addressing the operand is the address of where the data is to be retrieved or stored. In *inherent* addressing all of the information needed to complete the instruction is contained within the opcode so no operand is needed.

❖ A computer also contains *data memory* to hold temporary variables during run time.

❖ A computer also contains input and output ports to interface with the outside world.

❖ A *memory mapped* system is one in which the program memory, data memory, and I/O ports are all assigned a unique address. This allows the CPU to simply process information as data and addresses and allows the program to handle where the information is being sent to. A *memory map* is a graphical representation of what address ranges various components are mapped to.

❖ There are three primary classes of instructions. These are loads and stores, data manipulations, and branches.

❖ Load instructions move information from memory into a CPU register. A load instruction takes multiple read cycles. Store instructions move information from a CPU register into memory. A store instruction takes multiple read cycles and at least one write cycle.

❖ Data manipulation instructions operate on information being held in CPU registers. Data manipulation instructions often use inherent addressing.

❖ Branch instructions alter the flow of instruction execution. *Unconditional branches* always change the location in memory of where the CPU is executing instructions. *Conditional branches* only change the location of instruction execution if a status flag is asserted.

❖ Status flags are held in the condition code register and are updated by certain instructions. The most commonly used flags are the negative flag (N), zero flag (Z), two's complement overflow flag (V), and carry flag (C).

Exercise Problems

Section 13.1 – Computer Hardware

13.1.1 What computer hardware sub-system holds the temporary variables used by the program?

13.1.2 What computer hardware sub-system contains fast storage for holding and/or manipulating data and addresses?

13.1.3 What computer hardware sub-system allows the computer to interface to the outside world?

13.1.4 What computer hardware sub-system contains the state machine that orchestrates the fetch-decode-execute process?

13.1.5 What computer hardware sub-system contains the circuitry that performs mathematical and logic operations?

13.1.6 What computer hardware sub-system holds the instructions being executed?

Section 13.2 – Computer Software

13.2.1 Which elements of computer software are the individual operations that a computer can perform?

13.2.2 Which element of computer software is the binary code that tells the CPU which instruction is being executed?

13.2.3 Which element of computer software is a collection of instructions that perform a desired task?

13.2.4 Which element of computer software is the supplementary information required by an instruction such as constants or which registers to use?

13.2.5 Which class of instructions handles moving information between memory and CPU registers?

13.2.6 Which class of instructions alters the flow of program execution?

13.2.7 Which class of instructions alters data using either arithmetic or logical operations?

Section 13.3 – Computer Implementation – An 8-bit Computer Example

13.3.1 Design the example 8-bit computer system presented in this chapter in VHDL with the ability to execute the three instructions LDA_IMM, STA_DIR, and BRA. Simulate your computer system using the following program that will continually write the patterns x"AA" and x"BB" to output ports port_out_00 and port_out_01:

```
constant ROM : rom_type := (
    0     => LDA_IMM,
    1     => x"AA",
    2     => STA_DIR,
    3     => x"E0",
    4     => STA_DIR,
    5     => x"E1",
    6     => LDA_IMM,
    7     => x"BB",
    8     => STA_DIR,
    9     => x"E0",
    10    => STA_DIR,
    11    => x"E1",
    12    => BRA,
    13    => x"00",
    others => x"00");
```

13.3.2 Add the functionality to the computer model from 13.3.1 the ability to perform the LDA_DIR instruction. Simulate your computer system using the following program that will continually read from port_in_00 and write its contents to port_out_00:

```
constant ROM : rom_type := (
    0     => LDA_DIR,
    1     => x"F0",
    2     => STA_DIR,
    3     => x"E0",
    4     => BRA,
    5     => x"00",
    others => x"00");
```

13.3.3 Add the functionality to the computer model from 13.3.2 the ability to perform the instructions LDB_IMM, LDB_DIR, and STB_DIR. Modify the example programs given in exercise 13.3.1 and 13.3.2 to use register B in order to simulate your implementation.

13.3.4 Add the functionality to the computer model from 13.3.3 the ability to perform the addition instruction ADD_AB. Test your addition instruction by simulating the following program. The first addition instruction will perform x"FE" + x"01" = x"FF" and assert the negative (N) flag. The second addition instruction will perform x"FF" + x"01" = x"00" and assert the carry (C) and zero (Z) flags. The third addition instruction will perform x"7F" + x"7F" = x"FE" and assert the two's complement overflow (V) and negative (N) flags.

```
constant ROM : rom_type := (
    0     => LDA_IMM, -- A=x"FE"
    1     => x"FE",
    2     => LDB_IMM, -- B=x"01"
    3     => x"01",
    4     => ADD_AB,  -- A=A+B
    5     => LDA_IMM, -- A=x"FF"
    6     => x"FF",
    7     => LDB_IMM, -- B=x"01"
    8     => x"01",
    9     => ADD_AB,  -- A=A+B
    10    => LDA_IMM, -- A=x"7F"
    11    => x"7F",
    12    => LDB_IMM, -- B=x"7F"
    13    => x"7F",
    14    => ADD_AB,  -- A=A+B
    15    => BRA,
    16    => x"00",
    others => x"00");
```

13.3.5 Add the functionality to the computer model from 13.3.4 the ability to perform the *branch if equal to zero*

instruction BEQ. Simulate your implementation using the following program. The first addition in this program will perform x"FE" + x"01" = x"FF" (Z=0). The subsequent BEQ instruction should NOT take the branch. The second addition in this program will perform x"FF" + x"01" = x"00" (Z=1) and SHOULD take the branch. The final instruction in this program is a BRA that is inserted for safety. In the event that the BEQ is not operating properly, the BRA will set the program counter back to x"00" and prevent the program from running away.

```
constant ROM : rom_type := (
    0     => LDA_IMM,
    1     => x"FE",
    2     => LDB_IMM,
    3     => x"01",
    4     => ADD_AB,
    5     => BEQ,
    6     => x"00", -- should not
                    -- branch

    7     => LDA_IMM,
    8     => x"FF",
    9     => LDB_IMM,
    10    => x"01",
    11    => ADD_AB,
    12    => BEQ,
    13    => x"00", -- should
                    -- branch

    14    => BRA,
    15    => x"00",

    others => x"00");
```

13.3.6 Add the functionality to the computer model from 13.3.4 all of the remaining instructions in the set shown in Example 13.9. You will need to create test programs to verify the execution of each instruction.

Section 13.4 – Architectural Considerations

13.4.1 Would the instruction set need to be different between a Von Neumann versus a Hardware architecture? Why or why not?

13.4.2 Which of the three classes of computer instructions (loads/stores, data manipulations, and branches) are sped up by moving from the Von Neumann architecture to the Harvard architecture.

13.4.3 In a memory mapped, Harvard architecture, would the I/O system be placed in the program memory or data memory block?

13.4.4 A Hardware architecture requires two memory address registers to handle two separate memory systems. Does it also require two instruction registers? Why or why not?

13.4.5 A Hardware architecture requires two memory address registers to handle two separate memory systems. Does it also require two program counters? Why or why not?

Appendix A: List of Worked Examples

Index